An official publication of

THE AMERICAN SOCIOLOGICAL ASSOCIATION

WILLIAM D'ANTONIO, *Executive Officer*

SOCIOLOGICAL
THEORY
1984

Randall Collins

Editor

SOCIOLOGICAL THEORY ❧ 1984 ❧

 Jossey-Bass Publishers

San Francisco • Washington • London • 1984

SOCIOLOGICAL THEORY 1984
by Randall Collins, Editor

Copyright © 1984 by: Jossey-Bass Inc., Publishers
433 California Street
San Francisco, California 94104
&
Jossey-Bass Limited
28 Banner Street
London EC1Y 8QE

International Standard Book Number ISBN 0-87589-587-5

International Standard Serial Number ISSN 0735-2751

Manufactured in the United States of America

The paper in this book meets the guidelines for
permanence and durability of the Committee on
Production Guidelines for Book Longevity of the
Council on Library Resources.

JACKET DESIGN BY WILLI BAUM

FIRST EDITION

Code 8401

THE JOSSEY-BASS
SOCIAL AND BEHAVIORAL SCIENCE SERIES

SOCIOLOGICAL
THEORY
1984

PREFACE

Sociological Theory 1984 is the second in an annual series sponsored by the American Sociological Association to publish leading work in all the variety of approaches now being undertaken in sociological theory.

Among the various concerns that sociologists have with theory, one, I think, heads the list: the creation of new theory itself. Theory is the hard backbone of the discipline, the place where our knowledge, in whatever area it may originate, cumulates and becomes available for wider dissemination, further development, and application to new problems. The comment has often been made in recent years that this type of innovative theory is rare. Those of us who specialize in theory have been preoccupied, it seems, with writing *about* theory even at the expense of *doing* theory itself. Pursuing metatheoretical questions on the nature and limits of various kinds of theorizing is, of course, a legitimate and often valuable enterprise, just as it can be both valuable and intrinsically interesting to comment on the theories of the past or to generate programmatic lines for theory in the future. But we miss, sometimes, the presence of new theories in our own day, which is, after all, the end point of all these concerns *about* theory.

For these reasons, I am particularly pleased to be able to present in this volume of *Sociological Theory* a number of pieces that state important new theories. Just how those theories will fare in the future will be a matter for commentary, debate, and research. Several of the chapters provide general theories in the area of stratification, a topic of particularly central importance in our field in that so many aspects of sociology are tied into it. Others deal with microlevel phenomena, such as role acquisition, or "middle range" phenomena, such as the illicit economy of crime. Yet other chapters, though couched in terms of case studies of particular historical occasions, use these materials to develop theoretical models and arguments.

Current theoretical approaches differ in an often bewildering variety of substantive ways. One aim of *Sociological Theory* is to capture that variety. It is not possible, of course, to cover the full range of approaches in any one book; but this second volume, in conjunction with the first (*Sociological Theory 1983*), shows that some progress has been made in our tour of the many exotic and often mutually hostile territories of the current intellectual world. In addition to the substantive concerns just mentioned, this volume contains some central developments in modern neo-Marxism, in feminism and the sociology of gender, and in evolution and long-term societal change, as well as in the challenging new approaches to meaning, symbolism, everyday life, and communication that have gone under such labels as *phenomenology, ethnomethodology,* and *structuralism.* An effort is also made here to survey the borderline between quantitative and nonquantitative sociologies.

This volume continues *Sociological Theory*'s set of special features headed "Theory News: Reports on Recent Intellectual Events." Our roving intellectual reporters have brought back some first-rate contributions, I believe, on some of the hot spots of the current sociological world: the Marxian debate over world-system theory, some key issues in current feminism, and the revival of Parsons within current German theory. On the whole, I hope you will find this volume a theoretical feast.

San Diego, California   Randall Collins
January 1984

CONTENTS

    Models of Sociocultural Evolution   117
    Patrick D. Nolan

    Argues that the currently divergent approaches to processes
    of selection—intersocietal and intrasocietal—may potentially
    be integrated.

5. The Dual Labor Market of the Criminal
    Economy   140
    Kevin B. Bales

    Criminal careers, like those in the legitimate economy, are
    sharply stratified into a privileged primary sector and a
    secondary sector open to the pressures of the market.

6. Everyday Life as Text   165
    Mary F. Rogers

    Proposes that ethnomethodology may be best understood
    through an analogy with literary structuralism.

7. The Semantic Equation: A Theory of the
    Social Origins of Art Styles   187
    Albert Bergesen

    Analyzes abstraction and realism to show that elaborated
    and restricted codes exist in art as well as in language,
    reflecting the degree of solidarity of artistic communities.

8. Interaction as a Resource for Epistemological
    Critique   222
    Anne Warfield Rawls

    Demonstrates that sociological studies of everyday life
    provide a basis for critiquing existentialist philosophy.

9. The Problem of Epistemology in the Social
    Action Perspective   253
    John R. Hall

    Suggests that Parsons's strategy of "analytical realism"
    sacrifices the strengths of Weber's epistemology of
    Verstehen and ideal types.

Assesses what several German theorists are now doing to
extend Parsonian ideas.

CONTRIBUTORS

Jeffrey C. Alexander, professor, Department of Sociology, University of California, Los Angeles

Kevin B. Bales, London School of Economics

Albert Bergesen, associate professor, Department of Sociology, University of Arizona

Arnold Birenbaum, associate professor, Department of Sociology, St. John's University, Jamaica, New York

Rae Lesser Blumberg, associate professor, Department of Sociology, University of California, San Diego

Roslyn Wallach Bologh, associate professor, Department of Sociology, St. John's University, Jamaica, New York

John R. Hall, associate professor, University of Missouri, Columbia

Robert A. Hanneman, assistant professor, Department of Sociology, University of California, Riverside

Patrick D. Nolan, assistant professor, Department of Sociology, University of South Carolina, Columbia

Anne Warfield Rawls, assistant professor, Department of Sociology, University of Massachusetts, Boston

Mary F. Rogers, professor, Department of Sociology and Anthropology, University of West Florida

Jonathan H. Turner, professor, Department of Sociology, University of California, Riverside

Immanuel Wallerstein, professor, Department of Sociology, State University of New York, Binghamton

INTRODUCTION

Stratification has always been an important topic in sociological theory. One might well argue, in fact, that it is structurally the most central of all, in that a perspective on stratification ties together almost every other area of our field. It provides a link from small groups, families, and individuals to the large-scale macrostructures of the economy, the state, and the system of culture. The distributional processes of stratification—power, prestige, wealth, social mobility—might well be considered the dynamics of the entire society, as well as constituting the prime concerns and motivations of individuals. And the study of social change, both long-term and local, seems to boil down most of the time to the themes of stratification theory. Certainly in reading history, unconscious as historians may be of explicit themes of sociological theory, one constantly encounters the subject matter of stratification.

For this reason, it is particularly gratifying that this volume leads off with two chapters that present explicit general theories of stratification. The first chapter, by Jonathan Turner and Robert Hanneman, is consciously organized and titled in a way reminiscent of the famous article by Kingsley Davis and Wilbert Moore, "Some Principles of Stratification." The Davis–Moore thesis has probably been the subject of more extended debate than any other in the history of American sociology, although little progress emerged from that debate toward a more refined theory of stratification.

Indeed, the debate among Davis, Moore, Tumin, and others acted, more than anything, to reveal the chasm that was emerging between American sociology in the first half of the twentieth century and the more radical and iconoclastic approaches that have predominated in recent decades.

Turner and Hanneman's chapter thus has a certain historical interest, since it reveals how far we have come since 1945. This is not to say that Turner and Hanneman present a radical theory, in contrast to the functionalism epitomized by Davis and Moore. But one feature of the debate that followed Davis and Moore's publication was precisely that it revealed how much ideological issues were entwined with the functional theory of stratification, as well as with its critiques. Crudely put, the debate boiled down to the question whether stratification was "good for" society; the *mechanism* of stratification that Davis and Moore proposed was attacked largely in order to show that their implied defense of stratification was invalid. Davis himself once complained that the debate seemed to be concerned not with how to advance a scientific explanation of stratification but with which side was right and which was wrong. His complaint was certainly valid, since the years of debate did not produce either a more refined theory or even much explicit testing of the theory. It might also be said, however, that functional theory itself was by nature tautological and did not lend itself to a genuinely explanatory form—a damaging criticism, I would say, in that a theory that is not intrinsically testable cannot be considered a genuine causal explanation.

When I say that Turner and Hanneman enable us to measure how far we have come, I have in mind the ways they have taken up the explicitly scientific theory-building aim that Davis spoke of, which was never successfully carried out in the lineage of the original Davis–Moore theory itself. Turner and Hanneman state an explicit theory of the causal conditions determining various kinds and degrees of stratification. The theory does not hinge on whether one thinks stratification is good or bad for society, nor, I think, does it reduce to tautology. For better or worse, it is a genuinely explanatory theory, and couched at a higher level of generality than any we have seen before. Where Davis and Moore reduced stratification to the explanation of the distribution of wealth (and secondarily of prestige) and used social mobility as a mechanism explaining this distribution, Turner and Hanneman deal with a wider range of phenomena: They take wealth, power, prestige, and mobility alike as phenomena of stratification to be explained and add some significant refinements concerning the organization of ranked groups (what Weber would have called status groups). However accurate the Turner-Hanneman theory turns out to be in all its specifics, it clearly marks a step forward in our standards of what a theory of stratification should do.

The second chapter, by Rae Lesser Blumberg, also provides an ambitious and general stratification theory. It deals with an aspect of stratification not explicitly covered in the Turner-Hanneman model—gender stratification.[1] It also derives the theory in quite a different style: Whereas Turner and Hanneman build a formal and deductive model, Blumberg proceeds by the comparison and synthesis of contemporary, historical, and anthropological materials on the range of male/female domination, subordination, and equality found throughout the world. Again, we have a benchmark to see how far we have come in recent decades. Twenty years ago, the question of sexual stratification hardly existed in explicit sociological theories; it is nowhere to be found in the type of theory exemplified by Davis and Moore or even in the conflict-theory opponents that followed them in the late 1950s and 1960s.[2] Blumberg's theory, one might say, is somewhere between a "first wave" and a "second wave" theory of sexual stratification: It is second wave in that Blumberg critically reflects and improves on the sociological theories that emerged shortly after 1970, although it is also connected with the first wave, since Blumberg herself is the author of one of those earlier theories, which she further develops here. In its breadth and comprehensiveness, in any case, one sees again the kinds of progress that have been made.

Several other chapters are also related to the theme of stratification, though on different scales. Immanuel Wallerstein is, of course, the proponent of an extremely macro analysis of stratification, that which has existed historically among societies within the world system. Here he reflects on the obverse of a theme within his own intellectual tradition—not the "dependency" theme of "the development of underdevelopment" but the very way in which the mainline sociological theory of development is itself the product of a particular phase in the modern world system. Patrick

Nolan touches on the theory of development from a different angle, critically dissecting two different approaches to sociocultural evolution. Then, proceeding downward to the smaller scale of internal structures within a society, Kevin Bales shows how various issues in criminology take on a new light when put in the perspective of a recent stratification model. Bales shows that dual labor market theory applies to careers in the criminal world as well as in the "straight" one and that crime not only is an economy but is one that must be understood in terms of its stratification.

Next comes a series of chapters dealing with the micro and cultural levels of human consciousness. Mary Rogers attempts to show that ethnomethodology makes sense from the point of view of French structuralism, especially as practiced in the tradition of literary criticism and philosophy of autonomous symbolic systems. Her argument is that everyday life ought to be treated as a text for analysis, rather than as a realm of subjective meanings. Albert Bergesen also deals with the question of social semantics but pursues the line of theory emanating from Émile Durkheim and developed by Basil Bernstein and Mary Douglas. His specific subject matter is modern art; he attempts to show that differing art styles are related to the organization of social communities through a "semantic equation," which may have very wide application.

Anne Rawls uses Goffmanian sociology of everyday life to critique the type of epistemological constructs represented by the existentialism of Sartre. John Hall also deals with the issue of epistemology, arguing that Talcott Parsons's epistemological strategy of "analytic realism" sacrificed the strengths of Max Weber's alternative strategy of *Verstehen* and ideal types. Jeffrey Alexander draws on a Parsonian analytic scheme to consider the question of conflict at the political level as compared to the consensus at the level of culture. Here we see a variety of connections slanting out from a core of concern with culture, consciousness, and social organization. Arnold Birenbaum brings this section full circle by presenting a theory of the conditions in which social roles are acquired.

The last chapter takes up a question not of society but of our methods for approaching it. The thesis is that there is a sharp and growing division between statistical and qualitative sociology today. My chapter takes a rather combative stance on the hidden theoretical implications of various statistical methods and assumptions. Perhaps it is well to stress that my argument distinguishes between statistics, as a theory about how to treat data, and mathematics, as a vehicle for substantive theory itself, and that the criticisms directed against one have a very different implication in regard to the other.

The *Theory News* section in this volume contains some unusually interesting treatments. Albert Bergesen takes up the so-called Brenner critique directed by orthodox Marxism against the upstart heresy of world-system theory. Roslyn Wallach Bologh overviews recent feminist thinking on the issue of male/female differences and their possible moral implications. Jeffrey Alexander describes the revival of Parsonian theory that has recently been sweeping Germany and, in the process, offers what is undoubtedly the most lucid presentation available in any language of a highly abstract and difficult body of writings.

Notes

1. It has become very common to use the term *gender* rather than *sexual* to emphasize the distinction between biology and the varying social arrangements that are built around it. This is sometimes a useful distinction but is sometimes rather overdrawn. There is little danger of confusion in speaking of "sexual stratification." One might notice, incidentally, a tendency within "gender" sociology to talk as if such stratification had nothing to do with the sexes themselves.

2. I venture this statement even though Friedrich Engels published his theory of the origins of the family, private property, and the state in 1884 and Max Weber had a treatment of sexual stratification in the family (in *Economy and Society*) that foreshadowed many contemporary themes but that has been virtually overlooked. Within professional sociology—not only American but European—sexual stratification had to be completely discovered anew, for the most part less than fifteen years ago.

Randall Collins

SOCIOLOGICAL
THEORY
❧ 1984 ❧

We propose that sociological theory should comprise a series of elementary and abstract principles on the operation of distinctive and generic social processes. These processes intersect and interact in varying combinations to create diverse social forms, including stratification. Six elementary principles, stated as simple equations, are developed for the social processes implicated in societal stratification.

🍂 1 🍂

SOME THEORETICAL PRINCIPLES OF SOCIETAL STRATIFICATION

Jonathan H. Turner

UNIVERSITY OF CALIFORNIA, RIVERSIDE

Robert A. Hanneman

UNIVERSITY OF CALIFORNIA, RIVERSIDE

In this chapter we present six theoretical principles on societal stratification. Several assumptions have guided us in developing these principles. First, we assume that, in Radcliffe-Brown's (1948) words, "a natural science of society" is possible and that theoretical principles in sociology can and should resemble those in the other natural sciences. Second, we believe that theory in sociology should constitute a storehouse of elementary principles that are drawn on, in varying combinations, to explain some phenomenon of interest. Third, we argue that these principles should be highly abstract and simple, incorporating few concepts and articulating only the most basic relationships among concepts.

1

Although these assumptions invite controversy, our intent in enumerating them is to place into context the theoretical strategy to be pursued in this chapter. We do not visualize stratification as a unitary phenomenon about which "a" or "the" theory can be developed. For us, *stratification* is a name that sociologists give to the convergence of, and interaction among, several more basic social processes. In this chapter, then, we will attempt to isolate these underlying processes and then articulate an abstract principle for each.

Basic Social Processes and Stratification Systems

In this preliminary effort, we consider three generic processes to be implicated in what sociologists and anthropologists label "social stratification."

Distributive Processes. Valued resources are distributed unequally among members of a social system. At the most abstract level, we conceptualize these distributive processes in terms of the degree of concentration (C) of three basic resources: material wealth (MW), power (PO), and prestige (PR). The issue of concentration concerns the question of what proportion of persons in a social system possesses what proportion of a given resource (Mayhew and Schollaert, 1980). The following definitions will guide our analysis:

C_{MW} = the degree of concentration of material wealth in a system, with wealth defined as those material objects that people in a system value and find gratifying, or the capacity to purchase those objects with money

C_{PO} = the degree of concentration of power in a social system, with power defined as the capacity of a social unit to control the actions of other social units

C_{PR} = the degree of concentration of prestige in a social system, with prestige defined as the honor, respect, and esteem given by one social unit to another

In conceptualizing inequality, then, we are focusing on the issue of concentration. Indicators of the concentration of material wealth, such as income, are often defined as a Gini coefficient stating the degree of deviation of the actual distribution of income from a hypothetical distribution of perfect equality (Turner and Starnes, 1976:54). Our view is that inequality of power and prestige can also be defined by concentration measures.[1]

"Social Class" Processes. From our perspective, the term *social class* is too inclusive. Social class is the realization of underlying social processes and therefore cannot be viewed as a unitary property of social systems. Although we acknowledge that other processes are no doubt involved, we will focus on only two discrete social processes that sociologists seem to denote most often by such terms as *class, stratum,* and *rank.* These are defined as follows:

DF_{HO} = the degree and extent of differentiation of homogeneous subpopulations in a system, with homogeneity defined as the degree to which subsets of members in a system can be distinguished by common or similar behaviors and attitudes

RA_{HO} = the degree to which homogeneous subsets in a system can be linearly rank-ordered in terms of their imputed worthiness

These two processes might be viewed as "group formation" and "ranking" processes, respectively. When sociologists discuss social class, they appear to stress that people belong to ranked subpopulations, but too frequently they fail to view ranking and subpopulation formation as separate variables. That is, the degree of group formation and the degree of ranking can vary independently. Hence, we must develop separate principles for each process.

Mobility Processes. People in social systems move from position to position and from place to place. In the context of stratification, concern is with movement across ranked positions and/or ranked subpopulations. Hence, our inquiry will be guided by the following definition:

MO = the degree of movement of individuals or collectivities of individuals from one ranked subpopulation to another, with the degree of social mobility defined in terms of (1) the proportion of individuals in a society who are mobile and (2) the distance across rank-ordered subpopulations that those who are mobile travel

There is little that is original in our "discovery" of these processes; indeed, they often organize discussions in basic texts on stratification. But the full implications of distinctions like the foregoing are not always recognized. For example, if inequality in the distribution of wealth is a distinctive property of stratification (and of social organization in general), it requires a separate principle (in our terms, a principle on C_{MW}). The same is true for the other processes listed above—that is, C_{PO}, C_{PR}, DF_{HO}, RA_{HO}, and MO.

In the sections that follow, our goal will be to develop several elementary equations that explain the dynamics of the processes just listed. In this initial effort, we will confine our analysis to societal stratification, although the processes defined are relevant to other units and levels of analysis. Moreover, as will become evident, we will seek to simplify the equations by modifying somewhat conventional mathematical notation. And we should stress at the outset that our efforts are theoretical. At this stage we are not attempting to operationalize concepts or to test the principles. Such activities are obvious next steps, but they are beyond the space limitations of a single chapter.

Principles of Distributive Processes

As our earlier definitions imply, analysis of distributive processes requires an understanding of those conditions influencing the concentration of three basic resources—material wealth, power, and prestige. For each of these resources, somewhat different conditions affect the degree of concentration, and hence it is necessary to develop three separate theoretical principles for C_{MW}, C_{PO}, and C_{PR}.

Concentration of Material Wealth. In Equation 1 we present our views on those generic forces that are related to C_{MW}.

$$(1) \quad C_{MW} = W_1(P^{\exp}) \times W_2(NH^{-\exp}) \times W_3(NO^{-\exp})$$

where

P = the degree of productivity, or the total volume of products and services generated by the members of a social system, with products defined as material objects created by the conversion of environmental resources and with services defined as activities that facilitate the production and distribution of material objects

NO = the number of organizational units in a social system

NH = the number of hierarchies that link organizational units in a social system, with hierarchies defined as the vertical control of units in terms of power

and where

$$W_1 > W_2 > W_3$$

The notation system in Equation 1 and in subsequent equations requires some explanation. In our equations, we can potentially present six basic types of relations between the variables on the left-hand side of the equation and each of those on the right-hand side: positive linear, negative linear, positive logarithmic (log), negative logarithmic (-log), positive exponential (exp), and negative exponential (-exp). In Equation 1, C_{MW} is viewed as a positive exponential function of productivity (P) and a negative exponential function of the number of social hierarchies (NH) and the number of organizational units in a system (NO). Each of the variables in Equation 1 is weighted (as symbolized by W_1, W_2, W_3) so that the exponential relation between P and C_{MW} is given more weight than the negative exponential relation between C_{MW} and NH, which, in turn, is assigned more weight than the negative exponential relation between C_{MW} and NO. The terms in the equation are multiplicatively related because the effect of each independent variable on C_{MW} depends on the levels of the other independent variables.

Equation 1 borrows ideas from Marx ([1867], 1967), Weber (1968), Lenski (1966), and Turner (1972). Both Marx and Len-

ski have argued that inequality in wealth is a function of productivity and the concentration of power.[2] Under conditions of
low levels of productivity, extreme concentration of material
wealth would drive the majority of a population below subsistence, whereas under conditions of high productivity, there is
much material surplus to extract. This relation between productivity and the concentration of material wealth is exponential
because initial increases in P have less effect on C_{MW} than subsequent increases.

Rather than using the concentration of power (C_{PO}) as
the second term in Equation 1, we have conceptualized the impact of the distribution of power on C_{MW} in terms of the densities of organizational units (NO) and hierarchies (NH) in societies.
This formulation borrows heavily from Lenski's discussions of the
origins of the state, Marx's consideration of monopoly power, and
Weber's concern with the growth of bureaucratic authority. Hierarchical organization of units in a society involves the use of power by units high in the hierarchy to extract resources from units
lower in the hierarchy; in our conceptualization, it is the number
of hierarchies that is the critical force. That is, among two societies with comparable productivity and organizational density, the
one with more hierarchies will reveal the least concentration of
material wealth, for whereas resources will flow to the top of any
hierarchy (Michels, 1915), the existence of multiple hierarchies
disperses resources more than in systems with one hierarchy.
These processes help account for Lenski's (1966) finding that industrial social systems reveal less inequality than agrarian systems,
despite their increased productivity. One reason for this decrease,
we feel, is the increasing number of social hierarchies in industrial
societies, but additionally, much of the increase in equality is the
result of the third variable on the right side of Equation 1—the
number of organizational units in a system (NO). Weber (1968)
recognized clearly that organized subunits in a system require resources to sustain themselves; and the more organizational subunits in a society, whether kin-based, community-based, economic,
or political, the more dispersed will be resources. In sum, then, the
degree to which wealth is concentrated in social systems is a positive function of productivity and a negative function of the number of social hierarchies and organizational subunits in a system.

Concentration of Power. In Equation 2 we specify what we believe are the most generic conditions influencing the concentration of power (C_{PO}) in societal social systems:

(2) $\quad C_{PO} = W_1 \log(ET) \times W_2(P^{\exp}) \times W_4(IT^{\exp}) \times W_3(IC^{\exp})$

where

> ET = the degree to which members of a social system perceive threats from sources external to that system
> P = productivity (see definition in Equation 1)
> IC = the level of internal conflict, or potential for internal conflict, among units in a system
> IT = the total volume of internal transactions among members and units of a system

Equation 2 states that the concentration of power (C_{PO}) is logarithmically related to the level of perceived external threat (ET) and exponentially related to the level of productivity (P), the degree of internal conflict or conflict potential (IC), and the volume of internal transactions (IT). These factors stand in a multiplicative relation to one another with regard to their impacts on the concentration of power. That is, the effect of each factor on C_{PO} depends on the levels of the other factors. The weightings (W) argue that external threat is the most important influence on the concentration of power, followed respectively by productivity, internal conflict, and internal transactions.

The processes connecting these variables to C_{PO} and to one another in the ways specified in Equation 2 can be described as follows. As Spencer (1885) and Simmel (1956) recognized, societies engaged in conflict, such as war, become despotically organized in order to mobilize and coordinate resources for the conflict. We have stated this insight more abstractly in that any perceived threat to a society creates pressures for the centralization of authority to mobilize and coordinate resources to deal with the threat. We view this relation between ET and C_{PO} as logarithmic in that initial increases in perceived threat immediately activate and disproportionately affect the level of C_{PO} more than subsequent increases.

Productivity is related to C_{PO} in ways visualized by such thinkers as Marx ([1867], 1967, [1848], 1971) and Lenski (1966). Increases in P create material wealth, which is usurped by some sectors and used to buy power; and once power is initially consolidated, it can then be mobilized to acquire more wealth and employed again to garner even more power. However, this relation between C_{PO} and P is exponential, in that productivity must increase to a point where there is a sufficiently large economic and material surplus to usurp and utilize in consolidating political power (see Lenski, 1966, for empirical documentation).

Internal conflict and C_{PO} are also related exponentially, because initial conflicts, or early increases in hostilities and potential conflict, often disperse power or at least signal its lack of concentration. In systems where conflict has occurred or where it is a constant possibility, considerable centralization of power and its mobilization to deal with internal conflicts will be evident. Thus, although it may appear at first glance that conflict signals the dispersion of power (since to engage in conflict requires that each unit in the conflict have some power), our view is that the total level of power is expanded with conflict and that, over time, power becomes consolidated to deal with internal sources of tension.

Internal transactions are related to C_{PO} in a manner first given forceful expression by Spencer (1885) and more recently by organizational theorists (Blau, 1970). As the volume of interaction among units expands, and as their exchanges of resources increase, coordination, regulation, and control become severe problems, requiring the centralization of power to regularize exchanges. This relation between C_{PO} and IT is seen as exponential as well, in that initial increases in the volume of transactions do not require political regulation. It is only after a certain volume is reached that the capacities of system subunits to coordinate and control their own activities are exceeded.

As noted earlier, the factors ET, P, IT, and IC are seen to have an interactive relation with the degree of concentration of power. That is, the impact of each factor on the concentration of power is seen to depend on the levels of the other factors. The extent to which an increase in external threat will result in increasing concentration of power, for example, is greater in systems with high levels of productivity, internal conflict, and regulatory complexity than in systems that are lower in these factors.

Similarly, the impact of an increase in productivity, transactional complexity, or internal conflict on the degree of concentration of power is dependent on the existing levels of the other variables. Although it is not immediately relevant to the statement of the principle embodied in Equation 2, the levels of external threat, productivity, transactional density, and internal conflict also "interact" in that these forces may be causally related. As with all the principles stated in this chapter, however, specification of the determinants of the factors on the "right-hand side" of equations is beyond the scope of the current work.

Concentration of Prestige. In Equation 3, we specify some of the conditions influencing the concentration of prestige, or C_{PR}, in societal social systems.

$$(3) \quad C_{PR} = W_1\left[-\log\left(\frac{Po}{N}\right)\right] + W_2\left[\left(\frac{SK}{N}\right)^{-\exp}\right]$$
$$+ W_3\left[\left(\frac{FI}{N}\right)^{-\exp}\right] + W_4\left[\left(\frac{Mw}{N}\right)^{-\exp}\right]$$

where

N = the number of people in a social system

Po = the number of people in status positions that are *perceived* by members of a social system to possess high levels of power

SK = the number of people in status positions that are *perceived* by members of a social system to possess high levels of skill

FI = the number of people in status positions that are *perceived* by members of a social system to possess a high degree of functional importance

Mw = the number of people in status positions that are *perceived* by members of a social system to bring a high level of material wealth

and where

$$W_1 > W_2 > W_3 > W_4$$

Equation 3 states that the degree of concentration of prestige

(C_{PR}) is a negative logarithmic function of the number of positions, as a proportion of all persons (N), that are perceived to possess power (Po), or (Po/N), and a negative exponential function of the number of positions, as a proportion of all persons (N), that are perceived to possess skill (SK), functional importance (FI), and material wealth (Mw), or (SK/N), (FI/N), and (Mw/N), respectively. These variables are seen as additively related, with greater weight given to (Po/N), followed in order by (SK/N), (FI/N), and (Mw/N).

In this proposition, we have borrowed from the Davis–Moore (1945) hypotheses[4] and Bernard Barber's (1978) more recent theory of occupational prestige. As indicated in the definitions presented earlier, prestige involves bestowing honor and esteem; and when we analyze its concentration, we are addressing the question: What proportion of all people in a society is bestowed what level of honor and esteem? Equation 3 states that the concentration of prestige is an additive function of the number of people in a society (N) and the number of positions *perceived* by its members to carry at least some degree of power (Po), skill (SK), functional importance (FI), or material wealth (Mw). The more of these attributes people bestow on a position, the greater will be the honor, esteem, or prestige given to that position. The perceptions do not have to be accurate; people only have to *believe* that others have power, skill, functional importance, or wealth for them to be given prestige. As is evident, however, the number of people in a society is a critical variable in assessing the concentration of prestige. Our concern is not with the level of prestige of any one position but with the *proportion* of all positions in a society receiving honor. The greater the number of positions receiving prestige in relation to the total number of positions, and the greater the number of people in these prestigious positions, then the less concentrated is prestige in a society. And conversely, the fewer the prestigious positions, and the fewer the people in those positions, then the more concentrated is the prestige.

We should emphasize that prestige is a somewhat different resource from either material wealth or power, primarily because it is a perceptual and behavioral variable. It is *bestowed* when people *perceive* that a position has power, functional importance, skill, or wealth. We are assuming in this statement that people naturally assess positions in terms of these attributes and are willing to give varying degrees of honor in accordance with how much of any one attribute is perceived to exist and which combination of attributes a position is perceived to possess. That is, people want to know which positions are powerful, which ones involve skill, which ones are important for the society, and which ones carry wealth. We are also assuming in Equation 3 that people perceive power as the most deserving of honor, followed, respectively, by perceived skill, functional importance, and wealth. Again, these perceptions do not have to be accurate; people only have to believe that a position carries one of these attributes.

Principles on "Social Class" Processes

As noted earlier, one of sociologists' and anthropologists' most ambiguous concepts is denoted by the label *social class* or, alternatively, *rank* and *stratum*. What is typically termed social class is, at the very least, the intersection of two distinct processes: (1) the process of differentiation (DF_{HO}) of relatively homogeneous subpopulations in societies and (2) the process of ranking (RA_{HO}) of these homogeneous subpopulations.

Differentiation of Homogeneous Subpopulations. In Equation 4 we present our ideas on those properties that affect the degree of differentiation among, and homogeneity in, a society's subpopulations (DF_{HO}).

$$(4) \quad DF_{HO} = W_1 \log(N) \times W_4(DF_p{}^{\exp}) \times W_5 \log(DF_{T,S})$$
$$\times W_2(I^{\exp}) \times W_3 \log(D)$$

where

N = the total number of people in a social system

I = the degree of inequality in the distribution of rewards, or $C_{MW} + C_{PO} + C_{PR}$

D = the rate of discriminatory acts by members of the majority against members of minority subpopulations in a social system

DF_p = the degree of differentiation of productive positions in a social system

$DF_{T,S}$ = the degree of differentiation of productive positions in time and geographical space

and where

$$W_1 = W_2 > W_3 > W_4 > W_5$$

Equation 4 suggests that the degree of differentiation among, and extent of homogeneity within, subpopulations is a function of size (N), functional, spatial, and vertical differentiation $(DF_p, DF_{T,S}, I)$, and discriminatory behavior (D). These factors are seen as interactive in their impact on DF_{HO}. That is, the impact of each factor on the degree of differentiation of homogeneous subpopulations depends on levels of the other factors. Equation 4 also suggests that the effects of each factor on DF_{HO} are nonlinear and that size and vertical differentiation have larger effects than do discrimination (D), functional differentiation (DF_p), and spatial differentiation $(DF_{T,S})$.

As Spencer and Durkheim[5] argued a century ago, there is a basic relation between social differentiation and population size. Part of this relation is purely mathematical in that a small population cannot be divided into as many subunits as a large one. But there are also substantive lines of argument: (1) differentiation of productive and political activities is necessary to sustain and control larger populations; (2) differentiation of larger populations will result from the increasing difficulty of sustaining high rates of face-to-face interaction as the number of interacting parties increases; (3) differentiation of larger populations will ensue from the increasing difficulty of maintaining physical proximity of individuals as their numbers increase. Thus, certainly one of the driving forces behind differentiation is population size. Yet, although population size may increase the degree of social differentiation, it does not account for the degree of homogeneity of differentiated social units.

Our concern is not just with differentiation (DF) but also with those forces related to the creation of homogeneity among differentiated subpopulations (HO). This emphasis requires isolating those forces that are related to increasing not just differentiation itself but also homogeneity of differentiated subpopulations, or DF_{HO}. Inequality (I) is certainly one such force, since when people possess varying levels of resources, their perceptions and actions will also vary, for the level and configuration of one's resources enable one to do some things and not others; and we assume that people with similar levels of resources are likely to see and act in convergent ways. A high degree of inequality in the distribution of resources produces differences in people's shares of resources; and those with similar shares are, in general, likely to be similar in their attitudes and modal behaviors.

Another condition fostering homogeneity in subpopulations is discrimination, for when members of a society are consistently subject to discrimination (D), they are likely to be excluded from certain positions and forced into a relatively narrow range of productive roles, thereby differentiating them from others while forcing a convergence of attitudes and behaviors. Moreover, victims of discrimination are likely to band together as a way of insulating themselves from the abuses of discrimination, with the result that as their rates of interaction increase, they become more alike in outlook and behavior (which, of course, makes them easier targets of discrimination).

Differentiation of productive positions (DF_p) is another force creating homogeneity. Those in similar roles are likely to develop common outlooks, because (1) their experiences are similar, (2) their rates of interaction are high, and (3) their shares of resources converge. Moreover, if these roles are separated in time and space $(DF_{T,S})$, there are further pressures for the convergence of attitudes and behaviors; for when people are separated in time and region, especially when performing their major income-producing roles, they are likely to develop a common perspective and to engage in modal behaviors that distinguish them from others.

The weightings of the variables in Equation 4 follow from our comments above. Population size (N) is probably the most important initial force in increasing DF_{HO}, because in a small population, differentiation of a society is unlikely. Only in small populations, however, are the limiting effects of size on differentiation fully realized, as is indicated by the logarithmic form of the relation shown in Equation 4. The impact of distributional inequality (I) acts in the opposite direction, with "increasing marginal returns" to differentiation as inequalities increase. Discrimination (D) is the next most critical force, since it is a major factor increasing rates of interaction within groups. The logarithmic form of the relation between D and DF_{HO} suggests that relatively low levels of discrimination are sufficient to induce group interaction effects and that further increases in discrimination result in smaller increases in interaction. Differentiation of productive activities (DF_p) and separation of subpopulations in time and space $(DF_{T,S})$ are also critical forces in generating homogeneity, though less so than discrimination. The relation between DF_p and DF_{HO} is exponential in that early differentiation of productive roles leads to less differentiation of whole subpopulations than do subsequent increases in differentiation. The relation of $DF_{T,S}$ to DF_{HO} is logarithmic, since initial increases in the separation in time and space of productive workers have more influence on the homogeneity of differentiated subpopulations than do further increments of $DF_{T,S}$.

In Equation 4, size, discrimination, and the various forms of differentiation $(DF_p, DF_{T,S}, I)$ are shown as interdependent in their impacts on DF_{HO}. This multiplicative form is a way of specifying a series of assertions that we feel reflect many of the major ideas about the formation of subpopulations that exist in the sociological literature. The multiplicative combination of N, I, DF_p, $DF_{T,S}$, and D asserts, for example, that the impacts of differentiation $(DF_p, DF_{T,S}, I)$ on the formation of homogeneous subpopulations are greater in large populations than in small. It is also likely, though beyond the scope of this chapter, that size, differentiation, and discrimination effects on the formation of homogeneous subpopulations are accelerated by causal relations among these factors.

Ranking of Differentiated and Homogeneous Subpopulations. In Equation 5 we present our ideas on the conditions affecting the degree of rank ordering among subpopulations (RA_{HO}):

$$(5) \quad RA_{HO} = W_1 \log(CN_{VS}) \times W_2(DF_{HO}{}^{\exp})$$

where

CN_{VS} = the degree of consensus over value standards among members of social systems

DF_{HO} = the extent of differentiation of, and the degree of homogeneity in, subpopulations in a social system (see Equation 4)

and where

$$W_1 > W_2$$

Equation 5 states that the degree of linear rank ordering among homogeneous subpopulations (RA_{HO}) is a logarithmic function of the degree of consensus over value standards (CN_{VS}) and an exponential function of the degree of differentiation of homogeneous subpopulations (DF_{HO}). Consensus over value standards is weighted more heavily than subpopulation formation. And CN_{VS} and DF_{HO} are seen as multiplicatively related in that increases in the value of one increase the impact of the other on ranking.

Equation 5 borrows from Parsons's (1953) "analytical model" of stratification, which we view as a theory of ranking more than as a model of stratification.[6] To assess the worthiness of an object, it is necessary to have standards; and at the societal level of organization,[7] we argue, the degree of consensus over value standards is the critical force. In systems with high degrees of consensus, the criteria for ranking are clear, and it is relatively easy to assign a position in that system a rank in terms of its worth as measured against value standards. We have speculated that this relation between ranking (RA) and value consensus (CN_{VS}) is logarithmic because initial increases in value consensus set into motion efforts to apply those agreed-on standards to virtually any differences among the members of a society. We are assuming, of course, that people naturally tend to evaluate and rank one another—an assumption that we feel is reasonable.

In the context of social stratification, our concern is with ranking of homogeneous subpopulations (RA_{HO}), and if a system is to reveal ranked subpopulations, there must be distinct differences among some of its subpopulations. Otherwise, ranking under conditions of high CN_{VS} will be in terms of the attributes of individuals. For us, the degree of differentiation of homogeneous subpopulations (DF_{HO}) is the critical consideration in creating ranked "social classes," because homogeneity of behaviors and attitudes within different subpopulations gives members of a society a target or object for applying their value standards. But without fairly high degrees of DF_{HO}, rankings will not be clearly linear, since distinctions among subpopulations will be somewhat ambiguous. It is for this reason that the relation between RA_{HO} and DF_{HO} is exponential; that is, initial increases in DF_{HO} are much less critical than further increases, since it is only when DF_{HO} is high that RA_{HO} can also be high.

In Equation 5 CN_{VS} is given more weight than DF_{HO}, because considerable ranking occurs even in populations with quite low levels of differentiation. Yet DF_{HO} can, even at low levels of value consensus, lead to at least some efforts at ranking, we believe, because people in different subgroupings will seek to assess their relative standing (indeed, individuals are constantly engaged in "social comparison" processes). In fact, as people seek to assess their relative standing, they often create value standards to justify their assessments.

In Equation 5 value consensus and differentiation of homogeneous subpopulations are shown as multiplicatively related to RA_{HO}. This multiplicative form suggests that the impact of DF_{HO} on ranking is greater at high levels of value consensus and, conversely, that the impact of value consensus on ranking is greatest in highly differentiated societies. In addition, though beyond the scope of this exercise, the process of ranking in societies is further reinforced by relations between CN_{VS} and DF_{HO} such that increases in the two tend to be associated.

To the degree that stratification involves consideration of "classes" of individuals, then theory must separate those processes that create subpopulations and those that lead to ranking of these subpopulations. We are not arguing that Equations 4 and 5 exhaust the conceptual possibilities for isolating the constituent processes of social class, but we are asserting that it is necessary to view class as the outcome of a series of discrete processes that require separate theoretical principles. Two of these processes are DF_{HO} and RA_{HO}.

Mobility Processes

In Equation 6 we present our ideas on the process of vertical mobility (MO) as defined earlier:

$$(6) \quad MO = \left[W_1(DF_{HO}^{-exp}) \times W_2(RA_{HO}^{-exp})\right]$$
$$+ \left[W_3(NP^{exp}) \times W_4(CP^{exp})\right]$$
$$+ \left[W_5(C_{OR}^{-exp}) \times W_6(C_{IR}^{-exp})\right]$$

where

DF_{HO} = the extent and degree of differentiation of homogeneous subpopulations in a social system (see Equation 4)

RA_{HO} = the degree of linear rank ordering of subpopulations in a social system (see Equation 5)

NP = the absolute number of productive positions in a social system

CP = the rate of change in the types of productive positions in a social system

C_{OR} = the degree of concentration of organizational resources in a social system

C_{IR} = the degree of concentration of individual resources in a social system

and where

$$W_1 = W_2 = W_3 = W_4 > W_5 > W_6$$

In Equation 6 the rate of mobility is seen as a function of three basic terms. The first, RA_{HO} and DF_{HO}, may be thought of as the height of the barriers to mobility, or distances among the classes. The negative exponential form attached to these terms suggests that increases in interclass distances at low levels do little to dampen interclass mobility, while similar incremental changes in interclass distances at higher levels have much greater mobility-dampening consequences.

The second major element of Equation 6 refers to "structural" mobility—that is, moves facilitated by either the complexity of the positional structure (NP) or changes in structure (CP). As the number of positions increases, the number of possible moves between positions is seen as increasing exponentially. This is mathematically obvious and requires no further comment. Similarly, changes in the number of positions (CP) create "vacancy chains" such that the total number of possible moves increases exponentially for each new position created. NP and CP are seen as related to total mobility in a multiplicative way. An increase of one position in a quite simple structure (low levels of NP) is seen as setting off far fewer moves than a one-position increase in a more complex structure, because far more moves will be required to readjust the more complex structure to the changes induced by the addition of a new position.

The third element of the mobility equation (C_{OR} and C_{IR}) suggests that, controlling for structural mobility and barriers to interclass mobility, concentration of organizational and individual resources acts to reduce aggregate mobility. This part of the equation represents the "human capital" or "status attainment" approach to circulation mobility. It suggests that, to the degree that individual resources or access to organizational resources is unequally distributed in a population, aggregate rates of mobility are reduced. Such reductions of mobility rates due to unequal distribution of resources are not linear in their effect, in that increases in C_{OR} and C_{IR} at low levels are argued to have little impact on mobility, while marginal increases in C_{OR} or C_{IR} at high levels act to restrict mobility chances substantially.

The rationale for the relation specified in Equation 6 can be expressed in terms of the processes that connect the variables to one another. Rates of interaction within a homogeneous subpopulation are greater than those outside the subpopulation, creating pressures for similarity in behaviors and attitudes. Such similarities present a barrier to those who would enter this subpopulation, since there is likely to be dissimilarity between the attitudes and behavioral patterns of subpopulation members and those who would seek to enter a population. Unless anticipatory socialization occurs, or unless individuals can acquire the necessary behavioral and attitudinal repertoire quickly on entering a new subpopulation, entry will prove difficult. Ranking of subpopulations accelerates these processes by giving members of a subpopulation something to lose if those below them can penetrate their group, for the more persons who can occupy a given rank, the less will be its worth. Of course, high degrees of ranking of groups provide incentives for upwardly mobile individuals or groups of individuals, but other things being equal, these pressures are more than compensated for by people's desire to preserve their position and exclude those who would dilute its worth. Thus, as homogeneity and ranking of subpopulations increase, processes that inhibit mobility are increasingly operative; and hence DF_{HO} and RA_{HO} not only are multiplicatively related to each other but are related in a negative exponential curve to MO.

The number of productive positions in a society is, we feel, an obvious and very important force. If positions are few, opportunities for movement are limited. But as the number of positions increases, opportunities for people to move to new positions increase, since someone must fill the expanding number of productive roles. When such increases are associated with changes in types of productive positions, then there are even more new opportunities for individuals or groups of individuals.

Whether individuals (or collectivities) can take advantage of opportunities created by such changes is influenced by their organizational and individual resources. Access to resources also influences people's capacity to maintain their rank in the face of changes in the number and nature of positions. If organizational resources are highly concentrated, then those in higher positions can maintain their relative station in either static or changing systems. But if resources are widely dispersed, then pressures for change in people's positions can be generated. Moreover, once changes occur as a result of these pressures or for other reasons, people have the organizational resources to take advantage of the opportunities created by such changes. Dispersion of individual resources accelerates these processes by allowing more people to use their skills to create effective organizations that generate pressures for new opportunities and by increasing the number of persons who can take advantage of whatever opportunities become available.

Conclusion

In this chapter we have argued that theory in sociology should consist of a series of simple and abstract principles about generic social processes. Theory about composite phenomena, such as stratification, thus consists of an ad hoc juxtaposition of elementary principles. We have sought to illustrate the utility of this no doubt controversial strategy by developing six abstract and simple equations about the generic properties of the social universe that, when found operating together, create a social form usually termed *stratification*.

We do not assert categorically that these six are the only processes involved; there may be more. Our view, however, is that the processes delineated in Equations 1 through 6 are among the most critical; for, whatever else may be involved, stratification is a social form created by the intersection of those processes involved (1) in concentrating material wealth, power, and prestige, (2) in creating subpopulations that become rank-ordered, and (3) in accelerating or lessening the movement of people and groups as they move from one ranked population to another. A "natural science of society" seeks to explain the operation of these processes; and even though Equations 1 through 6 may require refinement or be subject to empirical refutation, they represent a sincere effort to develop scientific theory in the social sciences.

Notes

1. A similar approach to the concept "centralization" as the degree of concentration in the distribution of formal authority across actors in a system is elaborated in Hanneman and Hollingsworth (1978).

2. Marx's basic ideas can be represented as follows: $C_{MW} = W_1(P^{exp}) \times W_2\log(C_{CP})$, where C_{CP} is defined as the concentration of control in the means of production and where $W_1 > W_2$. Lenski's formulation can be expressed as follows: $C_{MW} = W_1(P^{exp}) \times W_2(ES^{exp}) \times W_3(C_{PO}^{exp})$, where ES is defined as the level of economic surplus and where $W_1 > W_2 > W_3$.

3. This formulation borrows much from Herbert Spencer's (1885) early analysis. Spencer's formulation can be expressed as follows: $C_{PO} = W_1\log(ET) + W_2(IC^{exp}) + [W_3(IT^{exp}) \times W_4(P^{exp})]$, where $W_1 > W_2 > W_3 > W_4$.

4. The Davis–Moore hypothesis can be expressed as follows: $C_{PR} = W_1 - \log(\frac{FI}{N}) + W_2 - \log(\frac{AP}{N})$, where AP is defined as the number of personnel available to fill positions defined as functionally important and where $W_1 > W_2$.

5. Spencer's (1885) formulation can be expressed as $DF =$

$N^{\exp}$, and Durkheim's ([1893], 1947) can be expressed as $DF = (N^{\exp}) + \frac{EC}{N}$, where EC is defined as the extent of geographical space.

6. Parsons's (1953) basic proposition can be summarized as follows: $I = \log(CN_{VS}) + DF_A^{\exp}$, where DF_A is defined as the differentiation of actors in terms of "qualities," "performances," and "possessions."

7. More abstractly, $RA = (CN_S) \times (DF_A)$, where RA is defined as ranking, CN_S as consensus over standards of evaluation, and DF_A as the differentiation of actors.

References

BARBER, BERNARD
    1978   "Inequality and Occupational Prestige: Theory, Research, and Social Policy." *Sociological Inquiry* 48(2): 75–88.

BLAU, PETER
    1970   "A Formal Theory of Differentiation in Organizations." *American Sociological Review* 35(2):210–218.

DAVIS, KINGSLEY, AND MOORE, WILBERT E.
    1945   "Some Principles of Stratification." *American Sociological Review* 10(Apr.):242–249.

DURKHEIM, EMILE
    1947   *The Division of Labor in Society.* New York: Free Press. (Originally published 1893.)

HANNEMAN, ROBERT A., AND HOLLINGSWORTH, J. ROGERS
    1978   "The Problem of Centralization: Health and Education Policies in Great Britain and the United States." Paper presented at the annual meeting of the American Political Science Association, New York.

LENSKI, GERHARD
    1966   *Power and Privilege.* New York: McGraw-Hill.

MARX, KARL
    1967   *Capital: A Critical Analysis of Capitalist Production.* Vol. 1. New York: International Publishers. (Originally published 1867.)
    1971   *The Communist Manifesto.* New York: International Publishers. (Originally published 1848.)

MAYHEW, BRUCE H., AND SCHOLLAERT, PAUL T.
  1980   "The Concentration of Wealth: A Sociological Model."
         Sociological Focus 13(1):1-35.
MICHELS, ROBERT
  1915   *Political Parties: A Sociological Study of the Oligarchal
         Tendencies of Modern Democracy.* New York: Hearst's
         International Library.
PARSONS, TALCOTT
  1953   "A Revised Analytical Approach to the Theory of
         Stratification." In R. Bendix and S. M. Lipset (Eds.),
         Class, Status, and Power. New York: Free Press.
RADCLIFFE-BROWN, A. R.
  1948   *A Natural Science of Society.* New York: Free Press.
SIMMEL, GEORG
  1956   *Conflict and the Web of Group Affiliations.* New
         York: Free Press.
SPENCER, HERBERT
  1885   *Principles of Sociology.* New York: D. Appleton.
TURNER, JONATHAN H.
  1972   *Patterns of Social Organization.* New York: McGraw-
         Hill.
TURNER, JONATHAN H., AND STARNES, CHARLES
  1976   *Inequality: Privilege and Poverty in America.* Santa
         Monica, Calif.: Goodyear.
WEBER, MAX
  1968   *Economy and Society.* (Translated by Guenther Roth.)
         New York: Bedminister Press.

This chapter sets forth a general theory of gender stratification. While both biological and ideological variables are taken into account, the emphasis is structural: It is proposed that the major independent variable affecting sexual inequality is each sex's economic power, understood as relative control over the means of production and allocation of surplus. For women, relative economic power is seen as varying—and not always in the same direction—at a variety of micro- and macrolevels, ranging from the household to the state. A series of propositions links the antecedents of women's relative economic power, the interrelationship between economic and other forms of power, and the forms of privilege and opportunity into which each gender can translate its relative power.

🌿 2 🌿

A GENERAL THEORY OF GENDER STRATIFICATION

Rae Lesser Blumberg

UNIVERSITY OF CALIFORNIA, SAN DIEGO

Stratification theories may be viewed as attempts to explain differential power and privilege, and how the former begets the latter (Lenski, 1966); this theory of gender stratification is no exception. For all the theory's complexity, one factor—economic power—stands out. Crudely, it could be summarized by paraphrasing the popular expression "Remember the Golden Rule—he who has the gold makes the rules." In my version, it would be expanded to *he* and *she,* the amount of gold controlled by each sex would be compared, and the result would be used to help predict the extent to which each could make the rules. And if there

I would like to thank Randall Collins, Mary Freifeld, Clare Langham and Jacqueline Wiseman for their helpful comments on an earlier version of this chapter.

is one thing that is clear about relations between *he* and *she* today, it is that the rules are changing.

C. Wright Mills's famous dictum (1959) tells us that we live our lives at the intersection of history and social structure. At this moment in history, the position of women in the social structure is in flux; and most of us are already feeling it in our personal lives. For some of us, the changes in the system of sexual stratification have come home in the form of "personal troubles"—the typical manner, Mills tells us, in which we experience the birth of new public issues. But for most of us, the changing relations between the sexes have brought new pleasures as well as new pains. In the bedroom, in the kitchen, on the job, on TV, in the world around us, we are experiencing new ways of being—and seeing—men and women.[1]

It was roughly in 1970 that the changing roles and status of women surfaced as a "public issue," in Millsian terms. Media attention in the United States began focusing on a fledgling women's liberation movement, and a new literature attempting to account for "women's place" began to grow. As with many new ideologically tinged issues, theories emerged faster than a new data base. In particular, solid new information was scant on the enormous diversity of gender stratification, both among humans and among nonhuman primates. Since then, many important new data, largely from anthropology, have become available. Since these data remain little known in sociological circles, yet have clear importance for theories of gender stratification, they will be detailed here. In light of these recent findings, it now appears that many of the early 1970s theories of female status overestimated the extent and universality of female subordination among human populations, underestimated the range and level of women's economic productivity, and overestimated the influence of certain biological factors —for example, male brawn as a source of dominance and female baby-making as a source of dependence.

The next section presents a reassessment of the over- and underestimates mentioned above, in terms of the new evidence and improved data base. In later sections I review relevant strands of theorizing about both gender and societal stratification, and then propose and explicate a general theory of sexual stratification. The argument is developed around a series of twenty-five propositions or hypotheses. (These hypotheses, it should be noted, are presented in eight subsets or clusters, with discussion interspersed.) The theory is intended to have broad cross-cultural and historical application, and represents a further development of previous versions (Blumberg, 1974, 1978, 1979a) in the light of the growing accumulation of knowledge of the dynamics and determinants of gender relations.

The argument is complex and multicausal. While biological and ideological variables are taken into account, the emphasis is structural. As in the previous versions, the major independent variable affecting sexual inequality is women's relative economic power. The most important component of economic power continues to be conceptualized—as first argued by Marx—as relative control of the means of *production* and allocation of surplus. But now, that power is seen as varying—and not always in the same direction—at a variety of micro- and macrolevels. In fact, a growing body of evidence indicates that women can have different (and changing) degrees of relative economic power at the level of the household, the community, the class, and the state. The remainder of the theory focuses on the antecedents of women's relative economic power, the relations between economic and other forms of power (most of which are much less easily accessible to women than is economic power), and the forms of privilege into which each sex can translate its relative power.

Recent Evidence on Gender Stratification

With the broader angle of vision offered by anthropological and historical lenses, sociologists can avoid the trap of generalizing from the present and recent past of their class and country—and concluding that "this is the way the world is." Let us use these lenses to reassess the still common picture of women as invariably subordinated, economically dependent, and strongly bound by biology.

Scenarios of Sexual Equality. Are women always the "second sex"? Although no evidence has surfaced of a society in which females have clear overall dominance, we now have data on several diverse groups where the overall position of men and women appears equal or virtually so. The apparently most egalitarian group ever discovered, the Tasaday of Mindanao in the Philippines, was first contacted in the early 1970s (see, for example, Fernandez and Lynch, 1972; Nance, 1975). Before their discovery, the gentle, twenty-six-member band apparently did not hunt, and they seemed to have no sexual division of labor in gathering, their main productive activity. Although the group was unstratified and communal, the individual who appeared to have the most influence and prestige was an older woman. Other foraging (hunting and gathering) groups shade off from the apparently complete sexual equality of the Tasaday, although ethnographic descriptions of the Mbuti pygmies of Zaire's Ituri forest (for example, Turnbull, 1961, 1981) and the !Kung Bushmen of the Kalahari Desert (for example, Lee, 1968, 1969; Draper, 1975) come close. Both, incidentally, have more of a sexual division of labor in subsistence activities than the Tasaday, with women doing more of the gathering and men doing more of the hunting.

It need not be concluded, however, that the absence of sexual differentiation in production is needed for sexual equality. A very different scenario prevailed among the Iroquois, a horticultural group of colonial North America that "approach most closely to that hypothetical form of society known as the matriarchate" (Murdock, 1934:302, cited in Brown, 1975:237). The Iroquois were characterized both by great separation of the spheres of men and women and matricentered kinship institutions. Residence was matrilocal (the groom moved into the longhouse of the bride's female kin), descent was matrilineal, and economic resources passed by inheritance from mothers to daughters (although the land was communally owned, the women *controlled* it). In fact, women controlled the entire economy: land, crops, stored food, dwellings (longhouses). They also did virtually all the agricultural labor. Chiefs were always male, however, and men controlled the formal political and military spheres, although a "council of matrons" nominated a chief and had the right to depose him if they disapproved of his performance. But women's control of the economic sector was so nearly total that they seemed to have veto power over political and military ventures not to their liking (see Brown, 1970, 1975).

Still a different scenario of relative sexual equality is provided by two Western Bontoc (Igorot) subgroups in the Philippines.

The Tanulong and Fedilizan peoples of Luzon are more technologically advanced than the Iroquois, cultivating irrigated rice in elaborate terraces. Women are described as having equal status by Bacdayan (1977), who studied these groups in 1974: Their way of life
involves intense cooperation and interchangeability of tasks in production and a strong orientation to the nuclear family. Both sexes
inherit. Astoundingly, 81 percent of all tasks may be done by
either sex. By way of comparison, Murdock and Provost's study
(1973) of 186 preindustrial societies revealed a worldwide average
of only 16 percent interchangeability of tasks.

Below I shall argue that the most important commonality
uniting these three very different scenarios of apparent sexual
equality (or virtual sexual equality) is that women wielded at least
half the economic power.

Here, however, three generalizations are relevant. First, we
know of no society more complex than the Iroquois or Western
Bontoc that has been described as having equal status for women.
In other words, once societies develop complex political economies and stratification systems extending beyond the community
level, these are dominated by men. Second, most of the more sexually egalitarian societies of the world tend to correspond to one
of the three scenarios described above. As a group, hunting and
gathering societies (which account for over 99 percent of human
history) most closely approach sexual equality. Two other clusters
of societies where women approach equal status at the household
and community levels are those horticultural societies—mostly in
Africa—where women control substantial economic resources
(land or trade) and those irrigationist societies—mostly in Southeast Asia—where both sexes inherit rice land and women tend to
trade in the market on their own account. Third, during recent
years, colonialism, trends in the world economy, and deliberate
development schemes have tended to undermine the position of
women in many of the groups where it had been highest (see Boserup, 1970; Tinker, 1976; Blumberg, 1976a, 1979b, 1981). In this
regard, Sanday (1981:158) found that 60 percent of the 156 preindustrial societies she studied in which women were coded as having no economic or political power had been described after 1925.
Conversely, 63 percent of the societies in which women had some
political power had been described before 1925. She concluded

that contact with male-dominated European society had a dele-
terious effect.

In short, it is clear from the ethnographic information presented here that it is simplistic and overstated to universally regard
women as the "second sex" (de Beauvoir, 1952).

Women as Parasites Versus Women as Producers. In 1955,
when Parsons and Bales (1955:151) generalized that men are the
principal providers, "whereas the wife is primarily the giver of
love," very few would have objected to a view of women as economically nonproductive through most of human history. But
from evidence compiled largely since the late 1960s, we now know
that precisely the opposite has been true.

Before presenting the evidence, it is necessary to provide
some background. The mainline of human evolutionary history is
characterized by only a handful of "technoeconomic bases"—ways
in which people achieved their livelihood. These are (1) *foraging*
(hunting and gathering), which for several million years apparently
characterized all human groups, (2) *horticultural,* which apparently
emerged first in Africa some 18,000 years ago, in the Middle East
about 10,000–12,000 years ago, and in Mesoamerica roughly 7,000–
8,000 years ago, (3) *agrarian,* which emerged in the Middle East
perhaps 5,000–6,000 years ago, and (4) *industrial,* which dates to
roughly 1800 A.D. in England and parts of northwestern Europe.
Horticulture is done with digging stick or hoe on small, garden-size
plots. Agriculture, most typically, involves plow cultivation on
large, cleared fields; it may be irrigated or "dry" (rainfall-based).

Among *foraging* societies, in virtually all but Arctic-latitude
groups, most of the food supply is gathered, not hunted: fully 60–
80 percent, according to Lee and DeVore (1968). Men are the predominant hunters and women are the main gatherers. For example, in my calculations based on the 1,170-society computer
version of Murdock's *Ethnographic Atlas* (1967), women were the
primary labor force in 86 percent of the 85 societies whose main
activity was gathering.[2]

Among *horticultural* societies, I found a predominantly
male labor force in only about a fifth of the 376 *Ethnographic
Atlas* societies whose main economic activity is hoe cultivation. In
fact, most archeologists (see, for example, Childe, 1964:65–66)
now credit women with the development of early horticulture.

Historically, foraging and horticulture account for all but the last fraction of 1 percent of our three- to four-million-year human history; and women were the primary producers in most such societies.

Among *agrarian* societies, history makes a dramatic reversal. In the nonirrigated ones (the great majority), women play only a minor productive role. Only in the minority where the main crop is irrigated paddy rice is female labor significant. But since all of today's industrial societies, both capitalist and socialist, spring from agrarian origins, the view of woman as nonproducer is not surprising. Furthermore, agrarian societies represent the overall low point of female status in human history (for example, Michaelson and Goldschmidt's 1971 study of forty-six peasant societies found almost universal female subjugation); since this is *our* recent past, it is little wonder that we tend to think of women as "second-class citizens" throughout all of human history.

The societies of the *Ethnographic Atlas* are overwhelmingly foraging, horticultural, and agrarian. Aronoff and Crano (1975) calculated women's contribution to subsistence in all the *Atlas* societies: Overall, females produced 44 percent of the food supply.

Turning to contemporary nations, most of us would be even more surprised to learn that, according to new United Nations estimates, the world's women, as farmers, produce fully 50 percent of the world's food (Leeper, 1978:129). Women account for "60 to 80 percent of the agricultural labour in Asia and Africa; in Latin America . . . the percentage is 40 percent" (United Nations, 1978: 5).

Until the recent compilations discussed above, women's role in food production had been largely invisible. Even today, national statistics in most Third World countries rarely record the work that poor rural women do (see, for example, Deere, 1977; Garrett, 1976), and they tend to underestimate women's participation in the urban labor force as well.

All these data help to correct the picture of women as economically dependent housewives. But in anticipation of the argument to come, let us note that women's economic productivity is not enough, in and of itself, to lead to equal status.

Male Brawn and Female Baby-Making: Changing Views of Biological Factors. The last area where recent findings and/or

"paradigm shifts" (Kuhn, 1970) modify long-prevalent views concerns the biological underpinnings for sexual stratification. Let us
avoid the temptation of setting up "straw men" (or women) of the
cruder biological determinists and then demolishing them by observing that whereas men were and are bigger and stronger than
women and that women continue to have 100 percent of the
babies, the status of women is not a constant. Rather, female status varies dynamically from era to era, country to country, class to
class, and even household to household. Instead, let us look to
more sophisticated theories that nonetheless base part or all of
their explanation on now empirically questionable views of biological constraints. Two examples that emerged in the first rush of
new theorizing around 1970 will be given: for "brawn," Collins's
conflict theory (1971; see also 1975) and for "babies," Firestone's
radical feminist "case for feminist revolution" (1970).

As underpinning to his complex conflict theory (to be discussed later), Collins makes some assumptions concerning the
greater size, strength, and sexual aggressiveness of human males.
He views these assumptions as "amenable to empirical test" (1975:
233) rather than given.

But his assumptions are drawn from the then-available data
on the relation between male/female size differences and male
dominance among *nonhuman primates.* And our understanding
has changed. First he notes that, among baboons, macaques, and
gorillas, males are considerably bigger—and dominate females. So
far so good. The problem comes in his statement of the other side
of the coin: "The tree-dwelling gibbons, orangutans, howler monkeys, and chimpanzees, on the other hand, have little male dominance and, for the most part, little stable sexual pairings (or 'sexual property'); it is in these species that the males and females are
similar in size" (1975:233). Subsequent compilations of primate
research (see, for example, Leibowitz, 1978) give a different picture. First, it should be noted that, of the animals Collins names,
gibbons, orangutans, and chimps are *apes,* closer to humans in evolutionary terms than monkeys are (the fourth major ape species is
the gorilla). Gibbons, in fact, are the ape species with the *least* size
difference between male and female (almost none), but we now
know that they have the *most* stable sexual pairing of all the apes.
Conversely, male and female orangutans are *not* similar in size;

males average 160 pounds and females 80 (Leibowitz, 1978:62)—
the most dramatic sexual dimorphism among the apes. But they
do not show the male dominance/protector/"sexual property"
pattern attributed to the baboons, macaques, and gorillas. Rather,
males and females tend to range separately, so that "the smallish
orang females are essentially self-sufficient, rearing their young
without benefit of a male breadwinner, companion, or protector
for years at a time" (Leibowitz, 1978:75).

Collins also posits male desire for sexual gratification as the
fundamental motive in domination of females. It is relevant, then,
to cite the Mae Enga of the New Guinea highlands, one of the
most male-dominant groups on earth, because among them male
dominance and lust definitely are *not* linked. Mae Enga men believe that copulation is bad for their well-being and avoid it as
much as possible. (It should be noted that the Enga are under considerable population pressure.) Every ejaculation depletes a man's
vitality, mind, and body, they hold. So bachelors tend toward sexual abstinence, and married men tend to limit intercourse to the
level believed necessary for procreation (see Meggitt, 1964; Langness, 1967; Lindenbaum, 1972, 1976; Goldhamer, 1973; Schlegel,
1977).

Given his insistence that his assumptions constitute hypotheses to be tested among humans, would Collins have proposed
them in the knowledge of the subsequent data just summarized? It
should be noted that although we do not agree on the relative importance of the variables in his sexual stratification theory, my argument here is not with the variables but rather with the presumed
biological constants invoked as assumptions for the theory.

Firestone (1970) concentrates on the female side of biological determinism, in contrast to Collins's focus on the male. She
takes as "fundamental fact" "that women throughout history before the advent of birth control were at the continual mercy of
their biology—menstruation, menopause, and 'female ills,' constant painful childbirth, wetnursing and care of infants, all of
which made them dependent on males . . . for physical survival"
(1970:8). Firestone's position has been described as the extreme
of radical feminism (Mayes, 1981). Radical feminist theory stresses
the primacy of *patriarchy*, rather than, say, class or capitalism, in
accounting for female subordination in today's world (see also

Mitchell, 1966, 1971). To Firestone, patriarchy is a transhistorical universal because of *female* biology.

Firestone then dates the advent of effective birth control to the industrial revolution (1970:16). This is the basis of her subsequent argument that women must use technology to free themselves from their enslavement to reproduction.

Would she have proposed this argument if she had been aware of the new data and theories concerning human reproduction that have since emerged?

- We have already seen that for most of human history females were major producers in their own right and *not* dependent on males for physical survival.
- New evidence from contemporary foraging groups shows that women space their children very widely (over four years apart) and that their average family size is quite low, averaging around 2.0 children (see, for example, Whiting, 1968:248-249; Birdsell, 1968:237, for child spacing and family size estimates, respectively). These estimates are projected back to our Pleistocene ancestors; if correct, that would indicate that for most of human history women were not the "baby-making machines" envisioned by Firestone.
- The methods used to accomplish this spacing included a variety of both passive and active means. In the former category are late weaning (forager women often nurse their children to age four) and low body fat ratios, both of which inhibit conception. Low body fat ratios have been found among such well-nourished but lean foragers as the nomadic !Kung of the Kalahari Desert (Kolata, 1974:932-934). Among the active means are not just infanticide and abortion but also the deliberate use of plants found to be effective for contraception.
- Since about 1972, a large new fertility literature has emerged linking births and spacing to prevailing economic conditions. (Early references include Polgar, 1972, 1975; Mamdani, 1972; Schnaiberg and Reed, 1974.) Since then, a new view has gained ground, in which fertility has been linked to the ratio of expected costs to benefits of children.[3]
- The evidence also indicates that the human groups and periods characterized by high fertility and closely spaced births are fairly

delimited. For example, it is in traditional and "developing" agrarian societies where (1) child labor is useful, (2) peasants are squeezed by landlords, and (3) women are both unimportant in cultivation and generally subjugated that we find the kind of high fertility and narrow spacing that Firestone took to be women's lot throughout history (see Blumberg, 1978, chap. 4). Spacing in horticultural societies tends to be intermediate between the wide spacing of foragers and the narrow spacing of agrarian groups under "indigenous" conditions, although the penetration of the world capitalist system frequently brings pronatalist pressure to the poor in many such groups (see, for example, American Association for the Advancement of Science, 1974).

Summing up, theories based on universal male domination and/or female dependency cannot stand up to the recent empirical evidence culled from human societies. Nor does the recent evidence based on nonhuman primates—especially apes—support the view that male size/strength/aggression is clearly related to dominance either over females or over other males. (In neither chimps nor humans, for example, is there evidence that the leaders or dominant groups are invariably the brawniest bullies.) This does not mean that male size/strength/aggressiveness and female fertility/lactation are irrelevant to theories of gender stratification. But it does indicate that they are overshadowed by other variables.

Which variables? A brief review of other theories accounting for sexual stratification is in order. Since my conceptualization of economic power (see below) invokes a Marxian view of the importance of the relations of production, let us begin with the "Marxist-feminist" theories. To what extent have they provided us with the basis for a general theory of gender stratification?

Toward a Theory of Gender Stratification:
A Selective Review of the Literature

Marxist Approaches. In his analysis of societal stratification and social change, Marx ([1867], 1967) emphasized the importance of control of the means of production. However, he was all but silent on the subject of women in his writings.

So perhaps it should not surprise us that the bulk of the Marxist approaches to gender relations provide little systematic exploration of the extent to which women's control/noncontrol of the means of production covaries with their relative oppression. Rather, most of the Marxist-feminist theories have either (1) built on Engels (1972) and concentrated on family arrangements and/or the extent to which women work in "social production" or (2) revolved around a long and convoluted debate on whether women's housework is or is not "productive labor" in the strict Marxian sense. Recently, a third school of analysis has emerged, focusing on women's role in the division of labor under capitalism.

In the first vein, Leacock, in her extraordinary introduction to the 1972 edition of Engels's *Origin of the Family, Private Property, and the State,* ultimately emphasizes the monogamous nuclear family (as an economic unit) as the locus of female subordination. Such a formulation is unable to account for the existence of one of the most male-dominant clusters of cultures on earth— the preclass "warrior complex" societies, which do not have the monogamous nuclear family. These societies are typified by general polygyny, female infanticide, patrilocal residence and patrilineal property control, horticulture, frequent warfare, male supremacy, male/female hostility, and, according to Harris (1974, 1977), protein shortage; examples include a number of New Guinea highlands groups and the Yanomamo (Chagnon, 1968) of Venezuela.

Sacks (1975), in another interpretation of what is important in Engels, stresses female participation in social production as the basis of social adulthood, which is seen as the key to women's status in the larger society. Only in the context of the household does Sacks look to control of property by sex: (1) the more household property a woman controls, the better her domestic position, with the caveat that (2) where women are not social adults in the larger society, their exercise of this domestic power (and even property) is likely to be restricted. I agree with Sacks about both 1 and 2. But her social production/social adulthood analysis does not account for women's subordinate status in contemporary capitalist or socialist states.

The second major Marxist approach contrasts sharply with the anthropological tradition based on Engels, focusing on whether housework in capitalist societies is or is not productive labor, as defined by Marx. The debate began in 1969 with Benston's influential article and went back and forth. Some (for example, Dalla Costa and James, 1972) advocated state-paid wages for housework; others urged socialization of housework. Despite a lengthy bibliography[4] (see Mayes, 1981, for a good summary), the debate underemphasized women's substantial (though low-paid) role as wage laborers under capitalism. The relatively unsocialized nature of most housework under socialism and the prevalence there of a "double day" for women are also slighted. Moreover, too little is made of the fact that if socialized housework is defined as "women's work," it will not free women—a fact made abundantly clear in the Israeli kibbutz (see Blumberg, 1976b). There, women's traditional domestic and childcare duties *are* socialized, but they are also generally lower in prestige than "productive" labor and have become about 90 percent of the occupational options open to women.

A third Marxist-feminist focus attempts to account for the sexual division of labor in the United States under industrial capitalism. Milkman (1980) explores how foot-dragging policies by organized labor at two historically crucial points helped congeal the present pattern of occupational sex segregation. Baron (1982) provides a case study of women printers from 1850–1880, which illustrates the influence of both capitalism and partriarchy. Burris and Wharton (1982) utilize segmented labor market theory to interpret the maintenance of sex segregation in male blue collar and female lower white collar occupations between 1950 and 1979. These studies are intended to increase our understanding of a delimited problem, rather than as general treatments of gender stratification in Marxian terms.

Non-Marxist Materialist Approaches. More work has been done by anthropologists than sociologists, despite the traditional sociological interest in stratification.

Peggy Sanday has moved from materialist analyses of female status in the public domain (1973, 1974) to a search for the origins of sexual inequality in, for example, the sexual symbols in a society's creation myths (1981). Her latest work offers some interesting insight into the sorts of preindustrial societies where women do have high ascribed status (for example, in addition to having female symbols in their origin myths, such societies are more likely to be plant than animal economies). But two of her earlier empirical findings have a more direct bearing on a theory of gender stratification applicable to the full range of human societies. First, in her 1973 analysis of twelve societies, she found that where women did not participate in production, their status was invariably low, but that mere work did not necessarily result in high status. Second, although her Guttman scale of female status in the public domain has changed somewhat over time, it still shows that women's control over *economic* resources tends to *precede* their *political* participation or influence (that is, the latter has a higher Guttman scale score). These findings agree with my work (see below). But Sanday's definition of high female status in the public domain remains very loose: She codes merely whether women have *any* economic control or political participation, not their degree of economic or political power. By Sanday's liberal criteria, incidentally, few societies are classified as sexually unequal (39 out of 139, to be exact).

Alice Schlegel's work is getting closer to a theory of sexual stratification, although her 1977 book still had not made the leap. Her 1972 work, based on a sample of sixty-six matrilineal societies, revealed that, in most, a woman was under the control of her husband (the most frequent case) or her brother. In only fourteen of these societies were women classified as "autonomous"—that is, dominated by neither husband nor brother. Her statistics are all bivariate, and her orientation is more concerned with cross-cousin marriage than with control of the means of production, so she did not follow up on the intriguing fact that in all fourteen of the "female autonomous" societies women had partial or full control of household property (apparently no other relationship encompassed 100 percent of the cases in a category). Nor did she link this finding to another intriguing one: Ten of these fourteen cases involved "pure case" matrilocal residence, where the bride remains in the environs of her *female* kin and the groom is the one to leave his immediate family. In short, a connection among control of household property, marital residence favoring the female, and women's autonomy can be inferred from the data but is never developed as a theory. In her 1977 book, Schlegel's conceptualization of gender stratification has become much more sophisticated.

She specifies some of the variables that should be included in a theory of sexual stratification, and her emphasis is on economic factors. Significantly, she stresses relations to production, rather than distribution, in her critique of Friedl (1975). I agree with her. She also decries the slighting of ideology by extant materialist theories. (I now agree with Leacock, 1972, that without attention to the ideological factors one is left without any inkling of the *process* whereby change occurs in material conditions.)

Ernestine Friedl (1975) invokes a number of explanatory factors in her rich description of various types of hunting-and-gathering and horticultural groups' systems of gender stratification. But, as noted, she focuses on the difference between men's and women's rights to distribute the products of their labor outside the household. Schlegel argues that the hunting-and-gathering groups Friedl (1975:39–45) depicts as male-dominant, the inland and maritime Eskimo, have *productive* institutions with positions of male authority. Schlegel thus offers an alternative interpretation to Friedl's stress on male dominance as the result of male control of the distribution of the scarce and valued meat supply. I would add that, in looking for economic power in the realm of distribution, control over the allocation of *surplus* seems more crucial than control over the allocation of basic subsistence. In preclass societies, withholding basic subsistence from members of the group is rarely an option. One area in which I am in agreement with Friedl is her proposition that the "spacing of children and the patterns of childrearing are everywhere adjusted to whatever kind of work women do" (1975:8).

Marvin Harris's theory of the male-supremacy complex under conditions of resource pressure has already been mentioned. Although not all societies with strong male dominance adhere to this pattern, the theory serves to focus attention on the weapons/organized-force issue. In societies with this pattern, males not only control the means of force, they also control the means of production. There is little question that the two dimensions synergistically enhance male control. Interestingly enough, even some Marxist and/or feminist anthropologists have invoked male control of means of force as the ultimate masculine trump card: Gough (1975:70–71) uses it to account for whatever degree of male subordination exists in "hunting societies." And Sanday (1981) finds

nothing in her analysis to contradict Harris. Just as not all male-supremacist societies conform to the warfare/force scenario, however, not all warfare societies are male-supremacist. Colonial-era
Iroquois men, though *internally* peaceful, were fierce warriors in
their frequent external wars. But there is no evidence of their
using this "ultimate trump card" on their womenfolk during this
period.

The topic of force and warfare makes an appropriate transition to Randall Collins's influential sociological theory of sexual
stratification. No other gender stratification theory in the literature has such a wealth of propositions, formally stated (twenty-
eight in the 1975 version)—and such a diverse array of insights.
Although we disagree on his use of biologically based assumptions,
the relative importance of the role of force (both personal and organized) in upholding sexual stratification, and other matters, we
agree on his notions about economic resources—for example, "In
general, the higher the relative income of a wife compared to her
husband, the greater her power within the family" (Collins, 1975:
250).

To Collins, "sexual property" ("the relatively permanent
claim to exclusive sexual rights over a particular person") is the
keystone of sexual stratification, but historical variation is introduced by differences in the patterns of social organization that affect (1) the use of force and (2) the bargaining/resource power of
males and females. He then posits an evolutionary sequence of
ideal types to exemplify these major patterns of force, resources,
and sexual stratification.

Collins is strongest on agrarian and modern societies and
weakest in his coverage of the anthropological literature on foraging
and horticultural societies. Hence, there are problems with his first
ideal type, "low-technology tribal societies." Because there is little surplus, Collins expects little sexual stratification in such societies, with male force used to enforce sexual property rights. In
fact, "low-technology tribal societies" encompass not only most
of the known variation in human kinship systems, which Collins
notes, but also most of the known variation in degree of gender
stratification, of which Collins seems unaware. The category includes the Tasaday and the Iroquois, at the high end of female
status, and the "warrior complex" societies such as the Mae Enga

and the Yanomamo. At the former end, however, there is little evidence that men resort to force to keep women down.

To Collins, the low point of female status is in his second type, the "fortified households in stratified society" (corresponding to such agrarian societies as medieval Europe). Here, the male head of household monopolizes the means of violence (as well as economic resources), and the casual use of force against women is most prevalent. Men enforce female chastity and fidelity. Once the state takes over this monopoly on legitimate violence, however, as in his third category, "private households in a market economy," men retain their control over economic resources but lose control over the instruments of force. The decline in family complexity and the rise of a market society are reflected in women's becoming potentially free to negotiate their own sexual relationships, "but since their main resource is their sexuality, the emerging free marriage market is organized around male trades of economic and status resources for possession of a woman" (1975:243). Romantic love emerges, as well as *women's* vigilance over their sexual purity as a bargaining tool. In the fourth type, the "affluent market economy," the state retains its monopoly of the means of violence, but expanded work opportunities for women increase their resource bargaining power. In general, women's jobs and hence economic resources tend to be inferior to men's. However, in particular households, the woman may dominate if her market resources (economic resources, sexual attractiveness, lower commitment to the relationship) exceed the man's. Thus, "the most favorable position of women is found in social classes where overt use of force is minimized and female economic resources are maximized" (1975:254).

Where Collins and I differ here is in the direction of causation. In this chapter, I argue that where women have attained a position of control over substantial economic resources (approaching or exceeding that of their menfolk), overt use of force against them will tend to be restrained. (I found a negative correlation of nearly -0.6 between my measure of women's relative economic power and men's use of personal violence—that is, wife beating— against them in my study of sixty-one preindustrial societies, as will be discussed below.) I recognize, however, that under certain circumstances personal and/or organized force *is* likely to be invoked. For example, where women—or any other subordinate group —are only beginning to acquire increased economic power, the dominant group may well resort to physical violence to prevent them from consolidating that power (new supporting data on Mexico City families [Roldan, 1983] are presented later in this chapter). History tells us that the results have been mixed, wielders of superior force not always emerging victorious—as, for example, in the overthrow of the shah of Iran.

Below, we shall explore the relative strength of force, political organization, and economic resources in accounting for female status. To Collins, "political organization is the organization of violence" (1975:230), and it can affect the use of both violence and economic resources in male/female relations: "When the political situation restricts personal violence and upholds a particular kind of economic situation, economic resources accruing to men and women can shift the balance of sexual power and, hence, the pattern of sexual behavior" (1975:230). This seems to imply the primacy of the political sphere, even over male biology. And once male biology *is* held in check, the remainder of Collins's theory of sexual stratification sounds more like a conflict theory of *societal* stratification.

Main Forms of Power Affecting Societal Stratification. How have the major theories of societal stratification conceptualized the main sources of power? Is their relative importance for sexual stratification different from their relative importance for societal stratification? My answers to these questions underlie my own theory of gender stratification and differentiate it from those reviewed above.

Stratification theories have been described as attempts to explain differential power and privilege and how the former begets the latter (see, for example, Lenski, 1966). The most relevant definition of power still seems to be Max Weber's: "the probability of persons or groups carrying out their will even when opposed by others" (Gerth and Mills, 1946:180). Differential privilege may be manifested in many ways—in differential possessions, perquisites, prerogatives, and freedoms or in differential forms of honor, status, deference, and prestige. But it appears that only a very few forms of power have been frequently proposed as crucial or determinative for a society's inequality systems. I have likened these sources of power to great "rivers flowing into a swampy delta, whereupon they split into a labyrinth of channels of privilege, more of which are blind or meandering than direct" (Blumberg, 1979a:117). Metaphors aside, fewer major forms of power are mentioned in the literature than manifestations of privilege and prestige.

Lenski (1966:57–58), for example, considers the power of force or coercion, as well as two forms of institutionalized power, the power of property and the power of position (in the group's political or other major hierarchies), to be the main sources of power underlying an inequality system. Others (Weber [1904–1905], 1958; Parsons and Bales, 1955) would add such ideational forms as ideology, religion, and/or values. In any concrete historical situation, the relative strength of these forms of power in affecting the stratification system will vary in a complex and dynamic way, so that examples can be found of instances in which one or the other or some particular mix proved determinant. Overall, however, ideology seems a somewhat weaker form of power—even though it is quite important in the day-to-day dynamics and processes of a stratification system. (It is especially relevant as a source of new ideas about equality or, more frequently, as a resource upholding the interests of the dominant group.) Concerning the relative strength of the other three main sources, power of force, economic power, and political power, controversy still rages.

In theoretical terms, the grounds for the debate were laid down by Marx when he posited that, in the final analysis, economic power is the "mainstream," the most important source. Specifically, he argued, it has been the forces of production and their control that have exerted the most important influences on the stratification system, social change, and the various other institutions of the society. Explicitly or implicitly, in agreement or in disagreement, the major theorists of societal stratification since then have had to wrestle with Marx's ghost.

In historical terms, the debate has been fueled by the fact that in some types of societies the importance of the productive forces and their control has been more readily apparent than in others. For example, in a capitalist system, surplus is reinvested, and the forces of production can expand so rapidly as to enhance the power of those who control them. In contrast, the economic

stagnation of most traditional agrarian societies meant that conquering people was a much more likely way of increasing the size
of the pie than conquering nature. Given the high rate of surplus
extraction (averaging around 50 percent of the crop worldwide),
peasant producers lacked incentives to increase output, and the
aristocrats of the ruling class rarely would have known how even
if they had wanted to. Under these circumstances, many might
argue, the importance of politicomilitary power would increase.

My view is that for *women,* for both empirical and theoretical reasons, the most important—and the most achievable—form
of power has been economic.

A General Theory of Gender Stratification

Empirical Importance of Economic Power for Women. We
have no concrete evidence of any society in which women wielded
more than a tiny percentage of the power of force or attained even
50 percent of the political power. Nor do we know of a society
with an ideology of female supremacy, despite the existence of a
few that posit that men and women are equal. But we have data
on a surprising number of societies where women controlled as
much property as their menfolk, or more. In other words, female
control of economic resources shows a greater range of empirical
variation than the other major sources of power and is the only
one to exceed the 50 percent mark. Indeed, as the example of the
Iroquois shows, women's relative economic power can approach
100 percent.

Let us first explore the empirical range of variation in the
powers of property, force, politics, and ideology. Then let us summarize the empirical evidence of the relative strength of the last
three in comparison with economic power.

Empirically, as we have seen, the types of societies where
women have substantial *economic power* are (1) most hunting-
and-gathering societies, (2) many horticultural groups, and (3) a
number of wet-rice peoples (with bilateral inheritance). In the latter two categories, women are likely to trade in the market on
their own account, an additional avenue to property and economic
power. In a few of these societies, women traditionally controlled
local markets (for example, in West Africa, parts of the Caribbean,

and the Andean highlands). Switching from the "ethnographic present" to today's real world, however, we find that men (often foreigners) have become dominant in the large-scale wholesale and export trade, so that women's traditional control is being undercut (see, for example, Boserup, 1970, for the classic statement of the problem). Even so, it is significant to find that in many societies women long have produced (surplus) for *exchange* as well as (subsistence goods) for *use*. As I noted in my discussion of Friedl, allocation of surplus is the more relevant dimension for relative female power and position than allocation of subsistence for use value. For example, Roldan (1983) found that poor Mexico City men whose wives began working (but earned less) explicitly kept veto and decision power over "big ticket" purchases—that is, surplus allocation.

Another empirical point mentioned earlier bears repetition here: We have no known example of women wielding even 50 percent of the economic power *above the level of the local group* in stratified, state-level societies. In other words, societies complex enough to have social classes and the centralized state invariably will have men dominating economic—as well as the other forms of power—at the level of the class and the level of the larger society. In such societies, however, we still encounter examples of women controlling the majority of the economic power in their household and even in their local village or group. But their power would seem vulnerable should their economic interests conflict with those of the male-dominated groups controlling the more macro levels of the political economy. It appears that women would find themselves constrained in the full exercise of their microlevel economic power in situations where they do not control the more powerful macrolevels.

Turning now to the *power of force,* there is *no* level, micro or macro, where women typically wield a significant amount of coercive power. Quite the contrary, women are much more frequently its victims than its wielders. Wife beating is distributed widely around the world, as are other manifestations of individual and organized male violence against women. Examples of women's use of organized force make for interesting reading but tend to occur only under special circumstances. Perhaps the most famous more or less contemporary example involves the 5,000 women warriors of the king of Dahomey. In 1845 it was estimated that 5,000 female soldiers served in the 12,000-person army of the king. They were celibate and were denied marriage until middle age, devoting themselves to their king until then (Sanday, 1981, cites Polanyi, 1966, Argyle, 1966, and Lombard, 1967, concerning these women the Europeans called "Amazons").

The most famous noncontemporary example, of course, is the various "Amazons" of antiquity. Most references pinpoint them as women of the nomadic and seminomadic groups of herders who roamed from North Africa to the Caucasus.[5] I have a speculative theory on the preconditions for the emergence of such Amazon groups. First, in many such groups warfare was endemic and women received some measure of military training. Second, it would appear plausible that if the group were attacked and most of the young warriors, and then even the older men and younger boys, were being slaughtered, women would be thrown into the breach. (After all, Israeli women fought in combat in the 1948 war —although not in subsequent conflicts, when the *man*power and strategic situations were not so desperate.) Third, on some occasions, this presumably turned the tide of battle at least to the extent that the remnants of the group were able to avoid defeat and capture. Fourth, it seems plausible, then, that in a few of these groups women may have decided that if they let the demographic pyramid return to normal, their status would return to what it had been before. (Although women in mobile herding groups cannot usually be as thoroughly subordinated as village and urban women in agrarian societies [see Boulding, 1976], herding groups are rarely known for their sexual egalitarianism). Fifth, it seems plausible that some of these women took actions to prevent the restoration of the demographic status quo ante. Finally, the warring milieu in which they lived presumably impelled some of these women toward at least some subsequent combat—and hence notoriety. Mythical or otherwise, Amazons are the exception. In societies with the normal sex ratio, women apparently have never obtained and maintained power by force.

It does not take such exceptional circumstances for women to wield some *political power*. The range is from no political clout to a fairly substantial amount. But we know of no society where women have a fifty-fifty share of political power. Among groups where women have considerable political weight are many West African matrilineal societies. There, women had their own powerful political representatives (most spectacularly, the "queen mother"). But there, as among the Iroquois, the male ruler was considered primary.

Why we have no cases of a fifty-fifty split on political power is an intriguing—and thus far unanswered—question. Although political organization does tend to involve the organization of violence, as Collins and others argue, formal political spheres (involving headmen, councils, and the like) are found in a number of relatively peaceful low-technology societies where control of force does not yet seem to be monopolized by the polity. Yet here, too, women seem to play the lesser role.

Women fare somewhat better with respect to *ideology* than either force or political power in that there *are* some societies that proclaim an ideology of sexual equality. Empirically, the range of variation is from a number of societies with highly male-supremacist ideologies (for example, most agrarian societies; "warrior complex" horticultural peoples) to a few groups with the belief that man and woman are equals. As noted, however, we know of no society proclaiming the ideological superiority of women.

It is significant that a group can espouse an ideology of sexual equality even though the actual position of women is less than equal. This is true of both the U.S.S.R. and the Israeli kibbutz, as discussed below. In today's world, it is clear that formal ideologies of equality (like formal voting rights) have spread around the globe faster than structural arrangements that permit the translation of ideological equality into de facto equality. But the mere fact that the ideology of equality is now so prevalent should have future structural consequences. It appears, then, that although the power of ideology is generally weaker than that of force, political position, or property, the impact of ideas on our lives is far from negligible.

For instance, sometimes a woman has money, but the macrolevel ideology that she has absorbed concerning her appropriate spheres of action effectively limits the extent to which she can even envision herself using it. Many contemporary older women, for example, first gain ownership of economic resources through widowhood. But after a lifetime of actual and ideologically internalized economic dependency, it is a rare widow who takes full and active control of her new resources. Having the prevailing societal ideology against them may not paralyze all women from acting, but it will reduce the numbers who try to buck the image (or the system). Basically, having the overarching ideology against her will mean that, in comparison with her spouse, a woman will not get 100 cents worth of economic power from every dollar she brings to the household. Thus, we find an illustration of the notion that the prevailing degree of male domination of the macro-levels of power can affect (and, in this case, brake) the exercise of female economic power at more micro levels.

But what happens when we compare the relative strengths of economic and other major sources of power at the *same* (micro or macro) level? Here, when comparing the strengths of the various forms of power at a given level (for example, the single household, the state), the prevailing pattern is that force, politics, and ideology *all* appear weaker than economic power. Recall that in my sixty-one preindustrial societies I found an overall inverse correlation between women's relative economic power and male use of force against them. Furthermore, both Sanday and I, with different ethnographic data sets and different methods (she constructed a Guttman scale), found almost no instances in which women had significant political input in the absence of autonomous economic power. My one exception, on closer examination, seems to provide additional support for the greater relative strength of economic power. The only case I found in which women had substantial political clout without any appreciable degree of control of the means of production was the Mende of Liberia. The Mende are a patri-horticultural group in which women do much of the productive labor. I thought of them as my "U.A.W. case." Like the United Auto Workers, the Mende women were organized (in the form of a formidable secret society, the Sande). They used their clout—as does the U.A.W.—to influence the political sphere, rather than to try to wrest control of the means of production from their owners. In fact, what is remarkable is that the strong and respected Sande did *not* share substantially in economic power. Finally, mention of "respect" highlights my finding that no society where women had high economic power had a blatantly male-supremacist ideology. For women, then, the river of power does not flow two ways: The current goes from economic power to some degree of influence over the other spheres, rarely vice versa.

But let us not overestimate the strength of economic power. It does *not* seem to translate directly into formal power in these other spheres, but rather into power's weaker (and more informal) cousin, *influence*. And even here it is not clear that women with autonomous economic power are able to achieve their *own* agenda in these other spheres. But as a minimum, their economic power seems to block highly negative, hostile manifestations of those other types of power; that is, it acts as a mediating force.

Theoretical Importance of Economic Power for Women. This section explores theoretically the economic and other power variables and the antecedents of economic power. The next section deals with the consequences of women's economic power for their life chances, including the relation between control of the means of production and control of the means of reproduction.

1. *Conceptualizing economic power.* Three issues are clarified under this rubric: (1) the definition of economic power, (2) the most meaningful comparison group in assessing women's economic power, and (3) the different micro- and macrolevels at which economic power may be manifested and their degree of interrelationship versus autonomy.

Regarding the first issue: as has emerged in the preceding discussion, I argue that for sexual stratification economic power is most relevantly defined in terms of

- degree of control of the means of production and
- degree of control of allocation of surplus or of surplus value.

As for comparison groups, also manifest in the preceding discussion is my contention that although there are many instances in which women in group A may be compared with women in group B, and women at time 1 may be compared with women at time 2, the most important comparison for a theory of gender stratification is the comparison of *women's* relative economic power with that of a particular group of *men*.

Finally, on the question of levels of power, a number of authors in the gender stratification literature have distinguished between woman's status in the *public* sphere and her position in the private or *domestic* domain (for example, Rosaldo, 1974; Sacks, 1975; Sanday, 1974; and many others). I suggest that it is useful to further disaggregate these domains, and I propose the following conceptual scheme.

A society's various micro- and macrolevels can be conceived of as a "nesting" system in which women's relative economic power and status may vary at least somewhat independently at each level. (By "nesting," I mean that the more micro levels are encompassed within larger, also interlinked, macrostructures.)

First, all societies have a minimum of two such "nesting" levels:

- the *household* level or other "most micro" focus, such as a male/female pair, and
- the level of the *community* or local group.

In simple, politically uncentralized, preclass societies, the community level coincides with the society level.

Second, in class-stratified and politically centralized societies, a minimum of two more levels must be taken into account:

- that of the *class* and
- that of the larger *society*, respectively.

(This scheme may be expanded to encompass the relevant institutional, ethnic, and geographical sectors of complex societies. Thus, we can explore differential sexual stratification in, for example, two ethnic groups.)

Third, it should be emphasized that change may enter the system at any (or all) of these "nesting" levels and that changes are not necessarily in the same direction; that is, women's relative power and position may be improving in different aspects in certain micro- and macrolevels while deteriorating in others. Moreover, in today's complex world, some of these changes may stem from trends in a level even more macro than the society—the position of a given nation-state in the overarching world capitalist economy. (One increasingly visible example is the shift of certain production jobs in labor-intensive industries from areas of higher labor costs in the "core" capitalist countries to new export-processing zones in developing countries with low labor costs. Many have commented on the fact that these jobs go disproportionately to young, nonunionized females; see, for example, Fernandez-Kelly, 1983; Safa, 1983.)

Fourth, as will be specified in the propositions below, the more macro levels—which historically have been more male-dominated—will generally function as a "discount rate" affecting the exercise of women's relative economic power at more micro levels. (What I mean by *discount rate* is that women will not receive full *face value* for their microlevel economic power; rather, it will be reduced in proportion to the level of male dominance of the macrolevels.) This is because macrolevels influence microlevels more than vice versa.

The argument to this point can be summarized in the following five propositions or hypotheses:*

H_1: For women, the most important source of power affecting their position in a sexual stratification system is economic.

H_2: The greater the control of the means of production, the greater the control of the fruits of production.

H_3: Since macrolevels influence microlevels more than the reverse, where women's relative economic power at the *macro*levels (society; class; at times, community) is less than at the *micro*level(s), the less favorable macrolevels will act as a "discount rate" to reduce (but not eliminate) the extent to which women can exercise their relative economic power at the more micro level(s); that is, women's actual micropower will be less than their potential power.

H_4: Conversely, if it should occur that women's relative economic power at the macrolevels is *greater* than in a particular microlevel instance, the more favorable macrolevels will cushion women's less favorable microlevel position—that is, the "discount rate" will be positive.

H_5: Within these "nested" levels, the higher the macrolevel, the more important the impact of the other major sources of power (for example, political, force).

*Additional subsets of propositions are presented and discussed later in this chapter.

2. *Interrelation of the power variables during stability and
change.* The empirical findings reported earlier about the greater
importance of economic power for women than of other types of
power involved situations of relative stability. In fact, since much
of the evidence is from cross-sectional analyses of ethnographic
data sets, change could not be considered. Although the distinction between stability and transition remains relative, it is theoretically important to make it. In more stable situations, wom-
en's greater economic power is expected to lead to influence over
the other sources of power. But in times of flux, when women's
economic power at a given micro- or macrolevel is rising, men
might resort to repression to block that rise (1) the more they perceive it as a threat and (2) the more they perceive their situation
as a zero-sum game.

Roldan's data (1983), from her study of poor Mexico City
women who worked in their homes as outworkers for manufacturing jobbers, are fascinating in this regard. Although the earnings of
these women (most with children under seven) were unstable, far
below the minimum wage, and less than their husbands' incomes,
major changes in household-level sexual stratification ensued.

In about two thirds of the 140-odd households—generally
the poorest—the spouses "pooled" their income. In these "pooling" households, wives put a claimed 100 percent of earnings in
the kitty, while husbands kept back a quarter or more of income
as a personal allowance (actually, nearly half the men withheld income information in what wives resentfully viewed as a control
technique to keep them dependent). As these wives renegotiated
power relationships on the basis of their new earnings, bitter fights
over the amount the husbands withheld became common, constituting the "main source of quarreling [and] verbal and physical
abuse among spouses" (1983:6). Nevertheless, 77 percent of the
husbands retained final say on how much they should keep for
themselves. One informant, "Doña B," describes her husband as
slapping her in the face when she criticized his spending money
drinking.[6]

Overall male violence or threat of violence emerged as a
main response in "pooling" households where husbands viewed as
a threat wives' new attempts to cut into male economic decision-
making power.

What such men fear may be seen in the few cases in which

women became the main contributors by default. In three cases when husbands had stopped regular "pool" contributions, the wives "openly 'lost respect' for their husbands in words, actions, and thought. They report going out without their permission; they do not wash, iron, or cook for them as they used to; they manage, rather than budget, the common fund; they got jobs as washerwomen without their consent, in fact, against their will; they resort to foul language if they feel like it; and they *even strike them back if husbands try to beat them the way they used to"* (1983:15; emphasis added). In Latino lower class culture, such defiance may be considered extraordinary.

Not all situations of change, of course, involve zero-sum games, in which group A's gain comes out of the hide of group B. Where the change is less threatening, less repression should be elicited.

The next group of propositions summarizes the relations between economic and other power sources:

H_6:   In general, the greater women's relative economic power, the more likely that it will result in *influence* (though not necessarily formal power) in the political sphere.

H_7:   *Once consolidated,* the greater women's relative economic power, the less likely that there will be *negative* manifestations (that is, ones harmful to female interests) in the other major spheres of power.

H_{7a}: The less likely will be the enactment of political policies prejudicial to women's interests (although in class societies lower-class women will be less able to check policies unfavorable to them).

H_{7b}: The less likely and frequent will be the exercise of male force and violence against women.

H_{7c}: The less male-supremacist will be the prevailing sexual ideology.

H_8:   Conversely, *during times of transition,* when women's relative economic power is growing, the more it is perceived as a threat/zero-sum game, the more repressive (physically and/or politically) the male response is likely to be.

3. *The general precondition for female economic power: work and the sexual division of labor.* As a long list of previous au-

thors have noted, for women, work is the first step toward high status. (The list includes Martin and Voorhies, 1975; Oboler, 1973; Leacock, 1972; Sacks, 1975; Benston, 1969; Lenin, 1972; and Sanday, 1973.) But work is not enough. The world's slaves, workers, and peasants still have not inherited the earth. In this section I invoke women's participation in production as a precondition to economic power and then propose some hypotheses concerning the factors influencing the sexual division of labor.

Actually, little more need be said about women's participation in production as a precondition to economic power and high status. In her sample of twelve preindustrial societies, Sanday (1973) found that where women did not contribute to subsistence, their status was invariably low, but even in some societies (such as the horticultural Azande of Africa) where women did most of the production, their status could be abysmal. As I discuss later, only where women's work in production is of high "strategic indispensability" may it be translatable into some degree of control over the means of production. Here I shall argue the other side of the coin and propose that where women lack economic power, they will tend to lack control over the allocation of their labor power. Under these circumstances, I argue, it is not *women's* convenience, preferences, or even urgent needs that shape their participation in production. More important are the convenience, preferences, and needs of those who control the means of production. In short, the characteristics of the female labor *supply* are less important than the nature of the *demand* for labor by those who have the power to command it.

It is only in relatively simple, preclass societies, that the characteristics of the labor supply might be determinative of the sexual division of labor. So, even though I wish to predict sexual division of labor across the entire gamut of human societal complexity, let us begin with the anthropological work on sexual division of labor.

This work is generally based on the analysis of ethnographic data sets, such as the *Ethnographic Atlas* (hereinafter, EA) or Murdock and White's (1969) *Standard Cross-Cultural Sample* (hereinafter, SCCS). There seems to have been a clear trend away from early explanations emphasizing the strength and other characteristics of the male (for example, Murdock, 1949) to a focus on the compatibility of tasks with the simultaneous childcare responsibilities (especially breast feeding) of the female (for example, Brown, 1970; Whiting, 1972; Ember, 1983). In fact, Brown (1970) and Burton, Brudner, and White (1977) convincingly downplay the importance of male strength. This last study, for example, argues that (given breast-feeding constraints) women will tend to avoid tasks that are distant and/or dangerous. As a result, males will be more likely to dominate the beginning stages of production sequences (such as raw materials extraction rather than secondary processing, or land clearing rather than harvesting). However, these authors argue, if women participate in the earlier stages of a production sequence, they will also participate in the subsequent phases. Their analysis of the SCCS supports their hypothesis on the sexual division of labor in several such production sequences.

But other anthropological studies indicate that compatibility with female nursing is not the whole story, either. First, Nerlove (1974) found that, in a sample of eighty-three preindustrial societies, where women were important subsistence producers they were likely to introduce supplementary foods to their babies at an earlier age. This, of course, frees more of their time for subsistence activities by reducing the frequency of nursing. Second, a new study of sexual division of labor in Africa (White, Burton, and Dow, 1981) has found evidence that in addition to nursing-compatibility factors, a quite different variable—slavery—affected the extent to which women worked in farming. In general, in the more stratified societies where slaves were present, women farmed less—a finding in keeping with the theory I am proposing. (Their main measure of a compatibility-type variable was horticultural root crops, as opposed to agrarian cereal crops; the former are grown under conditions that are more compatible with nursing.) The important point is that both Nerlove's and White, Burton, and Dow's studies show that nonbiological factors can condition or override women's nursing compatibility/constraint.

Finally, it is worth mentioning that Murdock and Provost's (1973) empirical exploration of sexual division of labor in fifty activities, using the SCCS, found many instances of women working in modally male and apparently incompatible activities. By the nursing compatibility/constraint criterion, in fact, almost all the formal-sector jobs in today's industrial societies, both capitalist and socialist, are highly incompatible. Yet women form between a quarter and half of the labor force in all contemporary industrial economies.

How did it happen? I argue that labor *demand* is much more determinative than the attributes and aspirations of the labor *supply* in accounting for contemporary labor force participation patterns. (This statement should not surprise those who, during the worst of the recession in 1981–1982, watched frequent vignettes on the evening news of thousands of people in some frostbelt city lining up for a handful of advertised jobs.)

Let us start with "incompatible" but largely female-filled jobs. Oppenheimer (1973) has admirably demonstrated the causal role of economic demand in shaping U.S. female labor force participation since 1900. By that year, women already had become sex-segregated (as they largely remain today) in precisely those labor force sectors destined to grow the most in subsequent decades—clerical and service jobs. (The previously cited Marxist-feminist writings on the U.S. sexual division of labor are very relevant in this regard.) In 1900, demand in such job categories could be filled with young women working before having children. By 1940, Oppenheimer shows, demand for (female) labor could not be met with the available supply of young, unmarried women workers. So older married women whose children were already in school were the next group drawn into the labor force. (In fact, World War II presented a situation combining the impact of higher labor demand in female jobs and a shortage of males. Even then, most women worked in "women's" jobs. But "Rosie the Riveter" received popular acclaim and high (men's) wages working in normally male manufacturing jobs in defense-required production. After the war, Rosie and 600,000 of her sisters were laid off— studies showed that few wanted to quit—and the in-plant day nurseries were closed; see, for example, Tobias and Anderson, 1973; Trey, 1973.) By the 1960s, demand once again required additional cohorts, and mothers of preschool children, the last major nonworking female group, were progressively drawn in. In 1900 only 20 percent of women aged eighteen through sixty-four worked; by 1983 almost 60 percent did—including about 45 percent of mothers of children under six.

Considering classically male-filled "incompatible" jobs, the example of the Soviet Union is instructive. The U.S.S.R. sustained such tragically high male death rates in World War II that women remained for many years the majority of the work force—including up to 73 percent of the labor in the heaviest, unmechanized *agrarian* activities (Goldberg, 1972). (Worldwide, both ethnographic and nation-state data show agrarian production to be overwhelmingly male.) Soviet women "own" half the means of production (the men "own" the other half). But the *control* of the means of production is in the hands of a small, overwhelmingly male elite (as in the United States and other countries, for that matter). And this elite shapes the allocation of labor. From 1958 to the late 1960s, it pursued a policy that restricted the percentage of women in the universities, especially in the science faculties (see Goldberg, 1972; Dodge, 1966). Thus, although Soviet women have perhaps the highest overall labor force status in the world (as gauged by professional participation, for example), that status is vulnerable to shifting demand factors—and the policies of those who control the political economy.[7]

Let us summarize the foregoing discussion and its implications in a series of propositions:

H_9:   Women's participation in production seems to be a generally necessary but clearly insufficient precondition to their achieving a relatively high level of economic power.

H_{10}:   The higher the economic power of a group, the greater its control over the allocation of its labor power.

H_{11}:   Women's participation in production in relatively unstratified preindustrial societies is primarily a function of (1) the demand for labor relative to the available supply and (2) the degree of compatibility of the activity with simultaneous childcare responsibilities (especially breast feeding).

H_{12}:   The more class-stratified and centrally controlled the society, the more labor demand overshadows childcare compatibility for the prediction of the sexual division of labor.

H_{13}:   Where women are important producers, childcare arrangements will be adjusted to accommodate their production.

H_{14}:   In general, one sex can be drawn in large numbers into activities that are modally performed by the other sex (even if "incompatible" vis-à-vis female nursing constraints) under the following two conditions: (1) the activity is economically valuable enough to the group (or those who control its means of production in stratified societies) to justify breaking sexual division of labor norms, and (2) there is a shortage of available members of the "modal" sex (or an equally acceptable alternative labor force such as slaves, "guest workers," and so on).

H_{14a}:   For *males*, however, there is an additional scenario whereby they may enter modally female activities in large numbers. This is under conditions of (1) sexual inequality (that is, where women have low economic power) and (2) the existence of a severe glut of available males relative to the demand for labor in the attractive modally male activities.

(In other words, this second situation—glut pushing the unemployed sex into the other's activities—does not occur under conditions of sexual inequality when it is *females* who are in oversupply.)

Finally, one additional hypothesis will be offered, although its full explication is beyond the scope of this chapter:

H_{15}:   In contemporary industrializing and industrial countries (all characterized by varying degrees of sexual inequality), the sexual division of labor is conditioned by at least three additional factors: (1) the overall stratification system (including ethnic stratification); (2) the strength, nature, and sexual composition of the labor movement; and (3) the position of the country within the world economy.

4. *The "strategic indispensability" of women's work:* three sets of resources contributing to female economic power. To preview the argument, I hypothesize three sets of contributing factors to women's relative control of the means of production. The first set involves factors enhancing the *"strategic indispensability"* of women's work (that is, under certain highly favorable circumstances, workers *can* convert their labor in production to some degree of control over the means of production). The second set flows from the nature of the *kinship* system. Third, the overarching

stratification system, or *social relations of production*, can facilitate or hinder women's acquisition of relative economic power.

The "strategic indispensability" factors bear strong relation to the variables that labor economists might consider in weighing the bargaining power of a given labor force. They include—

- The importance of the women producers' *activities*, as measured by (1) the proportion or value of total output/diet produced and (2) the short-run substitution costs at the margin.
- The importance of the women *producers* themselves, measured as above.
- The extent to which women producers *control technical expertise*.
- The extent to which women producers *work autonomously* from close male supervision.
- The size, nature, and cohesiveness of the women's *work groups* (including their suitability for economies of scale), which affect:
- The extent to which women producers are able to *organize* on their own behalf.
- The extent of *competition* (by countervailing groups) affecting (1) the output of the women producers and/or (2) the women producers themselves, as a labor force.

Let us discuss each in turn.

- Importance of women producers' *activities*. This means that if what the women do is economically valuable to the group (or, in stratified societies, those who control its means of production), and if it would be very difficult and costly to replace that activity on short notice, the labor force in that activity will have more leverage, other things being equal.
- Importance of the women *producers* themselves. Maybe the activity is supremely important and impossible to replace on short notice—but what about its labor force? Is it easily replaceable? The fate of the U.S. federal air traffic controllers who went on strike early in the Reagan administration is relevant in this regard. They were fired en masse—and immediately replaced by their supervisors and military air traffic controllers. And the planes kept flying. This example is particularly dramatic, but it should be

stressed that mere "substitutability at the margin" is enough to weaken (women) producers' position. In general, it appears that if even 5–15 percent of a labor force can be easily replaced, this is sufficient to undermine the group's bargaining power, however important or valuable its product or activity.

This factor can be invoked to explain many situations in which a group is extremely important as a labor force but nevertheless remains quite oppressed. Historically, it appears that women, like peasants, are frequently victims of a situation in which they *are* substitutable at the margin. They are providers of an activity for which underutilized people with their skills are available locally or can easily be brought in. Because I feel that this is an important but neglected factor in explaining sexual stratification, I shall develop the argument vis-à-vis peasants by way of background.

Concerning peasants, I invoke Lenski's (1966:281–284) assertion that in traditional agrarian (plow-agriculture-based) societies 5–15 percent of the population was composed of a class he terms the "expendables." In these highly stratified and exploitive societies, children (especially sons in nonirrigating agrarian societies) were very useful in helping the peasant stay ahead of the landlord, so peasants had lots of them. The "expendables" were the excess sons and daughters of the peasant population, whom the ruling class(es) was unwilling to support on the land as adults, even at a bare subsistence level. (Permitting all these offspring to take up land as adults would quickly have eaten up any surplus the landowners could extract.) Frequently, these "expendables" migrated to the cities, where their life conditions as coolies, beggars, prostitutes, petty thieves, and the like were so miserable that they rarely reproduced their numbers. But in every generation their ranks were replenished by more migrants from the land. Meanwhile, back in the rural areas, additional landless peasants struggled to survive on the margins of the local economy. The existence of these groups guarantees "substitutability at the margin." Bluntly, any individual peasant is replaceable, and by someone who had been raised as a peasant before being pushed off the land. Therefore, I propose, the existence of this surplus labor population is a principal reason that peasants almost everywhere have so little economic power in proportion to their economic contributions. So too for women, I propose.

In preindustrial societies where we find women who are important but powerless producers, I suggest that we will find substitutability at the margin built into the system—although the "surplus" women would not be randomly distributed. The extra women could be introduced or redistributed through raiding, slavery, polygyny, or other means. They would generally accrue to more powerful males; lower status/junior men might not have access to even one woman. Thus, the underlying sex ratio is overshadowed by how powerful men create a woman surplus for themselves.

In industrial capitalist societies, the role of the housewife as a reserve labor force has been much written about. Moreover, more than half of U.S. women remain concentrated in fewer than twenty female-dominated, overcrowded, underpaid "pink-collar ghetto" occupations. Many more women know how to type—or hold teaching or beautician credentials—than are currently pounding typewriters, teaching children, or styling hair. And many others are doing these kinds of jobs on a part-time or temporary/substitute basis; their lack of fringe benefits drives down compensation packages for full-time workers in their field. In short, if even a small reserve of potential replacements exists—and they need not all be women—women's chances for parlaying production into power are poor (unless, somehow, they have other sources of strategic indispensability that will prevent these extra bodies from being used against them).

What other sources of strategic indispensability can help overcome the disadvantages of excess numbers (for both power and pay)? Clearly, the position of a work force is strengthened to the extent that its members can gain control of the labor process. The next four factors facilitate such control.

• Female producers' control of *technical expertise*. Stinchcombe (1966) calls this the "technical culture," and where female producers control such knowledge their leverage should be increased. Stinchcombe's study of rural stratification offers a good example on this point. He argues that peasants sharecropping for absentee landlords are resentfully aware of the landlord's lack of contribution to production and hence are frequently rebellious. In any situation of political instability, these smallholder tenants will try to turn the situation to their advantage and gain control of the land for themselves. Such peasants also have the advantage of the next factor.

• Female producers' *freedom from close supervision* by the superordinate group. Do women work autonomously from direct male supervision? Oboler (1973) emphasizes this factor in her study of African market women. Their menfolk cannot supervise their trading (and make off with the lion's share of the profits) because they are not up on the latest price movements and market trends. African market women are also known for the power of their guildlike associations, and the next two factors address female solidarity groups.

• The nature of women producers' *work groups*. Do women work individually or in large groups? Are they in competition in a zero-sum game, or do they cooperate? Is their work such that it cannot benefit from economies of scale (for example, gathering)? To the extent that women work in concentrated, cohesive groups—and are free from close male supervision—their work-group situation can facilitate their banding together.

• The extent to which women producers can *organize* on their own behalf. Here we have the labor union classic, "Organize!" Where women have the legal right to do so and the work situation to pull it off, they can add the power of numbers to their labor power. (Historically, however, this has been infrequent.) Under favorable circumstances, organization can translate into formidable control over the work *process* and into the benefits of "bread-and-butter unionism." Under exceptional circumstances, organization can lead to varying degrees of control of the means of production (for example, from a union seat on the board of directors, as in German "codetermination," to the group's buying out—or seizing—the enterprise).

• *Competition among countervailing groups* involving female producers and/or their output. This is an external factor that can affect the strategic indispensability of female producers. To phrase it negatively, a producer group is unlikely to gain power if it is caught in the "only game in town"—that is, all power in the society is monolithically lined up in the same direction. Let us consider the historical example of what happened following the Black Death in England and in East Prussia (based on Reinhardt, 1974; see also Cartwright and Biddis, 1972). In both places, heavy peasant deaths created a labor shortage. Presumably, survivors should benefit. In England, many did. In fact, a free yeoman class arose, which became the ancestors of today's "county class" gentry (Ziegler, 1969). But in the frontier zone of East Prussia, a previously free yeoman group became serfs tied to the land. Why the difference? In England, the crown was already in competition with the nobility for power, and the peasants benefited from the conflict and competition of these countervailing groups (in Simmel's terms, *tertius gaudens*—the third party benefits). Conversely, in East Prussia, there was no crown/noble power struggle. The nobles were the only game in town, and they operated as feudal warlords. They were able to secure their now-scarce labor supply by brute force. In summary, the absence of countervailing power groups may reduce the advantages that producers may otherwise derive from economic importance, even in the presence of severe labor shortage; and vice versa. But the essence of the countervailing-groups' argument as applied to females is not demographic. Instead, it stresses that women should be in a position to benefit from the competition between (at least) two more powerful groups, both of which sometimes find it advantageous to concede advantages to the women for their support.

A good example of how some women benefited (though only briefly) from the struggles between two countervailing groups is provided by what happened to "Rosie the Riveter" and her sisters during World War II. Management urgently needed the women's labor for war production (and profits). Organized labor urgently needed to guarantee that its union members would have jobs to come home to at the end of the war. And the union also had a pressing need to make sure that those jobs would pay just as well after the war as they had when the union members left for the war. So the union pushed management to pay Rosie and her sisters "equal pay for equal work." (The union also wanted to make sure these women would not be given the jobs permanently.) In the subsequent jockeying between labor and management, the women did in fact get full men's wages for their work (see, for example, Milkman, 1980). But it proved to be only "for the duration"; as noted, such women were laid off en masse at war's end.

All of the foregoing can be quickly summarized in two propositions:

H_{16}:   The greater the "strategic indispensability" of a female labor force, the more likely that it will be able to translate its labor power into some degree of economic power.

H_{17}:   In wage-labor societies, the greater the "strategic indispensability" of a female labor force, the higher its wages and the smaller the "sexual gap in earnings."

5. *The kinship system:* a second set of resources contributing to female economic power. In general, the evidence of the EA supports the hypothesis that family and kinship organization becomes maximally luxuriant and complex at *intermediate* levels of societal complexity (Blumberg and Winch, 1972). Family and kinship organization is generally less complex among hunters and gatherers than among advanced horticultural societies and pre-state agrarian groups, among whom are found the most extended family organizations and the most corporate and powerful unilineal descent groups. With the rise of the state, the powers and prerogatives of the corporate kin group are deliberately curbed. Thus, the relation of familism to societal complexity is curvilinear: More complex state-level societies—like the simplest societies—are more likely to have bilateral (rather than unilineal) kinship systems and simple nuclear families.

Some aspects of the kinship system, such as the rules for calculating descent, tend to change slowly, even in the face of changing economic conditions. In contrast, other aspects, such as household composition and prevailing patterns of marital residence, are much more volatile and tend to mirror changing economic circumstances more closely and more rapidly (see, for example, Morgan and others, 1974, for evidence on the volatility of U.S. household composition in relation to economic conditions). The fact of differential rates of change in different kinship/familial variables means that not all kin power is necessarily lined up, monolithically, in the same direction: Women may benefit from some aspects of kin arrangements while being disadvantaged in others.

It does seem possible to rank-order the major kinship/familial variables with respect to their impact on women's economic power. Specifically, I propose that *inheritance* is most important, followed by *residence,* followed by *descent.*

• *Inheritance*. Women's de facto share of inheritance—that is, the nature and amount of property they *actually* control—is a direct component of their economic power.

• *Marital residence*/household composition patterns. These variables can facilitate both property control and allies, although generally less directly than inheritance does. The most favorable pattern is that the bride continues to reside with her *female* kin who control the residence and domestic property and provide her with solidarity group alliances and support. The least favorable pattern is that the bride leaves her home village to marry into a completely patri system. Many intermediate combinations exist.

• *Descent*. At a very gross level, women fare best in matri systems and worst in patri systems, with variable (but often intermediate) status in bilateral systems. But Schlegel's research (1972) shows that women do not invariably have high status in matrilineal groups. Property may pass from mother's brother to sister's son; residence may be with the male kinsmen of the groom's maternal uncle (technically, "avunculocal" residence); and women may be under the effective domination of their husbands or brothers. We have already encountered examples of high female economic power among the bilateral kinship groups found in many Southeast Asian, Philippine, and Indonesian wet-rice societies. (Not all bilateral systems, however, are favorable to women, as the evidence from medieval Europe shows.) Even in some patri societies, as in horticultural Africa, women have *use* rights in land they farm—even if rights of *alienation* of the land remain with the patri-kin group—and utilize their importance as a labor force to form solidarity groups of female producers. In short, we have to examine each case in its specific context to see how women's position in the various aspects of kinship affects their access to economic power.

Since, in general, women are more likely to control substantial domestic property in matrilineal societies with matrilocal residence (Schlegel, 1972), let us conclude this section with a brief look at the literature on matri residence and the kinds of societies where matri institutions flourish.

Concerning marital residence, there are two main theories. "The first is that the sexual division of labor in subsistence activities may favor cooperative male groups, cooperative female groups,

mixed cooperative groups, or independent homesteads, favoring in
turn virilocality, uxorilocality, bilocality, or neolocality" (White,
Burton, and Dow, 1981:829. Virilocality means patrilocal residence; uxorilocality, matrilocal; bilocality, both; in neolocal residence the nuclear couple live away from both their families). The
evidence from the major ethnographic data sets supports this view
for the Americas, especially North America, but not worldwide; in
Africa there is no relationship whatsoever.

The second major theory focuses on defensive activities and
specifically links matrilocal residence to a pattern of *external* warfare (Divale, 1974; Ember and Ember, 1971). In matrilocal groups,
brothers are scattered and the pattern of frequent feuding and internal warfare characterizing patrilocal groups is absent. In fact, a
number of observers have commented on the internal peacefulness
of matrilocal groups.[8]

Matri societies tend to inhabit a fairly delimited set of ecological niches (for example, they are very rarely found among
groups living in the heart of dense forests, according to Aberle,
1961). Martin and Voorhies (1975) stress the importance of a stable—and relatively lush—environment. Statistically, the high point
is reached in *horticulture.* For example, the calculations of Lenski
and Lenski (1982:155), based on some 915 EA societies, show 39
percent *matrilineal descent* among horticulturalists where male-
dominant herding or hunting accounts for less than 15 percent of
total subsistence. In my own EA calculations, I found approximately the same percentage of *matrilocal residence* among groups
with "incipient cultivation"—that is, simple, shifting horticultural
cultivation. Other EA calculations make it clear that matrilocal
residence "peaks" at a somewhat lower level of societal complexity than matrilineal descent. Overall, *foraging* societies have the
second-highest concentration of matri kinship. For example, Martin and Voorhies's calculations (1975:185–186), based on a subsample of 515 EA societies, show that in fifty-nine of ninety foraging societies, or over 65 percent, the *option* of permanent matrilocality exists. Pure matrilocal residence is dominant in only 19
percent of these ninety societies, however. Since European colonialism was particularly disruptive of matri kinship arrangements
(more "appropriate" arrangements often were vigorously imposed),
these figures are biased in unknown ways, possibly underestimat-

ing the prevalence of matri kinship. At any rate, it appears that, with internal competition and/or greater emphasis on deliberate accumulation of surplus, matri societies are selected against. And with the demise of matri societies, women lose the most frequent kinship route to economic power.[9]

In summary.

H_{18}:   For women, de facto *inheritance* is generally the most important and direct kinship-system input into economic power.

H_{19}:   Marital *residence* patterns that provide women with a co-resident group of female kinswomen and access to domestic property facilitate their relative economic power (though less directly than inheritance does).

H_{20}:   *Descent* patterns, though less directly linked to women's economic power than inheritance and residence, also can act as facilitators/hindrances. In general, matri descent is most favorable for women's economic power, patri descent is least favorable, and bilateral descent, though quite variable, is often intermediate.

6. *The prevailing social relations of production:* the third set of resources contributing to female economic power. Here we are concerned with who controls the *society's* means of production and allocates its surplus (if any). In general, women tend to do better in societies with communal relations of production. These, of course, are most prevalent among simple foraging societies that deliberately avoid significant surplus accumulation. However, some intentional utopian groups, such as the agrarian socialist Israeli kibbutz, both deliberately produce surplus and practice communal relations of production. Does communal ownership always mean communal control in which females share equally in economic power? In a word, no. Resources "owned" by the community may in fact be controlled by a subgroup not representative of the total community (as in today's socialist states). The example of the kibbutz is relevant here. The kibbutz espouses a formal *ideology* of sexual equality and actually achieves equality in *distribution*—that is, male members receive no more material rewards than do female members. But women have never been full

partners in control of the means of *production*. They were always underrepresented in the main agrarian production activities, and over the course of the first generation they were edged out of most such jobs they had held in the pioneering days. Their representation on the economic committees, where actual control over productive resources is most prominently exercised, followed this same pattern. Thus, despite a formal "town hall democracy," women's de facto control of the macrolevel political economy of the kibbutz never approached a 50 percent share. Occupationally, kibbutz women ended up concentrated in the (lower-esteemed) domestic service activities from which they had ostensibly been liberated. Over the years, women's dissatisfaction with the narrowness of their occupational choices has been a continuing problem for the kibbutz (see, for example, Spiro, 1963; Blumberg, 1976b). In other words, as predicted, with less than equal economic power, women have been less able to allocate their labor to their own satisfaction.

Although sex differences in economic control occur more than occasionally in classless communal societies, they tend to be considerably more pronounced in societies with class stratification. As mentioned, we know of no society with complex class stratification and the state where women share equally in economic power *beyond the level of the local community*.

Within complex class societies, women's "strategic indispensability" and access to kin resources may vary from one class to another (see, for example, Stack, 1974, on kin network sharing patterns among a black "urban underclass" U.S. group). In other words, knowing that a particular class forms 50 percent of the population and controls 10 percent of the society's resources does not tell us how that 10 percent is divided among the men and women of the class; empirical research among the various social classes is necessary. As a generalization, however, in societies where women have very limited rights to property, the de facto gap in economic power and privilege between men and women should shrink the lower we go in the class system. In sexually inegalitarian societies, among classes where *men* are virtually propertyless, their lot may be misery, but it is shared in a sexually more egalitarian manner than among the affluent.

H_{21}: The less communal and less egalitarian the manner in which the societal pie is controlled and cut up, the more obstacles to female economic power will be found at the macro levels of the society.

H_{22}: In class societies with sexual inequality, de facto differences in male/female economic power and privilege will be less among classes with little control of property.

Consequences of Women's Economic Power for Their Life Options. We come now to the realm of "dependent variables." Women's access to power of any type should translate into various manifestations of privilege, prestige, and freedom. The argument here is that women have more access to economic than any other of the major sources of power—and that, moreover, economic power is the *strongest* predictor of their overall status position (that is, those privileges, prestige rankings, and freedoms).

Two broad types of privilege can be summarized as "honor," on the one hand, and "opportunity," on the other. In the first type are various aspects of prestige, deference, and "status." Interrelationships among these variables are complex, and in general, the variables do not seem to be straight-line translations of women's position with respect to the major power sources. For example, some societies place a high premium on sexual attractiveness (many Polynesian peoples, for instance). A young woman may achieve a transitory status based on beauty at one stage of the life cycle (see Bart, 1969), independent of any power and privilege she may subsequently acquire by virtue of her economic efforts. *Deference* is equally problematic. For example, in some polygynous Ivory Coast horticultural groups, women grow and control the bulk of the food supply and trade the surplus in the market on their own account. But they still maintain deference customs to their husbands involving mealtime etiquette (Clignet, 1970). Conversely, in British Victorian times and the U.S. antebellum South, the deference customs went the other way: Upper- and upper-middle-class "ladies" were placed on a deference pedestal, but their rights (including their right to administer property after marriage) and their lives were rigidly restricted. In short, there is no clear relation between "honor" and freedom.

"Opportunity" measures, in contrast, are concerned with autonomy in controlling one's own life. And the extent to which one can control one's destiny at both micro- and macrolevels is associated with one's relative power resources.[10]

Take fertility, for instance. For women, this is potentially the greatest shaper of their adult lives. Women have 100 percent of the world's babies and are disproportionately likely to care for them while they are young. Therefore, a woman's fertility career crucially affects her autonomy, freedom, and opportunities in other spheres of life, at both macro- and microlevels. A number of variables are involved in a woman's fertility pattern, incidentally, and *each* has an impact on a woman's options in other areas of life. These variables include • the age at which a woman first gives birth, • the spacing between her children, • her age when she has her last child, • the total number of children she has, and • the ways in which she accomplishes this (what Davis and Blake, 1956, term the "means of intervention" resorted to—abstinence, contraception, abortion, infanticide, and so on).

We now know that there is a general relation between fertility patterns—that is, the variables listed above, plus others such as the prevailing sex ratio—and the economic arrangements of a group. (In macro terms, the mode of production affects the mode of reproduction.) At more micro levels, it has been proposed that a family's economic situation affects the benefits and costs of a given fertility pattern. But families are neither total dictatorships nor total democracies. For each of the fertility variables listed above, the cost/benefit ratio (that is, expected utilities) may differ for the woman, for the man, and for the larger family unit. To what extent is it the *woman's* utilities that are served? She, after all, is the one most affected by the actual fertility outcomes. In sum, for a woman, controlling her fertility (to the extent possible given the prevailing level of knowledge) is in many ways a more meaningful measure of status and overall autonomy than any amount of prestige or deference. And I hypothesize:

H$_{23}$: The greater women's relative economic control, the more control they will have to ensure that their fertility pattern serves their *own* interests.

Of course, not only the woman, the man, and the family have a vested interest in her fertility. Most traditional states and religions until recently have been highly pronatalist. In today's world, we have instances of states wanting to impose low fertility on a reluctant population (for example, China, India) and other instances of states trying to encourage higher fertility for some or all elements of their population (the Soviet Union attempts to encourage the fertility of ethnically Russian urban women, who reproduce well below replacement level, but does not encourage fertility among the explosively growing Asian and Islamic minorities). The evidence indicates that it takes a stiff level of coercion to cut fertility drastically when the individuals involved have high positive utilities in more than the state-decreed family size. And, to date, programs to enhance fertility among working women for whom fertility is burdensome have not been notably effective.

But even when the state, the church, and the husband oppose women's attempts to control fertility *and* female economic power is low, if a woman's utility calculations cause her to decide that a given pregnancy is harmful to her interests, the evidence indicates that she may resort to secret, illegal means. Kinzer's (1973) data on the high rates of then-illegal abortion in the heartlands of machismo, urban Latin America and Italy, are relevant in this regard. Fertility is that important an issue for most women when it goes against their utilities.

Significantly, a study by Weller (1968) in Puerto Rico found that when women entered the labor market, their household decision-making power rose—and initiating contraception was one of the first ways in which they exercised their greater control.

The data from Roldan's Mexico City study (1983) provide additional support. In households where spouses pooled income, Roldan dichotomized the group into those where wives' contributions were less than 40 percent of the kitty (recall that husbands withheld an average of 25 percent of *reported* income from the pool) and those where wives contributed more than 40 percent to the common fund. Where wives contributed less than 40 percent, the decision whether to have any more children was the woman's in 20 percent of cases (it was joint in 67 percent and the husband's in a mere 3 percent). But where wives contributed more than 40 percent of the household pool, the decision on number of children was the woman's alone in fully 50 percent of cases. (As a caution, it should be noted that Ns are small; moreover, since the study involved only working women, we have no way of knowing whether the minute proportion of cases where the husband has the main say in the wife's future fertility is lower than in households where the wife does not earn income.)

Fertility is not the only relevant female autonomy variable significantly affected by women's economic power, I posit, although it may well be the most important for a woman's life chances. I have put together a list of what I term "life options" known to exist in all human societies. Some affect woman's position at the microlevel of the household, others at more macro levels. The list deliberately excludes economic, political, and force variables to avoid tautology, although I have discussed some of the interrelations among these variables earlier in this chapter. It is by no means complete. The importance of the list, rather, lies in providing a measurable set of opportunities and freedoms that I suggest may be most strongly predicted by women's relative economic power. In other words, their degree of economic power is a stronger predictor of women's relative equality in "life options" than are any of the other forms of power discussed earlier.

1. *Fertility.* As noted, fertility variables include age at first birth, spacing interval, age at last birth, preferred sex ratio of children, total family size, and "means of intervention" (if any) resorted to. Although in contemporary societies there is an overall inverse relation between fertility and most common indicators of "female status" (for example, level of education, occupation), I suggest that even today there are circumstances in which women's utilities may favor fairly high fertility. The most prevalent example involves the increasingly hard-pressed rural women farmers in much of Africa. Numerous studies have shown that their work load is increasing and their resources (relative to their menfolk's and, at times, in absolute level) are decreasing. Out-migration takes away adult males, and rural schools draw older children (especially boys in many of these countries). Meanwhile, exhausted soil, increased time and distance required to bring decreasingly available water and firewood, and intensifying need for cash income add up to both more labor needs and strong pronatalist pressure. My in-

terest is in ascertaining women's relative control over each of the fertility pattern variables, so as to reflect their *own* perceived utilities.

2. *Marriage.* This is another microlevel variable that frequently has macrolevel consequences for women. Here I am interested in a woman's relative freedom, in comparison with the men in her "pool of eligibles," to decide (1) whether to marry, as well as (2) when and (3) whom.[11]

3. *Divorce.* All human societies provide for the termination or annulment of unions in some form. As with marriage, the rules come from more macro levels of the society but exert maximum effect at the micro level. To which spouse do these rules give (1) greater freedom and (2) more grounds to end a union? (In several of the African horticultural groups in my sample of sixty-one preindustrial societies—in which women were the primary labor force —their ability to divorce seemed to exceed that of men.)

4. *Premarital sex.* What is at issue here is control of one's body. To what extent is there a double standard permitting greater freedom for men? (Empirically, analyses of the major ethnographic data sets show that such factors as patri institutions, stratification, and "high gods" are associated with greater restriction of females premaritally; see, for example, Blumberg, Carns, and Winch, 1970.)

5. *Extramarital sex.* Standards for pre- and extramarital sex may vary. To what extent is there a double standard that more severely punishes women? An interesting wrinkle here is that in some societies the person punished for adultery is the wife's lover. In a number of African horticultural societies where women are the primary labor force, and adultery is endemic, the norms call for the woman's male lover to pay the husband a fine—or work for him.

6. *Control of the household* (that is, household power). This is a microvariable of great impact on people's lives. To the extent that male/female heterosexual households are "the only game in town," all sorts of decisions affecting our welfare are made there. "Family power" research has been exploring such decisions since the classic study by Blood and Wolfe, 1960. In the United States, for example, the sizable literature on husbands' and wives' inputs into family decision making (conceptualized as "family

power") typically reveals that the power of the employed work-ing-class wife to make certain household decisions is one that comes to her by default from the great separation between male and female spheres of activity. But employment itself usually en-hances the wife's household power vis-à-vis her husband, regardless of social class (see, for example, Scanzoni, 1972).

Among newer tacks, a fascinating focus is emerging in "women in development" circles comparing men's and women's household expenditure decisions. Among various groups of Third World poor, if new income enters the household and is controlled by the man, it tends to be spent on liquor, consumer items such as transistor radios, trips, paid female companionship, perhaps some toys for the children, and maybe some producer items (see, for example, Stavrakis and Marshall, 1978). In contrast, new in-come controlled by the woman tends to be devoted to nutrition, education, and other basic human needs.[12]

Also relevant is the extent to which the partners' income is pooled or separated. Many variations exist. For example, a com-mon household budget is still the exception in many parts of Africa where women are important producers and retain primary responsibility for their children's subsistence needs; there, the woman's income will cover one set of expenditures, and the man's will be devoted to others. Roldan's research (1983), in which 67 percent of the poor working-class Mexico City households studied had a pooled common fund, clearly showed that women exerted both greater autonomy and greater household control as the result of their economic contributions. In fact, "although all women in this group sought a paid job because of pressing economic needs, a second element was mentioned in 87 percent of the cases: women worked to secure an autonomous income as a means to diminish or counteract husbands' domestic power: not to have to beg him when the allowance is insufficient; not to be humiliated and told: 'You are good for nothing. I support you and this family'; to en-sure or . . . expand their sphere of autonomous management" (Roldan, 1983:12).

In short, although cultural variables (such as the extent to which the household is viewed as "women's domain") and person-ality factors clearly affect household power dynamics, I posit that overall, women's economic power is the strongest predictor of their degree of household power. Both Schlegel's findings (1972) on her sixty-six-society matrilineal sample and my own data from sixty-one preindustrial societies provide further empirical support.

Finally, one of the few contemporary examples of a group in which wives and husbands have identical economic resources is the Israeli kibbutz. There, the still-socialist distribution system gives the woman "100 cents for every dollar" given to the man (in fact, the woman typically also controls the small lump-sum payment given for household sundries over and above the individual allotments). As pointed out, women's actual economic power at the macrolevels of the kibbutz political economy is less than men's. But given kibbutz spouses' microlevel economic equality, it is interesting to note that the *husbands* spend more hours per day in *domestic and childcare endeavors* than in any other modern-world group of which I am aware (see Blumberg, 1983).

The examples clearly do not exhaust microlevel "life options." Nonetheless, let us conclude with one variable that seems to be part microlevel and part macrolevel and one illustrative, essentially macrolevel variable. In these less micro variables women's economic power may not be the only important predictor, but it is still posited as an influential one.

7. *Freedom of movement.* The extent to which women are restricted in their movements in the "public domain" clearly affects their life opportunities in the larger world. From a company's willingness to hire a woman for a job involving frequent overnight travel to the right of an attractive young woman to walk unescorted outside her house, the size and opportunity structure of a woman's world is affected by the extent to which she is geographically restricted in comparison with men. Historically, it has been village and urban women of the more affluent classes who have suffered the most stringent limits to geographical mobility (see, for example, Sjoberg, 1960; Boulding, 1976). Among these groups, seclusion (purdah), veiling, and footbinding reached their apogee. Although such women might have been materially privileged in comparison with peasant and working-class men, the restrictions on their lives were enormous in comparison with the men of their own class.

8. *Access to education.* To a certain degree, macrolevel factors completely independent of women's economic power shape

the extent to which educational, political, and occupational rights and options are offered to women (relevant here are considerations of the "global village" and the world economy that have arisen under advanced capitalism). Boulding (1972) and Safilios-Rothschild (1971) treat some of these considerations; both consider how development is affecting a list of women's opportunities that share a number of variables with my "life options." But I argue that women's economic power also influences their access to educational opportunities, from training as tribal shamans to admission to graduate school. The latter is particularly important in contemporary stratification systems, where most people get their income from their occupations rather than their property. And, increasingly, ours are "credentialed societies" in which educational requirements are undergoing steadily rising inflation. To the extent that women can command fewer than half the places at crucial educational levels (that is, those most determinative of life chances—different societies have different "threshold levels" for this), their future structural position in the society will suffer.

The preceding discussion concerning "life options"—and, indeed, the entire argument—can be summarized in two additional hypotheses:

H_{24}:   Women's relative economic power (in comparison with that of counterpart men at household, community, and more macro levels such as class and state) is the most important predictor of their overall relative equality in a wide variety of "life options."

H_{25}:   Women's participation in production, independent of their relative economic power (that is, independent of their compensation/economic return for such work),[13] is *not* predictive of their relative equality in "life options."

Conclusions

The gist of these twenty-five propositions can be summarized as follows:

1.   For women, their relative economic power (defined in terms of relative control of the means of production and allocation

of surplus) is the most important of the variables affecting their overall position with respect to sexual stratification.

2. Women's relative economic power may vary somewhat independently at a variety of micro- and macrolevels, such as the household, the local group, the class, and the larger society (for example, the state).

3. To the extent that the more macro levels (for example, class, larger society) of political and economic power are male-dominated, women's exercise of their relative economic power at more micro levels will be correspondingly "discounted."

4. Female participation in production seems to be a generally necessary but clearly insufficient precondition for subsequent economic power, independent of any compensation paid for that labor.

5. Female participation in production, especially in more stratified societies, is more a function of the demand for labor relative to the available supply than of the degree of compatibility of the activity with simultaneous childcare responsibilities (especially breast feeding).

6. Three groups of variables are proposed as antecedents of women's relative economic power:
   - "Strategic indispensability" factors that affect women's leverage as a labor force and, in the most favorable case, result in women's converting their labor power into some degree of economic power.
   - The extent to which the kinship system facilitates their acquisition of property, through its rules on inheritance, marital residence, and descent (listed in descending order of importance).
   - The larger society's stratification system (social relations of production); women generally fare less well in more stratified preindustrial societies.

7. The lower women's relative economic power, the more likely they are to be oppressed physically, politically, and ideologically.

8. The greater women's relative economic power, the greater their control over their own lives:
   - The greater a woman's relative economic power, the greater the likelihood that her fertility pattern will reflect her

own perceived utilities (rather than those of her mate, family, state, and so on).

- The greater her relative economic power, the greater her control over a variety of other "life options" as well (for example, marriage, divorce, sexuality, household authority).

These propositions have been refined by the growing codifications of data relevant to a theory of gender stratification that have emerged since the late 1960s. They have been stated in a way that is intended to permit their use across the entire range of societal complexity and at both macro- and microlevels in contemporary societies.[14]

It should be stressed that a number of the propositions of the theory are also relevant for the study of *societal* stratification: First, recall the argument that even a low level of substitutability at the margin (say, 5 to 15 percent) can undermine the bargaining power of a group. This argument was developed as a proposition for a general theory of stratification and was used to explain why peasants are almost everywhere so oppressed despite the crucial economic importance of their activities. Then its logic was extended to women, who were shown to be easily substitutable in most historical and contemporary labor force situations.

Second, all the "strategic indispensability" factors were developed from the standpoint of general stratification theory. I offer the list as a series of hypotheses about the factors that enhance the leverage and bargaining power of *any* subordinate group that functions as a labor force for a superordinate group:

- The greater the importance of the producers' activities and/or the producers themselves (as measured by the value of their output and short-run substitution costs),
- the greater their control over the labor process (including the extent to which they control technical expertise, work autonomously of close dominant group supervision, and labor in large and cohesive work groups),
- the greater their ability to organize on their own behalf, and
- the more they are beneficiaries of competition between countervailing groups,

the greater the "strategic indispensability" of the group, and the more likely that it will be able to gain control of at least some of the means of production, hence increasing its future economic power and position within the stratification system.

Third, the greater the economic power of a group, the greater its control over the allocation of its own labor power.

Fourth, as a manifestation of the preceding hypothesis, it is proposed that a higher-status labor force may enter the traditional economic activities of a lower-status labor force in large numbers when there is a labor *glut* in the higher group's activities. But the relationship is asymmetrical: The lower-status labor force may not enter the preferred activities of the higher-status group when there is a job shortage in the lower-status group's own activities.

Fifth, in general, the greater the control over the means of production, the greater the control over the fruits of production.

Additionally, the propositions linking women's economic power and their degree of control of fertility variables should be of direct relevance to a wide variety of demographic theories. What I am proposing is that the relation between "mode of production" and "mode of reproduction" is mediated through the economic activities and power of the woman. Where she is an important producer, childcare activities will be adjusted. Where she has low relative economic power, she will be less likely to have any real control over her fertility, and vice versa. These relations should have policy implications for family planning programs as well as theoretical relevance for population studies.

A final point of more general theoretical relevance is that I propose the *disaggregation* of the "new home economics" household production function as a way of untangling not only fertility but also income flows into the household and expenditure patterns out of the household. It is not only male/female calculations that have to be done separately, I suggest, but those of the other principal actors as well. To reiterate, households are neither perfect democracies nor perfect dictatorships, and their boundaries can encompass oppression and conflicting utilities as well as solidarity and consensus.

In conclusion, I suggest that we can come full circle: Once the impact of biology is relegated to the background, many of the propositions of a theory of gender stratification are relevant to general theories of stratification—and vice versa.

Notes

1. Moreover, it is increasingly evident that not all the trends are lined up in the same direction. Before moving on to theories, it may be useful to review some of the complex and contradictory changes in the "state of the sexes" since approximately 1970.

In 1970, around the time that a renewed interest in the position of women emerged, an important statistical milestone was reached: U.S. labor force participation of women in the "prime labor force years," 18 through 64, reached 50 percent (U.S. Department of Labor, 1971). Since then, women's labor force participation has continued to climb, and as of 1983, nearly 60 percent of females 18 through 64 are employed. But more than half of them continue to be crowded into fewer than 20 low-paid "pink-collar ghetto" occupations. And the "sex gap in earnings" for full-time, year-round workers remains as wide in the 1980s as it was in the 1970s: Currently such women earn 59 cents for every male dollar. In fact, the disproportion is greater now than during the peak years of the "feminine mystique"—in 1955 it was 64 cents to the dollar (Ehrlich, 1974).

Politically, there are a few more women in Congress, many more in local and state office, and a newly discovered "gender gap" in voting (which helped put the first woman on the Supreme Court). But the Equal Rights Amendment failed ratification by three of the 38 states needed. In our personal lives, we marry later, live together more, divorce more, have fewer children and have them later in life, and seem to have more nonmarital sex, more nonheterosexual sex, more orgasms—and more fear of genital herpes. Since the 1973 Supreme Court decision (*Wade* v. *Roe*), women have had more abortions, but a strong "right to life" movement continues to mobilize to reverse this trend. Meanwhile, a new phenomenon, male strippers, is packing in women patrons even in such presumably conservative "heartland" states as Kansas.

At the top of our political economy, some 367 women hold 527 directorships on the boards of the 1,300 largest corporations— 3 percent of the seats, a 400 percent increase in 10 years (Fleming,

1983). At the bottom, both the "feminization of poverty" and wife beating have been exacerbated by the severe recession of the early 1980s.

Worldwide, trends are even more contradictory. In 1970, Ester Boserup published her landmark book indicating that, contrary to the then-prevailing view, the forces of economic development and "modernization" often affected Third World women negatively—especially in areas where females had traditionally enjoyed economic autonomy as farmers and/or market traders. The United Nations proclaimed 1975 as International Women's Year and 1976-1985 as the "Decade for Women." But documentation continues to pile up illustrating Boserup's thesis on the deepening marginalization of many Third World women—an erosion of their resource base coupled with an increase in their work load (see, for example, Tinker, 1976; Blumberg, 1979a, 1981). But not all the changes have been negative. The ideology of equal rights for women and the secular religion of voting continue to spread. And, as a mixed blessing, the export of jobs in labor-intensive industries from the capitalist industrial countries to the Third World has resulted in the unexpected phenomenon that their recipients are disproportionately young, single women.

2. Murdock's *Ethnographic Atlas* (and its subsequent smaller, improved versions) has generated both supporters and critics galore. The latter justifiably fault it for a broad variety of methodological problems. It is certain that there are a number of errors scattered among its codes on some 1,200-odd societies. Nevertheless, over time, the *Atlas* has been used for dozens of studies whose findings have stood up to other data sources. In general, its economically linked variables have proved the most trustworthy. Moreover, these seem least likely to be affected by "Galton's problem" (where two variables seem to covary not because of any functional link but rather because of the happenstance of joint diffusion).

3. Expected costs and benefits of offspring may be different for the male and female parents. These differences can encompass one or more of a variety of fertility variables: age at first birth, spacing, preferred sex ratio, age at last birth, completed size of family, and means of intervention (contraceptives, abstinence, abortion, infanticide) used. I shall argue that one of the most rele-

vant payoffs for a woman of greater economic power is greater leverage in achieving *her* utilities in fertility outcomes. This may not always mean fewer children, since there are a number of circumstances in which women might opt for larger families. Nevertheless, in studies of contemporary developing and developed societies, the bulk of the evidence indicates a negative correlation between female status and fertility.

4. Building on Benston's article (1969), prominent contributions have been made by Seccombe (1974), Gardiner (1975), Harrison (1973), and Gough and Harrison (1975). The "wages for housework" argument of Dalla Costa and James (1972) has been criticized by Adamson and others (1976) and by Himmelweit and Mohun (1977). Finally, see also Coulson, Magas, and Wainwright (1975).

5. I ultimately hope to develop my "mini theory" on the preconditions for Amazon groups, first mentioned in this chapter, as a separate article. It should be noted that ancient references mention a geographically diverse array of Amazon groups. "Libyan" Amazons were supposed to have dwelled near the Atlas Mountains (in Roman times, the land known as Libya included in its territory present-day Morocco, Algeria, and Tunis). These women, who flourished "presumably in the early days of Egyptian glory" (Boulding, 1976:300), were described as having "red leather armor, snakeskin shoes, and . . . python-leather shields" (Diner, 1965:133, cited in Boulding, 1976). Another oft-cited Amazon group is the Gorgons, who lived near the Caucasus Mountains. They were described by Strabo as a people of great courage against whom Perseus waged war (Diner, 1965:134, quoted in Boulding, 1976); they favored tight-fitting clothes, Phrygian caps, and long, soft leather boots. Most frequently, the bulk of Amazon groups are depicted as Scythians from the Caucasus. Another area linked to Amazons in ancient writings is the area of the Thermodon River, where they were supposed to have thrived well before the time of Homer. In fact, the legends of a surprising number of peoples mention Amazons, from the Greeks to the Chinese (whose literature refers to a western women's realm located between the Black Sea and the Caspian Sea; see, for example, Sobol, 1972). A fine student paper (Tarr, 1980) treats Amazon geographical ranges as well as customs.

6. Roldan writes: "This is how [Doña] B. describes the new pattern":

> Now that I get my own money I feel better, less short of money because now I know how much money I have for the week. Before I used to ask him for everything [he gave her a daily allowance]. I obey and respect him, but I feel I also have some rights. . . . Before he used to shout at me if he thought I was spending too much on the children, or did not give him the food he wanted. Now I tell him: "With the small salary you earn and you go and spend it on drinking with your friends. Look at me, I am also earning, and I do not buy anything for me, but all I get I put in the house." It is not fair. Once or twice he slapped me in the face. He said I had shouted at him. I felt I was right. Mind you, it is not that I feel proud, or that I think I am better than he is, but I feel I have the right to tell him: "Look, why do you do this or that, like drinking, spending too much on cards, or the races." I am helping him, so somehow I have the right to expect him to change [Roldan, 1983:15].

Note that in the overwhelming machismo of the prevailing culture, the woman *twice* justifies her assertiveness (in curbing what she views as her husband's wasting too much of his earnings on his personal pleasures) on the fact that she, too, is now earning. This, rather than anything in the ideology, is what gives her what she feels is the new *right* to assert herself. In fact, she is careful *not* to present herself as a violator of traditional norms of respect and deference to males.

7. Goldberg (1972), writing from a radical perspective, credits (1) the Soviet Union's long-standing policy of economic expansion and development and (2) the horrendous death rates of Soviet men in World War II (at war's end the sex ratio stood at only 74 males per 100 females) as the main factors creating economic demand for women's labor, even in "nontraditional" occupations. Education is even more important than in the West in order to get a *good* job in the U.S.S.R., so university admission policies are crucial "gatekeepers" for women's occupational advancement or decline. By 1958, when the demographic pyramid

had returned to normal for the college-age population, political criteria were added to the entrance exam scores, previously the sole standard for university admission. In 1958 representatives from the overwhelmingly male ranks of the Komsomol (Young Communists) and trade union leaders were added to admissions committees. Now applicants were chosen on the basis of recommendations from their Komsomol or trade union as well as their test scores. Whereas women had been 52 percent of the students in higher education in 1955, by 1964, under the new rules, they were down to only 43 percent. Even more drastic was their low representation in the prestigious science faculties. By 1964 Moscow State University was admitting only 35 percent females to its science faculties, even though they remained 47 percent of applicants. These policies were softened during the strong economic expansion of the late 1960s, and female enrollment once again crept up to the 50 percent mark. But the precedent is clear and does not bode well for women if growth slackens again.

8. Martin and Voorhies (1975) stress this factor and go on to argue that matrilineal groups "provide a very adaptive superstructure for horticultural communities in stable environments. [Matrilineality] loses its adaptive value in the face of expansive, competitive, or more intensely exploitative technoeconomic systems" (1975:229).

9. Collins (1982) offers a theoretical and descriptive account of "courtly marriage politics" in Heian Japan (about 800–1200 A.D.) and the Nayars of South India's Malabar Coast that is very relevant for my theory. Specifically, he wishes to add a *political* element to "any general theory of the status of women" (1982:21). He describes two situations in which kinship marriage politics among the elite focused on getting the family's women to "marry up" and thereby advance the group's status and power. The case of the Nayar is better known, since this matrilineal, matrilocal, high-status warrior caste has been well studied for its unique system of "visiting husbands" (see, for example, Mencher, 1965). Women were allowed considerable sexual freedom, so long as they played by the rules: A visiting husband could never be of a lower caste (or even a lower-ranking Nayar) and could visit only in the night hours. Such women also had property rights and were literate. Much less well known is the case of Heian Japan. Although

the prevailing system was patrilineal, "courtly politics" during this period gave a matrifocal orientation to alliances among the elite. As among the Nayar, an attractive, intelligent daughter was a greater asset than a son to an ambitious family. Such daughters could become concubines or wives of higher-ranking nobility (the biggest prize being the emperor) and greatly advance their family's position. In both Nayar and Heian cases, the custom seemed to spread downward from the top aristocracy. The status of women in Heian Japan clearly rose (for example, women produced the most famous literature of the period), and they gained the right to control and inherit property in their own names. These rights gradually eroded after 1200 when a military dictatorship ended the period of courtly marriage politics. Collins introduces the concept of "courtly marriage politics" to account for both cases. Under a "court nobility" type of marriage politics, matrilocality and matrilineality are introduced (Heian Japan) or emphasized (Nayars). Furthermore, both elaborate status ranking and "prevailing sexual affairs amounting to polyandry" (1982:14) characterize such a system.

Collins views his theory of courtly marriage politics as complementary to my economic theory "in showing some of the autonomous dynamics of kinship politics which can bring about female property rights" (1982:21). His data illuminate the situation in which women's economic power derives from the kinship system rather than their own labor: In neither case did these elite women work. Instances in which women are the non-working "coupon clippers" of a matrifocal kinship system are empirically rather rare, however (hence the proposition that female participation in production is a *generally* necessary but invariably insufficient precondition for economic power).

10. I wish to stress that the major power variables dealt with in this chapter—economic, political, force, and (to a lesser extent) ideology—do not exhaust the list of variables that can be conceived of as *resources* in a male/female bargaining situation. *Sexual attractiveness,* stressed in Collins's theory, is one of these additional resources. When we see an older, unattractive person with a gorgeous young partner (regardless of the sexes involved), we assume that the less attractive partner is trading abundant resources for the other's sexual attractiveness. This brings up two

somewhat related variables that act as resources in a relationship. On the one hand, the partner with a *lower commitment* to the relationship gains more leverage because of the other's greater emotional investment. On the other hand, the *age gap* between spouses usually favors the older partner (unless that person is already so old as to be losing accrued power). The older partner brings greater experience, political contacts, and opportunities to have amassed wealth. In most societies, the age gap favors the male (in fact, female sexual attractiveness is held to decline faster with age), but how much of a resource it is remains to be determined. Finally, some theorists (for example, Rosaldo, 1974) have stressed that *male participation in domestic and childcare tasks* reflects a more egalitarian system. This last potential resource seems a bit more problematic than the others. We know that men do tend to help out a bit more around the house when women are important producers. But I would caution that the more time the man devotes to household affairs in the absence of a nonhousehold source of power for the wife, the more likely he may be to enhance his own power there, in what could well be her only possible arena for authority. Encel, MacKenzie, and Tebbutt (1974), writing about Australia, also make this point.

11. In this and the subsequent "life options," it should be noted that (1) the sexes may have virtually equal freedom in making their own (marriage) choices; (2) the sexes may have virtually *no* freedom (for example, if she disapproves of her family's choice, she can commit suicide; if he disapproves of his family's choice, he can opt for permanent exile—a more or less equal *lack* of freedom); (3) the male can have varying degrees of greater freedom than the female; (4) the female can have varying degrees of greater freedom than the male. Frequently, however, it would be misleading to view these outcomes in terms of the neoclassical economist's "tastes and preferences" view of choice. For example, an increasing proportion of the world's women are becoming heads of households (with or without a prior formal marriage) because of structural factors that militate toward this family form, rather than an autonomous decision to forgo a marital union (see, for example, Blumberg with Garcia, 1977). About a third of poor Third World women now are estimated to be de facto/de jure household heads.

12. In fact, there has been a recent upsurge of interest among the development community in various aspects of female income. First, income-generating projects have been frequently attempted as a concrete way of incorporating women into economic development. Most, however, have been so marginal and under-capitalized that any income generated has been insufficient to make a substantial difference in these women's abilities to meet their families' basic human needs. Second, interest is also keen in further exploring the differential expenditure patterns mentioned in the text. Third, control of income has become a focus of concern in the sense that each sex may retain autonomous control of any income earned, both sexes may pool their income (perhaps to different degrees), or one sex may turn over income earned to the household while the other partner retains independent control. In March 1983 the Population Council and the Rockefeller Foundation cosponsored a conference on "Women, Income, and Policy" that highlighted these issues. Still underemphasized, however, was a concern for what I have been emphasizing here: women's control of economic resources *in comparison with* their menfolk. This is surprising, since obtaining a crude measure of relative male and female household contributions, for example, seems much easier than the tedious and detailed process required to establish family budgeting information.

13. One enormously significant difference between women working in subsistence production in nonmonetized economies and women working for wages in contemporary societies is that those wages are paid in money and therefore embody a transformation to capital. If the woman's earnings do not permit any surplus but are merely exchanged for survival, one could argue that this difference is irrelevant. But in a money economy, for a woman to go from "no cents on the dollar" in comparison with her spouse's earnings to "X cents on the dollar" is sufficient to initiate microlevel changes in the power dynamics of the relationship, as Roldan's research clearly showed. Similarly, when a U.S. wife enters the labor force on a full-time basis, she can expect to earn about 59 cents for every dollar earned by her male counterpart. But, as has been argued in this chapter, going from zero to even 59 cents on the dollar will profoundly affect intimate relationships. This is especially true in a country such as the U.S. where a sub-

stantial majority of women now work, and public opinion polls show that disapproval of a married woman's working when her husband has a job has declined consistently as women's labor force participation rose. The working women in Roldan's study, in contrast, had to buck a still-strong societal attitude of disapproval of their economic activities, a historically macho culture, and the fact that they still represent a statistical minority of females. And yet even though their earnings were so small that they had little choice concerning the survival necessities on which they spent them, it was *they* who spent them—and felt an upsurge in autonomy in the process.

14. I have been accumulating empirical support for my theory as opportunity and funding have permitted. My first effort involved a sample of sixty-one preindustrial societies, chosen to provide about ten societies each from Murdock's main world culture regions and about ten societies each from the main productive bases found in tehnographic data sets (ranging from hunting-gathering to intensive agriculture). Each society chosen was included in the *Human Relations Area Files* (HRAF), the *Ethnographic Atlas,* and the *Standard Cross-Cultural Sample*—a "triple overlap" sample. The HRAF materials did not permit easy coding of the "strategic indispensability variables" (which were not as refined at that time) or fertility-linked factors (although here an attempt was made, in conjunction with Hazel Reinhardt). The two most powerful independent variables proved to be economic power and force. Women's relative economic power was measured as discussed above: the proportion of the means of production controlled by women, the proportion of surplus (if any) allocated by them, and, in addition, the extent to which women could accumulate wealth without restriction and share in inheritance. Force was measured by only a single indicator: the circumstances under which men beat their wives (ranging from apparently never to "at will"). Political power was measured in terms of relative clout in governance at the local level—that is, women's proportional representation in the council (or equivalent) as well as their relative overall political influence.

Life options, the dependent variable, was measured by a four-factor index of how women's degree of freedom compared with men's with respect to (1) marriage, (2) divorce, (3) premarital virginity, and (d) household control. Other independent or inter-vening variables measured included those relating to societal com-plexity and the prevailing degree of stratification, sexual division of labor in the main productive activities, the kinship system (es-pecially marital residence and the form of descent), ideology of male supremacy, and male participation in childcare and domestic tasks.

The various independent and intervening variables noted above accounted for a majority of the variance in the life options index (R^2 = 0.56). Women's relative economic power accounted for well over 80 percent of that 0.56 (namely, 0.47). But only force retained an independent net impact, over and above eco-nomic power, in the regressions predicting to life options. In fact, it accounted for almost all the remaining .09. (The intercorrelation between economic power and force, which approaches –0.6, is not quite high enough to make multicollinearity a problem requir-ing remediation.)

Ideally, I would like to explore the refined theory presented in this chapter will a full-scale coding project based on a major eth-nographic data set. But I have also been attempting to develop em-pirical support for the theory in contemporary societies around the globe. Toward that end, for example, I have undertaken case studies of the Israeli kibbutz, compared secondary data on the United States and other industrial societies, and attempted to in-corporate my paradigm into my development work (primarily in Latin America). In the last year or so, for example, I have had oc-casion to do fieldwork in Peru, Ecuador, and Colombia. The con-trasts within a single country in the position of women can be so dramatic that it does not take months of interviewing to see the difference. In regions of the Ecuadorian southern border zone where women play a role in farming and have income-producing activities of their own, one could always count on a few feisty females who would more than hold their own at group meetings against the overwhelmingly male majority (these were potential beneficiaries of credit and other farming assistance). In contrast, there are coastal fishing regions where only men fish and the wom-en have almost *no* income-producing activities. There, there were no women at group meetings. Even in their homes, the sense of dependency, fatalism, and subordination they projected was over-

whelming. I interviewed women worn out by excessive childbear-
ing who would like to avoid having their daughters share their
fate. But neither they nor their daughters held out any strong expectations that this would come to pass. Life was not in their
hands. Naturally, there is a tendency for researchers to "see" what
they are looking for. Clearly, a good deal more research is needed
before any of the propositions presented in this chapter can be
considered soundly grounded in empirical support.

References

ABERLE, DAVID F.
  1961   "Matrilineal Descent in Cross-Cultural Perspective." In
         David M. Schneider and Kathleen Gough (Eds.), *Matri-
         lineal Kinship*. Berkeley: University of California Press.
ADAMSON, OLIVIA, AND OTHERS
  1976   "Women's Oppression Under Capitalism." *Revolution-
         ary Communism*, No. 5(Nov.).
AMERICAN ASSOCIATION FOR THE ADVANCEMENT OF SCIENCE
  1974   *Culture and Population Change*. Washington, D.C.:
         American Association for the Advancement of Science.
ARGYLE, WILLIAM J.
  1966   *The Fon of Dahomey*. Oxford: Clarendon Press.
ARONOFF, JOEL, AND CRANO, WILLIAM D.
  1975   "A Re-examination of the Cross-Cultural Principles of
         Task Segregation and Sex-Role Differentiation in the
         Family." *American Sociological Review* 40:12-20.
BACDAYAN, ALBERT S.
  1977   "Mechanistic Cooperation and Sexual Equality Among
         the Western Bontoc." In Alice Schlegel (Ed.), *Sexual
         Stratification*. New York: Columbia University Press.
BARON, AVA
  1982   "Women and the Making of the American Working
         Class: A Study of the Proletarianization of Printers."
         Review of Radical Political Economics 14, No. 3
         (Fall).
BART, PAULINE B.
  1969   "Why Women's Status Changes in Middle Age: The
         Turns of the Social Ferris Wheel." *Sociological Sym-
         posium* 1, No. 3(Fall).

BENSTON, MARGARET
  1969   "The Political Economy of Women's Liberation."
         Monthly Review 21(Sept.):13–27.
BIRDSELL, JOSEPH B.
  1968   "Some Predictions for the Pleistocene Based on Equi-
         librium Systems Among Recent Hunter-Gatherers." In
         Richard B. Lee and Irven DeVore (Eds.), *Man the
         Hunter*. Chicago: Aldine.
BLOOD, ROBERT O., JR., AND WOLFE, DONALD M.
  1960   *Husbands and Wives: The Dynamics of Married Living.*
         New York: Free Press.
BLUMBERG, RAE LESSER
  1974   "Structural Factors Affecting Women's Status: A Cross-
         Societal Paradigm." Paper presented at the meeting of
         the International Sociological Association, Toronto.
  1976a "Fairy Tales and Facts: Economy, Family, Fertility,
         and the Female." In Irene Tinker and Michele Bo
         Bramsen (Eds.), *Women and World Development*. Wash-
         ington, D.C.: Overseas Development Council/American
         Association for the Advancement of Science.
  1976b "Kibbutz Women: From the Fields of Revolution to
         the Laundries of Discontent." In Lynne Iglitzin and
         Ruth Ross (Eds.), *Women in the World: A Compara-
         tive Study*. Oxford: ABC Clio.
  1978   *Stratification: Socioeconomic and Sexual Stratifica-
         tion.* Dubuque, Iowa: William C. Brown.
  1979a "A Paradigm Predicting the Position of Women: Policy
         Implications and Problems." In Jean Lipman-Blumen
         and Jessie Bernard (Eds.), *Sex Roles and Social Policy*.
         London: Sage.
  1979b "Rural Women in Development: Veil of Invisibility,
         World of Work." *International Journal of Intercultural
         Relations* 3:447–472.
  1981   "Females, Farming, and Food: Rural Development and
         Women's Participation in Agricultural Production Sys-
         tems." In Barbara C. Lewis (Ed.), *Invisible Farmers:
         Women and the Crisis in Agriculture*. Washington,
         D.C.: Office of Women in Development, Agency for
         International Development.

1983   "As You Sow, So Shall You Reap: A Structural Analysis of Sexual Stratification in the Kibbutz in the 1980s." In Michal Palgi and others (Eds.), *Sexual Equality: The Israeli Kibbutz Tests the Theories*. Norwood, Pa.: Norwood Press.

BLUMBERG, RAE LESSER, CARNS, DONALD, AND WINCH, ROBERT F.
1970   "High Gods, Virgin Brides and Societal Complexity." Paper read at the meeting of the American Sociological Association, Washington, D.C.

BLUMBERG, RAE LESSER, AND GARCIA, MARIA-PILAR
1977   "The Political Economy of the Mother-Child Family: A Cross-Societal View." In Luis Leñero-Otero (Ed.), *Beyond the Nuclear Family Model*. London: Sage.

BLUMBERG, RAE LESSER, AND WINCH, ROBERT F.
1972   "Societal Complexity and Familial Complexity: Evidence for the Curvilinear Hypothesis." *American Journal of Sociology* 77:898–920.

BOSERUP, ESTER
1970   *Woman's Role in Economic Development*. New York: St. Martin's.

BOULDING, ELISE
1972   "Women as Role Models in Industrializing Societies: A Macrosystem Model of Socialization for Civic Competence." In Marvin H. Sussman and Betty E. Cogswell, *Cross National Family Research*. New York: E. J. Brill.

1976   *The Underside of History*. Boulder, Colo.: Westview Press.

BROWN, JUDITH K.
1970   "A Note on the Division of Labor by Sex." *American Anthropologist* 72:1074–1078.

1975   "Iroquois Women: An Ethnohistoric Note." In Rayna R. Reiter (Ed.), *Toward an Anthropology of Women*. New York: Monthly Review Press.

BURRIS, VAL, AND WHARTON, AMY
1982   "Sex Segregation in the U.S. Labor Force." *Review of Radical Political Economics* 14, No. 3 (Fall).

BURTON, MICAHEL L., BRUDNER, LILYAN A., AND WHITE, DOUG-
LAS R.
  1977   "A Model of the Sexual Division of Labor." *American
         Ethnologist* 4(2):227-251.
CARTWRIGHT, FREDERICK F., AND BIDDIS, MICHAEL D.
  1972   *Disease and History*. New York: T. Y. Crowell.
CHAGNON, NAPOLEON A.
  1968   *Yanomamo: The Fierce People*. New York: Holt, Rine-
         hart and Winston.
CHILDE, V. GORDON
  1964   *What Happened in History*. (Rev. ed.) Baltimore: Pen-
         guin Books.
CLIGNET, REMI
  1970   *Many Wives, Many Powers*. Evanston, Ill.: Northwest-
         ern University Press.
COLLINS, RANDALL
  1971   "A Conflict Theory of Sexual Stratification." *Social
         Problems* 19:3-21.
  1975   *Conflict Sociology: Toward an Explanatory Science*.
         New York: Academic Press.
  1982   "Courtly Politics and the Status of Women: The Na-
         yars and Heian Japan." Unpublished paper.
COULSON, MARGARET, MAGAS, BRANKS, AND WAINWRIGHT, HIL-
LARY
  1975   "The Housewife and Her Labor Under Capitalism—A
         Critique." *New Left Review* 89(Jan.-Feb.):59-72.
DALLA COSTA, MARIAROSA, AND JAMES, SELMA
  1972   *The Power of Women and the Subversion of the Com-
         munity*. Bristol, England: Falling Water Press.
DAVIS, KINGSLEY, AND BLAKE, JUDITH
  1956   "Social Structure and Fertility: An Analytic Frame-
         work." *Economic Development and Cultural Change*
         4:211-235.
DE BEAUVOIR, SIMONE
  1952   *The Second Sex*. New York: Knopf.
DEERE, CARMEN DIANA
  1977   "The Agricultural Division of Labor by Sex: Myths,
         Facts, and Contradictions in the Northern Peruvian

Sierra." Paper presented at the Joint National Meeting of the Latin American Studies Association and the African Studies Association, Houston.

DINER, HELEN
1965   *Mothers and Amazons.* (Translated by John Philip Lundin.) New York: Julian Press. (Originally published 1932.)

DIVALE, WILLIAM TULIO
1974   "Migration, External Warfare, and Matrilocal Residence." *Behavior Science Research* 9:75-133.

DODGE, NORTON T.
1966   *Women in the Soviet Economy.* Baltimore: Johns Hopkins Press.

DOWD, DOUGLAS
1974   *The Twisted Dream.* Cambridge, Mass.: Winthrop.

DRAPER, PATRICIA
1975   "!Kung Women: Contrasts in Sexual Egalitarianism in Foraging and Sedentary Contexts." In Rayna R. Reiter (Ed.), *Toward an Anthropology of Women.* New York: Monthly Review Press.

EHRLICH, HOWARD J.
1974   *Selected Differences in the Life Chances of Men and Women in the United States.* Report No. 13. Baltimore: Research Group One.

EMBER, CAROL R.
1983   "The Relative Decline in Women's Contribution to Agriculture with Intensification." *American Anthropologist* 85:285-304.

EMBER, MELVIN, AND EMBER, CAROL R.
1971   "The Conditions Favoring Matrilocal vs. Patrilocal Residence." *American Anthropologist* 73:571-594.

ENCEL, SOL, MACKENZIE, NORMAN, AND TEBBUTT, MARGARET
1974   *Women and Society: An Australian Study.* Melbourne: Chesire.

ENGELS, FREDERICK
1972   *The Origin of the Family, Private Property, and the State.* New York: International Publishers.

FERNANDEZ, C. A., II, AND LYNCH, FRANK
1972   "The Tasaday: Cave-Dwelling Food Gatherers of South

Cotabato, Mindanao." *Philippine Sociological Review* 20:279-330.

FERNANDEZ-KELLY, MARIA PATRICIA
1983   *For We Are Sold, I and My People: Women and Industry in Mexico's Frontier.* Albany, N.Y.: State University of New York Press.

FIRESTONE, SHULAMITH
1970   *The Dialectic of Sex.* New York: William Morrow.

FLEMING, LOUIS B.
1983   "More Firms Welcome Women on Board at the Directors' Table." *Los Angeles Times,* April 24, business section, p. 1.

FRIEDL, ERNESTINE
1975   *Women and Men: An Anthropologist's View.* New York: Holt, Rinehart and Winston.

GARDINER, JEAN
1975   "Women's Domestic Labor." *New Left Review* 89 (Jan.-Feb.):47-58.

GARRETT, PATRICIA M.
1976   *Some Structural Constraints on the Agricultural Activities of Women: The Chilean Hacienda.* Madison: Land Tenure Center, University of Wisconsin.

GERTH, HANS H., AND MILLS, C. WRIGHT (EDS.)
1946   *From Max Weber: Essays in Sociology.* New York: Oxford University Press.

GOLDBERG, MARILYN POWER
1972   "Women in the Soviet Economy." *Review of Radical Political Economics* 4(3):60-74.

GOLDHAMER, FLORENCE KALM
1973   "Meri Bilong Mi: The 'Misfit' of Role and Status for the New Guinea Highlands Woman—A Comparative Study of Melanesian Male-Female Antagonism." Paper presented at the meeting of the American Anthropological Association, New Orleans.

GOUGH, KATHLEEN
1975   "The Origin of the Family." In Rayna R. Reiter (Ed.), *Toward an Anthropology of Women.* New York: Monthly Review Press. (Originally published in *Journal of Marriage and the Family,* 1971, 33(4):750-771.)

GOUGH, KATHLEEN, AND HARRISON, JUDITH
   1975   "Unproductive Labor and Housework Again." *Bulletin
           of the Conference of Socialist Economists* 4.
HARRIS, MARVIN
   1974   *Cows, Pigs, Wars, and Witches: The Riddles of Culture.*
           New York: Random House.
   1977   *Cannibals and Kings: The Origins of Cultures.* New
           York: Random House.
HARRISON, JUDITH
   1973   "The Political Economy of Housework." *Bulletin of
           the Conference of Socialist Economists* 4(Winter).
HIMMELWEIT, SUSAN, AND MOHUN, SIMON
   1977   "Domestic Labor and Capital." *Cambridge Journal of
           Economics* 1(March).
KINZER, NORA SCOTT
   1973   "Priests, Machos, and Babies; or, Latin American Wom-
           en and the Manichaean Heresy." *Journal of Marriage
           and the Family* 35:300–312.
KOLATA, GINA BARI
   1974   "!Kung Hunter-Gatherers: Feminism, Diet, and Birth
           Control." *Science* 185(Sept. 13):932–934.
KUHN, THOMAS
   1970   *The Structure of Scientific Revolutions.* (2nd ed.) Chi-
           cago: University of Chicago Press.
LANGNESS, L.
   1967   "Sexual Antagonism in the New Guinea Highlands: A
           Bena Bena Example." *Oceania* 38:161–177.
LEACOCK, ELEANOR BURKE
   1972   "Introduction." In Frederick Engels, *The Origin of the
           Family, Private Property, and the State.* New York: In-
           ternational Publishers.
LEE, RICHARD B.
   1968   "What Hunters Do for a Living, or How to Make Out
           on Scarce Resources." In Richard B. Lee and Irven
           DeVore (Eds.), *Man the Hunter.* Chicago: Aldine.
   1969   "!Kung Bushmen Subsistence: An Input-Output Anal-
           ysis." In Andrew P. Vayda (Ed.), *Environment and
           Cultural Behavior.* Garden City, N.Y.: Natural History
           Press.

LEE, RICHARD B., AND DEVORE, IRVEN (EDS.)
  1968   *Man the Hunter*. Chicago: Aldine.
LEEPER, DONALD S.
  1978   "Assistance, Hunger, and Malnutrition: The Commod-
         ity Systems Approach." Paper presented at the Inter-
         national Conference on Women and Food, University
         of Arizona, Tucson (mimeo).
LEIBOWITZ, LILA
  1978   *Females, Males, Families*. Belmont, Calif.: Wadsworth.
LENIN, VLADIMIR I.
  1972   *On the Emancipation of Women*. Moscow: Progress
         Publishers.
LENSKI, GERHARD E.
  1966   *Power and Privilege: A Theory of Social Stratification*.
         New York: McGraw-Hill.
LENSKI, GERHARD E., AND LENSKI, JEAN
  1982   *Human Societies*. (4th ed.) New York: McGraw-Hill.
LINDENBAUM, SHIRLEY
  1972   "Sorcerers, Ghosts, and Polluting Women: An Analysis
         of Religious Belief and Population Control." *Ethnol-
         ogy* 11:241–253.
  1976   "A Wife Is the Hand of Man." In P. Brown and G.
         Buchbinder (Eds.), *Man and Woman in the New Guinea
         Highlands*. American Anthropological Association Spe-
         cial Publication No. 8.
LOMBARD, JAQUES
  1967   "The Kingdom of Dahomey." In Daryll Forde and
         Phyllis M. Kaberry (Eds.), *West African Kingdoms in
         the Nineteenth Century*. London: Oxford University
         Press.
MAMDANI, MAHMOOD
  1972   *The Myth of Population Control: Family, Caste, and
         Class in an Indian Village*. New York: Monthly Review
         Press.
MARTIN, M. KAY, AND VOORHIES, BARBARA
  1975   *Female of the Species*. New York: Columbia Univer-
         sity Press.
MARX, KARL
  1967   *Capital: A Critical Analysis of Capitalist Production*.

Vol. 1. New York: International Publishers. (Originally published 1867.)

MAYES, SHARON S.
1981   "The Political Economy of Women's Liberation." In Scott McNall (Ed.), *Political Economy: A Critique of American Society.* Glenview, Ill.: Scott, Foresman.

MEGGITT, M. J.
1964   "Male-Female Relationships in the Highlands of Australian New Guinea." *American Anthropologist* 66: 204-224.

MENCHER, JOAN
1965   "The Nayars of South Malabar." In Meyer Nimkoff (Ed.), *Comparative Family Systems.* New York: Houghton Mifflin.

MICHAELSON, EVALYN JACOBSON, AND GOLDSCHMIDT, WALTER
1971   "Female Roles and Male Dominance Among Peasants." *Southwestern Journal of Anthropology* 27:330-352.

MILKMAN, RUTH
1980   "Organizing the Sexual Division of Labor: Historical Perspectives on 'Women's Work' and the American Labor Movement." *Socialist Review,* 10(1):95-150.

MILLS, C. WRIGHT
1959   *The Sociological Imagination.* New York: Oxford University Press.

MITCHELL, JULIET
1966   "Women: The Longest Revolution." *New Left Review* 40(Nov.-Dec.).
1971   *Women's Estate.* New York: Pantheon.

MORGAN, JAMES N., AND OTHERS
1974   *Five-Thousand American Families—Patterns of Economic Progress.* Ann Arbor: Institute for Social Research, University of Michigan.

MURDOCK, GEORGE P.
1934   *Our Primitive Contemporaries.* New York: Macmillan.
1949   *Social Structure.* New York: Macmillan.
1967   "Ethnographic Atlas: A Summary." *Ethnology* 6:109-236.

MURDOCK, GEORGE P., AND PROVOST, CATERINA
1973 "Factors in the Division of Labor by Sex: A Cross-Cultural Analysis." *Ethnology* 12:203-235.

MURDOCK, GEORGE P., AND WHITE, DOUGLAS R.
1969 "Standard Cross-Cultural Sample." *Ethnology* 8:329-369.

NANCE, JOHN
1975 *The Gentle Tasaday*. New York: Harcourt Brace Jovanovich.

NERLOVE, SARA B.
1974 "Women's Workload and Infant Feeding Practices: A Relationship with Demographic Implications." *Ethnology* 13:207-214.

OBOLER, REGINA E.
1973 "Economics and the Status of Women." Paper presented at the meeting of the American Anthropological Association, New Orleans.

OPPENHEIMER, VALERIE KINCADE
1973 "Demographic Influence on Female Employment and the Status of Women." *American Journal of Sociology* 78:946-961.

PARSONS, TALCOTT, AND BALES, ROBERT
1955 *Family, Socialization, and Interaction Process*. New York: Free Press.

POLANYI, KARL
1966 *Dahomey and the Slave Trade*. Seattle: University of Washington Press.

POLGAR, STEVEN
1972 "Population History and Population Policies from an Anthropological Perspective." *Current Anthropology* 13:203-211.
1975 "Population, Evolution, and Theoretical Paradigms." In Steven Polgar (Ed.), *Population, Ecology, and Social Evolution*. The Hague: Mouton.

REINHARDT, HAZEL H.
1974 Personal communications with author, Madison, Wisconsin.

ROLDAN, MARTHA
1983 "Intrahousehold Patterns of Money Allocation and

Women's Subordination: A Case Study of Domestic Outworkers in Mexico City." Unpublished paper circulated to participants in Women, Income, and Policy Seminar, Population Council, New York, March. (Drafted October 1982.)

ROSALDO, MICHELLE Z.
1974 "Woman, Culture, and Society: A Theoretical Overview." In Michelle Z. Rosaldo and Louise Lamphere (Eds.), *Woman, Culture, and Society*. Stanford, Calif.: Stanford University Press.

ROSALDO, MICHELLE Z., AND LAMPHERE, LOUISE (EDS.)
1974 *Woman, Culture, and Society*. Stanford, Calif.: Stanford University Press.

SACKS, KAREN
1975 "Engels Revisited: Women, the Organization of Production, and Private Property." In Rayna R. Reiter (Ed.), *Toward an Anthropology of Women*. New York: Monthly Review Press.

SAFA, HELEN I.
1983 "Women, Production, and Reproduction in Industrial Capitalism: A Comparison of Brazilian and U.S. Factory Workers." In June Nash and Maria Patricia Fernandez-Kelly (Eds.), *Women, Men and the International Division of Labor*. Albany, N.Y.: State University of New York Press.

SAFILIOS-ROTHSCHILD, CONSTANTINA
1971 "A Cross-Cultural Examination of Women's Marital, Educational, and Occupational Options." *Acta Sociologica* 14:96–113.

SANDAY, PEGGY REEVES
1973 "Toward a Theory of the Status of Women." *American Anthropologist* 75:1682–1700.
1974 "Female Status in the Public Domain." In Michelle Z. Rosaldo and Louise Lamphere (Eds.), *Woman, Culture, and Society*. Stanford, Calif.: Stanford University Press.
1981 *Female Power and Male Dominance: On the Origins of Sexual Inequality*. Cambridge: Cambridge University Press.

SCANZONI, JOHN
   1972   *Sexual Bargaining*. Englewood Cliffs, N.J.: Prentice-
           Hall.
SCHLEGEL, ALICE
   1972   *Male Dominance and Female Autonomy: Domestic
           Authority in Matrilineal Societies*. New Haven, Conn.:
           HRAF Press.
   1977   *Sexual Stratification: A Cross-Cultural View*. New
           York: Columbia University Press.
SCHNAIBERG, ALLAN, AND REED, DAVID
   1974   "Risk, Uncertainty, and Family Formation: The Social
           Context of Poverty Groups." *Population Studies* 28.
SECCOMBE, WALLY
   1974   "Housework Under Capitalism." *New Left Review* 83
           (Jan.–Feb.).
SJOBERG, GIDEON
   1960   *The Pre-Industrial City*. New York: Free Press.
SOBOL, DONALD J.
   1972   *The Amazons of Greek Mythology*. Scarsdale, N.Y.:
           A. S. Barnes.
SPIRO, MELFORD E.
   1963   *Kibbutz: Venture in Utopia*. New York: Schocken
           Books.
STACK, CAROL B.
   1974   *All Our Kin: Strategies for Survival in a Black Com-
           munity*. New York: Harper & Row.
STAVRAKIS, OLGA, AND MARSHALL, MARION LOUISE
   1978   "Women, Agriculture, and Development in the Maya
           Lowlands: Profit or Progress?" Paper presented at the
           International Conference on Women and Food, Univer-
           sity of Arizona, Tucson.
STINCHCOMBE, ARTHUR L.
   1966   "Agricultural Enterprise and Rural Class Relations." In
           J. L. Finkle and R. W. Gable (Eds.), *Political Develop-
           ment and Social Change*. New York: Wiley.
TARR, DENA
   1980   "Amazons." Unpublished student paper, University of
           California, San Diego, Department of Sociology.

TINKER, IRENE
    1976   "The Adverse Impact of Development on Women." In
            Irene Tinker and Michele Bo Bramsen (Eds.), *Women
            and World Development*. Washington, D.C.: Overseas
            Development Council/American Association for the
            Advancement of Science.

TOBIAS, SHEILA, AND ANDERSON, LISA
    1973   "What Really Happened to Rosie the Riveter: Demobi-
            lization and the Female Labor Force 1944-47." *MSS
            Module* 9:1-36.

TREY, J. E.
    1973   *Women in the War Economy—World War II*. Warner
            Modular Publication, Reprint 44. (Reprinted from the
            Review of Radical Political Economics, 1972, 4(3).)

TURNBULL, COLIN M.
    1961   *The Forest People*. New York: Simon & Schuster.
    1981   "Mbuti Womanhood." In Frances Dahlberg (Ed.),
            Woman the Gatherer. New Haven: Yale University
            Press.

UNITED NATIONS
    1978   *Effective Mobilization of Women in Development*. Re-
            port of the Secretary General. UN/A/33/238.

U.S. DEPARTMENT OF LABOR, BUREAU OF LABOR STATISTICS
    1971   *Marital and Family Characteristics of Workers, March
            1970*. Special Labor Force Report No. 130. Washing-
            ton, D.C.: Government Printing Office.

WEBER, MAX
    1958   *The Protestant Ethic and the Spirit of Capitalism*. New
            York: Scribner's. (Originally published 1904-1905.)

WELLER, ROBERT H.
    1968   "The Employment of Wives, Dominance and Fertil-
            ity." *Journal of Marriage and the Family*, 30(August):
            437-442.

WHITE, DOUGLAS R., BURTON, MICHAEL L., AND DOW, MALCOLM M.
    1981   "Sexual Division of Labor in African Agriculture: A
            Network Autocorrelation Analysis." *American Anthro-
            pologist* 83(4):824-849.

WHITING, BEATRICE
    1972   "Work and the Family: Cross-Cultural Perspectives."

Paper presented at the Conference on Women: Resource for a Changing World, Cambridge, Mass.

WHITING, JOHN M.
1968 "Pleistocene Family Planning." In Richard B. Lee and Irven DeVore (Eds.), *Man the Hunter.* Chicago: Aldine.

ZIEGLER, PHILIP
1969 *The Black Death.* New York: Harper & Row.

*The social sciences and the social movement were parallel
inventions of the nineteenth century, sharing epistemological and historiographical premises consonant with the
existing world order. Their central organizing concept was
"development." Changes in the world system in recent
years and prospectively in the years to come are leading to a
sea change in which social science is called upon the rethink
its epistemology, its historiography, and its links with the
social movement.*

☙ 3 ☙

THE DEVELOPMENT
OF THE CONCEPT
OF DEVELOPMENT

Immanuel Wallerstein

STATE UNIVERSITY OF NEW YORK, BINGHAMTON

A case can be made for the assertion that the concept of development is not merely one of the central components of the
ideology both of western civilization and of world social science
but is in fact the central organizing concept around which all else
is hinged.[1] I am not interested here, however, in the history of
western civilization. I am interested, rather, in the history of social
science—indeed, in the very notion that there is something called
social science, or, to be more accurate, that there are various disciplines that collectively make up the social sciences. This idea is
not, as any rapid glance at the historical evolution of the organization of universities will show us, self-evident. What today are
called the humanities have long been studied. What today are
called the natural sciences have a long history. The social sciences,

however, were invented and inserted into the curriculum only in the nineteenth century.

This is itself a remarkable fact, which is insufficiently observed and celebrated. For example, the *International Encyclopedia of the Social Sciences,* published in 1968, does not even have an entry for "social science(s)" as such. (It is true that the *Encyclopedia of the Social Sciences,* published in 1937, opens with an essay entitled "What Are the Social Sciences?" But it is a very weak essay, of a chronologically descriptive, discursive nature.) This is no accident but in fact reflects the dominant ideology of world social science.

The invention of the social sciences required a particular extension of modern secularism. The natural sciences are based on the assumption that natural phenomena behave in predictable (or at least analyzable) ways and are therefore subject to intervention and manipulation. The struggle to establish the legitimacy of this perspective, as we all know, encountered the resistance of many religious authorities and of all those who believed that such a view would stimulate hubris and undermine social stability. We have little patience today for any who still preach such a backward form of resistance to scientific inquiry.

The social sciences basically make a parallel assertion: Social phenomena behave in predictable (or at least analyzable) ways and are therefore subject to intervention and manipulation. I do not for a moment suggest that this belief was unknown before the nineteenth century; that would be absurd. But I do suggest that such a perspective did not really have *droit de cité* before then.

The French Revolution in many ways crystallized the issues involved in this concept and served as an ideological turning point. By legitimating the concept of "the rights of man," the revolutionary process bequeathed us the legitimacy of deliberate social change, which no amount of conservative ideologizing since has been able to undo. (Note that conservatives are reduced these days to arguing that social interventions ought to be "cost-effective," a dramatic comedown if ever there was one.)

If social intervention is legitimate, it can be so only because what is is not perfect but is perfectible. It is, in the end, only some variant of the idea of progress that justifies the enormous social energy required by social science, the most complex of all forms of knowledge. Otherwise, the whole exercise would be an esthetic game, in which case poetry or mathematics might be more appealing modes of activity. (And if what is is not perfect but is perfectible, we may be drawn to portray the alternatives as an antinomy of reified forces.) This is, of course, what did happen historically. In the wake of the French Revolution and all the ideological turmoil it generated, social commentators of human "development" began to make a distinction that was crucial for all subsequent analysis—the distinction of society and state.

In general, the state represented what was, and was not perfect, and society represented the force that was pushing toward the perfectibility of the state. At times, as we know, the imagery has been reversed. No matter! Without the distinction of society and state, social science as we know it would not have existed. But it is also true that, without the distinction of society and state, the social movement as we know it would not have existed; for both social science and the social movement have claimed to incarnate views about the underlying society against the pieties of officially stated analyses and policies.

Thus, the epistemological links between social science and the social movement are profound—which, to be sure, justifies the great suspicion that political conservatives have always shown toward the enterprise of social science.

Let us look more closely at the antinomy of society/state. An antinomy involves a permanent tension, a permanent misfit or contradiction, a permanent disequilibrium. In some sense, the intent of both social science and the social movement is to reduce this antinomy, whether by harmonization, by violence, or by some *Aufhebung* (transcendence) of the pair.

The question of course immediately arises, which society, which state? The difficulties involved in answering this query have been so enormous that the query itself has, for almost 200 years, been largely skirted. To skirt a query is not, however, to neglect to answer it. It is to answer it secretly, shamefully, by burying the answer in a largely unspoken premise.

The premise was that the state was those states that were "sovereign"—that is, those states that reciprocally recognized one another's legitimate existence within the framework and the norms of the interstate system. There were in addition aspirants to this status, entities not yet existing whose existence was advocated by various national movements. And there were candidates for elimination, usually small-sized units which larger states wished to absorb and whose legitimacy was thereby put into question by some ideologues.

But generally speaking, everyone "knew" which the states were, and a large part of the enterprise of nineteenth-century (and indeed twentieth-century) history has constituted essentially a reading back into the past of a continuing history for such "states."

If "society" was to remain in permanent tension with the "state," and if the states were particular, geographically bounded, juridically defined entities (which, however, had histories), then it seemed to follow that each state was a society or had a society, and each society had a state. Or, at least, it seemed to follow that this is how it ought to be. Nationalism is the name we give to such an analytical credo in the realm of politics and culture.

This thrust toward parallelism of boundaries of society and state had immense hidden implications for the epistemology of social science as it in fact historically evolved, for it determined the basic unit of analysis within which almost all of social science has been written. This basic unit was the state—either a sovereign state or a politicocultural claimant to state status—within which social action was said to have occurred. The "society" of such a "state" was judged to be more or less cohesive, more or less "progressive" or "advanced." Each "society" had an "economy" that could be characterized and that had "home markets" and "foreign markets." Each "society" had a culture, but it also had "minorities" with "subcultures," and these minorities could be thought of as having accepted or resisted "assimilation."

It may seem that anthropology, at least, represented an exception. Anthropologists scorned the modern state and usually concentrated on some other entity—a tribe or a people. But in fact all the anthropologists were saying was that in what today we call the peripheral areas of the world economy, which were in the late nineteenth century largely dominated by colonial powers, the formal state was a thin social layer lying over the real political entities that were the so-called traditional political structures. The starting point for an anthropologist dealing with an acephalous society was the same as for a historian dealing with central Europe—a primordial and largely fictive politicocultural entity that "governed" social life, within which the *real* society existed.

In this sense, both the anthropologists and the Germanic historians of the nineteenth century could be spurned by hard-nosed British empiricists as incorrigibly romantic. Much as I think the "romantics" were wrong, they seem to me less wildly off the mark than our hard-nosed and arrogant empiricists. In any case, the subsequent transformation of vocabulary indicates the "state-ness" orientation that was always there. Central European *Völker* and Afro-Asian "peoples" who came to dominate a sovereign state thereby became "nations." Witness the Germans and the Burmese. Those who did not get to dominate a sovereign state became in-stead "ethnic groups," entities whose very existence has come to be defined in relation to one or more sovereign states. Poles are an "ethnic group" in the United States but a "nation" in Poland. Senegalese are an "ethnic group" almost everywhere in West Africa except Senegal.

Thus, the state came to provide the defining boundaries of the "society," and the "societies" were the entities that were com-parable one to the other—in the famous billiard-ball analogy to in-dividuals within all of human society. (In Kingsley Davis's *Human Society* [1948], a famous American textbook of the 1950s, the message is that each separate society follows a set of rules, which is that of "human society" as a generic category.) Societies were seen as collective entities going along parallel paths in the same direction. That is to say, it was societies that were "develop-ing." Development (or, in older terminology, progress) was a mea-surable (or at least describable) characteristic of societies.

This use of societies as the basic units of social science had two clear consequences. It rendered plausible two fundamental op-tions of the philosophy of social science that were widely adopted in the nineteenth century. I call these two options "universaliza-tion" and "sectorialization."

Universalization is the presumption that there exist universal laws applicable to all of human society—or, rather, all of human societies. The objective of social science is said to be the clear statement of these universal laws (in the form of falsifiable propo-sitions). The limits to our ability to state these laws are the limits of our present ignorance. The enterprise of social science is the search to reduce this ignorance. This is a realizable task. Once such laws, or a significant number of them, are stated, we shall collectively be able to deduce applications that can be used at the level of policy. That is, we shall be able to "intervene" effectively in the operation of these laws. The model is that of classical physics and its applications in technology and engineering.

Of course, one can state or discover "universal" laws about any phenomenon *at a certain level of abstraction*. The intellectual question is whether the level at which these laws can be stated has any point of contact with the level at which applications are desired. The proponents of universalization never seriously debated whether such a conjuncture of levels was theoretically probable. Recognizing gaps in current ability to make these applications, the proponents merely insisted that these gaps could be bridged in some near future by the earnest application of scientific intelligence.

There were, to be sure, some who emphatically denied the existence of such laws. But these "particularizers" tended to go to the opposite extreme. They expounded a so-called idiographic, as opposed to a nomothetic, view of social science. They argued that no generalizations at all were feasible, since everything was unique, and only empathetic understanding was possible. Or in a slightly less restrictive version, it was argued that only very low level generalizations were feasible. A great deal of huffing and puffing between the two schools of thought occurred. But in fact they shared not merely the central unit of analysis but also the presumed parallelism of all "societies"—in one case because they were all alike, in the other because they were all different.

What both schools excluded, and what was largely absent from mainstream work, was the possibility that a middle way existed, that a significant level of generalization (the analysis of structures) was not only possible but essential, but that this level was below the arena of "all societies" and, rather, at the level of what I would term "historical systems."[2]

The effective exclusion of this methodological middle way was quite consonant with the other philosophical option of modern social science, which may be called "sectorialization." Sectorialization is the presumption that the social sciences are divided into a number of separate disciplines, each of which comprises an intellectually defensible distinct focus of discourse. Over the past 125 years, we have collectively more or less settled on the following categories of disciplines: history, anthropology, economics, political science, and sociology. With some reservations one might add geography. You will recognize here the names of academic departments in most universities and the names of national and international scholarly associations. Of course, there were/are other candidates for the status of "discipline"—for example, demography, criminology, urban planning—but by and large these other candidates have not found widespread support.

The reason is simple. The five agreed-on disciplines reflect the assumptions of nineteenth-century liberal thought. Civilized life was organized in three analytically (and politically) separate domains—the economy, the political arena, and what was neither the one nor the other (which received the label of "social"). Thus we have three nomothetic disciplines: economics, political science, and sociology. History was reserved to the largely idiographic account of each separate society.

Anthropology was given the domain of the noncivilized. (If a society was exotic but in some sense was thought to be "civilized" —that is, if it had a literature and a major religion—then it was consigned to "Orientalism," a kind of bastard combination of history and philology.) Anthropologists had a hard job deciding whether they wanted to be nomothetic analysts of grand historical sequences or idiographic recorders of "prehistorical" structures. Since they tended to do a bit of everything, their domain was safe only as long as their "peoples" were colonized and ignored. With the political rise of the Third World after the Second World War, everyone else began to impinge on the anthropologists' domain, and hence for survival the anthropologists returned the favor, with the emergence of such new concerns as "urban anthropology."

Before we can do an "archeology of knowledge," we should see clearly the "architecture of knowledge." The rooms were "societies." The designs were "universalizing" and "sectorializing." The ideology was that of British hegemony in the world system. As of 1850, the British dominated the world economy and the interstate system virtually without challenge. They were the most efficient producers of the most high-profit products. They were the leading commercial power and largely imposed an ideology of free trade on the world, securing this doctrine by their naval power. The gold standard was in effect a sterling standard, and the banks of London centralized a great proportion of world finance. Of this period, the so-called golden age of capitalism, it has been said that "between 1846 and 1873 the self-regulating market idealized by Adam Smith and David Ricardo came nearer to being realized than ever before or since" (Dillard, 1962:282).

It was natural, then, that Great Britain should set the tone not only in world science but in the newly emerging social sciences. French social thought was no counterbalance. It was basically on the same wavelength as the British, as is attested, for example, by the correspondence between John Stuart Mill and Auguste Comte. One might even make the case that Saint-Simon expressed the spirit of nineteenth-century capitalist entrepreneurs even better than Smith or Ricardo.

The most profound legacy left us by this group of thinkers is their reading of modern history. The questions they felt called on to explain were (1) Britain's "lead" over France, (2) Britain and France's "lead" over Germany and Italy, and (3) the West's "lead" over the East. The basic answer to question one was "the industrial revolution," to question two "the bourgeois revolution," and to question three the institutionalization of individual freedom.

The three questions and the three answers are really one catechism that justified, indeed glorified, monumental and growing inequalities in the world system as a whole. The moral implicitly preached was that the leader merited the lead because he had somehow shown his devotion earlier and more intensely to human freedom. The laggard had but to catch up. And the social scientist had but to pose the question incessantly: What explains that a particular laggard has been and still remains behind?

There were some who refused to play this game—the schools of resistance, as I think of them: the proponents of historical economics in Germany, later the *Annales* school of French historiography (see Wallerstein, 1978), and from the beginning (but outside the universities), Marxism. What these resistants shared was rejection of both the universalizing and the sectorializing postulates of modern social science. But these movements were weak in numbers, largely separated from each other, and ultimately ineffective on a world scale in limiting the spread of the dominant ideology.

Their ineffectiveness came in part from their dispersion but in part from a fundamental error in judgment. Although all the movements of resistance rejected the epistemology of the dominant social science, they failed to challenge the historiography. They accepted without too much thought the industrial revolution in England at the turn of the nineteenth century and the French Revolution as the two watershed events of the modern world. They thereby accepted the premise that the construction of a capitalist world economy itself represented progress and in this way implicitly accepted the whole underlying theory of stages of development for each separate society. By surrendering the historiographic domain, they fatally undermined their resistance in the epistemological realm.

The consequences of this contradictory stance of the schools of resistance became clear during the period after 1945. At that time, the United States had become the new hegemonic power, replacing a long-since-displaced Great Britain. Despite the enormous geographical expansion of world social science, American social science played an even more dominant role during the period 1945–1967 than had British during the period 1850–1873.

The counterpoint to American hegemony was at one level the Soviet Union and its "bloc" of states, which were in acute politicomilitary controversy with the United States. But it was also, at a perhaps deeper and more long-range level, the rise of the national liberation movements throughout the peripheral areas of the world economy. The Bandung Conference was made possible by the conjunction of three forces: the strength of social and national movements in the periphery, the political and ideological forces incarnated in the Soviet bloc, and the needs of American capitalists to eliminate the monopolistic access that western Europeans held to certain economic zones. Thus American hegemony and the rise of the Third World were linked in both symbiotic and antagonistic fashion.

This contradictory link was reflected in the ideology of social science. On the one hand, there was a renewed triumph of scientism, of a pervasive and often specious quantification of research, in terms of which the newly discovered research arenas of the peripheral countries were simply one more source of data. On the other hand, the complexities of the study of these areas pushed toward the building of area studies on an "interdisciplinary" basis —a timid questioning of sectorialization, so timid that the very name reinforced the legitimacy of the historic "disciplinary" distinctions. These two thrusts were reconciled in the invention of a new vocabulary to restate nineteenth-century verities: the vocabulary of "development"—economic, social, political—subsequently subsumed under the heading of modernization theory.

At the level of ideology, the world of official Marxism turned out to pose no real opposition to modernization theory, even though it was derived from an ideology of resistance. The official Marxists simply insisted on some minor alterations of wording. For society, substitute social formation. For Rostow's stages, substitute Stalin's. For Britain or the United States as the model, substitute the Soviet Union. But the analysis was the same: The states were entities that "developed," and "development" meant the further mechanization, commodification, and contractualization of social activities. Stalinist bureaucrats and western experts competed for which one could be the most efficacious Saint-Simonian. (On the role of the Saint-Simonian element in the Marxist tradition, see Meldolesi, 1982.)

As we know, the frenetic certainties of the 1950s began to come apart in the 1960s. The United States, France, and other western countries began to find their power undermined by the growing militance and successes of the movements of the Third World, without and within. The problems of the real world became the problems, both social and intellectual, of its ideological centers, the universities. The explosions of 1968 (and thereabouts) were the result.

It is fashionable these days to downplay the importance of these rebellions of the mid to late 1960s on the grounds that the student rebels of that period have since largely become either reintegrated into or expelled from the social fabric and that the successor student generations are quiescent. What good, it is asked, did the New Left really serve? The answer is very simple. It was the meteoric flames of this rebellion that were primarily responsible for burning away the tissue that maintained Establishment liberalism as the unquestioned ideology of U.S. universities in particular and of western universities in general. It is not that the Establishment was destroyed. But since then it has been unable to exclude competing views as illegitimate, and this has permitted the 1970s to be a time of much intellectual fertility.

The explosions in western universities were matched by the

destruction of the sclerotic world of official Marxism. The death of Stalin, Khrushchev's report, the Sino-Soviet split, the triumphs and then the failures of the Cultural Revolution have all resulted in what Lefebvre (1980) has called "Marxism exploded." Here too we should not be misled. The fact that there are today a thousand Marxisms amid a situation in which more and more people claim to be Marxist does not mean that orthodox Marxism (whatever that is) has disappeared as a major ideological force. It simply no longer has a monopoly in its corner.

The disappearance of both *consensuses*—the liberal and the Marxist—is not independent of the changing geopolitics of the world. With the demise not of American power but of American hegemony, which I would date to 1967, there has been a steady movement toward a restructuring of the alliances in the interstate system. I have argued elsewhere (Wallerstein, 1980b, 1982) that the de facto Washington-Peking-Tokyo axis that developed in the 1970s will be matched in the 1980s by a de facto Paris-Bonn-Moscow axis. Whatever the reasons for this regrouping (in my opinion, they are largely economic), it is clear that it makes no ideological sense, certainly not in terms of the ideological lines of the 1950s.

This geopolitical shift, itself linked to the ideological-cum-political explosions in both the western and the socialist countries, has begun to open up, for the first time since the 1850s, both the epistemological and the historiographical premises of social science.

In terms of epistemology, we are seeing a serious challenge to both universalization and sectorialization and an attempt to explore the methodology of holistic research (see Bach, 1982; Hopkins, 1982), the implementation of that "middle way" that had been excluded by the nomothetic/idiographic pseudo debate of the nineteenth century. For the first time, the imagery of the route of scientific advance is being inverted. Instead of the assumption that knowledge proceeds from the particular toward ever more abstract truths, some wish to argue that it proceeds from the simple abstractions toward ever more complex interpretations of empirical—that is, historical—reality.

This epistemological challenge has been made before, as already noted, but it is being made more systematically and solidly today. What is really new, however, is the historiographical challenge. Once our unit of analysis shifts from the society-state to that of economic worlds, the entire reification of states, of nations, of classes, of ethnic groups, even of households falls away (see Wallerstein, 1980c). They cease to be primordial entities, Platonic ideas, whose real nature we must somehow intuit or deduce. They become constantly evolving structures resulting from the continuing development of long-term, large-scale historical systems.

In such a context, the British industrial revolution of 1760–1830 or the French Revolution does not disappear; but it may be seen in better perspective. There will be an end to the incredible formulation of intellectual problems in the form "Why did not Germany have a bourgeois revolution?"; "Can the Kenya bourgeoisie develop an autonomous capitalist state?"; "Is there a peasantry in Brazil (or Peru or . . .)?"

We are living in the maelstrom of a gigantic intellectual sea change, one that mirrors the world transition from capitalism to something else (most probably socialism). This social transition may take another 100–150 years to complete. The accompanying ideological shift will take less time, however, probably only another 20 years or so. This ideological shift is itself both one of the outcomes and one of the tools of this process of global transition.

It follows that the intellectual tasks before us are important ones, that our intellectual responsibilities are moral responsibilities. First of all, we must (all of us) rewrite modern history—not merely the history that scholars read but the history that is infused into us in our elementary education and that structures the very categories of our thinking.

We must learn how to think both holistically and dialectically. I emphasize the words *learn how,* for much of what has claimed in the past to be holistic and dialectical was merely all-encompassing, sloppy, and unduly motivated by the needs of propaganda. In fact, a holistic, dialectical methodology is infinitely more complex than the probabilistic quasi-experimental one that is so widespread today. We have scarcely begun to explore how it can be done seriously. Most of us are more frightened by its difficulties than by those of linear algebra.

We must then use this methodology to invent (I deliberately use the strong word *invent*) new data bases. The ones we use now (or 98 percent of them) are the results of collecting for 150–200 years data about states. The very word *statistics* is derived, and not fortuitously, from the word *state*. We do not have serious data about the capitalist world economy (not to speak of other and prior world systems). No doubt there are manifold intrinsic and extrinsic problems in the manufacture of such data. But the methodological ingenuities of the last 30 years that have opened up for quantitative research fields such as medieval history, once thought entirely recalcitrant to the application of hard data, give reason to hope that enough energy applied with enough intelligence might bring us to the point 30 years from now that we have at least as much hard data on the functioning of the modern world system as a system as we have today on the functioning of the various states.

We must use these new data to theorize anew, but hesitantly. Too much damage has been done in the past by premature jumping into the saddle and creating reified constructs that block further work. It is better for the time being to have fudgy concepts that are too malleable than to have clearly defined ones that turn out to be poorly chosen and thereby serve as new procrustean beds.

Finally, I am convinced that neither using a new methodology nor theorizing will be possible except in conjunction with praxis. True, it is the function of intellectuals to reflect in ways that those at the heart of politics cannot, for want of time and distance. But it is through action that unexpected social truths (not only about the present and the future but about the past as well) are revealed, and these truths are not visible (at least not at first) except to those whose very activities are the source of the discoveries. The intellectual who cuts himself or herself off from political life cuts himself or herself off from the possibility of truly perceptive social analysis—indeed, cuts himself or herself off from truth.

The epistemological links between social science and the social movement were there from the inception of both. This link cannot be cut without destroying both. No doubt there are dangers to both in this close tie, but those dangers pale by comparison with the dangers of surgical separation. That is what was tried in the late nineteenth century, and it would not be too strong to assert that the many horrors of the twentieth were, if not caused by, then abetted by this putative separation.

The likelihood is that this long-standing alliance between social science and the social movement will take on a new direction and a new vigor during the next twenty years. Neither social science nor the social movement will be able to emerge from the culs-de-sac in which both presently are, without a transformation of the other. This, of course, makes the change doubly difficult. Each is being called on not only to question (and reject) long-standing premises but to recognize its dependence on the other's progress for its own progress. There is no guarantee that these fundamental hand-in-hand changes will occur, but it is likely.

Notes

1. "Of all metaphors in western thought on mankind and culture, the oldest, most powerful and encompassing is the metaphor of growth" (Nisbet, 1969:7). (Nisbet uses *growth* and *development* interchangeably for this discussion.) To be sure, the point of Nisbet's book is summed up in the title of the last section, "The Irrelevance of Metaphor," but his insistence on the "priority of fixity" does not undo his observation on intellectual history. Indeed, his book is a *cri de coeur* of someone who feels very much in a minority.

2. For a brief exposition of what is involved in this middle way, see Wallerstein (1980a). It is not at all the same as Merton's "theories of the middle range." Merton advocated "special theories applicable to limited ranges of data—theories, for example, of class dynamics, of conflicting group pressures, of the flow of power and the exercise of interpersonal influence" (1957:9). This refers to the *scope* of the data, but Merton's objective is to develop "universal" theories of the middle range, not theories that are valid only for given historical systems.

References

BACH, ROBERT
    1982   "On the Holism of a World-Systems Perspective." In Terence K. Hopkins and others, *World-Systems Analy-*

sis: Theory and Methodology. Beverly Hills, Calif..
Sage.

DAVIS, KINGSLEY
1948   *Human Society.* New York: Macmillan.

DILLARD, DUDLEY
1962   "Capitalism After 1850." In Contemporary Civilization Staff of Columbia College (Ed.), *Chapters in
Western Civilization.* (3rd ed.) Vol. 2. New York: Columbia University Press.

HOPKINS, TERENCE K.
1982   "World-System Analysis: Methodological Issues." In
Terence K. Hopkins and others, *World-Systems Analysis: Theory and Methodology.* Beverly Hills, Calif.:
Sage.

LEFEBVRE, HENRI
1980   "Marxism Exploded." *Review* 4(1):19–32.

MELDOLESI, LUCA
1982   *L'utopia Realmente Esistente: Marx e Saint-Simon.*
Roma-Bari: Laterza.

MERTON, ROBERT K.
1957   *Social Theory and Social Structure.* (Rev. ed.) New
York: Free Press.

NISBET, ROBERT A.
1969   *Social Change and History: Aspects of the Western
Theory of Development.* New York: Oxford University
Press.

WALLERSTEIN, IMMANUEL
1978   "Annales as Resistance." *Review* 1(3/4):5–7.
1980a "The Annales School: The War on Two Fronts." *An-
nals of Scholarship* 1(3):85–91.
1980b "Friends as Foes." *Foreign Policy,* No. 40:119–131.
1980c "The States in the Institutional Vortex of the Capitalist World-Economy." *International Social Science
Journal* 32(4):743–751.
1982   "Crisis as Transition." In S. Amin and others, *Dynamics of Global Crisis.* New York: Monthly Review Press.

Two general approaches characterize current theories of sociocultural evolution. The "external selection" approach stresses the importance of intersocietal selection; the "adaptive change" approach, the importance of intrasocietal selection. This chapter identifies and critically evaluates the strengths and weaknesses of these approaches and outlines strategies for integrating these divergent approaches into a single evolutionary perspective.

4

EXTERNAL SELECTION AND ADAPTIVE CHANGE: ALTERNATIVE MODELS OF SOCIOCULTURAL EVOLUTION

Patrick D. Nolan

UNIVERSITY OF SOUTH CAROLINA, COLUMBIA

Current evolutionary theories can be distinguished from the "immanent" and "progressive" theories (Harris, 1968; Bock, 1978) from which they evolved by their convergent focus on the role of variation and selection in producing cumulative trends in the development of human societies (Campbell, 1975; Skinner, 1981). This formal convergence in theoretical structure has not

I would like to thank G. Lenski, B. Mayhew, R. Miller, J. Skvoretz, E. Carlson, M. Webster; fellow members of the structuralist group P. Mariolis, J. M. McPherson, K. Shin, and L. Smith-Lovin; and a number of anonymous reviewers for their many helpful suggestions and comments on earlier drafts of this chapter. Portions of this chapter were presented at the 1981 meeting of the Southern Sociological Association, Louisville, Kentucky.

produced convergence in substance and explanation, however, because there remain major differences and disagreements over the
source of variation, the mechanisms of selection, and the levels at
which these processes operate within and between human populations. Different theories consequently posit very different mechanisms and dynamics of change. Nonetheless, procrustean measures
are not necessary to factor a number of currently prominent and
developing theories into two coherent and largely mutually exclusive groups.

One group, the "external selection" approach, assumes that
some degree of change is inherent in all societies but that the rate
of innovation will vary over time and across societies depending on
societal information-storage and information-processing capacities.
Sources of variation receive less attention than information limits,
and selection between societies is seen to be responsible for the
major trends observed in sociocultural development. The process itself is viewed from an abstract macrosocial and intersocietal perspective, with very little attention paid to the reasons for technological change or adaptive adjustment to changing environments.
Population size is argued to depend on the level of technological
development, and it is seen as an important parameter of societal
information-processing capacity. Prominent representatives of this
group are the theories of Walter Goldschmidt (1959), Gerhard
Lenski (1970), and Barbara Segraves (1974).

The other group, the "adaptive change" perspective, argues
that technological innovations cannot simply be assumed to occur
but must be explained. Two explanations of change are offered:
(1) the benefits or reinforcement offered by innovations (Langton,
1979; Skinner, 1981) and (2) the coercive pressure of population
growth or resource depletion (Wilkinson, 1973; Harris, 1977,
1979; Hayden, 1981). For both, however, cumulative sociocultural development is depicted as a product of selection operating at
the level of individuals or their behavior. Evolution is viewed from
a microsocial intrasocietal perspective, with attention directed
toward the motivation for change and its reinforcement consequences for individuals. Adaptive change—behavioral selection
rather than intersocietal selection—is seen as the key process responsible for sociocultural evolution.

Notable differences in the individual theories do not vitiate

the marked similarities within and contrasts between these theoretical clusters. Similarities in conceptual and theoretical focus
produce common weaknesses within clusters, and comparison
across categories reveals complementary strengths.[1] The chrono-
logical development of representative theories also suggests that,
rather than attenuating over time, these shared differences actually may be growing more pronounced as the theories develop. The
present chapter will examine the divergent trajectories of current
theories, consider their respective strengths and weaknesses, and
explore strategies for transcending existing conceptual and theoretical weaknesses by integrating the two approaches. A number
of criticisms have been raised against evolutionary theories, but the
fundamental divergence of these theoretical clusters has remained
unexamined and unaddressed. It is not necessary to assume (pre-
maturely) that a single perspective or theoretical approach will
prove capable of adequately addressing all questions of cumulative
technological and social development in order to see the importance of recognizing the existing gap and attempting to bridge or
circumvent it.

External Selection

External selection theories combine a focus on the internal
process of accumulating technological information, in the tradition of V. Gordon Childe, Leslie White, and William F. Ogburn,
with recognition of the importance of "external" competition between societies for finite resources and territory, perhaps in the
tradition of Herbert Spencer and Thomas Malthus. Discussion of
the process of intrasocietal selection, selection between competitive cultural items within societies (beliefs, technologies, behaviors, and so on) is largely overshadowed by concern with forces of
selection operating between societies, intersocietal selection, because it is argued that the differential survival rates of differing
sociocultural systems are responsible for the long-term trends and
patterns of development observed in the *population* of human societies.

It is further argued that although the process of intrasocietal
selection *can* be rational and deliberate and *can* affect overall system survival, more often than not, it is guided by shortsighted and

narrow interests. Hence it plays a somewhat inconsistent and unpredictable role in the process of sociocultural evolution. Ironically, choices made within a society may actually reduce the survival
chances of the group as a whole (Lenski, 1970:90). The role of intrasocietal selection is even further complicated by the fact that
even if decisions are made "rationally" in the apparent interests
of the whole society, the final outcome may still be determined by
forces outside the control or purview of the group. Therefore, the
cumulative trend is not seen as a direct product of individuals and
groups themselves but of the mechanisms that select from the variation generated by their actions (Goldschmidt, 1959; Lenski,
1970; Segraves, 1974).

The accumulation of technological information within societies, the variation on which selection "acts," is viewed in large
part as a natural consequence of human curiosity, intelligence, and
experimentation and the highly developed human capacity to
adopt "superior" methods of satisfying human wants and desires
when they are witnessed, discovered, or developed. This process is
depicted as progressing most rapidly in areas of material technology where direct comparisons of utility are possible (Lenski,
1970:89-90, *pace* Ogburn, 1922).

The directional trend is produced by "external" selection,
and in early versions of the theory, military power is explicitly
identified as the major mechanism of intersocietal selection (Lenski, 1970:90). As Goldschmidt (1959:128) put it so forcefully,
"The brute fact of the matter is that the policing of evolutionary
development ultimately rests in the external selective process: the
fact that each society lives in the context of other societies which
offer an immediate or potential threat to the society, against
which it must rally its forces." Later versions (Lenski and Lenski,
1974, 1978) have given more emphasis to the role of "information," thus increasing the generality of the theory and positing a
useful, if necessarily incomplete, parallel between sociocultural
and biological evolution. Systems that fail to survive or are destroyed, for whatever reasons (disease, famine, military conquest,
and so on), it is argued on a more abstract level, perished because
they lacked the requisite "information" that would have enabled
them to meet the particular threat to their institutional integrity
or survival (Lenski and Lenski, 1978:87). To avoid any confusion

on this point, however, it should be clearly understood that the "extinction" of a society for these theorists refers to the extinction of the *system* and does not necessarily, or even usually, imply the extermination of the society's population.

The focus on information and on the cumulative nature of technological development produces a concentration on factors that enhance the capacity of societies to accumulate, store, and process information in accounting for technological "breakthroughs" and the uneven but generally increasing rate of technological change observed over recent millennia. Discovery, invention, diffusion, and the store of information they give rise to are seen to provide the basic parameters of variation on which external selection acts. "External" factors are seen to determine the relative survival probabilities of societies with differing stores of information and are seen, therefore, as being responsible for trends in *general* sociocultural evolution (that is, changes in the relative frequency of societal "types"). Little, if any, attention is paid to the question of what might *motivate* or induce individuals and groups within societies to systematically change or "adapt" their behavior to changing circumstances. Implicit in this perspective is the notion that technological "advance" is often, if not always, materially beneficial and is therefore self-evidently desirable to those implementing change.

At the abstract, macrosocial level, information accumulates at varying rates in different societies. More information makes for more possible combinations of ideas (inventions), and inventions may increase the resource-producing capacity of the group and enable the population to increase. A larger population means more information-processing units, more possibilities for experimentation and invention. Societal expansion may also increase intersocietal contact and cultural diffusion. The processes of cultural and technological growth are thus seen to be mutually reinforcing and largely self-generating. If intrasocietal selection is often shortsighted, "external" factors and intersocietal competition will select out those systems and those cultural repertoires that are most effective in coping with biophysical and sociocultural environments.

An even more abstract example of this approach is provided by Segraves's (1974) "probabilistic," "macrostructural" theory of sociocultural "transformation." Put simply, it maintains that if the probability of an innovation that harnesses more energy (produces sociocultural "advance") is an increasing function of time (becomes more likely with the passage of time), and if the likelihood of an environmental "destabilization" (environmental crisis such as drought or plant disease) also increases with the passage of time, then those systems most likely to survive a destabilization because of redundancy in their resource base (backup sources of food and energy) are most likely to continue to survive and "advance" technologically. Ecologically generalized, or resource-redundant, societies should therefore constitute a growing proportion of societies over time. Aside from alluding to the fact that "loosely articulated," "more generalized" systems are more conducive to structural transformation than "tightly articulated," more "specialized" systems, however, Segraves's macrostructural approach considers even less of the internal dynamic of change than did Lenski's. Her primary focus is on one facet of "external selection"—the environment and the inevitable, if unpredictable, crises to which it is prone. She contends that more diversified systems are more likely to survive the loss or curtailment of a single resource and that they are consequently more likely to survive and by chance alone to discover, invent, or stumble on something that increases their ability to harness energy.

One point that is not especially clear in these theories is what it is that is evolving. The theories argue that a society evolves as information accumulates within it, but is it the information or the society that evolves? Diffusion, migration, and the physical encoding of information in symbols, tools, buildings, and so forth suggest that a particular society is only a temporary locus, or "carrier," of information. The continuity, apparent irreversibility, and transsocietal nature of information accumulation also suggest that it is a supra- or extrasocietal pool of information that has cumulated and evolved over time. The cumulative changes in social organization and development may merely reflect changes in it, rather than its reflecting changes in them.

This shared concern with external selection and with the size of the information and resource base available to societies may establish basic parameters of survival and innovation, but the lack of concern with features of the internal process of change leaves a number of important questions unasked and unanswered. Motivational and intrasocietal factors are merely assumed or are made to appear unimportant in the grand sweep of sociocultural evolution.[2] As Campbell (1975) has noted, the parsimony of the theory can be increased by arguing that sociocultural evolution (like biological evolution) is a product of "blind variation" and "selective retention."

However, this lack of concern with the dynamics of intra-societal change has led one critic (Houghton, 1976) to charge that these theories have merely identified "existential trends" in the structure and development of human societies without offering a sufficient explanation of *why* those trends occurred—that is, how change was generated within societies or, more important from Houghton's point of view, why individuals were motivated to change their behavior.

From another quarter, this general approach has been taken to task by critics who question the assumption of self-evident benefits for the individuals and groups that implement new technologies. It is argued that technological changes have often entailed more labor hours and have generated more restrictions and demands on the populations that implemented them (for example, Wilkinson, 1973; Pfeiffer, 1977). It has also been argued that the "eureka" theory of the advent of horticulture (that is, its "sudden" discovery by women and immediate widespread implementation), which is prominent in these theories, is not plausible in light of the high intelligence of premodern humans and the increased work loads and social problems (such as maintaining domestic order) that accompanied horticulture and the sedentary life-style it required. For instance, Pfeiffer (1977) maintains that Neanderthal women were easily capable of understanding the "secret" of plant cultivation as many as 100,000 years before it was "discovered." In addition, archeologists (Wendorf and others, 1979) have found evidence that knowledge of plant cultivation precedes its wide-scale implementation by thousands of years. The Wendorf study reports evidence that barley may have been "discovered" and used on a limited basis as many as 11,000 years before the "agricultural revolution." The lack of accompanying social transformation lead the authors to characterize the "discovery" as "one of the great nonevents of prehistory." Knowledge of techniques of cultivation may be a necessary, but apparently is not a sufficient, condition for its widespread adoption.

Boserup (1965) demonstrated that labor intensity in agriculture *increased* with technological advance and population growth, and Wilkinson (1973) has argued that general increases in working hours and declines in living standards not only accompanied the industrial revolution but in many ways continue into more advanced levels of industrialization. These observations and arguments raise serious questions about the assumption that technological "advance" is always or usually desired by the individuals and groups adopting it. These questions are, of course, complicated by the fact that in stratified societies elites may benefit from the continued exploitation of nonelites. But it is clear that exploitation is limited by technological, environmental, and ecological constraints, and as Duncan (1964) and Marx (for example, 1972) have argued, technological "regimes" are inherently unstable.

Therefore, although it is possible to argue from this perspective that external selection is capable of producing the observed global trends in social organization and technological development *if sufficient change or variation is generated within societies,* theories employing the external selection approach may not be able to account for sufficient variation for selection to produce directional trends in technological development and social organization. If changes cannot be expected to occur simply because they are possible, or because of the lure of benefits they offer to those implementing them, then other causes of change will have to be identified and incorporated into the theory.

Adaptive Change

Explaining and accounting for motivating factors is clearly the primary focus of the adaptive change theories. Harris (1977, 1979), Wilkinson (1973), and Hayden (1981) explain a number of basic evolutionary changes in terms of the ever-pesent, and at times acute, environmental and demographic pressures that societies have had to cope with in order to survive. In part because of the technological difficulties in controlling conceptions and births, population pressure has been, and remains in many areas, a major cause of resource depletions and a powerful motive for technological intensification and change within societies. Wilkinson (1973) and Boserup (1981) are quick to point out, however, that whether a particular society or set of societies controls its reproduction is less important than whether *all* do. Population pressure can be imposed from without, and evidence exists that unstable technologies (for example, agriculture) are the most likely to be spread by forced migration (Rindos, 1980). Therefore, no group can ensure that it will not be subjected to population pressure or resource depletion simply by regulating its own population. The initial reaction to increased demand for resources (if out-migration and societal fissioning are not possible) may be to intensify production with existing technologies, but the deviation-amplifying feedback (Maruyama, 1968) of intensification may only increase problems and shortages by reducing remaining resources at an accelerating rate (Harris, 1977). Finally, "backed into corners," societies—or, more accurately, the individuals in them—find it more advantageous to seek or to implement new, though more labor-intensive, technologies than to suffer the increasing hardships of shortages or increased costs that would result from continuing existing technological practices. For Harris (1977) in particular, *cost/benefit calculations at the individual level,* under the duress of population pressure and environmental degradation, are the simplest and most straightforward explanation of cumulative technological and social change. The observed trend of increasing amounts of energy harnessed by human societies over time is also seen by Harris (1977, 1979) and Wilkinson (1973) as a result of the increased difficulty of securing needed resources for ever-larger populations in progressively degraded environments. As the title of Wilkinson's book suggests, this is indeed a poverty theory of progress.

Langton (1979), Houghton (1976), and Skinner (1981) share this microsocial perspective and concern with the motives of individuals to change their behavior, but their focus on reinforcement rather than environmental constraints or population pressure leads to a more optimistic assessment of the process. Langton (1979), in fact, offers a theory of "progress" based on the fact that through reinforcement individuals progressively learn to do things better over time (for example, to make more effective arrowheads). Langton appears to assume that the term *extinction* should be applied only to behavior that is no longer sufficiently reinforced and is therefore abandoned, not to the disappearance of people and groups. Skinner's (1981) recent paper, however, though extolling the importance of reinforcement, is careful to frame its argument within the context of selection and possible "extinction" of the organism, group, or society. Learning and reinforcement are obviously important features of the process of sociocultural evolution, but motivation and reinforcement without selection do not provide an adequate explanation.

Unfortunately, we may think we understand a process when we construct or reconstruct the subjective intentions and experience of the participants (Durkheim [1895], 1966; White, 1969). We may fail by this method to recognize the possibility that others may have thought and experienced the same things yet failed to survive. One cannot simply work back from successful adaptations. It is necessary to take failures into account (at least theoretically) to get an appropriate model of the process. A particular distribution of organizations or societies may appear to be the product of "adaptive change" when in fact it is the product of the relative birth and death rates of different organizational types (Hannan and Freeman, 1977). It might well be the case that in all systems, successful and unsuccessful, individuals were responding to reinforcement and environmental contingencies the best way they knew how—yet not all survived. It may be difficult to collect information about the variety of things that failed, but not recognizing the importance of "filters" in selecting out a small and perhaps unrepresentative sample of what was attempted may lead to the unsupportable conclusion that "solutions" were developed as specific and conscious responses to the problems encountered.

Further, in the case of reinforcement, one must assume that all populations of human beings have had the same general ability to learn and to experience reinforcement. Therefore, one is tempted to predict that, through reinforcement and learning, most if not all human groups would be able to adjust to their circumstances and persist. *Yet very substantial evidence indicates that most societies have failed to survive* (for example, Lenski, 1979: 13). In fact, high mortality rates appear to be characteristic of most forms of social organization (Mayhew, 1982, especially pp. 134–138).

Harris's focus on behavioral selection based on costs and benefits structured by population pressure and environmental feedback overcomes some of the difficulties of the reinforcement theories, but it too leads to a deemphasis on the role of external selection in the process. Harris does not directly dismiss it, but he does largely ignore it in his explanations of change. One can find references to it, but one can also find evidence that his increasing focus on behavioral selection is producing a progressive disregard for intersocietal selection. As the following passage (Harris, 1979: 60–61) indicates, to the extent that selection remains, it is in a highly individualized and behavioral form: "Another way to phrase this imperative is to assert that the selection processes responsible for the divergent and convergent evolutionary trajectories of sociocultural systems operate mainly on the individual level; individuals follow one rather than another course of action, and as a result the aggregate pattern changes. But I don't mean to dismiss the possibility that many sociocultural traits are selected for by the differential survival of whole sociocultural systems—that is, by group selection. Because intense intergroup competition was probably present among early human populations, provision must be made for the extinction of systems that were biopsychologically satisfying to the individuals concerned, but vulnerable to more predatory neighbors, with consequent loss of certain cultural inventories and the preservation of others."

On further analysis, however, even this "group selection" turns out to be the "catastrophic consequence of selection operating on or through individuals." In addition, "if the sociocultural system survives as a result of patterns of thought and behavior selected for on the individual level, it is not because the group as such was successful but because some or all of the individuals in it were successful" (Harris, 1979:61). Intersocietal warfare is no exception, since "a group that is annihilated in warfare can be said to have been selected for as a group, but if we want to understand why it was annihilated, we must examine the cost-benefit options exercised by its individual members relative to the options exercised by its victorious neighbors" (Harris, 1979:61). This would appear to be a change from the position reflected in earlier (scattered) statements such as the following: "In culture, as in nature, systems that are the product of selective forces frequently fail to survive not because they are defective or irrational, but because they encounter other systems that are better adapted and more powerful" (Harris, 1974:173).

This extreme individualism and atomization of society and

social process appear to be a direct consequence of the focus on the role of individual decision making in the evolutionary process. Such individualism clearly avoids the problem of reifying "society," and we might split hairs over the distinction between processes that operate "on" individuals and processes that operate "through" them, but this reductionist requirement would appear to be, on the whole, both theoretically unnecessary and counterproductive. To fulfill this requirement, one would virtually have to consider the motives, decisions, and behavior of nearly everyone, everywhere, whose behavior (or inaction) hindered, helped, or merely permitted the survival or collapse of particular behavioral or sociocultural systems. Granovetter (1979) has ably described the difficulties of such an approach in accounting for "aggregate" and cumulative social outcomes (see also Nolan, 1981), and it should also be noted that Harris himself has been forced a number of times to go beyond the cost/benefit decisions of individuals and groups in order to explain certain evolutionary outcomes (for example, 1971:218, 1974:173). However, it appears that Harris is proceeding to develop an ever more individualistic explanation of sociocultural change. Additional evidence of this is offered by the more individualized explanation of "cow love" presented in later works (for example, *Cannibals and Kings* compared with *Cows, Pigs, Wars, and Witches*).

A concern with avoiding "metaphysical forces" in evolutionary theorizing is justified, but this need not imply that all evolutionary theories must be reductionist. Recognition of intersocietal competition, contact, and conflict contributes a great deal to evolutionary explanations, and it does so in a nonmetaphysical, nonteleological way. Certainly it makes sense to recognize that sociological phenomena *can* be traced through the behaviors of individuals, but this does not mean that theories must exclusively address problems at the individual level and build up macroevents and macroprocesses by assembling microbehaviors. Not only is there a principle of parsimony to contend with, but there is the additional danger of the functionalist fallacy (tracing back only successful adaptations). Systems and forms of organization are just as subject to selection as individual behavior is. Poorly organized systems are not as likely to continue as those more effectively organized. The organization of systems can be *expressed* in terms of what the individuals in them are doing, but it is likely to be the *form* of organization that is extinguished by selection, not the individuals that constitute them. In this sense selection at the individual level is no more real or realistic than selection at the group level, particularly if one is concerned with the changing distributions of organizational types over time.

Summary

The major differences between these theoretical approaches do not seem fundamentally irreconcilable or logically contradictory.[3] In fact, it can be argued that the primary difference is a focus on analytically separable but fundamentally interrelated aspects of a single process of change. The two theories' differing emphasis on adaptive change and external selection have, however, led to very different and in many ways complementary substantive developments. External selection theories, and Lenski's in particular, have assembled considerable evidence of major patterns and shifts in such things as settlement size, division of labor, structure of belief systems, ownership of capital goods, and the complexity and centralization of wealth and political power. Adaptive change theories, and Harris's in particular, have assembled a number of fascinating, if controversial, "explanations" of such things as how horticulture may have been both a cause and a consequence of population pressure, how reinforcement may explain progressive change in stone tools or in food sources, how warfare may reduce and stabilize population growth by convincing families that male babies are more valuable and important than female babies, and how the Aztecs may have been driven to massive institutionalized cannibalism by progressive environmental degradation and lack of a domesticatable herbivore.[4] Theorists from each perspective, of course, report and build on the research of many others, but their respective approaches weave the data into two very different patterns. Each appears to be telling a very different story. For one, societies, or the individuals within them, have successively adapted to changing conditions; for the other, more powerful systems have propagated themselves at the expense of, or despite the resistance of, their less powerful competitors. For one, it is a story of adjustment and change; for the other, a story of differential birth and death rates. Each of these stories is both true and false. Each has something to contribute to our understanding of sociocultural evolution but by itself is inadequate and misleading. A combination or synthesis of the two approaches might not only avoid this dichotomy but enrich our understanding of the evolutionary process as well.

Strategies for Synthesis

It would be impossible, in the space remaining, to effect a synthesis or integration of the two perspectives, but promising strategies and lines of development can be outlined and discussed. First of all, it seems fairly clear that the cost/benefit calculations of individuals and groups should be firmly lodged within the general framework of external selection, since in the long (or even the short) run, the motivation, will, or attempt to adjust is no guarantee of success. Motivation for adaptive change, whether from coercion or incentive, can be seen, however, as a factor responsible for increased variation and potential for change in societies. Sociocultural systems respond technologically to changing environmental circumstances, in part, when individuals and groups within them act to reduce threats to their standard of living or their supply of needed resources. This hypothesis, which, if true, *is true of all social groups,* does not promise an answer for all evolutionary questions; but it does introduce a set of mechanisms to account for greater variability and change in the pool of sociocultural candidates that are selected from by a variety of external factors. Recognition of the importance of motivation and adaptive change as sources of variation subject to selection would not require that cumulative sociocultural development be aggregated on the basis of innumerable unobserved, and perhaps unobservable, reinforcement contingencies and cost/benefit calculations. It would also keep clearly in focus the fact that, however rewarding or enjoyable the technological and institutional arrangements of a particular society, they are always subject to the possibility of unforeseen or "outside" disruption and interference. Thus it would seem that the process of intrasocietal change and selection should be nested within the process of external selection.

Further, to overcome some of the previously noted ambiguity, it might be useful to view the information pool as the primary factor that evolves, not the societies in which it is temporarily stored and modified through the actions of particular individuals and groups. Moreover, this pool of information should be clearly seen as being largely *supra- or extra*societal. This view is in line with the increasing recognition of ever more macro levels of information and economic organization (for example, White, 1969; Wallerstein, 1974), and it has the additional advantage of explaining a number of anomalies and puzzles confronting current theories, including the following: (1) Although individuals, groups, and societies implement and some add to the cumulative pool of technological information, the coming and going of particular individuals, groups, and societies rarely, if ever, *decreases* its content (Childe, 1936, 1951, 1954), and (2) the most highly developed societies at a particular technological level are not the most likely to break through to the next technological level; for example, the most advanced hunter-gatherers do not adopt horticulture, and the most advanced agrarians do not become industrial (Childe, 1954; Sahlins and Service, 1960).[5]

A suprasocietal conceptualization coupled with the observation that as size, complexity, and interdependence increase, systems become increasingly resistant to change (Spencer, 1967; Zipf, 1949) may help to explain these and other seeming evolutionary paradoxes. Information may increase most rapidly in the most "advanced," largest, and most complex societies, yet this very complexity and "advancement" may make them incapable of effectively implementing fundamentally different technologies.[6] If information flows and accumulates across societal (though perhaps not social) boundaries, then those systems that have access to the information but that lack a tightly integrated technological/ social structure may be able to implement fundamentally different, or "revolutionary," technologies and thereby surpass the technological and economic achievements of the societies in which the requisite information developed. In fact, an externally generated crisis (war, economic stagnation, drought) may be required in order to reduce structural resistance sufficiently for major change to occur in large, complex social systems (Wallerstein, 1974, 1980; Skocpol, 1979).[7] Veblen's (1915) "advantage of backwardness" and Sahlins and Service's (1960) "law of evolutionary potential" make much more sense when viewed from this perspective. It also vitiates Segraves's (1974) characterization of these ideas as "unscientific." Of course, they must be viewed as probabilistic statements, and one must assume that some minimum infrastructural development is necessary for implementation of a complex technology. One would not predict that a peripheral country would be likely to adopt and exceed the economic development of advanced core nations, but a semiperipheral nation certainly might—for example, nineteenth century Japan.

This conceptualization might also better focus the question of the causal priority of "within" and "between" processes. As the flows of people, goods, and information have increased over time, and as information has shifted to external and relatively permanent storage, the effective size of this suprasocietal information pool has grown enormously. As different "world systems" have emerged, expanded, and contracted (Wallerstein, 1974; Childe, 1954; Lenski and Lenski, 1982), the degree to which the information pool has been contained within a *single social system* has also varied. The modern world system is rapidly approaching incorporation of the entire globe into a single sociocultural system (Wallerstein, 1974), and therefore information and system boundaries are converging. To the extent that they do coincide, innovation and information growth occur within a single system, and change and adaptation within it may be more important than competition between and elimination of societies in affecting sociocultural evolution.[8] Yet in the past, there have been changes in the relative convergence and divergence of these boundaries. To the extent that the boundaries converge, change and adaptation *within* are more important in the process; to the extent that they diverge, competition and conflict *between* may be more important. As emphasized earlier, however, the essential issue in both situations, whether the units of analysis are parts or wholes, is survival, and external factors, outside the purview or control of individuals, groups, or societies, cast the final vote in determining the distribution of organizational "types" over time. The relative importance of processes of selection within and processes of selection between, however, varies systematically by states of this contextual variable.

In conclusion, what is proposed here is an even more macro

theory of the evolution of information (and consequently of the systems which implement, and whose structures and processes depend on, that information), which incorporates adaptive change, reinforcement, and cost/benefit calculations as mechanisms that increase variability and change within societies and, therefore, in the collective extrasocietal pool of information that is evolving. In the final analysis, the cumulative evolutionary trend is shaped not by the individual participants (be they individuals or societies) but by external selection. To adequately effect a true synthesis or complete integration, however, would require not simply that the adaptive change and external selection approaches be juxtapositioned or nested but that both be translated into a single conceptual framework. The progressive emphasis on information suggests the most promising line for accomplishing this. The concepts of information and uncertainty could be broadened to include the behavioral and crisis aspects of the component parts of the evolutionary process identified and discussed here, thereby making it possible to forge them into a single coherent theory of sociocultural evolution.

Notes

1. The conceptual issues that unify and distinguish these theory groups are not peculiar to theories of sociocultural evolution. They are issues which distinguish sociological theories of all kinds and which have engaged the attention of sociologists with a variety of substantive interests. In their most general terms, they are: Should change be viewed as originating from within or from without sociocultural systems? Is a macro- or a microlevel approach best suited to explaining the process of change? Are human motives and values necessary for adequate explanation of any or all sociocultural phenomena? Are individuals and groups in control of their social development, or is this an "anthropocentric illusion"?

2. Rindos (1980) maintains that questions of "intentionality" and "motivation" may be avoided for at least one important technological transformation, the domestication of plants, by viewing it as one step in the "coevolution" of plants and humans. This process can be seen as one in which certain plant species (in

competition with others) further their "interests" by manipulating human behavior so as to ensure their survival and propagation. Only our reluctance to impute "motives" to plants prevents us from offering this as an explanation of the process, since, as Rindos clearly shows, it is equally capable of accounting for the events in question. This suggests that in some contexts human "motives" may be just as superfluous as plant "motives" are to an adequate explanation of plant domestication.

3. Although there appears to be no inherent logical incompatibility between them, where one perspective is dominant or ascendant, it seems to drive out the other. External selection appeared to play an important role in Harris's early theoretical arguments, indicating an awareness and appreciation of its importance and utility in accounting for major features of sociocultural evolution. Yet external selection has been progressively downplayed in succeeding formulations, perhaps reaching its lowest point in *Cultural Materialism* (1979). Lenski's most recent work (Lenski and Lenski, 1982) indicates an awareness of many of the shortcomings and limits of his original approach, and a number of changes and additions have been offered to improve it. But the changes fall short of an adequate synthesis of the perspectives, perhaps indicating the difficulty of bridging this conceptual gap.

4. Despite the theoretical centrality of intersocietal competition and warfare in Lenski's external selection theory, the theory is largely optimistic. Increasing information and energy may even enable human groups to control the evolutionary process in the future. Harris, in contrast, although he emphasizes the role of motivation and choice, sees every technological and social-structural change as creating the conditions that will necessitate more change. Every substitute resource and replacement technology is merely a temporary solution to an existing problem and is likely to be the source of many new ones. Hence, for Harris the promise of technology is a hollow one, its rewards fleeting and ephemeral. His outlook is thus more pessimistic, with poverty and problems the engine of change, and progress the ideological smokescreen of the privileged.

5. Most external selection theorists, especially Segraves (1974), because of the ambiguity of what they view as evolving, appear to assume that only the most advanced societies can con-

tinue to advance, because only they have the requisite information to do so.

6. Germany and Japan, in their ability to implement the most advanced automated technologies, are recent examples of this thinking. Lacking the structural resistance of an intact industrial structure (for example, tooling, organized labor), they have been able to advance more rapidly than the societies within which these technologies were invented.

7. If biological analogies were not nearly so often fatal to social theories, it would be tempting to liken this suprasocietal information pool to a disease. The survival and propagation of a disease are affected by changes in the host population, and vice versa; further, infection (implementation) may require a crisis or reduction in resistance. This analogy might also serve to clearly distinguish evolutionary "advancement" from "progress" (Granovetter, 1979).

8. This would address Hawley's (1979:29) recent charge that increasing interdependence of societies renders evolutionary theories otiose since elimination through competition will be less important than expansion and change in explaining future social developments.

References

BOCK, KENNETH
    1978   "Theories of Progress, Development, Evolution." In T. Bottomore and R. Nisbet (Eds.), *A History of Sociological Analysis*. New York: Basic Books.

BOSERUP, ESTER
    1965   *The Conditions of Agricultural Growth: The Economics of Agrarian Change Under Population Pressure*. Chicago: Aldine.
    1981   *Population Growth and Technological Change: A Study of Long-Term Trends*. Chicago: University of Chicago Press.

CAMPBELL, DONALD T.
    1975   "On Conflicts Between Biological and Social Evolution and Between Psychology and Moral Tradition." *American Psychologist* 30:1103–1126.

CHILDE, V. GORDON
    1936   *Man Makes Himself.* London: Watts.
    1951   *Social Evolution.* New York: Henry Schuman.
    1954   *What Happened in History.* New York: Penguin Books.
DUNCAN, OTIS DUDLEY
    1964   "Social Organization and the Ecosystem." In R. E. L.
            Faris (Ed.), *Handbook of Modern Sociology.* Chicago:
            Rand McNally.
DURKHEIM, ÉMILE
    1966   *The Rules of Sociological Method.* New York: Free
            Press. (Originally published 1895.)
GOLDSCHMIDT, WALTER
    1959   *Man's Way: A Preface to the Understanding of Human
            Society.* New York: Holt, Rinehart and Winston.
GRANOVETTER, MARK
    1979   "The Idea of 'Advancement' in Theories of Evolution
            and Development." *American Journal of Sociology* 85:
            489–515.
HANNAN, M., AND FREEMAN, J.
    1977   "The Population Ecology of Organizations." *American
            Journal of Sociology* 82:929–964.
HARRIS, MARVIN
    1968   *The Rise of Anthropological Theory: A History of
            Theories of Culture.* New York: Thomas Y. Crowell.
    1971   *Culture, Man, and Nature: An Introduction to General
            Anthropology.* New York: Thomas Y. Crowell.
    1974   *Cows, Pigs, Wars, and Witches: The Riddles of Culture.*
            New York: Random House.
    1977   *Cannibals and Kings: The Origins of Cultures.* New
            York: Random House.
    1979   *Cultural Materialism: The Struggle for a Science of
            Culture.* New York: Random House.
HAWLEY, AMOS
    1979   "Cumulative Change in Theory and History." In Amos
            Hawley (Ed.), *Societal Growth: Processes and Implica-
            tions.* New York: Free Press.
HAYDEN, BRIAN
    1981   "Research and Development in the Stone Age: Tech-

nological Transitions Among Hunter-Gatherers." *Current Anthropology* 22:519–548.

HOUGHTON, JOHN

1976   "Evolutionism in Sociological Thought: A Socio-Historical Account." Unpublished Ph.D. dissertation, Department of Sociology, University of Texas at Austin.

LANGTON, JOHN

1979   "Darwinism and the Behavioral Theory of Sociocultural Evolution: An Analysis." *American Journal of Sociology* 85:288–309.

LENSKI, GERHARD

1970   *Human Societies: A Macrolevel Introduction to Sociology.* New York: McGraw-Hill.

1979   "Directions and Continuities in Societal Growth." In Amos Hawley (Ed.), *Societal Growth: Processes and Implications.* New York: Free Press.

LENSKI, GERHARD, AND LENSKI, JEAN

1974   *Human Societies: An Introduction to Macrosociology.* (2nd ed.) New York: McGraw-Hill.

1978   *Human Societies: An Introduction to Macrosociology.* (3rd ed.) New York: McGraw-Hill.

1982   *Human Societies: An Introduction to Macrosociology.* (4th ed.) New York: McGraw-Hill.

MARUYAMA, MAGORAH

1968   "The Second Cybernetics: Deviation-Amplifying Mutual Causal Processes." In W. Buckley (Ed.), *Modern Systems Research for the Behavioral Scientist.* Chicago: Aldine.

MARX, KARL

1972   "The German Ideology: Part I." In R. C. Tucker (Ed.), *The Marx-Engels Reader.* New York: Norton.

MAYHEW, BRUCE H.

1982   "Hierarchical Differentiation in Imperatively Coordinated Associations." In W. Sodeur (Ed.), *Mathematische Analyse von Organisationsstrukturen und Prozessen.* Duisburg: Sozialwissenschaftliche Kooperative.

NOLAN, PATRICK D.

1981   "A Behavioral Theory of Sociocultural Evolution: An

Illusive Answer to the Wrong Question." *American Journal of Sociology* 86:1410-1415.

OGBURN, WILLIAM F.
1922   *Social Change: With Respect to Culture and Original Nature.* New York: Viking Press.

PFEIFFER, JOHN
1977   *The Emergence of Society: A Prehistory of the Establishment.* New York: McGraw-Hill.

RINDOS, DAVID
1980   "Symbiosis, Instability, and the Origins and Spread of Agriculture: A New Model." *Current Anthropology* 21:751-772.

SAHLINS, M. D., AND SERVICE, E. R.
1960   *Evolution and Culture.* Ann Arbor: University of Michigan Press.

SEGRAVES, BARBARA
1974   "Ecological Generalization and Structural Transformation in Sociocultural Systems." *American Anthropologist* 76:530-552.

SKINNER, B. F.
1981   "Selection by Consequences." *Science* 212:501-504.

SKOCPOL, THEDA
1979   *States and Social Revolutions: A Comparative Analysis of France, Russia, and China.* Cambridge: Cambridge University Press.

SPENCER, HERBERT
1967   *The Evolution of Society: Selections from Herbert Spencer's Principles of Sociology.* (Edited by R. Carneiro.) Chicago: University of Chicago Press.

VEBLEN, THORSTEIN
1915   *Imperial Germany and the Industrial Revolution.* New York: Macmillan.

WALLERSTEIN, IMMANUEL
1974   *The Modern World System: Capitalist Agriculture and the Origins of the European World-Economy in the Sixteenth Century.* New York: Academic Press.
1980   *The Modern World System II: Mercantilism and the Consolidation of the European World-Economy, 1600-1750.* New York: Academic Press.

WENDORF, F., AND OTHERS
   1979   "Use of Barley in the Egyptian Paleolithic." *Science*
          205:1341-1347.
WHITE, LESLIE A.
   1969   *The Science of Culture: A Study of Man and Civiliza-
          tion.* New York: Farrar, Straus & Giroux.
WILKINSON, RICHARD
   1973   *Poverty and Progress.* New York: Praeger.
ZIPF, GEORGE K.
   1949   *Human Behavior and the Principle of Least Effort: An
          Introduction to Human Ecology.* New York: Hafner.

Dual labor market theory, developed as an explanation of underemployment and poverty within the economy, may also be applied to the illicit economy of crime. Criminal careers are differentiated into a primary sector, with occupational stability, low failure rate, and high chances of advancement; and a secondary sector, with instability, high failure rate, and lack of "market" control. The attraction of criminal careers, the likelihood of incarceration, and the effects of law enforcement are best understood in these contexts.

☙ 5 ☙

THE DUAL LABOR MARKET OF THE CRIMINAL ECONOMY

Kevin B. Bales

VANDERBILT UNIVERSITY

A great deal has been written about crime from a behavioral perspective. Many theories vie to explain motivation and career paths in illicit behavior. For the most part, these are theories of socialization, psychological at base and liberal in orientation. An emphasis of lesser consequence is the measurement of illicit activity in terms of its economic impact. Economic theories of criminal activity follow two major themes. The older and more developed of the two is the Marxian analysis of the legal system as an instrument of economic power and privilege. This macrotheoretical approach concentrates on the oppressive use of the justice system against the proletariat and the arbitrary way illegal behavior is defined by the economically powerful. The second approach is the

Special thanks are tendered for the critical aid of Robert C. Bibb, Michael Hughes, Columbus B. Hopper, Jack P. Gibbs, and Debra J. Umberson.

more recent microtheoretical econometric analysis. In this approach economic equations are used to explain decision making in crime; as in licit economics, cost, risk, profit, and so on are balanced to indicate the viability of various criminal activities.

The work at hand develops a theory "of the middle range." The theory of the dual labor market is applied to the illicit economy. The resulting mezzotheory posits a dual labor market in the illicit economy and outlines a dichotomy in illegal career paths. To arrive at this synthetic explanation, the conceptual underpinnings must first be examined. To do so, dual labor market theory and economic explanations of crime will be reviewed, and the central ideas of each that inform this theory will be illuminated.

Dual Labor Market Theory

In the late 1960s a number of researchers began to assert that underemployment, poverty, and career outcomes might best be explained by a theory of dual labor markets within the overall economy. This assertion was originally based on several studies of local labor markets in large industrial cities: Boston (Doeringer and others, 1969), Chicago (Baron and Hymer, 1968), Detroit (Ferman, 1963; Bluestone, 1970; Wachtel, 1970), and Harlem (Vietorisz and Harrison, 1970). From these studies grew the formal statement of the theory. Piore (1969, 1970, 1971) offered one of the first explanations of a distinct dual labor market model. Bluestone (1970) offered a "tripartite model of the labor market," the three sectors fitting within a dichotomized model. Gordon (1971) synthesized this research in order to compare the emerging theory with orthodox economic theory.

The dual labor market theory argues that the American labor market has become dichotomized over time into "primary" and "secondary" markets and that these two markets differ in employer and employee expectations, in pay scales and other attributes of jobs, and in the behavioral rules under which the markets operate. In the previously mentioned studies of local labor markets, researchers were hard put to explain why worker characteristics associated with productivity in orthodox economic theory had little or no effect on employment histories of many urban employees. When workers were referred to jobs, there seemed to be no significant difference between those workers hired and those rejected (Doeringer and others, 1969). Because of this discrepancy, the focus shifted away from worker characteristics to the characteristics of jobs held by low-SES and minority workers. The attributes of these jobs came to be associated with the secondary labor market: menial tasks, with little requirement for mental exercise; great instability of employment, the instability often planned into the job by the employer; low wages and no fringe benefits; poor, often unsafe working conditions. A key attribute of these jobs is that there is little or no chance for advancement; a bureaucratic block separates these jobs from any career ladder. If this exclusion is questioned by the employee, or if other grievances are raised, the grievance process is arbitrary and unregulated.

The characteristics of the primary labor market are the reverse. Whereas the former is predominately black and female, the latter is white and male. The primary labor market is characterized by good wages, good working conditions, and a chance for advancement. There are equity and due process in grievance resolution, and stability and low turnover on the job.

Piore (1970) argued that separation of the markets occurred and continues for five major reasons. First, the most important distinguishing characteristic between the two markets is "the behavioral requirements which they impose on the work force, particularly that of employment stability" (p. 101). Second, this exclusion is generalized across minority groups through discrimination. Third, the labor market dichotomy was determined historically rather than technologically. A wide range of occupations may be performed in either sector, and occasionally an occupation shifts from one sector to the other. Fourth, Piore notes, "the behavioral traits associated with the secondary sector are reinforced by the process of working in secondary jobs and living among others whose life-style is accommodated to that type of employment" (p. 101). Finally, Piore asserts, the boundary between the two sectors has become more defined and impermeable over time as employers attempt to stabilize their work force by determining which jobs require low turnover and extensive training and then filling the remaining jobs with less expensive, secondary labor. These five points are applied to career paths in the illicit economy later in this chapter.

Dual labor market theory has been criticized in several ways. Rosen (1976) and Welch (1975) have questioned the validity of its assumption that "human capital" variables fail to predict career placement, particularly in the secondary sector, as it omits satisfactory measures of "ability." In his review of the relationship of dual labor market theory and orthodox labor market theories, Cain (1976) argues that dual labor market theory is merely a modification and addition to orthodox theory in two ways: (1) the added emphasis given to the "idea of the endogenous determination of attitudinal variables among workers" (1976:1248) and (2) the added dimensions of inquiry into historical and institutional internal labor markets and especially the attention given to class interests.

However, some support has grown for dual economy and labor market theory. Cornwall (1977) developed a general model of the dual economy to be applied to developed as well as developing nations. His main conclusion was that "developed market economies operate in such a way that by continuing to stress their dual structure, real insights into the behavior of market capitalism are possible" (1977:73). Oster (1979) factor-analyzed eighty-three three-digit 1960 census code industries as a test of the theory of the dual economy. His findings supported the theory and stated that dual economy theory seems to represent "a viable taxonomic description of a predominant pattern of American industrial stratification" (1979:38).

To summarize, it is important to make several key distinctions. It is essential to separate dual labor market theory and dual economy theory, although one derives from the other. Dual labor market theory outlines the effects of the dual economy on the labor force. Because it explains human behavior rather than modes of production, dual labor market theory must be more flexible. For example, recent research shows the secondary labor market to be a " 'youth labor market' from which many young persons escape as they gain some experience in the work force" (Wallace and Kalleberg, 1979:9). Dual economy theory, in contrast, points to characteristics of industries and firms that are much less flexible—economic scale, capital intensity, firm size, and geographical location. Often separate issues are addressed; an analysis of the state's role in the dual economy (Bibb and Form, 1977) is important in the dual economy literature, but it is not central to understanding labor force consequences. This separation is supported by the finding that "there is less overlap between concepts related to the economic organization of firms and labor force consequences than has generally been assumed" (Wallace and Kalleberg, 1979:29). When dual labor market theory is applied to crime, the aim is to explain criminal careers, not the criminal economy. At best, criminal careers are indicators of the nature of the illicit economy. There are, however, other explanations of this illicit economy, which must be reviewed.

Economic Theories of Crime

Structural economic theories have long played a part in criminology; their impact, however, has been slight. Marxist criminology locates a single cause of conflict, capitalist economics, and suggests that conflict might be resolved through macroeconomic change. Central to this orientation is the interpretation of the legal system as an instrument for protection of the interests of the power-dominant group (Michalowski, 1977).

From the beginning, empirical research, primarily macroeconomic and demographic, has been carried out concerning crime. The results of this research provide the base for the development of macroeconomic theories of criminology. It would require volumes to relate the nature and outcome of such research in criminology, but a few of the generally accepted major demographic realities of crime can be easily listed. First, men generally are more criminally offensive than women, although the difference is decreasing. Second, ecological research links high rates of crime with indicators of physical and mental illness, familial disharmony, and the abuse of offspring. Third, ethnic groups exhibit different patterns of criminal behavior than the dominant culture or other ethnic groups. Fourth, higher rates of urbanization tend to be related to higher rates of crime, and some crimes are associated with areal density in large cities. Finally, when considering the relationship of economic indicators and crime rates, the validity of the statistics used to measure such phenomena as reported crime and unemployment is often called into question. Accepting that caveat, we may note that crime rates seem to be positively correlated with the general economic status of a society, with high levels of unemployment, and with the relative economic deprivation of groups within a society. Obviously, crime does not occur in an economic vacuum. Criminal activities are embedded in the national economic structure and are buffeted by the same economic winds as legitimate activities. Gould (1969, 1971), for example, has tied cash-coin supplies and automobile supplies to their corresponding theft rates. General economic trends alter the nature of crime in many ways. One major way involves changes in the illegitimate opportunity structures. These opportunity structures are the labor markets of crime, and they should parallel legitimate structures in their response to economic change.

Major economic theorists—Smith, Marx, Bentham—wrote about economics and crime, but while their work was enlarged by sociologists, it has been largely ignored by economists. During the last ten years, however, there has been a resurgence of the economic approach to criminology. Sullivan (1973) pinpoints the beginning of the current interest with the publication of Becker's (1968) statement on economics and crime. Becker's article became a model for the subsequent flood of econometric studies of crime. It provided a break with the predominating psychological explanations of crime and outlined the basic assumptions of this orientation.

"A useful theory of criminal behavior," states Becker, "can dispense with special theories of anomie, psychological inadequacies, or inheritance of special traits and simply extend the economist's usual analysis of choice." By this analysis the criminal is seen as the economic "rational man" who is simply trying to maximize his benefits or preference while being subject to certain costs or restrictions. In this scheme, a thief, for example, calculates the opportunities and potential profits from licit and illicit pursuits, the probability of apprehension if he acts illegally, and the probable punishment upon apprehension. He will include in the equation the possible future cost, especially in opportunity forgone, of going to prison if apprehended. Then he may choose the pursuit with the highest discounted returns. The criminal may, for any number of reasons, over- or underestimate any of the variables in the equation. But these miscalculations are not to be considered irrational any more than those made in legal activities. The recidivism of convicts is similarly explained. A criminal "made a rational choice before he went to prison," states Sullivan (1973), "acquired further criminal skills in prison, and faced rational, hostile employers when he was released. Given these circumstances this man would be irrational if he did *not* return to crime" (p. 149). Rational man is assumed as the subject in dual labor market theory, since labor market placement does not hinge on psychological adjustment in the licit or illicit economy.

The microeconomic approach of Becker and the macroeconomic explanations concern the activities of individuals. These individuals undoubtedly think beyond the immediate equations of cost and benefit. Yet it is doubtful that they plan their work or search for jobs with an eye only to macroeconomic trends. It is reasonable to assume that these individuals make criminal career decisions within their immediate economic context, weighing the attributes of each "job" available in their local labor market. It is necessary to examine the nature of this labor market to fully understand the choices made in a criminal career.

The Dual Labor Market of the Illicit Economy

A labor market theory of illicit economies is a theory "of the middle range" (Merton, 1949). There is a profound gap between the explanation of crime rates using social-structure variation and the analysis of the lonely criminal pondering the profit and loss of his pursuits. This gap may be filled by considering the criminal in the social context in which he pursues illicit activities and by examining the diverse relationships different criminals have to their occupations. Within this context of labor pools and career paths, there is room to analyze the economic structure and individual decision making; but we may assume that the criminal views his own world mezzoscopically, and it would be fruitful if we did so as well.

There is another reason that the criminal should be considered in terms of his career path and its socioeconomic context. It is the proclivity of criminology to study the most readily available subject, the criminal arrested or imprisoned. Because of this tendency, the results of most criminological research may be in serious doubt, for such research rests on the assumption that those apprehended are valid measures of the criminal population. As Trasler (1962) put it, "The criminologist is usually obliged to make the working assumption that those who are caught are in all material respects representative of those who escape detection" (p. 10). One might easily assume the reverse. It is no feat to imagine that a world of difference exists between the recidivist, small-time thief and the criminal businessman of organized crime—that these two individuals confront radically different structures of opportunity and that they exploit these opportunities in different ways. If some types of criminal careers are shielded from study by their placement in a dual labor market, our understanding of crime is skewed. Existing theories of crime are deficient if their support-ing data come from the secondary labor market of illicit activity alone. Dual labor market theory applied to crime suggests a way to correct this misinterpretation by directing our attention to the underrepresented and poorly understood areas of criminal ac-tivity.

Dual labor market theory is applied to illicit activity with the assumption that it is explaining career paths in economic crime, crime pursued for a profit. Crimes of violence, without the intent of profit, are rarely undertaken as a career. Although some econometric analysis examines the *social* cost and profit of mur-dering one's spouse, for example, this theoretical application is concerned with the *economic* component, and not of a single act but of a criminal career. Given this restriction, it is hypothesized that we should find a dual labor market in the illicit economy, one which parallels that of the licit economy. These illicit labor mar-kets should demonstrate many of the same attributes of licit markets; some illegal occupations should show good working con-ditions and the chance of advancement, others the reverse. Some should show occupational stability, low failure rate, and the abil-ity to influence the "market"; others should be unstable, with a high failure rate and no "market" control. Finally, these dichoto-mous occupational categories should be found within the same criminal "industry," as its upper and lower tiers, and should de-mand in their interaction different behavioral requirements. To determine whether such differentiation of criminal careers exists, I examine three areas of profit-based criminal activity: gambling, theft, and an inclusive category, organized crime.

Gambling. Gambling is an industry in America, both legal and illegal. The Institute for Social Research (1976) estimated the total outlays ventured in illegal gambling to be a little over $5 billion for 1974. Bell (1953), in discussing organized gambling "as a function of a mass consumption economy," termed this illicit activity "one of the queer ladders of social mobility in American life." Drake and Cayton (1945) examined a typical gambling enterprise—"policy," a type of numbers lottery, within which we find the delineation of primary and secondary job categories. Serving the "policy" industry at a secondary level are "walking writers" who work in the street canvassing for wagers. They are a hand-to-mouth lot and are the pieceworkers of illegal gambling. They are not eligible for employment in the occupational category that runs the "policy." These latter persons are described by Drake and Cayton as "a corps of well-trained white-collar experts." These "experts" control the "policy" over a wide area.

Reuter and Rubinstein (1977) have conducted an exhaustive analysis of gambling records seized from "numbers banks" and bookmakers in New York City. Their research sheds light on the ongoing stabilization of some gambling occupational categories and the alignment of other illicit occupations with parallel occupations in the licit economy. The modern "policy" or "numbers" racket shows an evolution of occupational categories from the "policy" studied by Drake and Cayton (1945) in the forties. The job category "walking writer," which included many secondary market attributes, has evolved into a position of more security and autonomy. The modern "collector" is well paid and may employ "subcollectors"; his position is entrepreneurial and yields a high profit margin; there is the possibility of advancement into the role of "controller," a sort of middle management position. This is not to imply that secondary job categories no longer exist in the "numbers" racket. The clerical workers in "numbers" have come to resemble in job attributes the secondary clerical workers of the licit economy. The "numbers" clerk has now evolved into a "female" job that is not likely to "acquire more responsibility, in contrast to collectors and controllers who frequently rise to more responsible positions" (1977:19). These two shifts in occupational category seem, in part, to be due to altered market structures. As previously noted, Drake and Cayton found central control of "policy" for a wide area. Reuter and Rubinstein, however, found a de-centralized "numbers" industry. The latter would benefit from an increased entrepreneurial role for the "collector" in a context of increased competition between "numbers banks." Although they state that the market may have been more centralized in the past, Reuter and Rubinstein have found the current market to be "high-ly competitive" (personal communication, 1980).

In order to understand modern urban gambling better, the authors interviewed federal attorneys in two states (personal com-munication, 1978, 1979). These sources outlined a large industry based on sports gambling; outlays for sports "books" and "cards" were estimated to be a little over $2.5 billion in 1974 (Institute for Social Research, 1976). This industry now has the stabilizing influ-ence of the federal government in its primary sector because in states in which gambling is illegal the federal government still col-lects a gambling tax. The returns for these taxes are not shared in any way with state agencies, and the persons who operate gam-bling enterprises and pay the federal tax need not fear federal in-tervention in their business. These taxpaying businessmen operate the largest gambling concerns, involving an extensive bureaucracy; the operations are secure and their clientele middle class. Below this group is a secondary labor pool that operates small-time gam-bling enterprises. This group usually pays no federal tax and so must fear state *and* federal intervention as well as pressure from the "es-tablished concerns." These secondary concerns are highly unsta-ble, and the high turnover is exacerbated by the fact that their operators are the ones most often arrested and convicted of gam-bling offenses, leading to a high failure rate among these enterprises.

The analysis of bookmaking in New York by Reuter and Rubinstein (1977) presents a picture of the market conditions in sports betting. The established urban bookmakers operate with relative stability. Although the sports betting industry could not be termed a monopoly or cartel, it is singularly free of violence and is characterized by a "total absence of blacks and Hispanics" (1977:33). The secondary gambling occupations of the modern urban market are also those that account for the majority of gam-bling arrests: pitches and portable or sidewalk card games.

Job categories within gambling may be divided into primary and secondary sectors. The racial breakdowns also show this. The major operators, or "syndicate officials," as Drake and Cayton (1945) call them, are more likely to be white than the "walking writer" or "numbers runner" who performs the fieldwork of the gambling enterprise; the stable urban bookmaking industry is owned and operated by whites (Reuter and Rubinstein, 1977). Secondary-sector personnel face outcomes similar to those of secondary workers in legitimate industry: bad working conditions, little chance for advancement, extreme job instability, and a high failure rate, failure in the illicit case exemplified by arrest and conviction.

Theft. Whereas we may expect to find primary and secondary sectors in a bureaucratized enterprise such as organized gambling, this is not as apparent for theft, usually considered an individual or small-group act. This view, however, results from a tradition in criminology of dichotomizing thieves into "professionals" and "amateurs," a delineation that, when examined, parallels that between primary and secondary sectors. Reckless (1950) states that "ordinary" criminals "usually have lower-class social origins" (p. 10). In contrast, the "professional career man" does not have such an origin or history, and his occupation requires a distinguishable group of behavioral requirements. The use of weapons, for example, "is an unpardonable error in the eyes of the professional. It shows a lack of resourcefulness" (p. 10). The professional does not associate with ordinary criminals, according to Reckless, nor is he recruited "from the 'sand lots' of delinquency and crime," the secondary labor pool of illicit activities. As Sutherland (1937) put it, the association with "ordinary" thieves is "limited by barriers which are maintained principally by the thieves themselves."

Perhaps the best description of this dichotomy is found in the research of Mack (1972; Mack and Kerner, 1974) and his description of the "able criminal." In a pilot study (Mack, 1964) that sought to examine "full-time criminals," he found that his eight subjects divided neatly into two groups. The first group of four had juvenile records, had "suffered from a lack of parental care and affection," and showed emotional disturbance in their behavior—in short, the "textbook criminal." The second four "gave every appearance of being psychologically well balanced," they had no juvenile record save one minor offense by one individual, and their early home life was "not known or not notably bad" (p. 40). A striking difference was found in the prison records; the first group had averaged 60 percent of their adult life in prison, the second group 12.5 percent. A second study (Mack and Kerner, 1974) considered 102 "full-time criminals" and found a close relation of criminal job category with time spent in prison. Even among these "able" criminals, the primary-sector categories (organizers, resetters, and providers of services) averaged 10–15 percent of their lives since age 17 incarcerated, while the figure for secondary categories (bank robbers, shoplifters, and "violents") was 25–30 percent.

Mack goes on to point out that "present criminologists are generalizing from the more to the less easily caught specimens" but that "the persistent able criminal appears to have little in common with the persistent criminal failure" (p. 10). If we divide these criminals into primary and secondary labor markets, the reason for faulty generalization becomes apparent. The secondary labor market is marked by instability and a high failure rate of enterprises; its bad working conditions and smaller profits would not provide the protection from arrest enjoyed by the primary sector. Thieves of the primary sector, however, exercise greater control over their "market" and adapt to new technologies and security measures. McIntosh (1971) termed this businesslike theft "project crime," involving bigger takes and more diffuse bodies of working knowledge. The larger profits enable primary-sector thieves to rationalize the higher cost of adaptation to new technologies in the same way that primary-sector industries rationalize higher technology costs through greater market control and larger profits.

Organized Crime. Organized crime provides a capsule dual labor market. Statistical estimates of its participation in the U.S. economy are necessarily sketchy, but it is undoubtedly to be measured in the billions of dollars. This discussion of organized crime centers on organizational hierarchy rather than career paths. The two sectors of the dual labor market are to be found with varying distribution in any large industry. Primary-sector industries have a predominance of primary labor market job categories but still rely on an assortment of secondary jobs to fulfill the menial tasks at the bottom rung of the job hierarchy. The more labor-intensive secondary-sector industry operates with a large group of secondary job categories over which a relatively small number of primary job categories maintain control. Examples of secondary industries are fast-food chains, garment manufacturing, and service-oriented or labor-intensive light industry (Harrison, 1972; Montagna, 1977).

By this definition, organized crime is the epitome of secondary industry. The legitimate industries that have been appropriated by organized crime are almost entirely secondary industries: food products, restaurants, services such as garbage disposal, and garment manufacturing. A few notable exceptions do exist—securities and real estate, for example. But the overall hierarchy of organization is secondary in nature (see Figure 1). Owing to the nature of the upper hierarchy, the primary job categories in organized crime are perhaps more impenetrable by the illicit secondary worker than primary jobs are by the secondary worker in legitimate industry. The division of the two sectors in organized crime occurs at

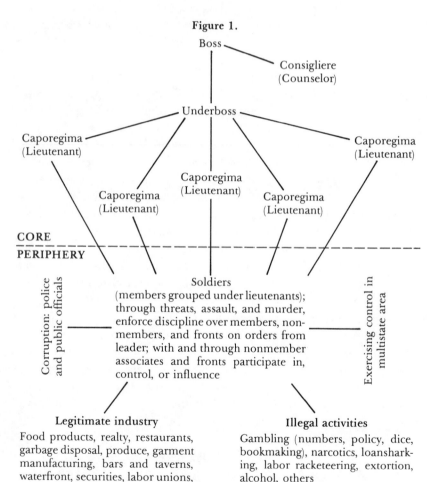

Figure 1.

CORE

PERIPHERY

Corruption: police and public officials

Soldiers (members grouped under lieutenants); through threats, assault, and murder, enforce discipline over members, non-members, and fronts on orders from leader; with and through nonmember associates and fronts participate in, control, or influence

Exercising control in multistate area

Legitimate industry
Food products, realty, restaurants, garbage disposal, produce, garment manufacturing, bars and taverns, waterfront, securities, labor unions, vending machines, others

Illegal activities
Gambling (numbers, policy, dice, bookmaking), narcotics, loansharking, labor racketeering, extortion, alcohol, others

about the level of "soldier" in Figure 1. Above that level in the hierarchy, in addition to the "family" administrators, are the personnel with specialized and expert functions who have found increasing employment in organized crime (Wolfgang, Savitz, and Johnston, 1970). Below that level are the secondary job categories of both legitimate and illegitimate activities.

Although the nature of the work differs between the licit and illicit sectors, the general occupational structure does not. The legitimate secondary-sector industry is particularly appealing to organized crime; its labor costs are low and its unorganized workers easily exploited. The high failure rate of secondary-sector industry provides a context for the "milking" of legitimate funds, which often drives the enterprise into bankruptcy. In the same way, illicit enterprises may be exploited into collapse, then revived in another location. Bad working conditions and high labor turnover take on added, ominous dimensions in the illicit enterprise.

Despite its ominous character, it is important to note that the organized crime described here has little relation to the "Cosa Nostra" that is regularly examined in the press. The division of the two sectors shown in Figure 1 must be considered historical. As long ago as the federal racket prosecutions of 1953-1959, there existed a decided lack of ethnic exclusiveness. This is not to say that labor force characteristics have been altered. Block and Chambliss (1981) note that for the decade 1960-1970 there was a decline in arrests of organized crime figures, and when arrested, such persons showed a strong immunity from prosecution and conviction. A stronger immunity suggests stronger "market position" for organized crime managers. As Block and Chambliss (1981) demonstrate, organized crime reflects its historical and economic context; indeed, organized crime has probably followed general economic trends into an expanded service economy with a high-technology emphasis. Some highly organized illegal activities fit this description: insurance and investment fraud based on control of interlocking computer systems; the high technology of drug importation and the large and expendable pool of salespersons needed to disseminate the drugs. Unfortunately, there are no data, except crime statistics, in which to follow these trends, and this discussion of labor force characteristics for organized crime must be considered only a point of departure.

Conclusions

I have hypothesized that there exists a dual labor market within the illicit economy and have examined three sorts of economic crime that seem to dichotomize their work forces in ways which might be explained by dual labor market theory. A final analysis might be to apply Piore's (1970) five connected arguments explaining labor market differentiation to the illicit economy. First, Piore suggests that the most important distinguishing feature is that each sector imposes different behavioral requirements. The diffuse managerial skills of primary-sector jobs in legitimate industry are mirrored by the skills required by the upper hierarchy of illicit enterprise. The descriptive literature abounds with dichotomized categories: "heavies" versus "operatives" (Mack and Kerner, 1974); "ordinary" versus "professional" criminals, each acting within separate behavioral requirements that might be summarized in the differences between the aggressive "heavy," or violent criminal, and the "smart" "cool operator."

Second, Piore notes that "certain workers . . . are trapped in secondary markets because their superficial characteristics resemble those of secondary workers" (p. 101). This mechanism operates through "statistical" or "pure" discrimination. Both forms of discrimination operate in the illicit economy. The racial and sexual dimensions of this discrimination occur with increased severity; the illicit businessman stands to lose nothing by not practicing equal employment opportunity. And two other dimensions take on increased importance, ethnicity and incarceration. Some primary labor markets are restricted to certain ethnic groups in the illicit sector, leading to an "ethnic succession in organized crime" (Ianni, 1973). Incarceration marks the convict in two ways in terms of labor market discrimination. First, it is the criminals of the secondary sector who are more likely to go to prison, so the ex-convict is seen as more likely to have been in the secondary sector before conviction. Second, the criminal skills a convict might learn while in prison are more likely to prepare him for the secondary sector.

Piore suggests that a third attribute of the dual labor market is that the two sectors are distinguished historically more than technologically. It is difficult to assess the illicit economy in this respect owing to the paucity of reliable longitudinal data on crime. In Block and Chambliss (1981) we find that organized crime in the 1930s occupied or was moving into those secondary economy industries and services that it is known to control today: garment making, trucking, food service, and gambling. In addition, the distinction between "professional" and "amateur" criminals has a long history in criminology, and criminology has long been concerned theoretically with differential structures of opportunity (Cloward and Ohlin, 1961; Merton, 1957; Sutherland, 1937; 1947), as will be discussed below.

Fourth, Piore notes that "the behavioral traits associated with the secondary sector are reinforced by the process of working in secondary jobs and living among others whose life-style is accommodated to that type of employment" (p. 101). Nowhere, perhaps, is that process of reinforcement more potent than for the secondary sector criminals who spend an average of 60 percent of their adult life in prison (Mack and Kerner, 1974). The job skills of the "walking writer" are not those of the "white-collar expert" in "policy," nor is the streetworking and streetwise "walking writer" likely to develop any sort of primary-sector expertise on the job. In contrast is the primary-sector criminal activity that operates as an ongoing business, its "businessmen" developing work patterns and life-styles virtually indistinguishable from those of their legitimate counterparts.

Finally, Piore argues that over time the two markets have become more strongly and rigidly separated. One of the major forces in this sharp separation is the trend of increasing skill specificity in the primary sector (Doeringer and Piore, 1971), combined with an increased emphasis on on-the-job training and intrafirm traditions of discrimination. These three trends are also found in the illicit economy. The illicit primary sector moves parallel to legitimate core industry in the ongoing sophistication, technological and social, of the enterprise. Organized crime, in particular, utilizes a wide range of specialists in its pursuit of "project crime" (McIntosh, 1971). The primary sector is trained in the nuances of businesslike crime and becomes more internally structured with each increment of instruction. The process is hastened through the maintenance of traditional patterns of discrimination; the "walking writer" of the 1930s was a resident of the ghetto he "worked," and so is the drug salesman at the street level today. Neither has an opportunity to climb into a primary sector of an entirely different ethnic, racial, or class composition. We see that with only minor adjustments Piore's basic arguments concerning dual labor markets can be applied to the dual labor market of the criminal economy.

A final question can be raised concerning illicit labor markets: What is their relation to previous work in differential opportunity structures in criminology? Cloward and Ohlin (1961) synthesized Merton's (1957) theory of anomie and Sutherland's (1947) theory of differential association. Cloward and Ohlin felt "that each individual occupies a position in both legitimate and illegitimate opportunity structures" (p. 10). They posited that Merton overly emphasized the legitimate opportunity structure and underemphasized "illegitimate avenues to success goals." Sutherland, however, according to Cloward and Ohlin, did not "recognize the significance of comparable differentials in access to legitimate means" (p. 10). Cloward and Ohlin also felt that Sutherland overemphasized the illegitimate career path. Their concept of differential opportunity structures permitted Cloward and Ohlin to unite the theories of anomie and differential association so that criminal careers might be considered "in relation to both legitimate and illegitimate systems." Both opportunity structures needed to be considered, since "there are marked differences from one part of the social structure to another in the types of illegitimate adaptation that are available" (p. 10). A dual labor market theory of the illicit opportunity structure serves to explain and enlarge on these "marked differences from one part of the social structure to another" in the same way that economic theories help to explain differential opportunity in the legitimate economy. It does so by defining the boundaries of these areas of opportunity and outlining typical levels of achievement for career paths within each of these areas.

But to merely outline illicit career paths is not enough; a theory of labor markets must explain and predict. In the study of dual labor markets in crime, it will be much more difficult to test theoretical predictions, because data are scarce. The "industry" data do not currently exist that would allow the student of illicit labor markets to follow the lead of Beck, Horan, and Tolbert, who found "significant differences [both] in . . . earnings levels and in labor force composition" in the licit economy (1978:718). The oligopoly of organized crime does not issue annual reports or complete government inquiries to provide the type of data used by researchers to illuminate segmentation in legitimate industries (Tolbert, Horan, and Beck, 1980; Bibb and Form, 1977; Oster, 1979). Nonetheless, the logic of dual labor markets may be applied to crime, and if we accept its assumptions, certain linked predictions follow.

First, because we would assume that law enforcement affects the two sectors in different ways, some predictions would follow concerning the overall crime rate. Depending on the relative sizes of the "worker" populations in the two sectors, we may assume that increasing police effort will not radically change the crime rate in a given area, because standard police practice is geared to the apprehension of secondary-sector offenders. The low incarceration rate and higher success rate of primary-sector criminals would provide a baseline crime rate not altered by increasing or decreasing secondary-sector arrests. Second, we would predict that the longer a primary-sector criminal is not caught, the less likely that he will be. This arises from the enhancement of "job" skill. As the primary-sector criminal gets better at what he does, assuming that he continues to be successful, he will forge into more arcane, obscure, and abstract crime that is complex to manipulate but has a low risk factor. As Hagan, Nagel, and Albonetti have shown, white-collar crime "is characterized by a diffuseness of victimization and an absence of unimplicated witnesses" (1980: 818). This enhancement and extension of "job" characteristics (also noted by McIntosh, 1971, in his discussion of "project crime") follows the logic of Doeringer and Piore (1971) in their explanation of the trend of increasing skill specificity as a force in the ongoing separation of labor market sectors. In this way a dual labor market approach explains the differential recruitment and adjudication of white-collar criminals found by Hagan, Nagel, and Albonetti. Third, a theory of dual labor markets in crime would interface with other theories that seek to explain criminal behavior. For example, dual labor market theory would suggest that deterrence theory cannot predict variation in the behavior of primary-sector criminals, whose chances of being punished are low and so hold little deterring force. Stated in terms of microeconomic theories, their cost/benefit ratios tend to render an outcome of profit. Finally, we would predict that primary-sector crime—white-collar crime, for example—would be less affected by general economic variation than secondary-sector crime. It is this last prediction that should be the most readily testable. Economists have previously linked fluctuations in the economy to variation in the crime rate.

This chapter adapts the theory of dual labor markets to add a new dimension to our understanding of crime. In doing so we discern the patterns suggested by dual labor market theory in illicit opportunity structures. If the patterns perceived do indeed exist and are not merely projections of the theory, several predictions are offered that arise from the logic of a dual labor market of crime.

References

BARON, H., AND HYMER, B.
  1968   "The Negro in the Chicago Labor Market." In Julius
         Jacobsen (Ed.), *The Negro and the American Labor
         Movement*. New York: Doubleday.
BECK, E. M., HORAN, PATRICK M., AND TOLBERT, CHARLES M., II
  1978   "Stratification in a Dual Economy: A Sectoral Model
         of Earnings Determination." *American Sociological
         Review* 43:704–720.
BECKER, GARY S.
  1968   "Crime and Punishment: An Economic Approach."
         Journal of Political Economy 1968:169–217.
BELL, DANIEL
  1953   "Crime as an American Way of Life." *Antioch Review*
         13(June):131–154.
BIBB, ROBERT, AND FORM, WILLIAM H.
  1977   "The Effects of Industrial, Occupational, and Sex
         Stratification on Wages in Blue Collar Markets." *Social
         Forces* 55:974–996.
BLOCK, ALAN A., AND CHAMBLISS, WILLIAM J.
  1981   *Organizing Crime*. New York: Elsevier.
BLOCK, MICHAEL K., AND HEINEKE, J. M.
  1975   "A Labor Theoretic Analysis of the Criminal Choice."
         American Economic Review 65:314–325.

BLOCK, MICHAEL K., AND LIND, ROBERT C.
1975 "Crime and Punishment Reconsidered." *Journal of Legal Studies* 4(Jan.):241-247.

BLUESTONE, BARRY
1970 "The Tripartite Economy: Labor Markets and the Working Poor." *Poverty and Human Resources* (July-Aug.).

BONGER, WILLIAM A.
1916 *Criminality and Economic Conditions.* (Translated by Henry P. Horton.) Boston: Little, Brown.

BROWN, WILLIAM W., AND REYNOLDS, MORGAN O.
1973 "Notes, Comments, and Letters to the Editor: Crime and 'Punishment'—Risk Implications." *Journal of Economic Theory* 6:508-514.

CAIN, GLEN C.
1976 "The Challenge of Segmented Labor Market Theories to Orthodox Theory: A Survey." *Journal of Economic Literature* 14:1215-1257.

CHAPMAN, JEFFREY I.
1976 "An Economic Model of Crime and Police: Some Empirical Results." *Journal of Research in Crime and Delinquency* 13(Jan.):48-63.

CHISWICK, BARRY R.
1973 "Schooling, Screening, and Income." In L. C. Solomon and Paul J. Taubman (Eds.), *Does College Matter?* New York: Academic Press.

CLOWARD, RICHARD E., AND OHLIN, LLOYD
1961 *Delinquency and Opportunity.* New York: Free Press.

CORNWALL, JOHN
1977 "The Relevance of Dual Models for Analyzing Developed Capitalist Economies." *Kyklos* 30(Fasc. 1):51-73.

DANZIGER, SHELDON, AND WHEELER, DAVID
1975 "The Economics of Crime: Punishment or Income Redistribution." *Review of Social Economy* 33(Oct.):113-131.

DOERINGER, PETER B., AND PIORE, MICHAEL J.
1971 *Internal Labor Markets and Manpower Analysis.* Lexington, Mass.: Heath.

DOERINGER, PETER B., AND OTHERS

1969   "Urban Manpower Programs and Low-Income Labor
       Markets: A Critical Assessment." Manpower Adminis-
       tration, U.S. Department of Labor.

DRAKE, ST. CLAIR, AND CAYTON, HORACE

1945   *Black Metropolis.* New York: Harcourt Brace Jovano-
       vich.

DUNLOP, JOHN T.

1957   "The Task of Contemporary Wage Theory." In George
       W. Taylor and Frank C. Pierson (Eds.), *New Concepts
       in Wage Discrimination.* New York: McGraw-Hill.

1958   *Industrial Relations Systems.* New York: Holt, Rine-
       hart and Winston.

EHRLICH, ISAAC

1973   "Participation in Illegitimate Activities: A Theoretical
       and Empirical Investigation." *Journal of Political Econ-
       omy* 81:521–565.

FELDSTEIN, MARTIN S.

1973   "Lowering the Permanent Rate of Unemployment: A
       Study, Joint Economic Committee Print." 93rd Con-
       gress, 1st session, September 18, 1973. Washington,
       D.C.: U.S. Government Printing Office.

FERMAN, LOUIS

1963   "The Irregular Economy: Informal Work Patterns in
       the Ghetto." University of Michigan (mimeo).

FOX, VERNON

1962   "Toward an Understanding of Criminal Behavior."
       American Journal of Economics and Sociology 21
       (Apr.): 145–158.

GORDON, DAVID M.

1971   *Theories of Poverty and Underemployment.* Lexing-
       ton, Mass.: Heath.

GOULD, LEROY C.

1969   "The Changing Structure of Property Crime in an Af-
       fluent Society." *Social Forces* 48:50–59.

1971   "Crime and Its Impact in an Affluent Society." In Jack
       D. Douglas (Ed.), *Crime and Justice in American Soci-
       ety.* Indianapolis: Bobbs-Merrill.

HAGAN, JOHN, NAGEL, ILENE H., AND ALBONETTI, CELESTA
1980   "The Differential Sentencing of White-Collar Offenders in Ten Federal District Courts." *American Sociological Review* 45:802–820.

HARRISON, BENNETT
1972   "Theory of the Dual Economy." In S. Sheppard, B. Harrison, and R. Spring (Eds.), *The Political Economy of Public Service Employment.* Lexington, Mass.: Heath.
1975   "Human Capital Theory: Education, Discrimination, and Life Cycles." *American Economic Review* 65(2): 63–73.

IANNI, FRANCIS A. J.
1973   *Ethnic Succession in Organized Crime.* Washington, D.C.: U.S. Department of Justice, Law Enforcement Assistance Administration, National Institute of Law Enforcement and Criminal Justice.

INSTITUTE FOR SOCIAL RESEARCH
1976   *Gambling in the United States.* Ann Arbor: University of Michigan.

KERR, CLARK
1950   "Labor Markets: Their Character and Consequences." *American Economic Review* (May):278–291.
1954   "The Balkanization of Labor Markets." In E. W. Bakke and others (Eds.), *Labor Mobility and Economic Opportunity.* New York: Wiley. Cambridge, Mass.: Technology Press of M.I.T.

LAYARD, RICHARD, AND PSACHAROPOULOS, GEORGE
1974   "The Screening Hypothesis and the Returns to Education." *Journal of Political Economy* 82(5):985–998.

MCINTOSH, M.
1971   "Changes in the Organization of Thieving." In S. Cohen (Ed.), *Images of Deviance.* New York: Penguin Books.

MACK, J. A.
1964   "Full-Time Miscreants, Delinquent Neighbourhoods, and Criminal Networks." *British Journal of Sociology* 15:38–53.

1972   "The Able Criminal." *British Journal of Criminology* 12-1:44–54.

MACK, J. A., AND KERNER, H. J.
1974   *The Crime Industry.* Lexington, Mass.: Heath.

MANSFIELD, ROGER, GOULD, LEROY C., AND NAMENWIRTH, J. ZVI
1974   "A Socioeconomic Model for the Prediction of Societal Rates of Property Theft." *Social Forces* 52:462–472.

MARX, KARL
1904   *A Contribution to the Critique of Political Economy.* (Translated from the 2nd ed. by N. I. Stone.) Chicago: Charles H. Kerr.
1970   *The German Ideology.* (Translated by C. Arthur.) London: International Publishers. (Originally published 1909.)

MEIER, ROBERT F.
1977   "The New Criminology: Continuity in Criminological Theory." *Journal of Criminal Law and Criminology* 67:461–469.

MERTON, ROBERT K.
1957   *Social Theory and Social Structure.* New York: Free Press.

MICHALOWSKI, RAYMOND J.
1977   "Repression and Criminal Justice in Capitalist America." *Sociological Inquiry* 46(2):95–106.

MONTAGNA, PAUL D.
1977   *Occupations and Society: Toward a Sociology of the Labor Market.* New York: Wiley.

OSTER, GERRY
1979   "A Factor Analytic Test of the Theory of the Dual Economy." *Review of Economics and Statistics* 61 (Feb.):33–39.

PIORE, MICHAEL J.
1969   "On-the-Job Training in the Dual Labor Market." In L. Weber and others, *Public-Private Manpower Policies.* Madison, Wisc.: Industrial Relations Research Association.
1970   "Manpower Policy." In S. Beer and B. Barringer (Eds.), *The State and the Poor.* Cambridge, Mass.: Winthrop.

1971   "The Dual Labor Market: Theory and Implications."
       In David Gordon (Ed.), *Problems in Political Economy:
       An Urban Perspective*. Lexington, Mass.: Heath.

RADZINOWICZ, LEON
1966   *Ideology and Crime*. New York: Columbia University
       Press.

RECKLESS, WALTER C.
1950   *The Crime Problem*. New York: Appleton-Century-
       Crofts.

REUTER, PETER, AND RUBINSTEIN, JONATHAN
1977   "The Structure and Operation of Illegal Numbers,
       Bookmaking, and Loansharking in Metropolitan New
       York." Unpublished manuscript, Center for Research
       on Institutions and Social Policy, New York.

ROSEN, SHERWIN
1976   "Human Capital: A Survey of Empirical Research."
       Discussion Paper 76-2, revised. Department of Eco-
       nomics, University of Rochester.

SJOQUIST, DAVID LAWRENCE
1973   "Property Crime and Economic Behavior: Some Em-
       pirical Results." *American Economic Review* 63:439–
       446.

SULLIVAN, RICHARD F.
1973   "The Economics of Crime: An Introduction to the Lit-
       erature." *Crime and Delinquency* (Apr.):138–149.

SUTHERLAND, EDWIN E.
1937   *The Professional Thief*, by Chic Conwell (interpreted
       by Sutherland). Chicago: University of Chicago Press.
1947   *Criminology*. Philadelphia: Lippincott.

TOLBERT, CHARLES M., II, HORAN, PATRICK M., AND BECK, E. M.
1980   "The Structure of Economic Segmentation: A Dual
       Economy Approach." *American Journal of Sociology*
       85(5):1095–1116.

TRASLER, G.
1962   *The Explanation of Criminality*. London: Routledge
       & Kegan Paul.

TRUONG, THAM VAN
1976   "Development of a Dual Economy With or Without
       Turning Point." *Growth and Change* 7(2):20–27.

VIETORISZ, THOMAS, AND HARRISON, BENNETT

1970 *The Economic Development of Harlem.* New York: Praeger.

WACHTEL, HOWARD M.

1970 "The Impact of Labor Market Conditions on Hard Core Unemployment: A Case Study of Detroit." *Poverty and Human Resources* (July–Aug.).

WALLACE, MICHAEL, AND KALLEBERG, ARNE L.

1979 "Economic Organization, Occupations, and Labor Force Consequences: Toward a Specification of Dual Labor Market Theory." Presented at the annual meeting of the American Sociological Association, Boston, August 30.

WELCH, FINIS

1975 "Human Capital Theory: Education, Discrimination, and Life Cycles." *American Economic Review* 65(2): 63–73.

WOLFGANG, MARVIN E., SAVITZ, L., AND JOHNSTON, N.

1970 *The Sociology of Crime and Delinquency.* New York: Wiley.

*The work of literary structuralists, particularly Roland
Barthes, provides sharper insights into ethnomethodology
than symbolic interactionism, labeling theory, or phenomenology. Further, it suggests that the metaphor of text may
be fruitful for analysts of everyday life. Greater theoretical
benefits derive from that metaphor, however, if one applies it
using the ideas of literary theorists outside the structuralist
tradition.*

☙ 6 ☙

EVERYDAY LIFE AS TEXT

Mary F. Rogers

UNIVERSITY OF WEST FLORIDA

During the past fifteen years or so, sociologists have tried in
various ways to make sense of ethnomethodology. Some (Dreitzel,
1970:vii–viii; Johnson, 1981:293; Collins, 1975:30) compare it
with symbolic interactionism, others (Leiter, 1980:185) with labeling theory. More commonly, sociologists look to phenomenology for access to ethnomethodology (Dallmayr and McCarthy,
1977:10; Heap and Roth,1978:288; Mayrl, 1977; Morris, 1977;
O'Neill, 1972:212). Though common, that approach has sparked
debate: Some analysts (Spurling, 1977:72; Zimmerman, 1979:
383) deny a close correspondence between phenomenology and
ethnomethodology. Other commentators claim that ethnomethodology is unintelligible to "outsiders." Lewis Coser (1975), who
criticizes its cultlike character, exemplifies that stance. Jonathan

I thank the anonymous reviewers whose comments helped me strength-
en this chapter.

Turner (1974) also leans in that direction. By delineating the social bonds among leading ethnomethodologists and emphasizing their geographical concentration, he implies that if ethnomethodology is no cult, it may nonetheless qualify as a men's club.

None of the foregoing approaches is adequate. Unlike symbolic interactionists, ethnomethodologists are not concerned primarily with symbols, selves, roletaking, or even interaction as such.[1] Their concern with common-sense activities, although it sometimes leads to considerations of labeling, focuses on what *underlies* labeling. Besides, ethnomethodologists' critiques of "conventional sociology" (Mehan and Wood, 1975b; Wilson, 1970) imply that established sociological models hold few clues about ethnomethodology. Some ethnomethodologists have emphasized that sociologists need to examine experience itself (Douglas, 1970: 376). Studying experience necessitates fresh methods of data gathering and theory construction, even shifts in the sociological idiom (Blum, 1974a, 1974b; Mehan and Wood, 1975b:225). By claiming to offer those alternatives, ethnomethodologists imply that their work lies closer to the fabric of common-sense experience than that of other sociologists. Yet their approach to experience as such seems without precedent in sociology.

Similarly, some ethnomethodologists claim a phenomenological basis for their work. Garfinkel (in Hill and Crittenden, 1968:114) has made that claim, for example. In addition, the work where Garfinkel (1952) laid the grounds of ethnomethodology is replete with references to Edmund Husserl, Alfred Schutz, and Aron Gurwitsch. In his programmatic *Studies in Ethnomethodology* (1967:ix) Garfinkel cites those three phenomenologists as major influences. Not all ethnomethodologists acknowledge an indebtedness to phenomenologists. Nonetheless, Garfinkel's position carries obvious weight, particularly for "outsiders" trying to get a handle on the development he masterminded. Those who look to phenomenology for insights into ethnomethodology, however, enter a blind alley. Ethnomethodology exhibits no consistent relationship to phenomenology. It largely dismisses phenomenological terminology and disattends the work of contemporary phenomenologists like Joseph Kockelmans, Maurice Natanson, and Robert Sokolowski. More fundamentally, ethnomethodologists make rare reference to, and adopt no clear, explicit perspective on, human consciousness, the paramount concern among phenomenologists. Overall, the gap between what some ethnomethodologists claim and what they do perhaps leaves many sociologists doubting their own grasp of ethnomethodology. In addition to its eclectic intellectual bases, then, some of ethnomethodologists' claims exacerbate the difficulty of understanding what ethnomethodology is as a sociological development.

Ethnomethodology does remain a sociological enigma and, to that extent, a prime candidate for a case study in the sociology of sociology. In their respective fashions Paul Attewell (1974) and Kenneth Leiter (1980) have undertaken studies along those lines. More generally, ethnomethodology remains an intellectual question mark and is thus a candidate for a case study in the sociology of knowledge. To date, only Charles C. Lemert (1979) has moved in that direction. Here I extend his argument that ethnomethodology and structuralism are homologues. The metaphor of text guides my analysis of ethnomethodology as an intellectual development that resonates with literary structuralism in its disregard for subjective meanings and its emphasis on the formal features of everyday life. Specifically, ethnomethodologists disclose the accountable features of everyday life by treating mundane discourse as if it were a text in need of the deconstructive efforts the French literary structuralists propound.[2]

The Textual and the Mundane

Originating in the thought of Friedrich Nietzsche and later Martin Heidegger, contemporary structuralism claims scholars as diverse as Claude Levi-Strauss, Jacques Lacan, Louis Althusser, Michel Foucault, and Jacques Derrida. Among literary scholars Roland Barthes advanced a structuralism that, together with some of Derrida's ideas, offers grounds for understanding ethnomethodologists' goals and techniques. Barthes's influence is widespread. Besides shaping contemporary literary criticism, his ideas have influenced such cultural critics as Susan Sontag. Even though his work seems not to have directly affected ethnomethodology, its resonance with that development is unsurprising. During the 1950s and 1960s Barthes's interdisciplinary interests landed him among French sociologists. Although his training was mostly in literature, grammar, and philology, from 1955 to 1959 he served as a research attaché in sociology at the Centre Nationale de Recherché Scientifique. During the following three years he chaired the section on social and economic sciences at the École Pratique des Hautes Études. Thereafter he became director of studies there in the sociology of signs, symbols, and representations (Barthes, 1977b:184). Thus, although he appears not to have directly influenced ethnomethodologists, one can trace a fundamental resonance between Barthes's and ethnomethodologists' approaches to their objects of investigation. Barthes's treatment of The Text,[3] in particular, illustrates that resonance.

Barthes's Text "is a tissue of quotations drawn from the innumerable centres of culture" (1977a:146). So conceptualized, any text is "valid for all the texts of literature." Although no single text "represents" literature, every text provides entry into the network of literature inasmuch as "literature itself is never anything but a single text" (Barthes, 1974:12). The Text is where language relations become transparent (Barthes, 1977a:164). It "always involves a certain experience of limits. . . . The Text is that which goes to the limit of the rules of enunciation (rationality, readability, etc.)" (1977a:157). As such, The Text represents a "methodological field" where practices "speak" according to particular rules. It exists in the movement of discourse; experiencing The Text derives from the activity of production. As the form limiting discourse, The Text remains profoundly taken for granted until a discourser struggles with its constraints while trying to produce a particular text.

Structuralists like Barthes focus on how The Text, as a discursive form, takes the shape it does (Barthes, 1977a:127). That focus leads to analyses not of authors and writing but of language and rules. Barthes says the search for literary sources and influences reflects the "myth of filiation." The citations making up a text are, at root, anonymous and untraceable (Barthes, 1977a: 160). Like language itself, texts are "off-centered." Foremostly, they reflect linguistic constraints, not individuals' imaginations. A text is a system of language relations based on the productive activity of writing. The textual analyst is a special sort of reader.

Ethnomethodologists' stances toward practical situations are similar. The situational ethnomethodologists,[4] who dominated ethnomethodology in its early days, assume that social situations exhibit an invariant structure regardless of their specific purposes or settings (Garfinkel and Sacks, 1970). Their work implies that any everyday situation elucidates the network of situations making up the practical sphere. Moreover, analyzing the production of any social situation reveals the limits of everyday discourse by exposing the "ground rules" and "background expectancies" that are constitutive elements of all social situations. In ethnomethodological terms, analyzing account-able features discloses the unquestioned and unnoticed rules that allow common-sense actors to demonstrate their competence as members. As the development of ethnomethodology implies, those competencies are essentially linguistic.

From the start, ethnomethodologists emphasized linguistic activities as the key to understanding the common-sense world. Garfinkel's (1967) early breaching experiments, for example, usually involved manipulating everyday language or conversations in order to expose the background features and formal structure of everyday life. The current prominence of linguistic ethnomethodologists is a culmination of ethnomethodology's continual preoccupation with everyday speech as the constitutive basis of the common-sense world. For ethnomethodologists, everyday life is a textual affair based on linguistic structures and competence. Its practical situations rest on the anonymous, untraceable rules that govern language use. Every situation is off-centered and open-ended; in ethnomethodological terms, every social situation involves reflexivity and indexicality (Bittner, 1973:116; Garfinkel, in Hill and Crittenden, 1968:1, 206–208; Heap, 1980:89; Heritage and Watson, 1979:136; Mehan and Wood, 1975b:90). That situations are inescapably reflexive means that they fold back on themselves independently of their participants' intentions, though not independently of their activities. That language is indexical means that the meanings of its terms shift from one situation to the next, making meaning significantly recondite as a situation takes shape. Everyday life is, then, The Text, a methodological field where reader-ethnomethodologists study members' productive (or constitutive) activities to disclose the ground rules that make those activities "visibly account-able and rational-for-all-practical-purposes." Unsurprisingly, ethnomethodological reports often appear redundant. Ethnomethodologists face, after all, a single Text (everyday life) whose features are accessible through any given text (mundane social situation) considered as a methodological field in need of a careful reading.

In Barthes's view the meaning of any text is overwhelmingly plural. In fact, the "multiplicity of writing" establishes objects amenable only to disentanglement, not decipherment (1977a: 147). Disentangling meaning requires understanding that "the meaning of a text can be nothing but the plurality of its systems" (1974:120). Thus a text's meaning is a plenitude that defies analytical capture. A text invites linguistic-structuralist attention as a field of signifiers whose infinity "refers not to some idea of the ineffable (the unnameable signified) but to that of playing" (1977a: 158). Barthes assumes that the linguistic play animating a text is more susceptible to structuralist description than to descriptions concerning motive, intersubjectivity, or communication.[5] Thus his model, like structuralist models generally, comprises categories that reduce meaning to the systemic functions that units of discourse serve.

For Barthes, meaning concerns the "functional nature" that segments of a narrative exhibit (1977a:88). A narrative consists of different functions that are more structural than artistic in nature (1977a:89). Thus the fundamental "reality" of a narrative sequence is the logic it exposes and satisfies (1977a:124). Action and temporality in no way determine the meaning of a narrative (see Barthes, 1977a:99), since they lie outside the "objective structure of the text" (1977a:131). That structure is parallel with the structure of a sentence. More generally, Barthes (1977a:83-84) assumes that all semiotic systems exhibit a similar formal structure: "Able to be carried by articulated language, spoken or written, fixed or moving images, gestures, and the ordered mixture of all these substances, narrative is present in myth, legend, fable, tale, novella, epic, history, tragedy, drama, comedy, mime, painting, . . . stained glass windows, cinema, comics, news items, conversation" (1977a:79). Narrative is a transcultural, transhistorical form of human life (1977a:79). Structurally, narratives are susceptible to summary and translation "without fundamental damage" (1977a:120-121).

To summarize or translate any narrative—broadly, any textual object—requires different sorts of structural analysis. Barthes (1977a:137–138) cites A. J. Greimas's actantial analysis, which treats the actors in a narrative according to their functions—that is, Subject, Object, Sender, Receiver, Opponent, and Helper. He also cites V. Propp's functional analysis, which considers narrative acts as functions stabilizing a narrative. Barthes's own approach, which resonates with both of those, comprises three types of considerations. First, *indicial analysis* inventories the biographical, psychological, and social attributes of the characters in a narrative. Second, *functional analysis* focuses on what the characters do "according to their narrative status." Third, *sequential analysis* inventories the actions that constitute sequences in the narrative's "pseudo-logical schema" (Barthes, 1977a:127–128). For the structuralist, then, the text is an objective form amenable to exacting analysis, even though its meaning eludes analysis.

Among ethnomethodologists meaning is similarly problematic. Although some ethnomethodologists (Cicourel, 1973; Douglas, 1970; McHugh, 1968) treat meaning explicitly, such work departs from the mainstream of ethnomethodology. For the most part, ethnomethodologists are not interested in interpreting mundane situations as individuals experience them in a meaningful field of action and interaction. As linguistic concerns become paramount, the plurality of meanings that inform everyday life move even more to the periphery of ethnomethodological inquiry. Ethnomethodologists turn increasingly to functional categories meant to account for the structure of everyday life. The lens those categories form is preeminently linguistic. Thereby ethnomethodologists imply that meaning is a structural derivative of the linguistic units that make up sequences and provide members the grounds of common-sense competence. The ethnomethodological conception of "member" illustrates that stance toward meaning. In contrast to the common-sense actor whose activities imply a self, the member is a competent user of natural language (Garfinkel, in Hill and Crittenden, 1968:119, 121). He or she produces utterances that function as units in the narrative specifying a social situation. A member is not a person with motives and subjectively meaningful experiences; a member is a course of activity (Garfinkel, in Hill and Crittenden, 1968:119).

The methods ethnomethodologists use to illuminate the textual quality of everyday life are similar to Barthes's methods for analyzing literary texts. Ethnomethodologists virtually translate everyday narratives by showing, most generally, the functions that narrative units serve in the reflexive "accomplishment" of a social situation. To an extent members are narrative characters subjected to indicial analyses. Moreover, ethnomethodologists treat members' utterances from a functionalist perspective. Finally, ethnomethodologists disclose members' logic through sequential analyses (for example, Atkinson, 1979; Pollner, 1979; Schegloff and Sacks, 1974). Throughout such analyses meaning remains an implicit problem. The sequencing of utterances in a social situation, for example, reveals little or nothing about the meanings those utterances or that situation hold for participants.[6] Within the ethnomethodological sphere, then, the structuralist refusal to confront human consciousness and authorship prevails.

Although Barthes (1977a:164) insists that a theory of The Text coincides with a "practice of writing," he follows other structuralists in rejecting the traditional conception of authorship. His position is deconstructionist: "Author" is a "figment of humanist ideology" (Norris, 1980:245). Both Barthes and Derrida suggest that throwing off the preoccupation with authors makes the "limitless freeplay" of texts accessible; reading becomes creatively independent (Norris, 1980:245). Under those circumstances the reader-commentator comes to the text "with unlimited freedom to make what he can of the open-ended discourse of signs" (Norris, 1980:250). Thus deconstruction has a "liberating" as well as a "skeptical" side (Norris, 1980:245).

From Barthes's standpoint the text "reads without the inscription of the Father" (1977a:160–161). The text differs from "the work"; its proper metaphor is network rather than organism. Considered from a textual perspective, writing becomes a "performative" rather than an activity of recording, noting, depicting, and representing (1977a:145–146). The modern "scriptor" exists alongside the text; he or she neither precedes nor exceeds the writing. Every text, according to Barthes (1977a:145), "is eternally written *here and now*." Moreover, "Succeeding the Author, the scriptor no longer bears within him passions, humours, feelings, impressions, but rather this immense dictionary from which he draws a writing that can know no halt: Life never does more than

imitate the book, and the book itself is only a tissue of signs"
(1977a:147). Originality is beyond the scriptor's scope (1977a:
146). The concept "author" thus distorts one's perspective on a
text (1977a:147). Barthes wants to avoid that concept and its traditional implications regardless of the humanistic losses. Thus his
scriptor, the one *who writes,* is not one *who is* (1977a:111-112).

Structuralists like Barthes (1977a:105) refuse characters
any "essence." Although narratives require characters as their
agents, the structuralist assumes that those characters cannot be
described in terms concerning "persons." Characters are not beings
but functions (1977a:105-106). As such, they occupy spheres of
action, few in number, that are amenable to classification (1977a:
107). Although a realistic view of character entails concern with
motives, a realistic view of discourse engenders concern with functions within the mechanism of, for example, a story or a conversation (Barthes, 1974:178). Discourse itself constrains its characters,
even though that constraint is usually "modestly 'forgotten' "
(1974:135).

Lemert (1979:292) implies that the preceding points define
the homology between ethnomethodology and structuralism. Both
perspectives give language priority over the social subject; they de-
constitute the idea of a human center. In Derrida's (1978:280)
terms, "It was necessary to begin thinking that there was no center, that the center could not be thought in the form of a present-
being, that the center had no natural site, that it was ... but a
function. ... This was the moment when language invaded the
universal problematic, the moment when, in the absence of a center or origin, everything became discourse." Rather than viewing
language and utterances as signs of selves, ethnomethodologists
take "selves" as signs that language itself needs explaining. Language thus displaces consciousness as the focus of investigation
(Lemert, 1979:297, 298). Like Barthes, ethnomethodologists
study "methods, not people as such—a fact which is dramatically
documented by the definition of *member* as a competent language
user, not a social actor" (Lemert, p. 297). Like Barthes's scriptor
and characters, then, members lack motives, memories, and passions. They are functionaries in social situations structured, first of
all, by language and the rules of discourse.

Philip Pettit (1977:i, ii) also argues that ethnomethodology represents, intentionally or not, an extension of structuralism. He says, "Perhaps the interpretation of a sentence in everyday life is an accelerated version of the procedure involved in interpreting poetry" (p. 25). In either case language serves as the principal topic and resource. The structuralist perspective necessitates disavowing the center of social life. For structuralists, language obeys its own laws and functions independently of human creativity (Lemert, 1979:291). In that sense ethnomethodology potentially ruptures the sociological tradition (Lemert, 1979:293). Its structuralist program poses a crucial question: "Is it possible to go so far toward eliminating voice, presence, origin, and the whole 'logocentric' tradition of Western discourse without in the process giving up the claim to communicate intelligible meaning?" (Norris, 1980: 255).

Most ethnomethodologists would probably deny that their work implies that question. After all, their references to members' *achievements* proliferate (Garfinkel and Sacks, 1970; Pollner, 1974). Moreover, Garfinkel (1967:68) insisted early on that ethnomethodology aimed to overcome the "judgmental dope" model implied in conventional sociology. Then, too, some ethnomethodologists emphasize the elegance of members' knowledge and methods (Sudnow, in Hill and Crittenden, 1968:51). Yet in most ethnomethodological reports the human center *is* missing. Motives, subjective meanings, and interests receive no explicit attention in most ethnomethodological studies. In fact, as James Heap (1976) indicates, ethnomethodology lacks a clear-cut conception of the social as such; that concept receives almost no explicit attention from ethnomethodologists. Their concerns lie elsewhere and are best grasped by understanding structuralist priorities. Whether or not they intend it, ethnomethodologists commonly reflect the structuralist program in their studies.

That circumstance is one reason many sociologists are hard put to understand ethnomethodology and fit it into the sociological sphere. By and large, sociologists are less familiar with structuralism than anthropologists are. Literary structuralism is even more alien to them. Thus sociologists commonly lack the cross-disciplinary grounds necessary for grasping ethnomethodological concerns, methods, and perspectives. In addition, some of ethnomethodologists' own claims aggravate other sociologists' problems in understanding ethnomethodology. Some ethnomethodologists emphasize, for instance, that sociologists need to examine experience itself (Douglas, 1970:376). Studying experience necessitates fresh methods of data gathering and theory construction, even shifts in the sociological idiom (Blum, 1974a, 1974b; Mehan and Wood, 1975b:225). Ethnomethodologists claim to offer those alternatives. Thereby they imply that their work lies closer to the fabric of common-sense experience than that of other sociologists. Yet experience as such is neither an explicit nor a consistent concern among ethnomethodologists.

In his analysis Lemert focuses on Levi-Strauss, Foucault, and Derrida to illustrate the homology between structuralism and ethnomethodology. But Barthes's ideas more sharply illuminate ethnomethodology. His works more acutely illustrate structuralists' commitment to decentering. Moreover, Barthes's focus on The Text provides a metaphor that clarifies the ethnomethodological perspective on everyday life. At the same time, that metaphor offers an alternative to the theatrical metaphors that social dramaturgists and symbolic interactionists sometimes use. Finally, Barthes's structuralism evokes attention to alternative literary approaches to texts capable of providing sociologists fresh interpretive grounds for analyzing everyday life.

Implications and Alternatives

The idea of everyday life as text is attractive. The metaphor centers attention on expression and communication and, therefore, on the grounds of social action and interaction. "Text" also leads to the questions of how the public and the private realms intermesh and how informal and formal discourse relate. The metaphor also invites considerations of meaning and purpose as well as of language and narrative conventions. Perhaps as the works of Kenneth Burke (1966), Ernst Cassirer (1962), and Hugh Dalziel Duncan (1968) variously suggest, everyday life does exhibit a distinctive grammar that enables common-sense actors to take for granted much of what they mean and to make sense of what they cannot take for granted in given instances. The metaphor offers sociologists a plenitude of theoretical possibilities. Adopted only in the structuralist sense, however, it threatens to undermine theoretical advances concerning the self, interaction, and the social construction of shared realities.

Fortunately, literary critics offer diverse approaches to texts. Norris (1980) suggests three on the basis of Barthes's positive influence on the critic or the critic's serious quarrel with the structuralist perspective. The frameworks belong to Harold Bloom, E. D. Hirsch, Jr., and William Empson. Although space permits only a passing glance at their frameworks, that glance suffices to illustrate alternatives to literary structuralism. In other terms, "text" might be a fruitful metaphor for sociologists, if they refuse to assume that "the psychological person . . . bears no relation to the linguistic person" (Barthes, 1977a:114). Similarly, sociologists need to reject the notion that "the reader is without history, biography, psychology: He is simply that *someone* who holds together in a single field all the traces by which the written text is constituted" (Barthes, 1977a:148). In more general terms, sociologists need to override the structuralist deconstructions that stymie explanation and theory construction (Norris, 1980:251).

The French structuralists have influenced many American scholars, including a trio of literary critics at Yale University—Geoffrey Hartman, J. Hillis Miller, and Harold Bloom. Of the three, Bloom stands out for trying to temper the structuralist posture. "In Bloom there is an undisguised hankering for some form of presence, or authorial voice, which asserts itself against the slippages and detours of textual meaning" (Norris, 1980:246). Bloom (1975b:175) favors "interpretation that seeks to restore and redress meaning" rather than "to make of demystification the principal end." In his view, structuralist deconstructions impoverish meaning "by deconstructing the thinking subject itself, by dissipating the ego into a 'rendezvous of persons' " (pp. 85–86). Bloom argues that structuralists undermine the ability to recognize textual illusions that gather meanings in the text or return the reader to the perspective the text demands (p. 85). Moreover, he decries the structuralist "flight from psychology and history" (p. 85). Finally, he notes that linguistic models address only linguistic problems: "The obsession with 'language' is one of the clearest instances of a defensive trope in modern literary discourse" (Bloom, 1975a: 105).

Bloom's alternative to deconstruction is eclectic. Basically, his framework rests on the kabbalistic tradition and Freudian psychology. Bloom uses the Kabbalah as a theory of rhetoric (1975a: 18, 25, 33). In his view, the Kabbalah offers a theory of influence centered on the concept of exile, which becomes belatedness in the literary sphere (1975a:83). From a kabbalistic perspective, "to interpret is to revise is to defend against influence" (1975a:65). All poetry—or writing—begins with interpretation, or the act of reading (1975a:101). Significantly, "literature is always misprision, and so is criticism, as a part of literature" (1975a:123). Interpretation is revisionism (1975b:126) aimed at "deciding" meaning (1975b:3). Like criticism, it is a metaphor for the act of reading (1975b:74). Yet both reading and writing involve misreading that originates in a primal scene of instruction (1975b:60). In that sense both involve belatedness. Both also involve distinctive tensions of consciousness. For example, "Poetry is written by the same natural man or woman who suffers daily all the inescapable anxieties of competition. This is not to say that the imagination refers to a world of things, but rather that a poet's consciousness of a competing poet is itself a text" (1975b:165).

Bloom's scheme presupposes human consciousness and authorship. It also circumvents the temptation to proceed as if the writer, reader, or critic acted in an intellectual, psychological, or social vacuum. Bloom emphasizes origins, the primal scene of instruction, influence, belatedness, and anxiety. Significantly, he treats reading as the basis of all writing, interpreting, and criticizing. He specifies a "sixfold trope" for the act of reading (Bloom, 1975b) as well as tropes of limitation and tropes of representation based on Kenneth Burke's work. Bloom's scheme is rich. Its social-psychological considerations alone make it worthy of sociological attention. In short, Bloom's framework may be adaptable to the study of everyday life.

E. D. Hirsch, Jr., offers a second alternative. Hirsch attacks the deconstructionist stance on phenomenological grounds. His scheme serves as a reminder that structuralists characteristically reject phenomenology (Pettit, 1977:39, 68, 69). Hirsch (1978:24) decries the "intrinsic criticism" that insists on treating literature as literature and never as anything else. He assumes that interpretation aims at construing "from a sign-system (for short, 'text') something more than its physical presence" (p. 75). Adapting Husserl's ideas, Hirsch distinguishes meaning from significance (pp. 79-80). The former is the "determinate representation" a text has for an interpreter; the latter is meaning related to something else. The interpreter's quest for meaning requires, Hirsch argues, that *"unless there is a powerful overriding value in disregarding an author's intention (that is, original meaning), we who interpret as a vocation should not disregard it"* (p. 90). On those premises Hirsch elaborates a scheme for studying authorial intentions. His framework resonates with the tradition of *Verstehen* in the social sciences. For that reason alone Hirsch's ideas merit the scrutiny of sociologists interested in interpreting everyday life so as to take into account actors' intentions and meanings.

Although William Empson's scheme differs from Hirsch's, Empson does assume, like Hirsch, that the interpreter must reckon with the author (Norris, 1980:243). Empson's perspective emphasizes the elusive quality of the author's voice. It focuses on the ambiguities, hints, and overtones that contribute to a text's meaning. Determining that meaning requires, for Empson, matching what constitutes the "credible intention" of the author (Norris, 1980: 243). His perspective thus concerns how a reader or listener comes to understand a sentence (Pettit, 1977:23). It also addresses the inevitability of much ambiguity. Empson (1953:235) analyzes the situational elements that give rise to particular types of ambiguity and make it coherent. His work shows that "literature . . . demands a sense, not so much of what is really there, as of what is necessary to carry a particular situation 'off' " (p. 245). Thus Empson's work has clear relevance for analysts interested in the ambiguities and fragility that stamp everyday life.

The work of Bloom, Hirsch, and Empson, among others (Booth, 1961; Iser, 1974, 1978; Sacks, 1967), suggests the heuristic value of "text" as a metaphor for everyday life. More important, their ideas offer sociologists fresh concepts and techniques for grappling with common-sense complexities. Their ideas hold richer theoretical possibilities than structuralism, if only because they take into account human consciousness, expression, communication, and interaction. In short, if everyday life is in some sense a text, we will read it better by looking to Bloom, Hirsch, and Empson for guidance than to structuralists.

In fact, Paul Ricoeur (1971:529) has already considered the

possibility that the subject matter of the human sciences displays "some of the features of the text as text" and that methodologies in the human sciences "comprise the same kind of procedures as text interpretation." Ricoeur concludes that the metaphor of text is probably fruitful for social scientists. He cautions, however, that written discourse differs considerably from spoken discourse. The metaphor demands careful use, then. Ricoeur's (1976, 1977, 1979:135-172) own work on text interpretation, on metaphor, and on explanation in the human sciences provides strong grounds for systematically exploring the heuristic value of "text" as a metaphor for everyday life. Significantly, Ricoeur himself sympathizes with structuralist approaches to texts and social reality. His sympathy is not unbounded, however. He assigns structuralist analyses a role that mediates between objective and subjective approaches (Ricoeur, 1971:558). Therein Ricoeur himself provides a clue about how ethnomethodology happens to exhibit similarities to structuralism, particularly such versions as Barthes's.

Perhaps both ethnomethodology and literary structuralism respond, consciously or not, to parallel developments in their respective fields. Perhaps, specifically, ethnomethodology emerged as a mediating force between quantitative sociology, which pays little attention to everyday life and social forms as such, and interpretive sociologies, which often focus on everyday life but attend more to its subjective features than to its fundamental forms. Garfinkel's (1952) abortive attempt to synthesize Parsons's sociology of forms with Schutz's phenomenology of the everyday world implies an interest in such mediation.[7] Perhaps, too, literary structuralism came to prominence as a mediating force between psychological criticism, which disattends forms in favor of authors' intentions and techniques, and phenomenological criticism, which focuses on textual sense and meanings. Structuralism, as we saw earlier, explicitly opposes phenomenology. Ethnomethodology implicitly opposes it. Despite his express indebtedness to phenomenologists like Schutz and Gurwitsch, Garfinkel in fact stretched the phenomenological umbrella so as to include "neo-Kantians" like Freud and Parsons (1952:110). Thereby he distorted "phenomenology" to the point of implying opposition to Husserlian phenomenology left to its own wiles. Perhaps, in short, reactions against phenomenology account for the similarities between structuralism and ethnomethodology. In the meantime sociologists more interested in everyday life than in the intellectual foundations of ethnomethodology have ethnomethodologists to thank for hinting at the aptness of "text" as a metaphor for everyday life.[8]

Notes

1. Ethnomethodologists are not, of course, all of one kind. Those who most interest me here remain discernibly aligned with Garfinkel's program regardless of how they label themselves. It strikes me that among those ethnomethodologists three groupings are at work. Those of a more theoretical bent with concerns lying close to the fabric of traditional sociology include Alan F. Blum, Jack Douglas, Peter McHugh, John O'Neill, Roy Turner, and (to an extent) Jeff Coulter. Those more inclined toward applying Garfinkel's methodology or using his terminology include Egon Bittner, Aaron V. Cicourel, Hugh Mehan and Houston Wood, D. Lawrence Wieder, and Don Zimmerman. Finally, those who have elaborated Garfinkel's methodology, mostly in linguistic directions, include Melvin Pollner, Harvey Sacks, Emmanuel Schegloff, and David Sudnow.

2. Culler (1975) provides an excellent overview of literary structuralism.

3. I follow Barthes in sometimes capitalizing *text*. The capitalized term refers to the fundamental form of written discourse; the uncapitalized version refers to any particular instance(s) of that form.

4. Douglas (1970:33-34) contrasts situational ethnomethodologists, who focus on contextual meanings and social interaction, with linguistic ethnomethodologists, who focus on conversation.

5. Derrida's (1973:147) position is similar. Derrida labels human consciousness as a "determination" or "effect" rather than as a potent "presence." Further, he says structuralism cannot contribute to a history of the imagination and human affect (Derrida, 1978:4).

6. An ethnomethodological reader of this chapter replies, however, that little or nothing about meaning can be discerned

without reference to the sequential position of utterances or other actions in interaction.

7. The attempt was abortive inasmuch as Parsons's and Schutz's ideas are incompatible; see Filmer (1972:218-219); Grathoff (1978).

8. Aaron Cicourel (1975) moves in the direction I have advocated here. Cicourel, however, is explicitly concerned with the differences between *written* texts in social life (such as organizational documents, with all their effects on the careers of juvenile offenders, school pupils, and other subjects of bureaucracies) and oral discourse.

References

ATKINSON, J. MAXWELL
    1979   "Sequencing and Shared Attentiveness to Court Proceedings." In George Psathas (Ed.), *Everyday Language: Studies in Ethnomethodology.* New York: Irvington.

ATTEWELL, PAUL
    1974   "Ethnomethodology Since Garfinkel." *Theory and Society* 1(Winter):179-210.

BARTHES, ROLAND
    1974   *S/Z.* (Translated by Richard Miller.) New York: Hill and Wang.
    1977a *Image-Music-Text.* (Translated by Stephen Heath.) New York: Hill and Wang.
    1977b *Roland Barthes.* (Translated by Richard Howard.) New York: Hill and Wang.

BITTNER, EGON
    1973   "Objectivity and Realism in Sociology." In George Psathas (Ed.), *Phenomenological Sociology.* New York: Wiley.

BLOOM, HAROLD
    1975a *Kabbalah and Criticism.* New York: Seabury.
    1975b *A Map of Misreading.* New York: Oxford University Press.

BLUM, ALAN F.
    1974a "Positive Thinking." *Theory and Society* 1(Fall): 245-269.

1974b *Theorizing.* London: Heinemann Educational Books.

BOOTH, WAYNE C.

1961   *The Rhetoric of Fiction.* Chicago: University of Chicago Press.

BURKE, KENNETH

1966   *Language as Symbolic Action: Essays on Life, Literature, and Method.* Berkeley: University of California Press.

CASSIRER, ERNST

1962   *An Essay on Man: An Introduction to a Philosophy of Human Culture.* New Haven, Conn.: Yale University Press.

CICOUREL, AARON V.

1973   *Cognitive Sociology: Language and Meaning in Social Interaction.* New York: Penguin Books.

1975   "Discourse and Text: Cognitive and Linguistic Processes in Studies of Social Structure." *Versus* 12:33-83.

COLLINS, RANDALL

1975   *Conflict Sociology: Toward an Explanatory Science.* New York: Academic Press.

COSER, LEWIS A.

1975   "Presidential Address: Two Methods in Search of a Substance." *American Sociological Review* 40:691-700.

CULLER, JONATHAN

1975   *Structuralist Poetics: Structuralism, Linguistics, and the Study of Literature.* Ithaca, N.Y.: Cornell University Press.

DALLMAYR, FRED R., AND MCCARTHY, THOMAS A.

1977   *Understanding and Social Inquiry.* Notre Dame, Ind.: University of Notre Dame Press.

DERRIDA, JACQUES

1973   *Speech and Phenomena—and Other Essays on Husserl's Theory of Signs.* (Translated by David B. Allison.) Evanston, Ill.: Northwestern University Press.

1978   *Writing and Difference.* (Translated by Alan Bass.) Chicago: University of Chicago Press.

DOUGLAS, JACK D.

1970   "Understanding Everyday Life." In Jack D. Douglas (Ed.), *Understanding Everyday Life.* Chicago: Aldine.

DREITZEL, PETER
  1970   "Introduction: Patterns of Communicative Behavior."
         In Peter Dreitzel (Ed.), *Recent Sociology No. 2: Patterns of Communicative Behavior*. New York: Macmillan.
DUNCAN, HUGH DALZIEL
  1968   *Symbols in Society*. New York: Oxford University Press.
EMPSON, WILLIAM
  1953   *Seven Types of Ambiguity*. London: Chatto & Windus.
FILMER, PAUL
  1972   "On Harold Garfinkel's Ethnomethodology." In Paul Filmer and others, *New Directions in Sociological Theory*. London: Collier-Macmillan.
GARFINKEL, HAROLD
  1952   "The Perception of the Other: A Study in Social Order." Unpublished doctoral dissertation, Harvard University.
  1967   *Studies in Ethnomethodology*. Englewood Cliffs, N.J.: Prentice-Hall.
GARFINKEL, HAROLD, AND SACKS, HARVEY
  1970   "On Formal Structures of Practical Actions." In John C. McKinney and Edward A. Tiryakian (Eds.), *Theoretical Sociology*. New York: Appleton-Century-Crofts/ Meredith Corporation.
GRATHOFF, RICHARD (ED.)
  1978   *The Theory of Social Action: The Correspondence of Alfred Schutz and Talcott Parsons*. Bloomington: Indiana University Press.
HEAP, JAMES L.
  1976   "Reconceiving the Social." *Canadian Review of Sociology and Anthropology* 13:271–281.
  1980   "Description in Ethnomethodology." *Human Studies* 3:87–106.
HEAP, JAMES L., AND ROTH, PHILLIP A.
  1978   "On Phenomenological Sociology." In Alan Wells (Ed.), *Contemporary Sociological Theories*. Santa Monica, Calif.: Goodyear.
HERITAGE, J. C., AND WATSON, D. R.
  1979   "Formulations as Conversational Objects." In George

Psathas (Ed.), *Everyday Language: Studies in Ethno-methodology*. New York: Irvington.

HILL, RICHARD J., AND CRITTENDEN, KATHLEEN S. (EDS.)
1968   *Proceedings of the Purdue Symposium on Ethnometh-odology*. Lafayette, Ind.: Institute for the Study of Social Change, Purdue University.

HIRSCH, E. D., JR.
1978   *The Aims of Interpretation*. Chicago: University of Chicago Press.

ISER, WOLFGANG
1974   *The Implied Reader: Patterns of Communication in Prose Fiction from Bunyan to Beckett*. Baltimore: Johns Hopkins University Press.
1978   *The Act of Reading: A Theory of Aesthetic Response*. Baltimore: Johns Hopkins University Press.

JOHNSON, DOYLE PAUL
1981   *Sociological Theory: Classical Founders and Contemporary Perspectives*. New York: Wiley.

LEITER, KENNETH
1980   *A Primer on Ethnomethodology*. New York: Oxford University Press.

LEMERT, CHARLES C.
1979   "De-Centered Analysis." *Theory and Society* 7:289–306.

MCHUGH, PETER
1968   *Defining the Situation: The Organization of Meaning in Social Interaction*. Indianapolis: Bobbs-Merrill.

MAYRL, WILLIAM W.
1977   "Ethnomethodology: Sociology Without Society?" In Fred R. Dallmayr and Thomas A. McCarthy (Eds.), *Understanding and Social Inquiry*. Notre Dame, Ind. University of Notre Dame Press.

MEHAN, HUGH, AND WOOD, HOUSTON
1975a   "The Morality of Ethnomethodology." *Theory and Society* 2:509–530.
1975b   *The Reality of Ethnomethodology*. New York: Wiley-Interscience.

MORRIS, MONICA
1977   *An Excursion into Creative Sociology*. New York: Columbia University Press.

NORRIS, CHRISTOPHER
  1980 "Derrida at Yale: The 'Deconstructive Moment' in Modernist Poetics." *Philosophy and Literature* 4:242–256.
O'NEILL, JOHN
  1972 *Sociology as a Skin Trade: Essays Towards a Reflexive Sociology.* New York: Harper & Row.
PETTIT, PHILIP
  1977 *The Concept of Structuralism.* Berkeley: University of California Press.
POLLNER, MELVIN
  1974 "Sociological and Common-Sense Models of the Labeling Process." In Roy Turner (Ed.), *Ethnomethodology.* New York: Penguin Books.
  1979 "Explicative Transactions: Making and Managing Meaning in Traffic Court." In George Psathas (Ed.), *Everyday Language: Studies in Ethnomethodology.* New York: Irvington.
RICOEUR, PAUL
  1971 "The Model of the Text: Meaningful Action Considered as a Text." *Social Research* 38(Autumn):529–562.
  1976 *Interpretation Theory: Discourse and the Surplus of Meaning.* Fort Worth: Texas Christian University Press.
  1977 *The Rule of Metaphor: Multi-disciplinary Studies of the Creation of Meaning in Language.* (Translated by Robert Czerny, Kathleen McLaughlin, and John Costello, S.J.) Toronto: University of Toronto Press.
  1979 *Main Trends in Philosophy.* New York: Holmes and Meier.
SACKS, SHELDON
  1967 *Fiction and the Shape of Belief: A Study of Henry Fielding with Glances at Swift, Johnson, and Richardson.* Berkeley: University of California Press.
SCHEGLOFF, EMMANUEL, AND SACKS, HARVEY
  1974 "Opening Up Closings." In Roy Turner (Ed.), *Ethnomethodology.* New York: Penguin Books.
SPURLING, LAURIE
  1977 *Phenomenology and the Social World: The Philosophy of Merleau-Ponty and Its Relation to the Social Sciences.* Boston: Routledge & Kegan Paul.

TURNER, JONATHAN
  1974   *The Structure of Sociological Theory*. Homewood, Ill.: Dorsey.
WILSON, THOMAS P.
  1970   "Normative and Interpretive Paradigms in Sociology." In Jack D. Douglas (Ed.), *Understanding Everyday Life*. Chicago: Aldine.
ZIMMERMAN, DON H.
  1979   "Ethnomethodology." In Scott G. McNall (Ed.), *Theoretical Perspectives in Sociology*. New York: St. Martin's.

*Art is a language. Art objects are therefore decipherable into
more or less elaborated and restricted codes. These codes
change with the relative solidarity of the community in which
they are produced. The more solidary the group, the more
restricted the code; the less solidary the community, the more
elaborated the artistic codes they produce. In general, realism
is a more elaborated code and abstraction a more restricted
code, and accordingly more solidary communities should produce more abstract art and less solidary groups should produce
more realistic art. This theoretical relationship between artistic
codes and group solidarity is captured in the idea of a
"semantic equation" and is applied to changes in the styles
of New York art from the 1940s through the mid 1980s.*

%7%

THE SEMANTIC EQUATION: A THEORY OF THE SOCIAL ORIGINS OF ART STYLES

Albert Bergesen

UNIVERSITY OF ARIZONA

If we define language as a symbol system that transmits information, then it is obviously not limited to speech and verbal behavior. Art, music, poetry, literature, drama, film, and dance also
transmit meaning and communicate. Language, argued Saussure, is
not a content but a form, a structure, and these expressive arts
represent a structuring of various elements: body movements in
dance; sounds in music; plots, characters, and themes in literature;
images, sounds, and words in poetry; and color, shape, and line in
painting. The visual structure of art is no less a language than the

I would like to thank Howard S. Becker, Randall Collins, Paul DiMag-
gio, Otis Dudley Duncan, Andrew M. Greeley, Robert L. Heilbroner, Flo
Hout, Michael Hout, Stanley Lieberson, and Harrison White for helpful comments on an earlier version of this chapter.

187

verbal structure of speech. Both involve the systematic organization of basic elements, whether verbal or visual, and both carry and communicate social information.

When an individual paints or sculpts, that activity expresses personal intent. But artists do not work entirely alone; they are part of a larger social community composed of other artists and an elaborate support structure of dealers, galleries, museums, patrons, and art critics (Becker, 1982). The community aspect of artistic production is also expressed in the very structure of the art. Every work of art reflects the input and nuances of its immediate author; but it also has elements common to a number of artists, which we call style. Art styles such as impressionism, abstract expressionism, minimalism, pop art, neorealism, or neoexpressionism represent a set of conventions used by a social community of artists. These social conventions, or distinctive ways of applying and structuring paint and image—say, the expressive splashing and gestural smearing of pigment that define the style called abstract expressionism—can be viewed as an element of a group's shared assumptions and collective expectations. To the extent that the elements of a common style represent what a number of individual artists share, the style itself can be considered a unique group product. From a Durkheimian point of view, styles of art are the property of the group, not the individual, as they are only what all members share, not what is unique to each artist. For art communities defined by their distinctive style, the common stylistic element represents the collective reality of the group. Just as norms or common moral sentiment unifies other groups, so does, say, the gestural smearing and splashing of paint unify the collectivity defined as abstract expressionism. Styles of art represent cultural communities where the use or non-use of the style defines membership and group boundaries.

Style, as a kind of Durkheimian representation of the group as a whole, is transformed with changes in the group's solidarity. The more the collectivity is constituted as a corporate actor, having a life of its own, with its own collective purposes above and beyond those of its individual members, the more the style will be well defined and clearly articulated. In more corporate communities, the elements of style are also internalized as the personal style of member artists, and there is greater moral pressure to use these stylistic devices as signs of group membership. For example, with the growth and acceptance of the abstract style of the New York school, artists who wished to be considered avant-garde (one of the collective purposes of the New York school) felt pressure to express themselves using the normative style of an ever more minimal and sparse abstraction. When the sense of centrality and importance of the New York school began to decline in the late 1970s and early 1980s, however, artists felt freer to express themselves in other styles.

This pattern or structure of art, the art's style, can be broken down into vocabulary and syntax. *Vocabulary* comprises the basic building blocks of paint and color; materials such as wood, bronze, clay, plaster, and plastic; and shapes and forms that the artist can arrange. The rules for arranging this vocabulary constitute the artistic *syntax* and include, for example, rules of perspective, principles of compatible and incompatible colors, and techniques of drawing, painting, or sculpting—in short, all the things one would learn in art school. Any particular style, then, represents the organization of vocabulary and syntax into an identifiable structure. Art is a language, and to the extent that we can decode verbal behavior, we should also be able to identify codes in the visual structure of painting and sculpture.

The sociolinguist Basil Bernstein (1975) has identified two kinds of linguistic codes, elaborated and restricted, that will provide a starting point for a theoretical discussion of the social origin of artistic styles. "A restricted code will arise where the form of the social relation is based on closely shared identifications, upon an extensive range of shared expectations, upon a range of common assumptions. Thus a restricted code emerges where the culture or subculture raises the 'we' above the 'I.' . . . The use of a restricted code creates social solidarity at the cost of verbal elaboration of individual experience. The type of social solidarity realized through a restricted code points toward mechanical solidarity, whereas the type of solidarity realized through elaborated codes points toward organic solidarity. The form of communication reinforces the form of the social relation" (p. 147).

A restricted code uses a smaller vocabulary pool and a narrower and less flexible range of syntactical alternatives. Symbols and images also tend to be more collective and general, rather than personal and particular. It is a code that assumes the relevant others know what is being talked about, which results in the use of in-group slang and referents not immediately intelligible to outsiders. Elaborated codes are just the opposite, using a larger vocabulary and a more supple syntax along with more precisely articulated images and particularistic referents. Bernstein associated this kind of code with the middle classes, characterized by frequent contact between people of different occupations, in contrast to the close-knit working-class neighborhoods where he found the restricted code. Here people shared the same workplace, friends, and neighbors, creating little need for a very explicit mode of communication, since everyone shared the same assumptions and could understand one another with a language of agreed-on in-group terminology. Restricted codes are more implicit, elaborated codes more explicit and, as such, less context-dependent.

With these ideas as a starting point, I would like to expand and generalize Bernstein's initial insight. First, these codes are not limited to particular social classes. The more general principle is the linkage between the solidarity, or corporateness, of the group and the pattern of language that develops. In effect, if the solidarity of Bernstein's working-class neighborhoods were to decline, I would expect their codes of speech to become more elaborated, and if middle-class groups were to share more assumptions, their codes should become more restricted. The general proposition, then, is that solidary groups or communities with high degrees of shared assumptions produce more restricted codes, and when that solidarity declines, the code shifts and becomes more elaborated. Second, the idea of the code is general. It is not limited to speech. Following the earlier assumption that various expressive arts communicate and that they can be considered kinds of languages, it is possible to identify elaborated or restricted codes in artistic as well as verbal communications. Therefore, variations in the solidarity of communities should produce variations in their artistic codes, and since codes are styles, variations in group solidarity should produce variations in styles of art.

This relation between artistic codes and the community in which they appear is complex. More restricted codes are a form of ritual, in that they carry social information and as such act to periodically reaffirm collective sentiments (Douglas, 1970; Bergesen, forthcoming). One is less able to signal personal intent using a set of general symbols and a limited pool of vocabulary and syntax. What is communicated, though, are the common assumptions of the group, things everyone knows and recognizes, and such a communication acts to reinforce group culture.

Artistic Codes as Visual Rituals

Painting or sculpture can be considered a kind of visual ritual whose performance is encoded in the arrangement of physical and spatial materials. Verbal rituals constituting, if you will, "styles of speech" are performed every time someone talks since the code is the overarching plan of the verbal elements and appears whenever something is said. To speak at all is to speak in some sort of code, because language is, by definition, a structured—hence coded —set of sounds and symbols. The same holds true for the visual arts, except here the performance of the ritual is visual rather than verbal. Art is not the random arrangement of color and form but a particular combination of elements to create a particular visual structure. This visual structure encodes the fundamental social assumptions of the group in which it is produced.

Every time the art object is seen, therefore, the ritual is performed, for the apprehension of the style is the visual transmission of the art code. If speaking in code is a ritual reaffirmation of social order, so too is the "frozen speech" in paint or granite. One apprehends the substantive assumptions of the social order through the visual absorption of meanings encoded in art. Rituals are not limited to behavioral ceremonies, such as birthdays, weddings, or harvest festivals. Order and structure are also immanent within cultural objects, which are incarnations of information about their society and as such are constantly "performing rituals." To see a painting or sculpture is, in effect, to hear someone speak—as is often heard in the comment "That painting speaks to me." Every time art is seen, it speaks, and in this way the ritual is performed.

Abstract and Realistic Codes

In general, the more restricted the artistic style, the narrower the range of vocabulary and the more simple and rigid the syntactical rules. For example, consider color as a basic unit of artistic vocabulary. A painting in a more restricted style would be composed of a narrower range of colors, with less variation in hue and intensity and less mixing of colors. In effect, all the options of using color would be restrained, limited, or restricted. Similarly, the application of paint, itself a syntactical device, would be simplified. Brushstrokes as a means of expressive communication would be reduced or removed, and in extreme cases the human hand could be eliminated altogether, being replaced by mechanical techniques such as silk-screening or by collage, in which found objects replace images drawn by the artist.

In general, the more vocabulary is reduced and the more syntax is simplified, the more abstract the art. This is almost of necessity. A narrower range of artistic materials makes it difficult to accurately replicate a realistic image. Thus abstract art tends to be a more restricted code, and conversely realism tends to be a more elaborated code. By definition, realism spells things out in full, and it therefore requires a full range of color, shape, form, line, and so on to realistically reproduce an image. It is simply difficult to paint anything very realistically with just a few abstract gestures.

Linguistically, realism contains more of its meaning within its own internal structure than does abstraction, which is a more context-dependent form of communication. For instance, a realist painting of a bowl of fruit is just what it appears to be, as opposed to, say, an abstract expressionist painting, which in principle could be mistaken for spilled paint or a child's scribbles. Without mastering the skills of drawing and painting—that is, without utilizing the vocabulary and syntax of art—one could not paint a realist portrait or seascape. But one could drip paint on a canvas à la Jackson Pollock or dabble pigment in expressive gestures like any other abstract expressionist. I am not speaking of esthetic quality but simply of whether some paint is defined as art or as a mistake or child's play. As a general rule, the more minimal and abstract the painting, the more alternative interpretations become possible. Is a drip of paint a drip of paint or art? This may seem trivial, but it must be remembered that much of the minimal and conceptual art of the 1960s involved art objects that were stacks of railroad ties, mounds of dirt, pieces of cloth, piles of scrap metal, or assorted found objects stacked, piled, or flung on museum floors. These art objects readily lent themselves to being defined as something other than art, if they were not encased in supplemental art theorizing that gave them their distinctly artistic significance. The important theoretical point is that in and of itself a drip of paint cannot signify its appropriate classification. It does not contain enough internal meaning to denote its status, as it does not employ enough variation in vocabulary and syntax to internally generate context-free meaning the way, say, the painted vase of flowers can. At least that is a painting. Whether it is good or bad is a moral evaluation, which is secondary to its factual classification as art.

This importance of context, not only for interpreting art but, more fundamentally, for the very definition of art, suggests a theoretical connection between restricted codes and more solidary groups. Art, like all languages, not only appears in a social context but is a part of that very context. A restricted code is filled in and decoded by the commonly held assumptions of the group. More important, an intelligible restricted code, in speech or art, could not appear without assumptions provided by the broader group context.

There is a reciprocal relation between shared assumptions and restricted communication. More abstract art appears in communities with higher levels of shared assumptions, but these restricted artistic codes, in turn, function to reaffirm those shared assumptions. When a restricted code is employed, it automatically brings to life the community's shared culture, as those shared assumptions must be activated to understand highly coded communications. In a sense the source of meaning of a restricted code is divided between what is actually said and what people already know. The complete significance of abstract art is not contained solely in the abstract gestures themselves, as they are too minimal. The other half of the painting's meaning comes from the interpretive context in which it is apprehended. For Bernstein's codes of speech, the shared assumptions resided in neighborhood working-class culture. In modern art the shared assumptions of the art world are articulated by the various theories and critical interpretations of abstraction provided by art critics and by the artists themselves. From the point of view of the art community, the presence of critics reflects a high level of shared assumptions. The social role of critic or art theorist is an emergent property of well-defined art movements or communities. For example, the more post-1945 modern art assumed a corporate form, with its own purposes and goals, the more emergent structural apparatus appeared that articulated these collective sentiments. This structural apparatus takes the forms of social roles such as critic; formal organizations such as art schools, galleries, and museums, along with other institutions such as art journals; and special sections of more general newspapers and magazines devoted to new developments in art—any social arrangement, formal or informal, through which the collective purposes of the art movement can be articulated.

The first clear manifestation of this in post-1945 New York art were the famous critics Clement Greenberg and Harold Rosenberg, whose interpretations of the new American abstraction were considered very important. Later, with conceptual art, the roles of critic and artist merged, and the artist became his or her own interpreter, both producing an art object and explaining its meaning. The importance of these interpretations for understanding art also increased. Although the Greenberg/Rosenberg criticism was admired and was considered part of the overall art world, the explanations of the conceptualists were even more vital because without them it was not clear at all that their art objects were art. With increasing abstraction there is a growing separation of the artist from the actual construction of the art object, either because the artist puts less and less into the object—the deobjectivization and minimalization aspect of an ever-increasing abstraction—or because the use of found objects limits the artist's input to saying, "This is art and here is why." With found objects the artistic significance is not derived from the internal syntax of the object's raw materials, since they were not created by the artist. Found objects, without context, could be legitimately interpreted in terms of their original nonart function, making their art-theoretical context imperative for their proper classification as art. With found objects the art communication comes less from the art object than from what is said or assumed about it. In effect, the art object itself no longer speaks. What is talking is the artist's verbal explanation, or, more technically, the provision of meaning that should have been supplied by the internal semantic structure of the art object in the first place. The realist painting of a vase of flowers says, without any interpretation, "I am a painting of a vase of flowers." But the conceptual artist's block of melting ice, for example, might be construed as saying all sorts of things, including "I am just a block of melting ice." It is only with the supplemental information, the theorizing of the artist, that this block of ice is understood, first, as art, and, second, as a philosophical exploration of time and space or of the transformation of reality into different forms. Then the ice becomes an artistic statement. Note that the ice cannot define itself as art without context, whereas the realist painting of flowers can; that, in this somewhat crude example, is the heart of the semantic difference between realism and abstraction as forms of communication.

The Semantic Equation

This relation between supplemental information (theorizing, interpreting) and the restrictedness of the style can be theoretically represented as an equation, the semantic equation. On the right-hand side of the equation is the art object itself, on the left-hand side the supplemental information. Both sides contribute to the intelligibility of a piece of art. To attain intelligibility, which I assume is a constant, a balance is required between the extensiveness of the artistic vocabulary and syntax and the extensiveness of the supplemental information provided by the artists themselves or by the critics and theorists of the larger community. When the art object becomes more abstract and minimal, supplemental theorizing and critical interpretation within the art community will increase. When the art becomes more realistic and elaborated, theorizing and supplemental information will decline. The art communication will be more explicit and hence less context-dependent when it is more realistic, and more implicit and context-dependent when it is more abstract.

This relation can be visualized as a kind of semantic teeter-totter, with the extensiveness of the art object's vocabulary and syntax on the right-hand side and the extensiveness of the supplemental information on the left-hand side. When vocabulary and syntax go down (more minimal and abstract art), theorizing and interpretation (supplemental information) go up, and vice versa. Styles of art and the role of criticism go hand in hand. They are both part of the overall social organization of art as a means of communication. The shift from realism to abstraction, and from some abstraction to more abstraction, is accompanied by ever more explanations and extra-art information. That is the principle of the semantic equation.

An Example: Changing Styles of the New York School

To better convey the operation of the semantic equation, I turn to a brief consideration of developments in post-1945 modern art produced in New York.[1] Here we have a community of artists, gallery owners, museums, art critics, and an intelligent comsuming art public. In short, all the social roles required to examine the semantic principles just outlined are present in a concrete community whose solidarity has also varied between the mid 1940s and mid 1980s.

We will see how the emergence of a community of artists in New York provided sufficient social conditions to generate an abstract form of artistic communication, abstract expressionism, and its supplemental art theory and criticism. Then, as the popularity of New York art grew, and the assumptions of abstract art became better known, the community became better defined, gaining a corporate identity as the "New York school." Following the principles of the semantic equation, the art became increasingly abstract with the minimalism of the 1960s, until in conceptual art it reached a point where it was so restricted that the art object itself virtually disappeared. Here the supplemental meaning, the artist's explanation of what his or her art meant, carried most of the communicative burden. Then, with a weakening of the centrality of the New York art world in the later 1970s and 1980s, there was a move toward more realistic styles in the form of photorealism and neoexpressionism. With this came a decline in the importance of art criticism and theory, as these more elaborated realistic codes were more self-contained forms of communication and therefore required less supplemental information.

The New York school of the 1940s and 1950s was a close-knit community.

> Given the concentration of artists, it was reasonable for a New York school to have emerged. . . . Artists of an avant-garde disposition who met fortui-

tously more often than not developed a loose network
of acquaintances. This in time led to the development
of a "scene," which centered on a number of semi-
public and public meeting places. Stimulating the
growth of an artists' "ghetto," as Motherwell called
it, was "the enormous pressure of the social world
around us," as Dzubus recollected. "You had a feeling . . . of you and your friends against everyone else
on the outside" [said Robert Motherwell]. They
shared a more or less common sensibility, an awareness of what was dead and alive in art. Therefore,
they provided the primary audience for each other's
work. They also gathered frequently because of a simple desire to socialize; every memoir of the period
dwells nostalgically on the frequent parties and shared
meals—the fun, spirit, and communion. Furthermore,
there was a collective need for assurance, a need to
talk out one's insecurities with one's peers [Sandler,
1978:29].

This emerging social community had many of the same
properties as Basil Bernstein's working-class neighborhoods, where
he found a restricted code in speech patterns: Artists lived in the
same neighborhoods, knew one another on a face-to-face basis,
exhibited in the same galleries, and socialized at common taverns
and restaurants.

Vanguard artists in New York organized themselves with relative ease because most lived in the
same neighborhood in Manhattan: a low-rent area
downtown in and around a belt between Eighth and
Twelfth Streets on the south and north, and First and
Sixth Avenues on the east and west. Indeed the section came to be called Tenth Street, since the stretch
of that street between Third and Fourth Avenues was
roughly the center. On that one city block alone in
middle and late fifties young artists organized cooperative galleries, and most were located on the same
block: the Tangier, Camino, Brata, Area, and March
galleries. Not only did significant numbers of artists
live, work, and show in the vicinity of East Tenth

>Street, but within easy walking distance were to be
>found the primary gathering places: The Cedar Street
>Tavern and the Club; as well as the art schools that
>fostered modernism: Hofmann's school, Amedee
>Ozenfant's school, the Subjects of the Artist School,
>and Department of Art Education of New York Uni-
>versity, and Stanley William Hayter's Atelier 17
>[Sandler, 1978:30].

It was a small world. As the art patron Robert Scull commented,
"Abstract expressionism was a little club down on Tenth Street.
There were never more than 100 people in on it" (quoted in
Wolfe, 1976:68). To the extent, then, that the New York art
world represented a close-knit community, it had the potential to
produce an abstract artistic code.

The first style to emerge from this community of artists was
abstract expressionism, which involved the application of paint in
expressive gestures—the pigment appears to be slapped, splashed,
smeared, or dripped on the canvas. "If the term *abstract expressionist* means anything verifiable, it means painterliness: loose,
rapid handling, or the look of it; masses that blot and fuse instead
of shapes that stay distinct; large, conspicuous rhythms; broken
color; uneven saturations or densities of paint; exhibited brush,
knife, finger, or rag marks" (Greenberg, 1969:361). For the most
renowed abstract expressionist, Jackson Pollock, this was literally
true—he would stand over his canvas, dip a stick into a can of
paint, and let it drip onto the canvas below. Abstract expressionism is associated with the work of Pollock, Franz Kline, Willem
de Kooning, Hans Hoffman, Clyfford Still, and others.

What makes this style of painting a restricted code? First,
any kind of abstraction is a shorthand way of saying something.
It may reflect the essence of an issue, but it is nonetheless an outline, blueprint, or symbolization of something that could, in principle, be spelled out in a much more elaborated fashion. The point
is clearly made in "The American Action Painters," a famous 1952
article by the New York art critic Harold Rosenberg, who was trying to define what was unique about the gestural abstraction that
was emerging in New York: "In this gesturing with materials the
esthetic, too, has been subordinated. Form, color, composition,
drawing, are auxiliaries, any one of which—or practically all . . .
can be dispensed with" (Rosenberg, 1969:343).

In this style the range of artistic vocabulary and syntax is reduced. Form, color, composition, drawing, and so forth are things that can be "dispensed with." Abstract art is also a kind of code in that its meaning is not entirely apparent on the surface of the painting. This, of course, is somewhat true of all art, abstract or realist. By definition, though, abstraction is not the thing itself, whatever the thing is, and so it requires additional information not present within the painting to fill out its meaning.

When art becomes ever more abstract, there *has* to be an increase in additional information that will classify and define these painterly gestures, and with the rise of abstract expressionism came the growing importance of art critics whose theories provided the additional information required by the balance assumption of the semantic equation.

> Contributing to the organization of a New York school community were art critics Greenberg, Hess, and Harold Rosenberg, and art historian Schapiro, all of whom made a practice of visiting studios and bringing together kindred artists. Schapiro's frequent lectures were attended by nearly all vanguard artists. His role as mentor in the development of two generations of the New York school was nothing short of inspirational. . . . Greenberg had been a discoverer of Pollock and an early champion of abstract expressionism. His art criticism in the *Nation* and *Partisan Review* was more closely read and respected than that of any other critic. Hess was executive director of *ARTnews,* then America's leading art magazine, and was largely responsible for turning it into the "family journal" of the New York school in general, and in particular, of de Kooning and his circle downtown. Rosenberg rarely wrote about individual artists, but his general essays, notably "The American Action Painters," published in 1952, focused attention on abstract expressionism and provoked interest in the controversy about its esthetic premises [Sandler, 1978:35-36].

It was no accident, then, that art critics and art theory simultaneously grew in importance with the emergence of abstract expressionism. Both sides of the semantic equation, artistic codes (abstract painting) and supplemental information (theory and criticism), were part of the overall semantic machinery of the New York art world. You cannot have abstraction without supplemental information, and criticism will seem important only when there is abstract art that is context-dependent and requires decoding. The explanations of modern art provided by Greenberg and Rosenberg were as fundamental a part of the communicative ability of abstract art as the dabs of pigment, and these art theorists understood their role perfectly. Said Harold Rosenberg: "A contemporary painting or sculpture is a species of centaur—half art materials, half words. The words are the vital, energetic element, capable, among other things, of transforming any materials (epoxy, light beams, string, rocks, earth) into art materials. It is its verbal substance that establishes the visual tradition in which a particular work is to be seen—that places a Newman in the perspective of abstract expressionism rather than of Bauhaus design or mathematical abstraction" (1973:151).

Rosenberg is implicitly speaking of the semantic equation. The "half art materials" is the right-hand side of the equation, the communicative act itself, the vocabulary and syntax of the art object; the "half words" is the left-hand side, the supplemental information. Rosenberg further suggests: "Of itself, the eye is incapable of bringing into the intellectual system that today distinguishes between objects that are art and those that are not. Given its primitive function of discriminating among objects in shopping centers and on highways, the eye will recognize a Noland as a fabric design, a Judd as a stack of metal bins—until the eye's outrageous philistinism has been subdued by the drown of formulas concerning breakthroughs in color, space, and even optical perception (this, too, unseen by the eye, of course). *It is scarcely an exaggeration to say that paintings are today apprehended with the ears*" (1973:153; emphasis mine).

The critic Hilton Kramer makes a similar point in a casual observation, "Frankly these days, without a theory to go with it, I can't see a painting" (quoted in Wolfe, 1976:4). During a period of abstract styles the eye alone cannot tell art from nonart because minimal gestures do not provide enough meaning in and of themselves, and so interpretive explanations, Kramer's "theory," are necessary. When realism predominates, the eye can tell what is supposed to be art and what is supposed to be a stack of bins or a fabric design. Explanatory art theory is less necessary because realism more explicitly spells out its assumptions within its internal structure and hence is less context-dependent. "Realism does not lack its partisans, but it does rather conspicuously lack a persuasive theory. And given the nature of our intellectual commerce with works of art, to lack a persuasive theory is to lack something crucial—the means by which our experience of individual works is joined to our understanding of the values they signify" (Kramer, quoted in Wolfe, 1976:4).

What started out in the 1940s and 1950s as a small community of avant-garde artists became, in the 1960s, a highly publicized and well-organized art movement. With New York as the center, the abstract art styles that began with abstract expressionism became an intersubjective sign system that constituted a cultural community, the "New York school," which extended beyond New York proper. "The term *New York art,* in fact, includes most of the significant American art produced in the past three decades. The school of Paris was an umbrella that covered Russia as well as Spain. Regardless of where a work is made, unless it is primitive, anachronistic, or truly eccentric, it becomes associated with the center of its day, the city whose style it reflects. Thus we unblushingly include Morris Louis and Kenneth Noland, the acknowledged leaders of what Washington likes to call its school of color painters, because their exhibiting history, the sources of their art, and most cogent influence have all been located in New York" (Geldzahler, 1969:15).

Whereas the solidarity of the 1940s and 1950s came principally from face-to-face neighborhood contact, this was supplemented in the 1960s by extensive attention from the media and the art public, which was now voraciously consuming New York art. In effect, increases in solidarity and taken-for-granted assumptions can come from within or without the group. The community of artists sits within a larger social matrix, which can turn its attention on the subgroup and heighten its collective identity and more clearly articulate the primordial premises on which it is founded. This new social situation of publicity, media heroes, and increased art sales was quite a change from the earlier decades. "Publicity had not been an issue with artists in the forties and fifties. It might come as a bolt from the Philistine blue, as when *Life* made Jackson Pollock famous; but such events were rare enough to be freakish, not merely unusual. . . . Television and the press . . . were indifferent to what could still be called the avant-garde. 'Publicity' meant a notice in the *New York Times,* a paragraph or two long, followed eventually by an article in *ARTnews* which perhaps five thousand people would read. . . . But in the 1960s all that began to change, as the art world gradually shed its idealist premises and its sense of outsidership and began to turn into the Art Business. . . . The art world . . . during the sixties became more and more concerned with the desire for and pursuit of publicity" (Hughes, 1982:6–7).

Media coverage in the 1960s progressed, and some artists began to write sympathetic criticism of their fellows in *ARTnews* and *Art Digest.* The cause of the New York school was also being championed by the Museum of Modern Art, which in numerous shows at home and abroad helped build the school's growing reputation (Sandler, 1978:265).

Along with the external dramatization of art in the media, the internal closeness of the New York art world was also tightening, with dramatic growth in galleries and sales (Simpson, 1981). Some of these galleries were cooperatives, organized, financed, and managed by the artists themselves, further reflecting the internal connectedness and shared identity of the New York school. "The cooperatives also became focal points of communal activities, places where artists could always find fellow artists to talk to, and on the joint Friday night openings of all the galleries, where they could participate in festivities that resembled big block parties" (Sandler, 1978:38). Artists also recommended one another for inclusion in galleries, resulting in a more ingrown and self-reaffirming art community. "Dealers almost without exception consulted with their 'stable' of artists before taking on anyone new. This process of mutual selection was crucial to artists' success, since it concentrated in a few galleries—known to curators, critics, and collectors—the artists generally considered the best of their generation, who, whether they were or not, had an edge over their peers in less prestigious galleries" (Sandler, 1978:258).

In short, as the 1950s moved into the 1960s, the exposure and attention focused on modern art grew dramatically, and the

New York school became not only accepted but honored, revered, and even sacred. The New York school was becoming an institution.

The more the New York school became a publicized and well-defined social movement, with a center (New York), leading figures (Jackson Pollock, Franz Kline, Hans Hoffman, and others), and an identifiable style (abstract expressionism), the more modern art became MODERN ART, a Durkheimian collective entity with a life of its own independent of the painters who were its constituent members. As the New York art community became more and more a "scene," a place to be and be seen, rituals of collective reaffirmation increased. Events like "happenings," mixing art with personal expressiveness, flourished in lofts, which also became the center of numerous parties, exhibitions, and general gathering places for artists, would-be artists, and hangers-on. The social scene of the 1960s New York art world was one gigantic ritual of self-importance, where the common culture of what had begun as avant-garde art became more and more a ritual gesture signaling membership in the community rather than expressing unique personal feelings and private artistic visions. "Abstract expressionism was, and is, a certain style of art, and like other styles of art, having had its ups, it had its downs. Having produced art of major importance, it turned into a school, then into a manner, and finally into a set of mannerisms. Its leaders attracted imitators, many of them, and then some of these leaders took to imitating themselves" (Clement Greenberg, quoted in Sandler, 1978:283). Abstract expressionism became something like a social role that artists performed when they came to New York. The process here fits Berger and Luckmann's (1966) description of social realities that exist as externalities which individuals internalize and experience as themselves. When a young artist is asked to identify himself and says, "I am an abstract expressionist," or later a "pop" or "conceptual" artist, he has internalized one of the totemic emblems of the New York school, and he experiences himself as one of the school's different collective selves.

As the New York art world became a more clearly bounded community, the collective purposes of that collectivity assumed greater importance in the lives of member artists. The theoretical process here centers on the transformation of an aggregation of individuals into a more corporate group, what Swanson (1964) has called the construction of a corporate collectivity with its own set of purposes that exist independent of those of its constituent members.

During the earlier decades, the New York art world was more an aggregation of artists, but outside attention and growing inner connections transformed it into a more corporate movement, with its own purposes and goals. Modern art developed a conscious history, with critics and artists discussing the direction and needs of modern painting. Styles were viewed in temporal succession and as part of the unfolding of the larger purposes of the modern movement. The changes in painting seemed part of some organic process, as if modernity had its own logic that propelled it forward, making one stylistic innovation after another the natural unfolding of the inner destiny of modern art. "Minimal art was historically inevitable, given the twentieth-century artist's preoccupation with stripping painting and sculpture nude in order to fathom their essential properties. Conceptual art, minimal's footnote, was the final state in this century-long process" (Tomkins, 1981:153).

This social process also changed the status of artists, as they came to internalize the movement's collective goals and in turn became agents of its purposes. The direction of abstract art increasingly became the concern of individual artists who internalized its purposes into their own aspirational structures. William Barrett recalls encountering a young artist who saw herself as "advancing the medium" of modern art rather than expressing her own feelings. "She had just completed a large painting that was not without its merits, and we congratulated her on it. At which she only shook her head ruefully, stared somberly at her own canvas, and remarked, 'Yes, but does it do anything for painting?' Afterward, my friend and I agreed that her response seemed sadly presumptuous: instead of looking at the individual work in its own terms, she had become her own art historian and was speculating on her possible place in the line of history. She was not alone here; quite run-of-the-mill talents began to be preoccupied with advancing the medium" (Barrett, 1982:52). As the sculptor Carl Andre commented about the 1960s minimalist painter Frank Stella, "Stella is not interested in expression or sensitivity. He is interested in the necessities of painting. . . . His stripes are the paths of brush on canvas. These paths lead only into painting" (quoted in Sandler, 1978:309). In effect, Stella is more concerned with the goals and objectives of modern art ("the necessities of painting") than with his own personal feelings ("expression" or "sensitivity").

The growing fame and shared assumptions of New York art had a direct effect on the styles that were produced. While abstract expressionism became something of a ritualistic exercise for many, a more fundamental change involved artistic communications becoming more abstract and minimal. The style that had dominated since the mid 1940s was now, in the 1960s, giving way to a sparser, cleaner, and simpler means of expression. If abstract expressionism had been a blueprint of earlier art, the new minimalism was a blueprint of a blueprint.

Although abstract expressionism was something of a restricted code, there was room for an even greater reduction of vocabulary and simplification of syntax. "As gesture painting became the established vanguard manner of the fifties, growing numbers of painters turned against its spontaneity, ambiguity, and complexity and adopted instead preconception, relative clarity of design and color, and simplicity" (Sandler, 1978:174). This decline in spontaneity, ambiguity, and complexity meant that more standardized syntactical formats appeared, the emotional expressiveness of gestural abstraction giving way to a more rigid and simple style. "The stylistic common denominator of fifties art was the 'hot,' 'dirty,' painterly look, and of the sixties art, the 'cool,' 'antiseptic,' mechanistic look" (Sandler, 1978:292). This new minimalism included the hard-edge abstraction of Frank Stella, Ellsworth Kelly, Jean Polk Smith, and Myron Stout, the stained color-field abstraction of Morris Louis, Kenneth Noland, and Jules Olitski, and the unitary or minimal sculpture of Robert Morris or Donald Judd. The painting of representational objects (flags, targets, letters) by Jasper Johns, which became known as pop art through the work of Andy Warhol, Roy Lichtenstein, Claes Oldenberg, James Rosenquist, Jim Dine, and others, can also be considered part of the more restricted expression of the 1960s.

Where abstract expressionism had already reduced its structure to a two-dimensional plane that eliminated depth and perspective, this already limited style could be narrowed even further. First, the thickness of paint was reduced. Where abstract expressionists often applied paint in thick gobs, minimal paintings were much flatter. Second, minimalism involved a reduction in drawing and a shift to much more precise and tightly controlled outlines of shapes. Gone were the expressive stabs and splashes of the abstract expressionists; images were now controlled and formal. "They simplified their formats, often to two planes of a different color each of black and white, abutted in clear juxtapositions rather than interwoven in intricate patterns. As Kelly remarked, his purpose was to *divide* the whole space of a picture and not to arrange forms. The focus of hard-edge abstraction, then, was not on the relationship of shapes but on the color-shape as *Color-Shape*" (Sandler, 1978:218). Third, color became more important as the arrangement of shapes, lines, and forms declined. But even here the range of color was reduced. Minimal paintings are plain, stark, and constant in tone. This simplification of form can be seen in the silhouettes and stark color forms used by Ellsworth Kelly or the more formal quasi-geometric layout of controlled design and intense colors of Kenneth Noland. One of the most important minimalist painters was Frank Stella, whose code of communication was quite minimal and restricted. "Abstract painters also saw in Stella's pictures an alternative to fifties painterly painting, that is, they were nongestural; nonreferential in image, color, and space; nonrelational in design; and above all, nonillusionistic or flat. Stella so ruthlessly banished every traditional painterly variation, accent, and nuance that his pictorial space seemed ironed out to an unprecedented flatness" (Sandler, 1978:310).

This minimal use of traditional artistic skills was publicly acknowledged by artists like Stella, who "claimed that his own painting aimed for unoriginality. . . . What interested him most was a good idea rather than the process of painting; he could not see why it was bad for an artist who had a good idea just to paint it. So intent was Stella on presenting his pictorial concepts that he said he would welcome mechanical means to paint his pictures, that is, to translate ideas into painting. . . . He also said that his idea of a picture was one that was the same all over and the same in the next painting, one in which only paint was used and none of himself. Stella concluded by saying that he did not know why he was an artist, or even if he was one" (Sandler, 1978:284). This interest in "ideas" is theoretically linked to the simplification of style. The balance assumption of the semantic equation states that there must be a trade-off between the implicit, the extra-art information implied in an ever more solidary art community, and the explicit, the actual painting. When the implicit increases, the explicit decreases. As the style shortens, the other half of the equation contributes more and more to making the artistic communication intelligible. In effect, Stella's art became more and more about his "ideas" and less and less about what was actually painted; or, to put it another way, what he painted had meaning only in terms of his ideas, not as an isolated visual statement.

This growing emphasis on "ideas" anticipated the later development of conceptual art, in which the semantic equation became so one-sided that the art object virtually disappeared, and the burden for meaning fell almost entirely on the side of extra-art information supplied by the artist.

A more minimal artistic vocabulary can also be found in the images of 1960s pop art. This is not to say there is no esthetic judgment or ability in selecting and reproducing mass media images or combining them with other colors and forms in an overall design. There obviously is. But there is a reduction in the means for personal expression when ready-made images or found objects are used and when mechanical techniques such as Andy Warhol's silk-screening replace hand and brush.

Reproducing media images—Warhol's soup cans and Brillo boxes or Lichtenstein's cartoon figures—means that the artist uses shapes and forms already composed. The arrangement of color, shape, and form is to a large extent already completed by the time the pop artist encounters the image, and although his or her reproduction does provide some variation, the artist's personal input is more limited than if he or she were to compose the image in the first place.

Not only do restricted styles involve a reduction and simplification of the formal elements of language, but the vocabulary employs more collective referents. The "we" and "us" take priority over the "I" and "me" as restricted styles are generated in better-defined groups where the collective takes precedent over the individual. With the generalized symbols of a restricted style, the individual loses his or her ability to signal precise meanings. In the very appearance of pop art in the 1960s, the use of common commercial symbols implied more shared understandings than the private artistic gestures of the earlier abstract expressionists. Painting comic book figures, gas stations, Coke bottles, or soup cans activated the common knowledge of all group members, since they instantly recognized these symbols without further elaboration. "People could immediately see and grasp what Warhol was painting. They were used to soup cans, movie stars, and Coke bottles" (Hughes, 1982:8).

If I may digress for a moment, there is a similarity here to elaborated and restricted musical codes found in black American music. I have noted elsewhere (Bergesen, 1979) that spirituals represent more restricted musical codes, generated in the tightly bounded group life of slavery, and blues more elaborated codes, generated by the dispersion of group solidarity during the migration north in the early twentieth century. Spirituals contain more common symbols in the form of biblical references to Moses, Pharaoh, Hebrews, Israelites, and the Promised Land. As with the mass media images in pop art, common symbols are used that will be understood throughout the group. The blues are more personal, with a greater emphasis on "I" and "me," and involve more personal statements, much like the more personal gestural painting of the abstract expressionists. The theoretical point is general: More tightly formed, well defined, solidary groups with more extensive shared expectations generate more common symbols, whether Pharaoh or Coke bottles. Conversely, in more loosely formed, less well-defined groups with less shared sentiments, the codes of communication, whether art or music, will generate more personal statements, whether the personal gestures of abstract expressionism or the personal anguish of the blues singer.

The ultimate abstract style is the conceptual art of the 1970s. Restrictedness did not stop with minimalism. It continued to its logical conclusion: the virtual elimination of the art object altogether. If the art object is restricted out of existence, the semantic burden falls entirely on the left-hand side of the equation, on the artist's theories and conceptual ideas, creating a style, or code of communication, known as conceptual art.

> If you push the process of abstraction far enough, you end with the emptiness of minimal art; and with so little now left on the canvas, you have but to take a small step further and declare with conceptual art, that the idea alone will do for a work of art [Barrett, 1982:52].

By 1970 it was clear that a new type of art was emerging in the New York and European art worlds. Quickly labeled conceptual or idea art . . . works of idea art frequently did not actually exist as objects. Rather, they remained ideas; frequently, what did exist was only some kind of documentation referring to the concept [Battcock, 1973:1].

Conceptual art, a catch-all term, includes artistic events, activities, and objects of a cerebral, purposely nonvisual kind. Permeating this art form, which developed in the late 1960s, is the notion that the idea, event, or activity and [its] execution or embodiment . . . are more important than the finished product, which merely documents the idea, or event, or activity. Documentation may be in the form of printed statements, photographic or other mechanically reproduced records, or discrete objects. Such traditional esthetic considerations as style, taste, permanence, and craft may be jettisoned in favor of the presentation of primary information. *Conceptual art expresses what the artist had in mind rather than the result of making. The conceptual artist sees himself as part of an information system rather than as the creator of an object* or as one who instructs [Baigell, 1979:75; emphasis mine].

Conceptual art involves a variety of activities. Some artists have looked at aspects of disposable art. "*The Stock Exchange Transplant* (1970) involved the transportation of debris from the floor of the New York exchange to a new location; after several hours it was removed and thrown away again" (Battcock, 1973: 4–5). Other artists deal with questions of process and change, as in "Les Levine's *The Process of Elimination* (1969), an experiment with pieces of white plastic on a vacant Greenwich Village lot" (Battcock, 1973:5).

Finally there are conceptual art "pieces" which consist of statements only in which the movements of the mind alone constitute the "art" experience. The following, by Donald Burgy, may serve as an example:

"Name Idea No. 1

"Observe something as it changes in time. Record its names.

"Observe something as it changes in scale. Record its names.

"Observe something as it changes in hierarchy. Record its names.

"Observe something as it changes in differentiation. Record its names.

"Observe something as it changes under different emotions. Record its names.

"Observe something as it changes in different languages. Record its names.

"Observe something which never changes. Record its names.

"September, 1969" [Lucie-Smith, 1981:344-345].

In conceptual art the artistic communication is now solely the extra-art information, the conceptual artist's idea, for which the artist provides "documentation." This documentation—the debris on the floor of the New York Stock Exchange, Levine's white plastic sheets on vacant lots, or Burgy's verbal statement *Name Idea No. 1*—is not so much the traditional artistic vocabulary and syntax of the right-hand side of the semantic equation as part of the left-hand side, acting as the medium for realizing the conceptual artist's idea, or extra-art information. Here you do not study the art object—the painting or sculpture—for there is none. The visual reality of the art is now on the left-hand side of the equation, for the artist is also critic and theorist. It would be as if Clement Greenberg, as conceptual artist, dripped some paint on canvas, à la Jackson Pollock, to illustrate his theories of modern art. Since the ideas are all that is left, they can just as easily be verbally stated and written down, which in many conceptual pieces is just what is done, creating a great deal of confusion over whether conceptual art is art, criticism, literature, or philosophy.

Conceptual artists seem to fully realize this transformation of the semantic equation. Douglas Huebler, for instance, when asked how we see a piece of conceptual art, answered: "Through a system of documentation which includes the use of maps, drawings, photographs, and descriptive language. The documents are not intended to be necessarily interesting; that is, *they* are not 'art.' For example, the 'image' of my *New York Variable Piece #1* is a description of space made from the location of 'points' that are either static or move vertically and horizontally in a random position. *There is no possible way in which this piece can be experienced perceptually.* It can be totally experienced through its documentation" (quoted in Rose, 1973:143-144; emphasis mine). As the critic Gregory Battcock noted, "Such matters of technique as color, hue, drawing, composition, and pictorial depth become all but useless when applied to the new form" (1973:1). Precisely. The semantic equation has shifted as far as it can go, and there is nothing "explicit" remaining. The right-hand side of the equation has become so restricted that it has disappeared. What remains, as the title of an exhibition of conceptual art stated, is "0 Objects, 0 Painters, 0 Sculptors" (Battcock, 1973:6). When the conceptual artist Kosuth said, "The shift from the perceptual to the conceptual is a shift from the physical to the mental" (Rose, 1973:6), he could not have been speaking more clearly of the semantic equation. The perceptual is the paint, clay, bronze, or canvas that is organized to produce a physical work of art. When that is gone, all that is left is the mental, or the idea, and that is conceptual art. The extra-artistic information, the theory or idea behind the paint and canvas, becomes the de facto "art"—although this is a strained use of the word *art,* since nothing is painted or sculpted.

This emphasis on ideas represents a gradual process of role fusion. During the 1940s and 1950s, the two sides of the semantic equation were socially realized in the separate roles of artist (the right-hand side) and critic (the left-hand side). During the 1960s artists spoke out about the implicit meaning of their work and assumed some of the role of critic. Minimal artists were taking on some of the critic's function of providing the extra-art information and interpretation for their ever more minimal paintings. In this process the social role "artist" was becoming one of interpreter or theorist of implicit meanings that were only hinted at in an ever more economical mode of artistic communication. The complete fusion of critic and artist finally comes with the role "conceptual artist," whose artistic communication is not in the form of an object at all but of "documentation," presentation of the idea on the left-hand side of the semantic equation.

Imbalance in the Semantic Equation

It is not clear how minimal and abstract artistic communication can become, but conceptual art seems very near the limit. The art object proper had virtually disappeared. The only activity going on was theorizing and interpretation. The art object, the painting or piece of sculpture, was no longer "speaking" to the audience; its interpretation was now doing all the talking.

Theoretically this situation may create an imbalance in the semantic machinery, requiring a resetting of the semantic equation with more equality between the explicit and implicit, between what is actually painted and what is assumed and taken for granted. Perhaps, then, movements of ever more abstraction will eventually become unstable and give way to more realistic formats. In New York art this is what seems to have happened, for after conceptual art came a rebirth of realism, variously called photorealism, new realism, superrealism, hard-edge realism, hyperrealism, studio realism, sharp-focused realism, or radical realism, associated with such artists as Philip Pearlstein, Audrey Flack, Alfred Leslie, Chuck Close, Alex Katz, John Baeder, Robert Cottingham, Robert Bechtle, Malcolm Morley, Don Eddy, Janet Fish, Richard McClean, and Richard Estes (Battcock, 1975; Lindey, 1980; Arthur, 1980). The terms *photo-*, *hyper-*, and *superrealism* reflect the incredible attention given to detail in this new realism. These paintings have a very nonallegorical and literal quality, being glimpses of the most mundane everyday life, whether landscapes, cityscapes, or portraits.

The first and most obvious difference in the chronology of styles covered so far is the switch from various kinds of abstraction to a full-blown realism. Things are no longer hinted at. They are now spelled out in full detail—in fact, in incredibly copious detail. Where abstraction presented something of an architectural blueprint, the new realism not only constructed the complete house but brought every splinter and nail to life. The shift in style is clear: The impulse to remove more and more from the canvas was now replaced by a collective urge to put more and more on the canvas and paint more literal detail. The traditional vocabulary and syntax of art were becoming more available for artistic expression; the artistic code was becoming more elaborated. "The painters of this tradition [neorealism] do share certain traits that distinguish them from the main stream of late modernism [various kinds of abstraction]. . . . They display a deep concern for the traditional craft of painting—the mixing of color, the drawing of the figure, the modulation of light" (Stevens, 1982a:66).

The balance has shifted back to the right-hand side of the semantic equation. There is less, or no, need for extra-art information to give these paintings meaning. What meaning they have is in front of you on the canvas; realism is not a code for some other hidden meaning. The new realism "resolutely excludes any possibility of interpretation that would involve translating the visual 'given' into terms other than its own, or reducing it to a mere transparent surface for an all-important 'something more' lurking beneath" (Nochlin, 1975:123). That is, the overall source of meaning derives from the artistic infrastructure of painted images, not from the more implicit theoretical context. "It is exactly this sort of 'meaningless' detail that is essential to realism, for this is what nails its productions down so firmly to a specific time and anchors realist works in a concrete rather than an ideal or poetic reality" (Nochlin, 1975:122).

The semantic working of this form of communication is the exact opposite of that in conceptual art, where there was no art object at all—let alone a full-blown realism—and where meaning was transmitted implicitly. "Painters demand that our responses be restricted to the . . . pictorial statements themselves rather than to the subjects of these statements. Pearlstein and Leslie, for example, are not painting ugly people or deliberately asserting a pessimistic view of human nature in general or feminine appearance in particular. They are simply painting their subjects as they actually see them, probing the appearance of naked human flesh under very strong front illumination and from a very close vantage point" (Nochlin, 1975:125). Here meaning is transmitted from the right-hand side of the equation, from the explicitly painted realism. So much is explicitly put forth that there is little use for the theoretical side of the equation. The semantic burden is now carried by what is painted, and the meaning is glued to the actualities on canvas, not the set of ideas on the other side of the equation, as in conceptual art and the earlier abstraction.

By the 1980s modern art seemed to be in a state of flux, with a number of styles competing, and none exercising the kind of moral hegemony that abstract expressionism or minimalism had earlier. "The inevitable reaction to the Minimal/Conceptual end game gave rise in New York to the period of 'pluralism' in art. Many of the new approaches—pattern and decoration, new image, narrative, and the current catchall New Wave—have been based on some form of recognizable-image-making, as though in rejecting minimal one had to reject abstract art as well" (Tomkins, 1981:153).

The 1980s also saw a resurgence of another form of nonabstraction, neoexpressionism. As in neorealism, the art object was again being brought to the center of attention. Neoexpressionism uses "idiosyncratic, usually figurative imagery realized in brash colors, lush surface textures, and very large scale" and involves "a disdain for the reductive, formalist esthetics of the 1960s and for the conceptualism of the '70s" (Phillips, 1982:66). Again the right-hand side of the semantic equation was assuming more responsibility at the expense of theorizing and interpretive explanations. Neoexpressionism involved a return to the use of expressive vocabulary and syntax to communicate individual feelings rather than illustrate abstract principles. As a kind of elaborated code, it allowed for the more precise articulation of individual intent at the expense of dramatizing the broader art community culture that was the issue with all the theorizing in minimalism/conceptualism.

The new expressionism was the opposite of the previous minimalism. Where one was cool and detached, the other was hot, emotional, and involved; where one banned brushstrokes and applied paint in a flat manner, the other used thick oils and brushy stroke marks; where one was devoid of concrete images, the other was filled with pictures of people and animals and historical/cultural referents. The shift in styles is noted by the artist Eric Fischl in commenting on Max Beckmann's nineteenth-century expressionist painting *The Departure*.

> What I discovered was that I could grasp the intention of the picture exactly, without understanding the allegory, without knowing this or that figure was a particular mythical character. I could see it simply as a complete narrative . . . *The Departure* made me feel how bankrupt abstraction had become, that it had somehow gotten to the point where I didn't trust

what I was seeing in an abstract painting. The image
always seemed to mean something hidden, so that I
had to know outside references in order to know the
particular meaning of that painting. And there was
Beckmann's *Departure,* a work of art whose meanings
were all inside it. Its references weren't art references.
They were cultural, so I could hook up certain parts
of the image to political violence or historical moments or religious values—all those things that belong
to the general culture [quoted in Ratcliff and others,
1982:61].

When Fischl says Beckmann's painting was "a work of art whose
meanings were all inside it," he means that its internal structure
was elaborated enough that it required no extra information to
give it meaning. It stood on its own. Further, that the images were
not just "art references" but part of the more general culture,
above and beyond the issues of the narrow community of modern
art, is in direct contrast to the references of minimalism/concep-
tualism. Where Frank Stella's brushstrokes lead only to painting
and the issues of postgestural abstraction, neoexpressionism leads
to the more readily identifiable images of western culture.

Change in the Social Base

There is no longer an obvious capital of art, as
New York was since the 1950s and 1960s [Stevens,
1982a:68].

Contemporary art is no longer a New York exclusive [Tomkins, 1981:146].

During the 1981–82 season, gallery goers [in
New York] were introduced to the work of nearly
fifty artists from Germany, Italy, and France, most of
whom had never been seen in this country before.
Taken together, these new names represent the first
major groundswell of artistic activity in Europe since
the end of World War II [Phillips, 1982:66].

Manhattan is undergoing an invasion of extremely promising young painters from Europe, wrote
critic Carter Ratcliff, who, like several other observ-

ers, sees in the current influx an end to the postwar domination of American art and to the New York art world's lingering, if until now largely unconscious, provincialism [Phillips, 1982:66].

American [artistic] hegemony is at an end [Ratcliff, quoted in Phillips, 1982:66].

This movement away from abstraction to the more concrete, explicit, and particularistic images of neorealism and neoexpressionism has involved more than just a shift from one style to another. This shift in the semantic equation reflects a change in the centrality and solidarity of the art community. There is the sense that New York is no longer the hegemonic center of modern art. It is not that New York has been replaced by another city—at least not yet—but that the agreed-on centrality and dominance of New York and the styles that were generated there no longer have the power they previously enjoyed. "For the first time in at least a dozen years the esthetic currents seem to be running in both directions between Europe and America" (Tomkins, 1981:154).

"What makes the recent European painting interesting to us right now, I am beginning to think, is its specific German or Italian frame of reference. Minimal art, the last significant new art to emanate from New York, was virtually without reference to place and time; it could be (and was) done as naturally in Tokyo and Dusseldorf as in New York. Conceptual art, minimal's footnote, was the final stage in this century-long process; if the essence of art was idea, then a way had to be found to convey the idea without the benefit of a 'work.' At that point, art disappeared into philosophy" (Tomkins, 1981:153). Exactly. When art disappeared into philosophy, the left-hand side of the semantic equation, the philosophy, was carrying all the semantic burden, as the right-hand side had virtually disappeared. The code had become so minimal that it gave no hint of the specifics of its origin. What it did signal was membership in the by now world community of modern art, of which New York was the agreed center. The decomposition of the stylistic hegemony of New York abstraction meant a reaffirmation of images and styles that reflected more regional tastes and cultural traditions. From a world point of view, regional images were a more concrete and personal means of expression than the neutral shapes of minimalism. "Paintings by German and Italian artists using recognizable imagery are also quirky and deliberately regional. They overturn the cool, universal abstractions of modernist art that look basically the same whether they originated in Paris, New York, or Rome" (Phillips, 1982:69).

This slippage in the importance of New York is linked to the erosion of that city's cultural position within the United States and the noticeable erosion of America's position within the larger world system. This loss of centrality affected New York's sense of superiority and hegemony and the art styles it pioneered. The result was a community with less confidence, less solidarity, which in turn affected the kinds of artistic codes produced. The appearance of photorealism in the late 1970s and neoexpressionism in the early 1980s marked a clear move away from the secret language of abstraction to a more explicit and elaborated code. As the sense of centrality and importance of New York declined, the accumulated shared assumptions about the meaning and significance of modern art also began to dissipate, forcing a shift in the semantic equation from the left-hand side of in-group artistic referents to the right-hand side of actual explicit signs. As things could less and less be assumed, they had to be spelled out in detail, and doing so entailed a greater use of the traditional artistic tools that had previously been consensually banned. These postabstract styles brought increases in the range of colors, thickness of paint, visibility of brushstrokes, and use of realistic images.

As the semantic equation predicts, the assumptions and interpretations spelled out by critics, art theorists, and often the artists themselves are less important in postmodernist styles. "I think it's a confusing time for critics because they are faced with a bunch of artists who are doing exactly what they've been told all these years not to do, and the artists are saying, 'That's too bad, we're going to do it anyway' " (Stevens, 1982b:58). The importance accorded the art critics Greenberg and Rosenberg for explaining the meaning of abstract expressionism, or the explanatory comments of minimalists like Frank Stella, or the very conscious theorizing by the conceptualists, is clearly absent with neorealists and neoexpressionists. In effect, their paintings speak for themselves.

The Life Cycle of Art Styles

One final interpretation of the semantic equation is a mixture of the imbalance and social-base ideas. Styles of art may have their own social/semantic cycle, embracing changes both in social context and in artistic code. The growing acceptance of an art style—such as the abstraction of the New York school—brings with it social acceptance and popularity, which in turn make the shared assumptions of the movement more explicit and well known and thus enhance in-group solidarity among the artistic communicators. This results, by the semantic equation, in a more abstract/restricted code of communication. The artistic code becomes so in-group that the artists come to be talking only to themselves and are cut off from the larger community that was their original source of support and success. This growing isolation then prompts a move toward more concrete, literal, realistic, and elaborated styles so the artists can once again reach out and make contact with the larger world. From this perspective the very success of an art movement plants the seeds of its later failure. Popularity and attention make artistic values better known, driving the art toward ever more restricted formats. But this so narrows the art community that soon only they, or those fully versed in their explanations and theories, are able to comprehend the art, which cuts them off from the larger art public and brings about the demise of their ever more minimal/restricted style.

This is probably the semantic principle underlying the common observation that success often breeds contentment and a rigidification of style that results in scholasticism, in which people eventually lose interest. Hence, the cycle begins again, with new styles and new innovation. Following this analysis, one would expect alternating cycles of more realistic and abstract art.

Note

1. The general idea of the semantic equation was inspired by Tom Wolfe's (1976) discussion of two trends in modern art, its deobjectivization and the growing importance of some kind of art theory to explain these ever more minimal artistic gestures. In discussing the history of modern art from early modernism through abstract expressionism, pop, op, minimal, earth art, and conceptual art, Wolfe observed the general trend of removing more and more content from the art object itself. "In the beginning we got rid of nineteenth-century storybook realism. Then we got rid of representational objects. Then we got rid of the third dimension

altogether and got really flat (abstract expressionism). Then we got rid of airiness, brushstrokes, most of the paint, and the last viruses of drawing and complicated designs (hard edge, color field, Washington school)" (Wolfe, 1976:97–98). He points out that modern art next got rid of the standard picture frame (Frank Stella's shaped canvases) and then the picture altogether, art being done directly on the walls of the gallery (Robert Hunter and Sol Lewitt). Then modern art got rid of the walls, creating sculptures that filled the museum (Carl Andre, Robert Morris, Ronald Bladen, and Michal Steiner), and then got rid of the gallery itself with earth art, such as Robert Smithson's Spiral Jetty in the Great Salt Lake. And finally, with conceptual art, the modern movement got rid of the idea of a permanent work itself, so that "there, at last, it was! No more realism, no more representational objects, no more lines, colors, forms, and contours, no more pigments, no more brushstrokes. . . . Art made its final flight, climbed higher and higher in an ever-decreasing tighter-turning spiral until . . . it disappeared up its own fundamental aperture . . . and came out the other side as Art Theory! . . . Art Theory pure and simple, words on a page, literature undefiled by vision . . . late twentieth-century Modern Art was about to fulfill its destiny, which was: to become nothing less than Literature pure and simple" (Wolfe, 1976:107–109). Here Wolfe seems to have captured the complex relationship between the vocabulary and syntax of an art object, as manifested in questions of color, form, line, brushstrokes, and so on, and the broader a priori cultural context, art theory, in which the art object is embedded. Together they form the two elements of the semantic equation, which must be balanced for the artistic communication to be intelligible.

References

ARTHUR, JOHN
  1980   *Realismphotorealism*. Tulsa: Philbrook Art Center.
BAIGELL, MATTHEW
  1979   *Dictionary of American Art*. New York: Harper & Row.
BARRETT, WILLIAM
  1982   "The Painter's Club." *Commentary*, January, pp. 42–54.

BATTCOCK, GREGORY
   1973   "Introduction." In Gregory Battcock (Ed.), *Idea Art.*
          New York: E. P. Dutton.
BATTCOCK, GREGORY (ED.)
   1975   *Super Realism.* New York: E. P. Dutton.
BECKER, HOWARD SAUL
   1982   *Art Worlds.* Berkeley: University of California Press.
BERGER, PETER L., AND LUCKMANN, THOMAS
   1966   *The Social Construction of Reality: A Treatise in the
          Sociology of Knowledge.* New York: Doubleday.
BERGESEN, ALBERT
   1979   "Spirituals, Jazz, Blues, and Soul Music: The Role of
          Elaborated and Restricted Codes in the Maintenance of
          Social Solidarity." In Robert Wuthnow (Ed.), *New Di-
          rections in the Empirical Study of Religion.* New York:
          Academic Press.
   Forth- "The Social Anthropology of Mary Douglas." In Rob-
   coming ert Wuthnow and others (Eds.), *Cultural Analysis: The
          Work of Peter Berger, Mary Douglas, Michael Foucault,
          and Jurgen Habermas.* London: Routledge & Kegan
          Paul.
BERNSTEIN, BASIL
   1975   *Class, Codes, and Control.* New York: Schocken Books.
DOUGLAS, MARY
   1970   *Natural Symbols.* New York: Pantheon Books.
GELDZAHLER, HENRY
   1969   *New York Painting and Sculpture: 1940-1970.* New
          York: E. P. Dutton.
GREENBERG, CLEMENT
   1969   "After Abstract Expressionism." In Henry Geldzahler,
          New York Painting and Sculpture: 1940-1970. New
          York: E. P. Dutton.
HUGHES, ROBERT
   1982   "The Rise of Andy Warhol." *New York Review of
          Books,* February 18, pp. 6-10.
LINDEY, CHRISTINE
   1980   *Superrealist Painting and Sculpture.* London: Orbis.
LUCIE-SMITH, EDWARD
   1981   *Art Now.* New York: William Morrow.

NOCHLIN, LINDA
  1975   "Realism Now." In Gregory Battcock (Ed.), *Super Realism*. New York: E. P. Dutton.
PHILLIPS, D. C.
  1982   "No Island Is an Island: New York Discovers the Europeans." *ARTnews*, October, pp. 66–71.
RATCLIFF, CARTER, AND OTHERS
  1982   "Expressionism Today: An Artists Symposium." *Art in America*, December, pp. 58–75.
ROSE, A.
  1973   "Four Interviews." In Gregory Battcock (Ed.), *Idea Art*. New York: E. P. Dutton.
ROSENBERG, HAROLD
  1969   "The American Action Painters." In Henry Geldzahler, *New York Painting and Sculpture: 1940–1970*. New York: E. P. Dutton.
  1973   "Art and Words." In Gregory Battcock (Ed.), *Idea Art*. New York: E. P. Dutton.
SANDLER, IRVING
  1978   *The New York School*. New York: Harper & Row.
SIMPSON, CHARLES R.
  1981   *Soho: The Artist in the City*. Chicago: University of Chicago Press.
STEVENS, MARK
  1982a "Revival of Realism." *Newsweek*, June 7, pp. 64–70.
  1982b "Who Needs Art Critics?" *ARTnews*, September, pp. 55–60.
SWANSON, GUY E.
  1964   *Birth of the Gods: The Origin of Primitive Beliefs*. Ann Arbor: University of Michigan Press.
TOMKINS, CALVIN
  1981   "An End to Chauvinism." *New Yorker*, December 7, pp. 146–154.
WOLFE, TOM
  1976   *The Painted Word*. New York: Bantam Books.

*The existentialism of Jean-Paul Sartre is critiqued from the
point of view of Goffmanian sociology of everyday life.
Despite many parallels between the two positions, the
philosophical viewpoint should not be taken as necessarily
more sophisticated than the sociological. Meaning, self,
and institutional order are interactional achievements, and
thus studies in conversational analysis and ethnomethodology become the basis for a critique of epistemology.*

ꙮ8ꙮ

INTERACTION AS A RESOURCE
FOR EPISTEMOLOGICAL
CRITIQUE

Anne Warfield Rawls

UNIVERSITY OF MASSACHUSETTS, BOSTON

The work of Jean-Paul Sartre has been characterized as a
counterpart of a Goffmanian version of role theory, albeit a glorified version (Craib, 1976; Hayim, 1980; Lofland, 1980). Sartre is
one of the very few "grand" theorists who have tried to ground
theory in description and observation of microprocesses. Goffman,
in contrast, has not made much of the theoretical implications of
his position. Indeed, a frequent criticism of Goffman is that he

The arguments in this chapter may be found in greater detail in Rawls
(1983a). This chapter attempts a less comprehensive presentation of those arguments, by way of a comparison of Goffman and Sartre. My most sincere
thanks to Jeff Coulter and George Psathas for their many years of support, to
Jay Meehan and Gila Hayim for careful reading of earlier drafts, to J. M. Ross
for technical assistance, and to Boston University, without whose generous
support none of this research would have been possible.

lacks any consistent theoretical foundation whatever (Lofland, 1980; Psathas, 1980; Craib, 1976; Manning, 1976). I believe, however, that the theoretical sophistication that Goffman can add to Sartre's argument provides a much sounder foundation for an extrapolation to social structure from the individual.

The work of Goffman and Sartre overlaps explicitly on the issue of the development and presentation of self in interaction. That the two authors appear to agree on a description of the gross features of the presentation of self has been generally acknowledged (Lofland, 1980; Hayim, 1980; Craib, 1976). They characterize the situation similarly:

> This person who I have to be is a representation for others and for myself, which means that I can only be he in representation. . . . I can only play at being the person who I have to be. . . . My reactions, to the extent that I project myself toward the other, are no longer for myself but are rather mere representations; they await being constituted as graceful or uncouth, sincere or insincere, etc. [Sartre, 1971: 102-105].

> One character presents himself in the guise of a character to characters projected by other players. . . . Control [of self-presentation] is achieved largely by influencing the definition of the situation which the others come to formulate. . . . thus when an individual appears in the presence of others, there will usually be some reason for him to mobilize his activity so that it will convey the impression to others that it is in his interests to covey [Goffman, 1959:xi, 4].

Where Goffman's and Sartre's positions diverge, there is a tendency to view Sartre's as the more sophisticated. Indeed, it has been suggested that where Goffman differs from Sartre, Sartre can be taken as a corrective for Goffman's shortcomings (Craib, 1976). This is quite typical of the perceived relation between sociology and philosophy.[1] When a philosopher and a sociologist show a marked similarity in some area, it is frequently assumed that any divergence over other matters is due to the sociologist's philosophical naiveté. For example, Natanson takes this issue to be at the heart of the debate between Parsons and Schutz (Grathoff, 1978).

Natanson chastises Parsons for rejecting what many have treated as a noble attempt by Schutz to introduce some philosophical clarity into Parsons's argument.[2] Sociologists are, in general, "blamed" for such oversights. This bypasses the critical question whether sociologists might have good reasons for their resistance to philosophy—that is, whether the social world might be considered a resource from which to generate a critique of philosophy.

There is a theoretical and a "political" significance to pointing out that the study of the mundane routines of everyday life might provide a full theoretical view of social structure and meaning. It is generally assumed that microstudies can have little relevance for a "larger" (that is, macro) understanding of meaning and order.[3] When they are viewed charitably, studies of the achievement of meaning in everyday life (such as ethnomethodology and symbolic interaction) are usually treated as methods for filling out our understanding of microprocesses in society but as themselves in need of theoretical grounding. The findings are then mated in conflicting ways to existing theoretical positions. If, however, it can be argued that they focus on the foundation of meaning and order, rather than on products of meaning and order, their significance for social theory is cast in a new light.

My argument is that some of the findings of microstudies (particularly ethnomethodological findings) challenge the very epistemological assumptions with which philosophy and social theory have often begun. To the degree that microstudies have addressed the achievement of meaning and social structure as process, they are fundamentally theoretical *by implication*. One could argue that what Weber, Mannheim, Garfinkel, and many other contemporary sociologists have been engaged in is a debate over the epistemological character of the social world[4]—not a philosophical debate in the ordinary sense, however, but a debate that assumes that the logical character of human action can be defined only with reference to empirical studies of practical action.

This chapter will address these issues through a comparison of Goffman and Sartre. The criticism is not directed against Sartre or against philosophy but, rather, against some prevalent assumptions concerning the nonnegotiated character of meaning. Sartre and Goffman happen to diverge on this issue, while having many other things in common. Through a comparison, I hope to illustrate both the point and its consequences in concrete terms.

Meaning and Action

Despite their agreement on the general features of presentation of self, Goffman and Sartre differ over the fundamental relation between meaning and action. Is it a fixed "institutionalized" meaning that structures the possibilities for action, or do my actions negotiate the possibilities for meaning? Clearly, in either sense, the possibilities for action are circumscribed by a certain standardization of acceptable behavior—that is, the ways in which roles can be recognizably played. But if actions constrain or constitute meaning in an important sense, the possibility is left open that the self constitutes social meaning in and through playing a role, instead of emerging out of a fabric of socially given meanings (thereby simply reflecting "social structure"). If actions negotiate meaning, then interaction is not simply a reflection of an institutional order, which it mirrors in microcosm, but is the actual birthplace of the meanings that continually renegotiate the institutional structure.

The following passage from Sartre, known as "the waiter," appears in full in Goffman. The distinction between "fixed" and "negotiated" meaning can be examined through a consideration of the differences in their interpretation of this passage:

> Let us consider this waiter in the café. His movement is quick and forward, a little too precise, a little too rapid. He comes toward the patrons with a step a little too quick. He bends forward a little too eagerly; his voice, his eyes express an interest a little too solicitous for the order of the customer. Finally there he returns, trying to imitate in his walk the inflexible stiffness of some kind of automaton while carrying his tray with the recklessness of a tightrope-walker by putting it in a perpetually unstable, perpetually broken equilibrium which he perpetually reestablishes by a light movement of the arm and hand. All this behavior seems to us a game. He applies himself to chaining his movements as if they were mechanisms, the one regulating the other; his gestures and even his voice seem to be mechanisms; he gives himself the quickness and pitiless rapidity of things. He is playing, he is amusing himself. But what is he play-

ing? We need not watch long before we can explain it: he is playing at *being* a waiter in a café. There is nothing there to surprise us. The game is a kind of marking out and investigation. The child plays with his body in order to explore it, to take inventory of it; the waiter in the café plays with his condition in order to *realize* it. This obligation is not different from that which is imposed on all tradesmen. Their condition is wholly one of ceremony. The public demands of them that they realize it as a ceremony; there is the dance of the grocer, of the tailor, of the auctioneer, by which they endeavor to persuade their clientele that they are nothing but a grocer, an auctioneer, a tailor. A grocer who dreams is offensive to the buyer, because such a grocer is not wholly a grocer. Society demands that he limit himself to his function as a grocer, just as the soldier at attention makes himself into a soldier-thing with a direct regard which does not see at all, which is no longer meant to see, since it is the rule and not the interest of the moment which determines the point he must fix his eyes on (the sight "fixed at ten paces"). There are indeed many precautions to imprison a man in what he is, as if we lived in perpetual fear that he might escape from it, that he might suddenly break away and elude his condition [Sartre, 1971:101–102; Goffman, 1959: 75].

Goffman (1959:30) stresses the need for the performance in order for meaning to be achieved. It is not that I must play out a certain performance because I am a tailor or a grocer but that *in order to claim to be* a tailor or a grocer I must perform the part: "When an individual projects a definition of the situation and thereby makes an implicit or an explicit claim to be a person of a particular kind, he automatically exerts a moral demand upon the others, obliging them to value and treat him in the manner that persons of his kind have a right to expect. He also implicitly forgoes all claims to be things he does not appear to be" (1959:13). Goffman says that "this role of the witness in limiting what it is the individual can be has been stressed by existentialists, who see it as a basic threat to individual freedom. See Jean-Paul Sartre, *Being and Nothingness*" (1959:13).

In contrast, Sartre emphasizes the problems faced by a social being whose *rights* are defined by the relation of his or her social performances to roles and statuses recognized by society at large. The waiter "knows well what it 'means': the obligation of getting up at five o'clock, of sweeping the floor of the shop before the restaurant opens, of starting the coffee pot going, etc. He knows the rights which it allows: the right to the tips, the right to belong to a union" (Sartre, 1971:102). In other words, I have rights to things like tips and unions only by being something that I am not. As a simple human being, I have no access to such rights.

Goffman stresses the rights and obligations that the interactional performance of a role entitles one to as a performer. For Goffman the performer's access to rights and obligations is not differentially conferred on particular status positions in the social world.[5] Rather, all participants in face-to-face interactions, within which these performances are brought off, have equal access to and equal protection from what Goffman variously calls a "working consensus" or a "moral consensus."

The implication is that, far from the ritual guarantees of interaction impinging on individual freedom, Goffman considers individual freedom to depend on those guarantees. The individual has an obligation, not because of his or her status within society at large as a grocer, for example, but an obligation occasioned by participation in interaction, to maintain a "working consensus" between participants, which makes certain demands on each other's performances.

Sartre is concerned with performances as they take on a meaning in relation to social institutions and the differential distribution of rights and goods. Goffman claims something more for the performance. A performance is not what it is because of a relation to some given and fixed set of meanings in the world. Rather, the performance has meaning, in particular a moral meaning, through its relation to the interaction within which it is played out.

It is in the *Critique* that Sartre develops a hierarchy of groups: serial groups, pledged groups, and institutional groups. He argues that at the level of serial groups there is no intrinsic meaning, no intrinsic order, and no intrinsic morality. In fact, such orders are described as the antithesis of human freedom and meaning. Pledged and institutional groups are characterized by an explicit pledge among members to some common enterprise. They are no longer simply organized by a relation to materiality but now have this in common as their agreed-upon project. Sartre extols institutional totalization as the high point of human interaction.

So, although Sartre offers a theory that moves from micro to macro descriptions of social organization, it is a developmental theory. That is, the micro levels of interaction are considered deficient of human meaning, which is finally achieved only at more macro levels of organization. Further, the meaning and orderliness of all micro-organizations are in reality simply a product of their particular orientation to a macro-organization that confers meaning and order on them. The reverse is true for Goffman: *Meaning is an in situ creation, not conferred by a relation to institutional givens.* It is for this reason that the management of impressions is a delicate and moral affair (Goffman, 1969a:84,94, 1961a:76). Interactions that Sartre would call simple seriality are not devoid of humanity and meaning for Goffman. They are, in fact, the source of the order, meaning, and morality that we bestow on the rest of the social order.

If Goffman's descriptions of interaction constitute an alternative to the institutional definition, and therefore relativity, of meaning, and if they can be substantiated, then philosophical assumptions about self, freedom, value, and meaning will have to be reconsidered. The constraints on freedom and meaning would in an important sense be not "institutional" or "structural" but "interactional." If the criteria for meaning, action, and value are relative to interaction and not institutions, then questions of value relativity, morality, and freedom have to be understood anew. The importance of ethnomethodology and conversation analysis consists, in part, in having contributed to the understanding and documentation of the achievement of meaning in interaction. It is in this regard that I have argued elsewhere (Rawls, 1983b) for the unavoidable epistemological relevance of that work and for its implications for the adequacy of general social theory and philosophy. This chapter suggests only the basic framework for those arguments.

Two Views of a Necessary Relation Between Individual and Group

Though claiming to derive a theory of social structure from the individual (that is, consciousness), Sartre nevertheless casts the sense of conscious experience against a relation to institutional order. Goffman, in contrast, chooses to begin not with consciousness itself but with the interaction within which consciousness takes on a public and communicable form. "We may say that the starting point for all that is to come later consists of the individual performer maintaining a definition of the situation before an audience" (Goffman, 1959:81).

Goffman and Sartre both consider the relation of the individual to the group a necessary one. For Sartre, however, this necessity is a consequence of the logical order of the material world and of "otherness." Selfhood is a simple transposition of "otherness"; therefore possession of a self requires the presence of others and of a material world. Interactional order is defined by a "given" relation to external conditions.

In contrast, Goffman presents a picture of constraints on interaction that are *internal* to interactional scenes. He paints a picture of the emergence of social order, wherein social order and meaning require a particular interactional relation between individual and group. Meaning is, according to this view, a constitutive production *in* and *through* group performance. Actions do not acquire their meaning primarily through a direct relation to external ends.

As a consequence, Goffman states, where there is "order," there must be a "working consensus."[6] For Sartre, there are levels of organized relationships on a continuum from no consensus at all to a high degree of consensus, and what Sartre calls the "pledge" appears only in relationships characterized by a "contract," an explicit verbal agreement. These forms of organization are considered "better than" unpledged relationships, which, Sartre argues, are merely matters of natural or mathematical order. Unless there is an explicit articulated pledge, the order is assumed to have only an institutionally defined, or, as Sartre says, a "serial," significance. For Goffman, there is no meaningful relationship where there is not a tacit pledge of some sort. "Participation in *any contact with others is a commitment* . . . an involvement in the face of others that is as immediate and spontaneous as the involvement he has in his own face" (Goffman, 1969a:6). When the "working consensus" is violated, interaction collapses. "Individuals collapse as units of minimal ceremonial substance and others learn that what had been taken for granted as ultimate entities are really held to-

gether by rules that can be broken with some kind of impunity"
(1969a:94); "We must be prepared to see that the impression of
reality fostered by a performance is a delicate, fragile thing that
can be shattered by very minor mishaps" (1959:56).

Sartre's attempt to explain the "totalization" of institutions
from fragmented and disconnected individual actions assumes that
in their initial state actions are unorganized and have *an institutional relevance and meaning, and only that.* Meaning is not considered an emergent property of actions. It would seem that Sartre
is treating meaning as a given, yet he is expressly concerned with
the coming into being of the humanly meaningful. For Sartre, the
existentialist, the problem is now to explain how meaning, or humanity, could ever be truly free of institutional or material constraints, since it appears to be defined by these constraints. Therefore, freedom becomes the ultimate existential problem. Freedom
in this sense is not problematic for Goffman, because meaning is
an interactional creation, not an institutional artifact or residue.

One feels compelled to ask what sort of an existential consciousness this is. Institutions appear to be wholly contingent on
material conditions. If individual consciousness is nothing more
than a contingent relation to contingent matters of fact, then
there is nothing special characterizing consciousness that we could
properly refer to as human. For the existentialist, the quest for
the essence of the human and of human freedom is the primary
concern. Therefore, it is not surprising to find Sartre ending on the
ironic note that what is common to all consciousness is this very
relation of contingency to contingency. What is ultimately constitutive of humanity is a process of rising above contingency by
somehow totalizing it into a consciousness of itself *as contingency.*
This recognition itself becomes a bond, a pledge between copartic-
ipants in futility. It is in this bond between members of the "opposition" that human meaning is created. Human meaning, therefore, stands in a purely negative relation to institutional constraints
(with no "positive" content). Seriality, for Sartre, is the initial
form that this negativity takes on.

Critique of the Institutional Relativity of Action
and Meaning: Seriality and Bondage

In Sartre's view, seriality is dehumanizing because persons
not bound by a pledge simply play out institutional scripts that

are devoid of human or interactional meaning. Seriality is intrinsically meaningless, dependent for its meaning on a relation to external ends. A line at a bus stop or a supermarket queue is an example of serial order. Sartre characterizes the orderliness of the line as a function of the separate relation of each person in line to some institutional goal such as "getting to work," rather than as a function of an interactional commitment between those in line to constitute themselves as an orderly line for something. "They are waiting for a bus at a bus stop in front of the church. I use the word *grouping* here in a neutral sense: we do not yet know whether this gathering is, as such, the inert effect of separate activities, or whether it is a common reality, regulating everyone's actions. . . . To begin with, it should be noted that we are concerned here with a plurality of isolations: These people do not care about or speak to each other and, in general, they do not look at one another; they exist side by side alongside a bus stop" (Sartre, 1976: 256).

Sartre argues not only that there is an underlying apathy at this level of interaction but that the structure of such action itself poses an active barrier to the realization of ourselves and others as human beings: "At this level, it is worth noting that their isolation is not an inert statute; rather, it is actually lived in everyone's project as its negative structure. In other words, the isolation of the organism, as the impossibility of uniting with others in an organic totality, is revealed through the isolation which everyone lives as the provisional negation of their reciprocal relations with others. . . . [He] has encountered [his neighbor] in his practical field as a general individual defined by waiting for the bus" (Sartre, 1976: 256).

Because Sartre considers daily life to be composed for the most part of serial relations, he considers it a form of bondage. The individual must break free of such "inert" relations in order to create a "common reality" to which an existential freedom is possible. This is a very pessimistic view of the value of the mundane features of everyday life and could not be more in opposition to a view of these same mundane features as a source of freedom.

Goffman describes what Sartre has called serial groups in much the same way as Sartre, but they take on a very different character in his work. There is, for Goffman, no arena of human interaction that is meaningless. The seemingly random and "in-sane" behavior of patients in an "asylum," or people queueing up in a line, is not intrinsically meaningless activity but, rather, heav-ily endowed with interactional significance for the participants. In Goffman's view, such situations provide an important arena within which interactants continually renew their interactional commitments.

Sartre has described the "pledge" as an articulated phenom-enon, a social contract in a Hobbesian sense. For Goffman, the "working consensus" is an implicit pledge that is necessary to en-sure the order and meaning of interaction. Therefore, it cannot come into being during an interaction but must already be presup-posed before any interactions (even supermarket queues) are pos-sible.

Through their actions individuals implicitly display a com-mitment to the "working consensus," renewing and affirming their relationship to one another. The contract is not written or articu-lated. Thus, for Goffman the social performance is a moral event that can "highlight the common official values of the society in which it occurs." In fact, "we may look upon it . . . as an expres-sive rejuvenation and reaffirmation of the moral values of the com-munity" (1959:35). If a social performance can reaffirm the moral values of the community, then its acceptability will be assessed ac-cording to the degree to which it accomplishes that affirmation. Goffman, in fact, argues that failing to reaffirm moral values in and through social actions is viewed by parties to the event as a moral transgression (1969a:10, 1959:1-17). If there is a moral is-sue inherent in the relationship between individuals during an interaction, then it should manifest itself in the protective and pre-ventive procedures engaged in by the interactants. It should, there-fore, *be available to detailed studies of those procedures.* For example, Goffman argues that embarrassment plays a role in main-taining a moral balance in interaction: "The expectations relevant to embarrassment are moral . . . we should look to those moral ob-ligations which surround the individual in only one of his capaci-ties, that of someone who carries on social encounters" (1969a: 105). These are moral commitments not because a particular soci-ety or organization has defined them as such but because *the inter-action itself requires these commitments for its very possibility as an interaction.* This is a functional requirement, yes. But the requirement is posed not on behalf of a particular institutional form but, instead, on behalf of the dynamics of interaction prior to a surrender to institutional constraints. The orderliness and meaningfulness of interaction are *emergent features* of the reciprocal commitment to the "working consensus": "An encounter exhibits sanctioned orderliness arising from obligations fulfilled, expectations realized, and . . . therein lies its structure" (1961b:19).

The constant threat of annihilation hangs over both the interaction and the social selves in and through whose commitments and performances it is created and sustained: "When an incident occurs and spontaneous involvement is threatened, then reality is threatened" (1969a:135); "To be awkward or unkempt, to talk or move wrongly, is to be a dangerous giant, a destroyer of worlds" (1961b:81). It is more prudent to act in accordance with projected expectations because to violate them would upset the interaction and thereby very probably prevent the attainment of the individual's own self-interests. We might characterize this principle in the following fashion: *Persons ignorant of their future status in this or other interactions honor an implicit agreement to accept at face value the "fronts" of all participants, thus protecting all positions that they themselves might come to occupy in the future.* This is a reformulation of the "working consensus," which calls on similar formulations in moral philosophy. This particular form of the principle adapts nicely to an explanation of conversational preferences and their relation to an underlying moral principle.

The social individual depends for security and understanding on an assessment of the character and intentions of fellow interactants. All need to know where the others stand in relation to their respective moral obligations. This information, however, is not immediately available. The interaction provides a vehicle through which this mutual identification can be accomplished. Participants "will be forced to accept some events as conventional or natural signs of something not directly available to the senses" (Goffman, 1959:2). Persons who fulfill their social interactional obligations may then be assumed to be ones who will respect their moral obligations as well. "A state where everyone temporarily accepts everyone else's lines is established. This kind of mutual acceptance seems to be a basic structural feature of interaction, especially the interaction of face-to-face talk. . . . As a main focus of attention talk is unique, however, for talk creates for the participant a world and a reality that has other participants in it . . . we must also see that a conversation has a life of its own and makes demands on its own behalf. It is a little social system with its own boundary-maintaining tendencies; it is a little patch of commitment and loyalty with its own heroes and its own villains" (Goffman, 1969a:11).

The importance of the activity in which the persons are engaged is for these purposes irrelevant. Rather, it is the attitude they adopt toward that activity that has relevance, for it is that attitude which confers interactional meaning on the activity. For example, I may be in a line to buy food to feed my family because they are hungry. What has interactional significance, however, is my attitude toward the other members of the line and toward the order of the line itself. What tells me something, what constitutes my commitment, is not the personal end but the respect of the collective accomplishment. "Regardless of the person's relative social position, in one sense he has power over the other participants and they must rely on his considerations. When others act toward him in some way, they presume upon a social relationship to him, since one of the things expressed by interaction is the relationship of the interactants. Thus they compromise themselves, for they place him in a position to discredit the claims they express as to his attitude toward them" (Goffman, 1969a:28).

Individuals must be in a position to evaluate the interactional commitments of others. These commitments, in turn, must be displayed *in* the interaction if they are not to be derived from institutional relations or to depend on explicit and optional articulation. Conversation analysis can be interpreted, in part, as a documentation of such displays. In particular, the early lectures of Sacks can be read as an attempt to work out in detail the implications of Goffmanian interactional obligations for the interpretation of conversational sequences.[7] In his early lectures Sacks shows that the need to create meaning (assuming that it is not institutionally defined) is exploited within the interaction (by participants) in order to display and evaluate (through various organizational features of talk) commitments to social and interactional obligations.[8] The details of conversation can thus be inspected for their moral and epistemological implications.

Institutional Order and Freedom

Sartre argues that the self must transcend seriality in order to achieve a "common reality" with others. For Goffman, a "common reality" is achieved in and through what Sartre calls seriality. Critically, for Goffman a "common reality" does not support the status quo as an ideal relation, because institutions are not the foundation of meaning. As long as one argues that interactional meaning does not depend on institutions for its sense, then to argue for seriality as a "common reality" is to challenge, not support, the status quo as ideal. This implication is usually overlooked. As a result, studies of everyday life are accused of being conservative descriptive accounts of the fine points of structural order. This is true for Sartre but not for Goffman, as is best illustrated by the differences in the characterizations of institutional order and freedom from the two perspectives.

For Goffman there are only certain times when institutions are experienced as visible, felt, organic realities (typically only when their existence is called into question). There is some evidence that when seriality itself provides a basis for membership in, for example, the scene of a robbery, blackout, or assassination, the participants will interact accordingly and grant one another the requisite speaking rights. For example, reports of public reaction after the John F. Kennedy assassination and the 1968 blackout are full of stories of persons in lines, in elevators, and with strangers in many settings who suddenly found themselves engaged in interactions that were more intimate than one would ordinarily expect under similar circumstances (Shibutani, 1966).

It is not that in these instances we rise above our ordinary circumstances. Rather, the institutional order has momentarily risen to the high level of organic solidarity experienced continually in the mundane encounters of everyday life. Institutional order rarely escapes to organic and authentic unity. Yet, insofar as Sartre considers human action and meaning to be institutionally defined, these situations would provide the *only* escape to an organic relationship of trust between persons.

Sartre glorifies a revolutionary and temporary overthrow of the established order. His primary example of a high point in history is the storming of the Bastille (Sartre, 1976:351-363). It is not the outcome that is applauded. Sartre shares with Marx a belief that all outcomes, all times of peace, are characterized by institutional bondage.[9] Consequently, Sartre applauds the spontaneity of the gathering. In his characterization, the mob is an immediately moral enterprise. The crowd has collected to achieve a common purpose, but the purpose is not institutional. Rather, it emerges directly and spontaneously from the human needs of the moment. The leader is not one who has an institutionalized status but one who simply emerges from the crowd; the crowd propels "the third party" toward their joint destiny. "The crowd in situation produces and dissolves within itself its own temporary leaders. . . . who give the entire crowd the biological and practical unity of its organism as the rule of common unification" (Sartre, 1976: 382).

Such a perspective on freedom ultimately leads to advocacy of an institutionless society. Yet, from Sartre's view, meaning and organization are possible only against a background of institutional ends. Even the riots and revolutions are defined by a relation to institutions—a negative relation, but an institutional relation nevertheless. There is tremendous circularity in assuming an institutional basis for meaning, organization, and self while arguing that one has to rid oneself of institutional determination in order to be free.[10]

Because Sartre considers all ordinary meaning to be institutionally defined, he misses the important possibility that participants in the mundane encounters of everyday life might also be bound by a common purpose—a purpose that is not particular and institutional but essentially moral.

Goffman, in contrast, presents a picture within which personal freedom can at any moment be achieved through interaction. Freedom is a continual achievement in and through the mundane interactions of everyday life. Of course, to the degree that interactions are dependent on institutions for some of their meaning, the human within them is still not free. But as Goffman argued in *Asylums,* even in a total institution (a mental hospital), patients manage to invest seriality with a personal, preinstitutional meaning. In fact, their need to invest the most meaningless of institutional places and events with a human interactive meaning of their own suggests that seriality is simply meaningless without such an investiture (even though such seriality bears a direct institutional relation that might be supposed to fill it with meaning). "The small talisman-like possessions that inmates use as symbolic devices for separating themselves from the position they are supposed to be in. . . . The practice of reserving something of oneself from the clutch of an institution is very visible in mental hospitals . . . I want to argue that this recalcitrance is not an incidental mechanism of defense but rather an essential constituent of the self. . . . Our status is backed by the solid buildings of the world, while our sense of personal identity often resides in the cracks" (Goffman, 1961a:307, 319, 320).

The important idea suggested here is that there is something more fundamental than institutions and that it can be found in the primary social relations of face-to-face encounters. This does not mean the family or communal life, as these are already highly institutionalized. One is speaking of finding those instances that take place every day within the shadow of institutions, which are nevertheless constitutive of institutions, not the reverse.

Sartre conceives of interaction as essentially inert and at best violent (that is, as a free rejection of inertia). Goffman assumes that the "working consensus" is contracted spontaneously in the mundane interactions of day-to-day life. Commitment to a "working consensus" is reaffirmed through a set of interaction obligations and rituals that hold for all members and that pledge them to treat one another, irrespective of inequalities among them, in terms of those involvement obligations.

Strategic Interaction

Assuming that the primary form of interaction is strategic seems to be an unavoidable consequence of arguing that a group has organic unity only if it is the product of activities unified with respect to external or institutional ends. Because everything must be analyzed in relation to material ends, a strategic posture must be assumed. It must also be presumed that participants adopt this posture as well. Actors are characterized as essentially strategic.

Regardless of Goffman's apparent preoccupation with strategic action (especially in his later work), he allows that many ordinary actions are *not* strategic.

For Goffman, not only is strategic interaction only one form of action, but it is quite clear that he believes an injunction against strategic interaction is embedded in the "working consensus."[11] "When an individual senses that others are insincere or affected (in their assumed role), he tends to feel that they have taken unfair advantage of their communication position to promote their own interests: *He feels they have broken the ground rules of interaction*" (Goffman, 1969a:24). This is possible because interaction is conceived of as intrinsically orderly; therefore the interaction can be understood without reference to strategic ends. A strategic model of interaction would characterize this intrinsic orderliness as nonexistent. Therefore, it matters a great deal whether or not one is entitled to take a strategic view.[12]

Sartre presents us with a view of people who are "united though not integrated through work, through struggle, or through any other activity in an organized group common to them all" (1976:256). They are united through a contingent relation to external events. A gathering is merely serial if it is the "effect of separate activities" (1976:256). It is organic if it is a "common reality, regulating everyone's actions" (1976:256). This assumes that the relatedness of activities in a gathering can and should be assessed through an analysis of ends and renders the actual process of individual interactional projects null and void. It assumes that there is no intrinsic sort of relatedness that could be found in any gathering regardless of ends.

A strategic view places the prerequisites for social order outside the social phenomenon (the event) itself. The principles of order are thereby thought to be above contingency, because they themselves are not situated. The organizing principles are considered to be ideal entities and are therefore not thought to be empirically discoverable. It is a curious dilemma: Although the importance of understanding social organization firsthand has been argued for, the principles of explanation are nowhere to be found.

Although both Goffman and Sartre have argued that the meaning of actions must be a continual accomplishment, for Sartre that accomplishment bears a necessary relation to some fixed, known-in-common, institutional given. Goffman argues for the recovery of that constitutive process through an understanding of actions themselves, while Sartre suggests it is recoverable only through a reflexive analysis of the contents of consciousness.

Sartre (1976) provides an elaborate theoretical explanation of how the dialectical unfolding of praxis could contain, as a moment of itself, its own consciousness of itself, as a process.[13] Therefore, that process is alleged to be recoverable through introspection. We would expect a novel account of the dialectical genesis of order from this perspective. What is produced are action descriptions. Sartre's descriptions do not have the character of uncovering the contents of anyone's consciousness; rather, they are the same sort of action descriptions that Goffman provides—hence the curious fact that Sartre and Goffman use similar examples on many occasions (which has led to the assumption that their theoretical positions are also similar). Sartre has presented an empirical reconstruction of the unfolding of meaningful action and called it a reflexive method. He describes situations as a location for consciousness, not consciousness as a location for situations. Furthermore, he describes consciousness as conditioned by the dialectics of situations, not situations as conditioned by the dialectics of consciousness. Yet, having taken the position that the principles of order are not situated, Sartre must claim that these descriptions of empirical circumstances are themselves unsituated.

Sartre's solution involves a circular argument in which all meaning is institutionally bounded and yet a necessary and valid critique of institutional praxis from the human standpoint is presumed. In order to preserve enough humanity to perform such a critique, however, one needs an individual who is not entirely institutionally defined.

Where meaning is a constitutive feature of actions, as we find in Goffman, and is not institutionally bounded, we have no such problem. Institutional meaning is bounded by interactional praxis; therefore interactional praxis has the natural prerogative of criticizing institutional praxis. This suggests that the actual process of interaction should be the object of study. The constitutive process will be examined as a production account of the achievement of meaning, rather than as "what it all amounted to in retrospect."[14]

Implications for the Problem of
Social Order and Human Freedom

For one interested in the problems inherent in combining freedom, social order, and moral value, the differences between Sartre and Goffman raise critical questions. Although Sartre promised a bridge between macro- and microsociology, he offered essentially the same perspective on moral relativity as Weber, with only an existential commitment to freedom (expressed as negativity) as a universal.[15] If individuals are bound to an institutional order with respect to which their values are defined, and from which they cannot escape, then it would seem that moral value itself is a function of an institutional relation and therefore relative.

Goffman has offered an important and generally overlooked characterization of the interactional being as primarily free. There are, of course, special problems with this position as well. Given such a position, one can avoid relativity only if the situated organizing principles of interaction are generalizable. This requires (1) a comprehensive theory of language, which renders preinstitutional meaning possible, and (2) a method for empirically observing the genesis of meaning in interaction.

The suggestion is that empirical studies of everyday life do indeed provide a viable critical standpoint immune to significant problems inherent in a view that takes institutions as a foundation. Furthermore, the debate has important implications for a characterization of the fundamental nature of the human. Sartre's human is defined initially by immoral material relations, which one must struggle to rise above. Goffman's interactional being possesses an initial freedom and moral worth, as does the interaction he or she inhabits.

Within Goffman's view, stability and order are not enemies of the individual: They are the *source* of the individual's freedom and individuality. It is those who would challenge the orderliness of seriality who are to be feared. It is not that Goffman and Sartre disagree about the immorality and dehumanizing effects of institutional relations. On the contrary, they share an anti-institutional perspective. *Goffman's position is not an endorsement of the "status quo," because interactions are considered to have a preinstitutional and therefore a pre-status-quo order.* Therefore, simple interactions like supermarket queues play an important role in providing an atmosphere within which humans need not fear one another —where the orderliness of the interactions can be taken as a display of trust.

Sartre's individual cannot escape institutional definition and has only negativity as a critical standpoint, whereas the "working consensus" supplies an intrinsic value structure through which Goffman's individual can escape complete institutional definition.[16] This intrinsic value structure provides the foundation from which to pose a critique of institutional values, order, and meaning. If, however, we allow that meaning is defined with respect to institutions, the critique destroys the very structure of meaning on which interactions, and therefore the critique itself, stand.

Only by allowing that meaning, order, and self may be interactional achievements can we fully appreciate Goffman's position. The problem is that this is plausible only if meaning is really negotiated in interaction. Closure on this theoretical debate awaits detailed documentation and understanding of interactional process. The information we so badly need has been delayed by the neglect, and even open hostility, of sociology as a discipline toward such work. Once we accept the possibility that meaning is an interactional achievement, then studies in conversation analysis and ethnomethodology suddenly become relevant to important theoretical debates. They become a resource for epistemological critique. Furthermore, they offer the promise of an uncompromising critical position.

Notes

1. See Winch (1958) for a discussion of the relation of philosophy to social science. In addition, Levison (1974) takes a typical view that sociology is confined to the context of justification (which is also defined by philosophy), while philosophy explores the context of discovery.

2. See Schutz's argument with Parsons over whether Parsons ought to accept a philosophical foundation for his sociology in Grathoff (1978). Also see Natanson's introduction to this collection. Valone (1979:3) suggests that it was not so much a mutual misunderstanding—as Parsons suggested—as "differing views

on the role philosophy should play in relation to the social sciences."

3. One important exception is Randall Collins (1981), who argues for the importance of microstudies for macrotheory. Although I applaud Collins's general position, I have misgivings about his interpretation of ethnomethodology and conversation analysis. As Collins interprets ethnomethodology, its primary assumptions are (1) that human cognition is limited, therefore necessitating a taken-for-grantedness in everyday life, and (2) that interactions, because of this cognitive deficiency, are meaningless as they occur and get a meaning constituted for them only in retrospect. In consequence, all rules or techniques for sense making are considered retrospective constructs, as interactants have to be satisfied with a tacit assumption that ongoing interaction has meaning, in lieu of any actual meaning. My interpretation, as presented in this chapter, assumes not only that there is meaning in interactions but that interactants collaborate to achieve such a meaning and that such a collaboration is active and patterned. I think it is not human cognition that is limited but rather our model of the social actor and social action.

4. Many contemporary sociologists have examined the construction of the social world (Berger and Luckmann, Weber, Mannheim, Garfinkel, Sacks) and the social self (Mead, Cooley, Durkheim, Toennies, Goffman, Sartre). If the social order is a creation with respect to social construction practices, if it has a negotiated status, this fact makes some demands on how such a world can be studied. Assumptions about the social world set the limits for the adequacy of theories that might describe that world. See in particular Bittner (1974).

5. It is true that Goffman often focuses on the interactional achievement of status. The working consensus orients toward a particular definition of the situation, which includes status and roles. But for different settings there will be different definitions of the situation, some of which include status and some not. In my classroom, for instance, I *can* effectively maintain my social superiority by successfully performing as a teacher. Goffman is careful to point out, however, that I can do so only through the cooperation of others. When I go home on the trolley, however, the definition of the situation does not include any particular sta-

tus of mine. In such a situation the working consensus must treat all as equals (although there is an apparent consensus that old ladies have rights that others do not). There are also nonstatus aspects of situations heavily endowed with status quo significance. It is these situations, where the working consensus appears to have no status quo, or "institutional" content, or situations where meaning is negotiated above and beyond institutional content, that I am concerned to argue for as analytically separable interactional sequences. Although Goffman explicates strategic actions and the negotiation of status and role, he is also committed to revealing a noninstitutional level of interaction. Even where he focuses on interactions that have obvious status implications (Goffman, 1951, 1969b), he focuses on those features of the "working consensus" that create order and are not defined by order.

6. See, for instance, in *Presentation of Self*: "Real agreement will also exist concerning the desirability of avoiding an open conflict of definitions of the situation. I will refer to this level of agreement as a working consensus" (Goffman, 1959:10). See also Goffman (1969a:11, 28, 37, 49, 95, 105, 117, 122, 129, 1959:9, 13, 35, 36, 248, 250, 251).

7. See in particular Sacks (1972a, 1972b, 1974a, 1974b); see also Garfinkel (1963, 1967, 1974), Schegloff (1967, 1972, 1977), Jefferson (1972), and Pomerantz (1975). Of course, Sacks's view underwent modification, and a major break with Goffman ensued along the way. Nevertheless, the assumptions are in important and fundamental ways the same. See also Goffman (1981), where he works out in some detail the ways in which he views his own theory as relevant to the analysis of interaction through talk.

8. Sacks's lectures are unpublished and therefore generally unavailable. Since it is in these lectures that Sacks worked out a foundation for conversation-analytic thinking that reflects some Goffmanian organizational considerations, I will reproduce several passages from the lectures:

> Suppose we take as *one restricted constraint of a party to a conversation "willingness to speak"*: that he is willing to speak if he is addressed with some first-pair member; that is, he's willing to do some sec-

ond-pair member. Otherwise, so far as we're concerned now, he's not going to talk. Under that constraint, what kind of listening is required of him so as to be able to produce a second-pair member when a first-pair member has been addressed to him?

One such resource-consequence turns on just the sort of argument I just gave you. The problem can be posed: A makes a Q [question] to B, B makes an A [answer] to that Q; there are also in the conversation [persons] C, D, and E. How could we ever know that C, D, and E listened to that answer? The ways we can come to know involve tracking from this particular Q & A, their tiedness "forward," such that we came upon an utterance which C spoke which was a first-pair member of a pair tied to a prior utterance, and which may then have been found to be tied to A's answer.

That is to say, then, that the fact that one party at a time talks and, for example, only one party answers a given question doesn't mean that we're prevented from seeing that others are listening to that Q. But the operation of the tying structures will involve us in seeing throughout a conversation that persons were listening to utterances they didn't speak directly after and show thereby that they were listening. In just the way that they show, by some utterance, that they listened to a last, they show by some utterance that they listened to a last –N—that is, an utterance which occurred, for example, five utterances ago.

The upshot of this sort of argument is that some motivations for any participant's listening to each utterance of a conversation are taken care of by the rules for structuring conversation. The techniques for structuring conversation have as a consequence that in order to possibly speak in some next utterance to something done in the last, one may have to listen to some indefinite sequence of prior talk.

That provides for a kind of self-containedness to the rules of conversation. Such a motivational structure doesn't require, for example, necessary reference to class position and other sorts of motives. It's an abstract structure in that regard. And it holds for any conversation and any participants in any conversation.

So that, given that Q answered by B, he has "a first chance" to show that he understood that Q. If he ties to it, and then somebody ties to him, then somebody who is, for example, answering the next question will be showing that he understood it; to understand it he would have had to understand the utterance whereby B answered the question, and in order to understand that, he would have had to understand the question. And, therefore, that person, three utterances down, had had his chance to show that he understood the initial utterance.

And in that regard, then, that others see that you understand an utterance is something that they can show via the next utterance. And then you can see that, while tying proceeds locally, not only will a person eventually have a chance, say, to show that he also understood some utterance you showed you understood, but in doing that he will show that he understood that you understood [Sacks, 1967, Lecture 11:4-10].

The idea that participants are attending to tying techniques as they move "forward" through a conversation, in order not only to make sense of the conversation for themselves but also to assess the understanding of others, stands in direct opposition to the interpretations by Collins (see note 3) and Habermas (see note 12) of conversation-analytic and ethnomethodological assumptions about interactional order. Harvey Sacks is "the founding father," so to speak, of conversation-analytic work.

9. Sartre's emphasis on a moment of institutional "totalization" is similar to Marx's argument that there are times when praxis becomes organic (as in revolutions). For Marx, in these moments the artificial differentiation between persons breaks down, and they become totalized in their relationships with one another: "At those times when the state is most aware of itself, political life seeks to stifle its own prerequisites—civil society, and its elements —and establish itself as the genuine and harmonious species-life of man. But it can only achieve this end by setting itself in violent

contradiction with its own conditions of existence, by declaring a permanent revolution. Thus the political drama ends necessarily with the restoration of religion, of private property, of all the elements of civil society just as war ends with the conclusion of peace" (Marx, quoted in Tucker, 1978:36). These revolutionary instants are characterized as high points in human history. Humans are portrayed as having reached out to each other as humans, transcending the bondage of the status quo and its rules, which establish the separateness and differentness of people. According to Marx, the essential feature of civil society is this differentiation and alienation of each human being from the other and from himself or herself. Humanity seeks desperately to break free of its imprisonment in institutionality. The possibility of freedom can become permanent only when the initial moment of integration can be actually united with the general interest. "In the bureaucracy the identity of state interest and private aim is established in such a way that the state interest becomes a particular private aim over against other private aims. The abolition of the bureaucracy is only possible by the general interest actually—and not, as with Hegel, merely in thought, in abstraction—becoming the particular interest, which in turn is only possible as a result of the particular actually becoming the general interest" (Marx, quoted in Tucker, 1978:25). The moment when the particular and the general become one is the moment that transcends the particular. It is important to note that this is not the perfection or totalization of an institutional moment but, rather, the coming to unity of the underlying undifferentiated moment with the whole.

10. To the degree that Marx relies on an initial level of organization for the grounding of meaning, he escapes Sartre's dilemma. If the humanity of persons is founded on some underlying social relations, then there is an important sense in which the self is immediately a social self and only secondarily, or even artificially, an individual in the classic sense. In the *Grundrisse* Marx touches on this issue of the primacy of sociality over individuality: "The human being is in the most literal sense a political animal, not merely a gregarious animal, but an animal which can individuate itself only in the midst of society" (Marx, 1973:83–85). Marx goes on to say that "only in the eighteenth century, in 'civil society,' do the various forms of social connectedness confront the individ-

ual as mere means toward his private purposes as external necessity" (Marx, 1973:223). Marx accused the intellectuals of his day of having invented the "individual" as a foil for their conception of economic behavior. He might level this same criticism at Sartre as well for having conceived the primary level of organization as a relation of individual actions to institutionally defined ends. We should expect Marx to offer social gatherings and social agreements as the primary unit of social explanation. He describes the process of individuation as a sort of "taking the role of the other" (to borrow from Mead). For a discussion of the similarities between Marx and Mead, see Rawls (1980a).

11. The working consensus is in large part characterized as insurance against strategic interaction. But of course the existence of expected patterns of behavior at any level makes strategic action possible (see in particular Goffman's, 1953, discussion of the Shetland Islanders). Mistaking Goffman's preoccupation with this possibility for a sanctioning of it as the basic mode of interaction is to miss the point.

12. If one takes a purely strategic view, noninstitutional interaction is likely to look fragmented and disconnected. This is a problem for Habermas, who interprets the Goffmanian model as a purely strategic model. He will then say about ethnomethodology: "A more realistic picture is that drawn by ethnomethodologists— of a diffuse, fragile, continuously revised and only momentarily successful communication, in which participants rely on problematic and unclarified presuppositions and feel their way from one occasional communality to the next" (Habermas, 1983). Failing to acknowledge the possibility of a pure negotiational quality to interactional performance obscures the interpretation of ethnomethodology. If we allow however, that there is a noninstitutional negotiation of meaning, founded on a "working consensus" that is held in common, then Habermas's characterization of ethnomethodology (which is all too typical) has missed the essential underlying orderliness of everyday life, which is "really," after all, what ethnomethodology is all about (see note 8).

13. To the extent that Sartre's method depends on the reflexive consciousness being a moment within its own praxis and not outside it, it is vulnerable to a standing debate in philosophy concerning the adequacy of this version of self.

14. The difference between a retrospective and a prospective view is important. If a retrospective view is significantly different, a distinction results between everyday life and the position of the observer, as does the concomitant distinction between formal and practical reason. In the Schutz–Parsons debate, Schutz argues for a retrospective view, Parsons for a prospective view (Grathoff, 1978). Garfinkel (1967), Sacks (1972b:293), Jefferson (1972: 303), and Mannheim (1971:90–91) address the crucial problem of understanding the prospective view.

15. Aron (1976, chap. 3) has argued that Weber approached the idea of existential commitment in the guise of "personal conviction."

16. Marx's human can realize itself as species being in freedom only through unity with others. Within this unity the human transcends the alienated nature imposed on it by "civil society" —for example, institutional being. Marx is arguing that the belief that individuality and meaning are institutionally organized is itself occasioned by participation in "civil society" and therefore cannot be the primary mode of being. Institutional organization creates the impression of itself as the essential character of the relationships between humans. But this is a characterization by civil society, of itself. Although Sartre has tried to rebel against institutions, claiming that they place the self in bondage, he accepts civil society's characterization of order and meaning as dependent on institutions (that is, civil society) for its foundation. He is therefore unable to escape the vicious circle.

References

ARON, RAYMOND
  1976 *Main Currents in Sociological Thought.* Vol. 2. New York: Basic Books.
BITTNER, EGON
  1974 "The Concept of Organization." In Roy Turner (Ed.), *Ethnomethodology.* New York: Penguin Books.
COLLINS, RANDALL
  1980 "Erving Goffman and the Development of Modern Social Theory." In Jason Ditton, *The View from Goffman.* New York: Macmillan.

1981 "The Microfoundations of Macrosociology." *American Journal of Sociology* 86:984–1014.

CRAIB, IAN
1976 *Existentialism and Sociology: A Study of Jean-Paul Sartre.* Cambridge: Cambridge University Press.

GARFINKEL, HAROLD
1963 "A Conception of, and Experiments with 'Trust' as a Condition of Stable Concerted Actions." In O. J. Harvey (Ed.), *Motivation and Social Interaction.* New York: Ronald Press.

1967 *Studies in Ethnomethodology.* Englewood Cliffs, N.J.: Prentice-Hall.

1974 "The Rational Properties of Scientific and Commonsense Activities." In Anthony Giddens (Ed.), *Positivism and Sociology.* London: Heinemann Educational Books.

GOFFMAN, ERVING
1951 "Symbols of Class Status." *British Journal of Sociology* 2:294–304.

1953 "Communication Conduct in an Island Community." Unpublished doctoral dissertation, Department of Sociology, University of Chicago.

1959 *Presentation of Self in Everyday Life.* New York: Doubleday Anchor.

1961a *Asylums.* New York: Doubleday Anchor.

1961b *Encounters.* Indianapolis: Bobbs-Merrill.

1969a *Interaction Ritual.* New York: Doubleday Anchor.

1969b *Strategic Interaction.* Philadelphia: University of Pennsylvania Press.

1981 *Forms of Talk.* Philadelphia: University of Pennsylvania Press.

GRATHOFF, RICHARD (ED.)
1978 *The Theory of Social Action: The Correspondence of Alfred Schutz and Talcott Parsons.* Bloomington: Indiana University Press.

HABERMAS, JURGEN
1970 "Toward Communicative Competence." *Inquiry* 13: 205–218, 306–375.

1983 "Theory of Communicative Comeptence." In T. McCarthy (Ed.), *Reason and the Rationalization of Society.* Vol. 1. Boston: Beacon Press, in press.

HAYIM, GILA
  1980   *The Existential Sociology of Jean-Paul Sartre.* Amherst: University of Massachusetts Press.
JEFFERSON, GAIL
  1972   "Side Sequences." In David Sudnow (Ed.), *Studies in Social Interaction.* New York: Free Press.
LEVISON, ARNOLD
  1974   *Introduction to the Philosophy of the Social Sciences.* New York: Irvington Press.
LOFLAND, JOHN
  1980   "Early Goffman: Style, Structure, Substance, Soul." In Jason Ditton (Ed.), *The View from Goffman.* New York: Macmillan.
MANNHEIM, KARL
  1971   *From Karl Mannheim.* (Edited by Kurt Wolff.) Oxford: Oxford University Press.
MANNING, PETER
  1976   "The Decline of Civility: A Comment on Erving Goffman's Changing View of Life." *Canadian Review of Sociology and Anthropology* 13(1):13-25.
MARX, KARL
  1973   *Grundrisse.* New York: Penguin Books.
PARSONS, TALCOTT
  1949   *The Structure of Social Action.* New York: Free Press.
POMERANTZ, ANITA
  1975   "Second Assessments: A Study of Some Features of Agreements/Disagreements." Unpublished doctoral dissertation, University of California, Irvine.
PSATHAS, GEORGE
  1980   "Early Goffman and the Analysis of Face-to-Face Interaction in Strategic Interaction." In Jason Ditton (Ed.), *The View from Goffman.* New York: Macmillan.
RAWLS, ANNE
  1980a "Alienation and the Concept of Self in Marx." Unpublished manuscript.
  1980b "Critique of Max Weber: Epistemological Basis for a Science of Social Action." Unpublished manuscript.
  1983a "Constitutive Justice: A Contribution to the Understanding of Social Order and Human Value." Unpublished doctoral dissertation, Boston University.

1983b "An Ethnomethodological Perspective on Social Theory." In Helm Anderson and others, *Ethnomethodologies*. New York: Irvington Press, in press.

SACKS, HARVEY

1967 Unpublished lectures, University of California, Los Angeles.

1972a "An Initial Investigation of the Usability of Conversational Data for Doing Sociology." In David Sudnow (Ed.), *Studies in Social Interaction*. New York: Free Press.

1972b "Notes on the Police Assessment of Moral Character." In David Sudnow (Ed.), *Studies in Social Interaction*. New York: Free Press.

1974a "A Simplest Systematics for the Organization of Turn Taking in Conversation." *Language* 50(4):696–735.

1974b "Everyone Has to Lie." In B. Blount and R. Sanchez (Eds.), *Ritual Reality and Innovation in Language Use*. New York: Academic Press.

SARTRE, JEAN-PAUL

1957 *Transcendence of the Ego*. New York: Farrar, Straus & Giroux.

1971 *Being and Nothingness*. New York: Washington Square Press.

1976 *Critique of Dialectical Reason*. London: NLB.

SCHEGLOFF, EMMANUEL

1967 "The First Five Seconds: The Order of Conversational Openings." Unpublished doctoral dissertation, University of California, Berkeley.

1972 "Notes on Conversational Practice: Formulating Place." In David Sudnow (Ed.), *Studies in Social Interaction*. New York: Free Press.

SCHEGLOFF, EMMANUEL, WITH JEFFERSON, GAIL, AND SACKS, HARVEY

1977 "The Preference for Self-Correction in the Organization of Repair in Conversation." *Language* 53:361–382.

SHIBUTANI, TOMATSU

1966 *Improvised News: A Sociological Study of Rumor*. New York: Bobbs-Merrill.

TUCKER, ROBERT (ED.)
    1978   *The Marx-Engels Reader.* New York: W. W. Norton.
VALONE, JAMES
    1979   Review of "The Theory of Social Action." *Phenomenology and Social Science Newsletter* 7:3.
WINCH, PETER
    1958   *The Idea of a Social Science.* London: Routledge & Kegan Paul.

Parsons's epistemology of "analytical realism" could be developed only by first displacing Weber's alternative epistemology within the social action perspective. Reconsideration of Parsons's epistemological moves shows that he came to conclusions unsupportable within the social action perspective. Reassertion of the postulate of Verstehen *retrieves his achievements from the pure functionalism and positivism he opposed, by establishing a comprehensive action scheme centered on ideal-type analysis.*

❧ 9 ❧

THE PROBLEM
OF EPISTEMOLOGY IN THE
SOCIAL ACTION PERSPECTIVE

John R. Hall

UNIVERSITY OF MISSOURI, COLUMBIA

In the case of social collectivities, precisely as distinguished from organisms, we are in a position to go beyond merely demonstrating functional relationships and uniformities. We can accomplish something which is never attainable in the natural sciences, namely the subjective understanding of the action of the component individuals.

Max Weber, *Economy and Society* (1977:15)

Extended version of a paper presented at the "Theory and History" panel of the annual meeting of the American Sociological Association, San Francisco, September 1982. I wish to thank Guenther Roth, Andrew Walker, Stephen Warner, and Dean Gerstein for their comments on earlier versions of this chapter, which no doubt helped me avoid some pitfalls of the topic.

> He [Weber] is no naive monist. . . . But his
> "pluralism" tends, by hypostatization of ideal types,
> to break up, in a sense not inherent in analysis as
> such, the organic unity both of concrete historical in-
> dividuals and of the historic process.
> Talcott Parsons, *The Structure of Social Action* (1937:607)

Of the disparate social theorists whom Talcott Parsons studied in *The Structure of Social Action,* Max Weber proved both the
most enriching and the most frustrating. Weber provided the most
elaborated conceptual base for consolidation of a voluntary action
schema. But he also posed the most profound obstacles to Parsons's program of establishing general theory by means of an epistemology of "analytical realism."

The other theorists whom Parsons considered in *The Structure of Social Action* were either unproblematic or irrelevant to
his methodological intentions. Marshall merely foreshadowed the
theoretical "convergence" on the voluntary action schema that
Parsons sought to establish, and his ideas did not depart from conventional utilitarian theories sufficiently to provide a systematic
methodological position keyed to the new perspective. Durkheim
made moves to reconcile positivism with the problem of social
meaning and action, but in the process, in Parsons's view, he became trapped in difficulties of "reification" and "misplaced concreteness." "In fact Durkheim in escaping from the toils of positivism has overshot the mark and gone clear over to idealism" (Parsons, 1937[hereinafter, SSA]:445). If Durkheim went too far,
Pareto did not go quite far enough. Pareto acknowledged theoretical categories as playing a role in generating "facts" and conceived
the task of a logicoexperimental science as the specification of
"laws" or at least "empirical uniformities" (SSA:180-185).[1] For
Parsons, "Pareto had a clearer conception than Weber in the general methodological context" (SSA:294). Yet, perhaps because of
his nomological approach, Pareto did not explicitly develop a
methodology keyed to the voluntary action schema, wherein the
status and conceptualization of meanings, values, and norms would
have to be established (SSA:294-295).

For Parsons, the convergence toward the voluntary action
schema of the theories of Marshall, Durkheim, Pareto, and Weber

was the more remarkable for the diverse epistemological stand-points from which they worked (SSA:722). But this very diversity left open the question of what epistemology could provide a base adequate to the voluntary action schema. As theorists, Marshall, Durkheim, and Pareto had converged on the action perspective, if at all, out of epistemologies that were rendered increasingly problematic the closer their substantive movements came to the action schema. But they never rectified these tensions between epistemology and theory by recasting their epistemological positions.

Weber, however, had explicitly forged an epistemological base for his *verstehende Soziologie*. But although Weber did not deny the possibility of systematic social and economic theorizing, his own sociological interests were directed to analysis of historical development, and hence his epistemological solution was not geared to underpinning a general social theory. For this reason, he presented Parsons with a peculiar kind of obstacle. Substantively, his work represented an achievement of the highest order, developed explicitly within the very perspective that Parsons wanted to advance. But Weber's epistemology based on use of ideal types in empirical analysis staked a claim to the intellectual terrain Parsons had to occupy, but in a different way, to develop a general theory of action. While Parsons lauded Weber's substantive achievements, he went to great lengths to reject ideal-type analysis in favor of a "more parsimonious" epistemology of "analytical realism." Under this approach, Parsons argued that there is a real world, external to any observer (SSA:753). But for sociology to advance theoretically, it is necessary to study the world analytically, not empirically, with concepts that "are not fictional, but adequately 'grasp' aspects of the objective external world" (SSA:730). Spelling out the universal elements and functions of action, and their ranges of variation and interrelations, was to yield a formal schema to serve as the master key to social science.

The epistemological struggle by Parsons against Weber's methodology marks a key divergence in the sociological perspective that posits understanding of socially meaningful action as a cornerstone of theoretical discourse. Although the divergence in the social action perspective does not hinge on much more than the problem of ideal-type analysis, the consequences of Parsons's solution are substantial. In *The Structure of Social Action,* Parsons's emergent epistemological position, situated in a three-way rejection of pure idealism, utilitarianism, and empiricism, provided a foundation on which to build his substantive digressions toward Durkheim, away from Weber—namely, his organicism, his teleology, and his pronouncedly normative reading of Weber. Differentiating "analytic factors" allowed him to define sociology as a distinctive theoretical domain where the problem of normative integration is the preeminent focus (Burger, 1977). Parsons thereby effectively relegated the classical political economic concerns of such analysts as Marx and Weber to other social scientific disciplines (SSA:768ff.). It was Parsons's epistemology that allowed him to balkanize the intellectual domains of social theory, by linking separate analytic fields of study through the functional interrelations of the social system.

In the more general movements of sociological theory over the past forty-five years, the establishment of Parsons's general action theory has given rise to a disjuncture between two sociologies within the social action perspective: a historical-comparative sociology that attends to individual cases of action complexes and their alternative developmental tendencies and a thoroughgoing functionalism that focuses on the general emergent properties of action "systems" and the uniformities of relations among properties. Although at their epistemological cores the two social action sociologies are mirror images of each other, and although outstanding work within the social action perspective tends to transcend the polar positions, still Parsons's solution has a serious shortcoming. His use of analytic factors rather than ideal types makes it impossible to adequately conceptualize the temporal, hence meaningful, character of social action. Analytical realism thus detaches Parsons's approach from the study of social action itself, rendering his general action schema theoretically unstable, with the result that, his intentions notwithstanding, functionalism can easily be subsumed in a more comprehensive positivism. Under such a tendency, the potential of Parsons's unique contribution to the social action perspective is eclipsed completely.

Jeffrey Alexander (1978:178) has called Parsons's sociological epistemology "his most fundamental theoretical contribution." It does not stand or fall with Parsons's interpretations of others' or his own social theories, both of which have come under strong attack. Although Parsons's work has the potential for synthetic accommodation with Weber's approach in a way that would consolidate the advance of a single social action paradigm, his own epistemological choices and the resulting theoretical instability and disjuncture tend to deflect social theory from the kinds of considerations that would solidify such an advance. To the degree that Parsons's critique of Weber's epistemology allowed him to transcend conceptualization of social action, and to the degree that his analytic factor approach has engendered a functionalist slippage toward positivism, the original voluntary action schema has been pushed into a theoretical cul-de-sac.

Parsons might well have regretted this consequence. True, he was strongly committed to general theory over empiricism (Parsons, 1977a). But he always remained convinced of the continuities between his early "convergence" voluntary action schema and his later functionalist systems theory. Potentially, accommodation between the divergent epistemological emphases of Weber and Parsons keyed to the postulate of *Verstehen* would not undermine Parsons's achievements; rather, it would retrieve them from crude operationalization within a pure functionalism and positivism essentially at odds with the voluntary action schema. But such *rapprochement* cannot be achieved by sleight of hand, like a rabbit pulled out of a hat; it requires careful consideration of Weber's and Parsons's alternative approaches to sociological concept formation and analysis—their points of agreement and points of debate.

This enterprise can be best advanced by first reviewing Parsons's critique of Weber, which gave rise to his alternative of "analytical realism." I will then explore the limits and insights of this critique and, finally, sketch a modified epistemology for a consolidated social action paradigm that would alter the basis for consideration of Parsons's substantive theoretical work.

Parsons's Critique of Weber's Epistemology

Like Alfred Schutz (1967; see Hall, 1981), Talcott Parsons praised Max Weber's sociological work but went to great lengths to revise the epistemological base for his achievements. Schutz wanted to found Weber's *verstehende Soziologie* in a phenomenology of social action and the lifeworld. He sought to refine Weber's basic concept of subjectively meaningful action but treated Weber's analytic strategy employing ideal types as unproblematic.

Parsons was not unfamiliar with phenomenology. Indeed, he maintained that the phenomenological dimension "remains implicit in any use of the action schema" (SSA:750–751). But he recognized that his moves toward general theory and causal explanation took him beyond phenomenology. These moves gave rise to an epistemological critique of Weber that differed substantially from Schutz's.[2] If for Schutz, Weber's methodological instincts were sound but underdeveloped, for Parsons, they were inadequate and misleading.

Parsons interpreted Weber's epistemology as a reaction against nineteenth-century idealist historicism. This application of idealism to the domain of history had sought to unmask the unique *Geist* of a culture; it necessarily repudiated any search for social scientific laws and delimited for science the role of reconstructing the empirical historical "facts" out of which the *Geist* could be discerned. Weber consolidated a tendency in German scholarship to break up the historicist-idealist complex by shifting the hermeneutic method toward considering the relativity of diverse social actors, with multiple and often conflicting goals. Epistemologically this move was sustained by an approach that asserts *Verstehen*—understanding of subjectively meaningful action—as a criterion of adequacy in concept formation and explanation, and ideal-type analysis as a strategy consonant with that criterion (Roth, 1971; Burger, 1976).

Although Parsons extensively critiqued Weber's epistemology, his differences with Weber should not be inflated. His discourse (SSA:591–597) on methods in natural and social science amounts to no more than a quibble with Weber, and he accepted the postulate of *Verstehen* virtually without discussion. The real problem was ideal-type analysis.

Weber did not assert a difference in the *general* logics of natural and social scientific inquiry; he simply added *Verstehen* as a criterion of the adequacy of social scientific explanation and asserted that value interests in social inquiry tend to render explanations of historical individuals[3] of greater interest than the formulation of general laws.[4] Parsons, for his part, considered *Verstehen* a special possibility of social science that did not have to violate general scientific canons (SSA:634-635). Indeed, he claimed the essential conformity of his voluntary action schema with *Verstehen* as a postulate requiring reference to "real subjective processes" (SSA:750-751). Further, he agreed that the fact of access to the subjective aspect of action "constitutes an objective difference between the subject matters of the two [natural and social] groups of sciences, and one of central importance" (SSA:583). For his part, Weber (1975) had never questioned the possibility that general laws about social phenomena might be specified; he simply doubted, on the basis of the value relevance of individualizing explanation in historical analysis, that such general laws would prove to be of much significance. In short, in the *Naturwissenschaft-Geisteswissenschaft* debate, there is little *logical* basis to distinguish the two positions.[5] Parsons had warrant to establish a system of general propositions, but that project could be judged best by its achievements. Here, as Parsons (SSA:596) himself admitted, general theory faces an uphill battle, for social science relevance is established more easily in concrete explanation of individual cases.

Despite these areas of broad agreement, Parsons rejected Weber's epistemology, largely because of its almost exclusive reliance on ideal-type analysis as a methodology. Weber created ideal types as sociologically clear concepts based on a principle of internal meaningful consistency; such concepts could then be used as "benchmarks" in empirical investigations, to see to what degree given cases could be subsumed under particular ideal-typical models of social action, organization, and dynamics. But Parsons argued that Weber had failed to integrate ideal types on a formal theoretical basis by spelling out their logical relations with one another in terms of a general set of element concepts. This move, in Parsons's view, would achieve a basic scientific goal—namely, greater parsimony than is possible in Weber's approach: A larger number of ideal types can be specified from a smaller number of element concepts by varying the values of the elements (SSA:618).

It is true, as Parsons (SSA:640ff.) himself recognized, that Weber defined his types by building from more elemental sociological concepts—for example, concepts of rational and other forms of action, relationship, organization, and the like (see Roth, 1971, especially p. 115). For Parsons, however, this is not enough, for it leaves the types suspended in ambiguous theoretical isolation from one another: There is no logical system of interrelations of types, nor does each type consist of a particular constellation of a general system of elements. But even if this problem were to be resolved, Parsons found what he believed to be a deeper problem of ideal-type analysis exposed. On the theoretical level, Parsons asserted that each type constitutes a constellation of elements in fixed relation to one another, while in empirical phenomena, the elements may vary independently. This differential creates a source of bias in empirical investigation. Since concrete phenomena are complex and ambiguous, they vary beyond the boundaries of any given ideal type or battery of types; hence, they can be adequately described only by, as it were, liberating the analytic elements from the fixed relations by which types are constituted (SSA:619).

In principle, for Parsons, ideal-type analysis and his own approach of "analytical realism" are what might be called mirror images of each other. Since ideal-type analysis implies a more general theoretical system, once that system is elaborated formally, any type can be specified by a fixed set of values of the general elements, and conversely, elemental dimensions describe a range of types and cases. The former tack gives rise to a social science of ideal types applied to concrete empirical cases; the latter permits the study of concomitant variations in conceptual elements, thus making possible the testing of "laws" about the causal relations between elemental dimensions.

But in Parsons's view, the translatability, in principle, between ideal-type and element-variable analysis does not prevent grave theoretical consequences from arising out of adopting the former approach rather than the latter. Exclusive reliance on ideal types sets up a dilemma, to which any resolution simply poses new difficulties. At the heart of the problem is what Parsons termed "atomism"—the result of constituting ideal types that, because of their character as abstract, internally consistent models, pose rigid separations between aspects of concrete phenomena (SSA:631; for a later formulation of the critique, see Parsons, 1967:73ff.). The result is a tendency toward reification in one of two phases—either (1) a "mosaic" theory that traces a diverse set of departures from ideal-type constructs or (2) a rigid evolutionism (SSA:607, 621,

626). Although Parsons did not elaborate his views in any detail, it must be presumed by his use of the term *mosaic* that element values not covered in the batteries of ideal types escape analysis altogether or at least are lost to analytic continuity owing to their lack of specification in their own terms. In any event, the atomistic separation of ideal types implies, in Parsons's view, that the empirical connection between certain conceptual elements (his example is of adventurer and rational bourgeois forms of capitalism) tends to be ignored (SSA:631).[6] If reification remains pluralistic, Parsons argues, the mosaic outcome yields a kind of fragmented and ad hoc empiricism. If, however, reification is tied to a systematic theory, its result is a "rigid evolutionary scheme" (SSA:621). The only other alternative open to ideal-type analysis is to retreat to a position in which concepts are taken to be simply "convenient fictions," which, "since they are not empirically true, do not explain anything" (SSA:626). "The only means of breaking this mosaic rigidity without recourse to skepticism is generalized theory which breaks down the particular element combinations in the ideal types, but by seeing in them a manifestation of common elements in constant modes of relationship with each other, transfers knowledge to a more flexible, yet at the same time more realistic basis" (SSA:626).

Countercritique

Parsons's attack on Weber's methodology of the social sciences was designed to dislodge it from occupying the conceptual space where Parsons would have to establish his own approach of analytical realism. Discounting areas of basic agreement—on the logic of science in general and the significance of *Verstehen* for social scientific inquiry—Parsons's attack focused on ideal-type analysis and occurred on two main fronts: (1) the purported tendencies of ideal-type analysis toward methodological atomism and (2) parsimony in theory. On the former basis, Parsons wanted to show the limitations of Weber's approach; the latter front offered a way to show the superiority of his own methodological solution. But neither kind of claim is sufficiently strong to reject Weber out of hand, and hence Parsons (for example, 1965:60) was careful to acknowledge that Weber's approach was "legitimate," although it involved "certain limitations" and was "only one of a number of necessary components of the social sciences." Parsons's critique was not designed so much to displace Weber's sociology as to subsume it; consequently, each of his lines of critique points for its resolution toward a comprehensive methodology that includes ideal-type analysis but establishes general theory at the center of discourse.

But Parsons's critique is based on a different set of presuppositions from those of Weber. Understanding the basis of Parsons's methodological quarrels with Weber establishes the grounds for delimiting the difficulties of Parsons's own solution. Because Parsons failed to treat Weber's analytic strategy as an integrated solution, and because he made moves that are at odds with necessary ontological assumptions about meaningful social life, he came to conclusions that must be judged unsupportable within the social action perspective.

The Problem of Organicism. Ironically, Parsons admitted to the usefulness of ideal types in sociological analysis and often used them in his substantive analyses; this in itself casts doubt on his commitment to his own critique of them. If he thought that use of types involves a "methodological atomism" that breaks up the "organic unity" of societies, leading either to reification or to a "fictional" form of theory, then how could he succumb to using them at all?

Conversely, it might be argued that Parsons's alternative of "analytical realism" itself breaks up the "organic unity" of social complexes of action, at the same time that it establishes a reified set of abstractions whose systemic interrelations create a fictional theoretical world. The sins of the "master-at-a-distance" (as Merton, 1980:68, considered Weber for Parsons) may be projections by the apprentice! Although this issue needs further consideration in assessing Parsons's own solution (see below), to begin with, it is important to consider briefly the way Parsons adopted organicism as a criterion for rejecting Weber's ideal-type methodology.

Weber (1977:13) consistently argued that, for purposes of sociological analysis, collective entities (such as the "state") could not be attributed a reality other than "as solely the resultants and modes of organization of the particular acts of individual persons, since these alone can be treated as agents in a course of subjectively understandable action." Such collective concepts and their use *by actors* who invoke "normative authority" (1977:14) may be a proper *subject* of analysis, but there are limits to the functionalism that follows in the wake of an "organic conceptualization of society": Functionalism can provide only a "provisional orientation," and "if its cognitive value is overestimated and its concepts illegitimately 'reified,' it can be highly dangerous" (1977:14–15).

Although Weber was a bit of a functionalist, he was no organicist. For Parsons to fault Weber on this basis would have required that Parsons establish the criterion of organicism by some independent line of argument. But in *The Structure of Social Action* Parsons's promotion of organicism really proceeds only by metaphor, and by default, in his assertions about Weber's "atomistic" approach. The metaphor (SSA:32) can be dismissed summarily: It is fantastic to point to Aristotle's argument about the human hand existing as what it is only by its connection to the rest of the body and to argue for a similar model for societies. To do so is to assume organicism in order to prove it.

Ideal Types, Parsons's Dilemma, and Historical Analysis. Parson's rejection of ideal-type analysis on the basis of its purported atomistic consequences really rests on Parsons's own preference for development of a general sociological theory, an approach that Weber did not pursue. Here Parsons simply assumed that theory must take a general form—that is, that it must be detached from its historical subjects to be worthy of the name. Although he effusively praised Weber's accomplishments in interpretive historiography, his considerations of Weber's ideal types (SSA, chap. 17)—what Parsons called Weber's "systematic theory"—failed to show recognition that, for Weber, the theoretical domain of ideal types and general laws (that is, for Weber, sociology properly conceived) serves as handmaiden to historical analysis, not as a domain to be integrated in its own terms (see Roth, 1976). It is Parsons's disregard for the essential continuities Weber elaborated between use of type concepts and thorough historical analysis that produces Parsons's charges of atomism and a dilemma between reification and a fictional theory of type concepts. Such a dilemma exists only for a sociology conceptually isolated from historical analysis.

For Weber, there was no dilemma; type concepts have to be

"fictions" because of the need for clear and consistent concepts reflecting "the highest possible degree of adequacy on the level of meaning" (1977:20; see Burger, 1976:123). But simply because types are "ideal" does not require that they be totally ahistorical; rather, they represent pure concepts *relevant* to the interpretation of extant and historical formations. It is for this reason that Roth (1979:125) prefers to call ideal types "sociohistorical models." If they are useful, it is because they are distillations of dynamics of various kinds of social action and organization. True, they are fictions, and this means that *by themselves* the furthest they can be carried is to analysis of their structural properties (see Roth, 1971: 126). But since they are meaningfully adequate models, to the degree that a given empirical case approximates one or another model, explanation of that case is subsumed under the "general" case —that is, the dynamic of the model. Thus, Weber did not limit the use of ideal types to abstract theorizing; indeed, he devoted the greater part of his energies to interweaving whole batteries of types with accounts of historical events, as a way of laying out "secular theories" (Roth, 1979) about concrete courses of historical development. In interpretive sociology, types and sequences thereof cannot properly stand on their own as theory; instead, they have to be brought to bear in historical analysis, where they provide an efficient means for discerning and highlighting the meaningful sources of diverse juxtapositions, conjunctures, and shifts of actual complexly interrelated social phenomena.

The ways Weber integrated ideal types into his own methodology of historically focused interpretive sociology do not involve the dangers of "reification" and a "fiction theory" that Parsons worried about. Weber regarded attempts to develop a grand theory that would establish causal relations among variables as largely futile. Instead, he held that the duality of analytic concepts and meaningful events requires a methodology that draws on the former as a way of trying to discern the causal processes at work *in the events themselves*.

Parsons was perhaps correct to describe Weber's approach as involving a methodological atomism—the inevitable outcome of creating ideal types as clear, unambiguous concepts reflecting meaningful action. But types also are historically relevant models, and if they are not taken as historical explanations themselves, but

instead are used carefully in conjunction with one another in substantive analysis of history, they offer the possibility of developing
secular theories that are neither evolutionistic nor teleological and
are not mosaic reifications. Indeed, this is what Weber provided in
Economy and Society: "a statement of the general historical relationships between economic and social organization and of the
general relationships between economic and social organization
and of the general developmental directions of changes ('rationalization')" (Roth, in Schluchter, 1981:xxv). Parsons came to a
negative assessment of this approach because of his own organicist
assumptions. Once these assumptions are abandoned and the
working relation between sociology and history in Weber's approach is understood, Parsons's charges against ideal-type analysis
lose their force.

   History, Verstehen, *and the Limits of Parsimony.* Ironically,
Parsons's argument in favor of an analytic-element approach over
ideal-type analysis flows from his own discursive atomism—his tendency to discuss different methodological issues in isolation from
one another, rather than grasping Weber's methodological solution
as a whole, predicated on and adjusted to the principle of subjective understanding. If *Verstehen* were not a consideration, the assertion of greater parsimony in a general theory would be established more easily: If each ideal type is described by a fixed
constellation of values of analytic elements, then a larger number
of types can be generated from a smaller number of variables. It
would make some sense to investigate interrelationships between
variables, rather than haphazardly considering various types as
constellations of variable values on an ad hoc basis.

   But the distinctive features of *social* sciences undermine this
parsimony in two closely connected ways. First, social analysis is
directed to a meaningfully finite set of interconnected and historically emerging phenomena (there are, for example, somewhat fewer than 200 nation-states in the world). Given any set of universal
variables that could be established, the extant and historical cases
should fall far short of approaching their possible range of variation. The alternative would be to assume (as does Gehlan, 1963)
that possibilities of social life and organization have already been
nearly exhausted. Even if we consider large numbers of individual
social actors (for example, in their motives in relation to work),

the tendency may be for cases to cluster together in radically alternative complexes of action, rather than varying continuously (this,
of course, is an empirical question). In any event, whether the
cases available for analysis are few or many, insofar as they represent a subsample of all possible cases, with no way of determining
the bounds of that subsample, sampling difficulties would prevent
any valid inference about general theoretical propositions.[7]

This argument can be placed in a more positive light by
briefly considering a related second matter, the value relevance of
social inquiry. As Parsons (1951:151ff.) occasionally affirmed,
since the number of historical formations is finite, and since the
tendency is toward an interest in historical individuals, greatest
parsimony can be achieved by considering the limited number of
ideal types that are relevant to the issues under consideration. In
this respect, Parsons was simply wrong to assert that Weber's types
are fixed and rigid and therefore incapable of dealing with variation, say, in one attribute that goes into the constellation of establishing a type. To the contrary, Weber often specified subtypes
(for a concise example, see his discussion of collegial authority,
1977:271ff.) that are tremendously useful in historical analysis
precisely because they typify, in meaningfully consistent ways,
closely related alternative patterns of social organization and the
factors (elements, if you will) of transition between types that are
relevant to differentiation within even a relatively narrow range of
variation of concrete social phenomena. Because Parsons wanted
to establish general theory as an enterprise that is in principle self-
contained, and because he therefore tended to divorce Weber's
conceptual categories from his secular historical theories,[8] he argued in *The Structure of Social Action* for the *formal* parsimony
of an integrated theoretical system. But this parsimony breaks
down in favor of an *analytic* parsimony once the connections between history and sociology are emphasized.

The arguments so far in favor of theoretical versus empiricist
parsimony are predicated on different conceptions of the sociological enterprise, and the choice between the two has to derive from
strategic rather than ontological considerations. But there is an
additional question, one in which the core principle of an interpretive sociology is at stake. Does Parsons's movement from an
ideal-type approach to concept formation to a position of "analy-

tical realism" mark a departure from concern with subjectively meaningful action? Some writers (for example, Martindale, 1959; Scott, 1963; Savage, 1981) have argued that the further Parsons moved toward general theory (that is, during the post–World War II era), the more he relegated socially meaningful action to a subsidiary and hypothetical role. Others (Turner and Beeghley, 1974; Gerstein, 1975; Munch, 1982) want to show the essential continuity between Parsons's voluntary action schema, the pattern variables (Parsons, 1951), and his social system theory (Parsons and Shils, 1951; Parsons, Bales, and Shils, 1953). Gerstein's demonstration merely sharpens the issue: Although the AGIL functions are clearly shown to be *grounded* in the voluntary action schema, they simply mark a more clear formulation of the model that, as Munch (1982:780) holds, is implicit in *The Structure of Social Action,* in which social action becomes significant especially for its functional or dysfunctional consequences, defined in terms of the resonance between goals of the personality system and the ultimate goals of the social system.

The methodological question turns on whether the move toward a basically functional consideration of social action violates the principle of *Verstehen.* There is good reason to think it does. Subjectively meaningful action, as Parsons (SSA:732–733) himself clearly understood, is occasional and concrete. As opposed, for example, to atemporal, potentially "eternal" norms, myths, and symbols (that is, cultural meanings), meaningful action has an inherently temporal structure involving a historicity of past, present, and future, linked together in the stream of consciousness of the actor (Husserl [1905], 1964; Schutz, 1967). The capacity to specify a structure of subjective temporalities can be considered a decisive test of whether a sociological concept remains true to the principle of *Verstehen* (Hall, 1980, 1981). Because ideal types are hypothetical cases, they are well suited to serve as concepts reflecting subjectively meaningful action, for the case can be a hypothetical actor or complex of actors, with attendant temporally articulated motives (Schutz, 1973:3–47).[9]

But it is precisely the temporal structure of action that "drops out" in the move from an ideal-type to an analytic-factor approach (see Giddens, 1979:62). For example, the pattern variable universalism/particularism does not carry a temporal structure. In itself, the dimension, or either pole of it, is not a (hypo-thetical) existential moment of being-in-the-world. The same argument holds for the four-function AGIL paradigm. It is true, as Gerstein (1975) has argued, that two of the AGIL functions—adaptation and goal attainment—have as one of their bases a relation to one form of action, rational action, in which means are directed toward previously established ends. But the AGIL functions are indeed functions, not types of action. In reference to any one of them, at a theoretical level it is possible to specify only the significance of functional fulfillment for system maintenance, not the temporal structure of action whereby the function is (or is not) fulfilled. In short, it is only in association with other elements or functions in a concrete or hypothetical case that an element or function can be aligned with a temporal structure.

The atemporal character of Parsons's categories is keyed to his identification with Husserl's ([1901], 1970b) early atemporal essentialism, which contrasts with the emphasis Husserl ([1913], 1962, [1905], 1964, 1970a) gave later to the essential temporal character of consciousness and its lifeworld setting. It was the latter approach that inspired Alfred Schutz, who worked much more consistently within an action perspective than Parsons did.[10] If, for Schutz (1967), Weber moved from a sociology of subjectively meaningful action to a sociology of observers' meanings about action, it must be concluded that Parsons went even further: from a sociology of observers' meanings about action to an abstract set of independently varying factors that cannot embody a subjective temporal structure and hence cannot conceptualize subjectively meaningful action. It is this move on the epistemological level that brought Parsons beyond the action perspective on the substantive level, allowing him to align the *functions* of actions with the atemporal Durkheimian collective cultural domain of norms, myths, symbols, and system goals.

Although Parsons charged that Weber violated the organicism of a (postulated) society-as-a-whole with his so-called methodological atomism, Parsons ignored the organic character of action itself. He claimed that ideal-type analysis cannot accommodate analysis of "emergent" features of social reality that occur in the admixture of various ideal-typical patterns of action (SSA:631), but he failed to recognize the emergent features of action; when action is conceptualized as the interplay of various elements, it must be understood that its meaningful character is more than the simple sum of the atemporal elements themselves. Put another way, the existential structure of action marks a "unit" (to use Parsons's term) that cannot be decomposed further without destroying its temporal, hence meaningful, character.[11]

Parsons's (SSA:616ff.) complaint against the "fixed" character of the interrelations between elements in a given ideal type is predicated on an absence of recognition that certain emergent features of "unit actions" derive from those fixed relations of elements to one another. This lacuna, in turn, stems from Parsons's own predilection to parcel out "elements" of theoretical analysis for separate treatment; because he dealt separately with the issue of *Verstehen* (SSA:583–591) and that of ideal-type analysis versus generalizing concepts (SSA:601ff.), he could not contend with the logical connection between *Verstehen* and ideal types as part of an integrated epistemological solution. By breaking down ideal types into their component variable elements, Parsons breached the bounds of *Verstehen*.

Parsons critiqued Weber's epistemology in order to set forth an approach appropriate to the voluntary action schema whose convergence, he argued, was established in the works of those who preceded him. But in his own elaborations of "analytical realism," Parsons undermined that convergence by advancing a position in which the core focus of that schema—subjectively meaningful action—tends to "drop out" of the theory.

Consequences of Parsons's Epistemological Move

The epistemological shift to analytical realism makes possible specific features of Parsons's theory that have been the subject of a good deal of controversy. The theory has also given rise to tendencies that Parsons might well have regretted. But there is another side to Parsons's work, in which he had geared his system theory to substantive analyses that explicitly or implicitly employed ideal-type analyses (for example, Parsons, 1951:151ff., 1954, 1977b, 1978). The alternative difficulties and possibilities are marked by the boundary between two conflicting tendencies in Parsons's work—an isolated general theory, on the one hand, and a comprehensive action schema, on the other.

The Path of General Theory. This is not the place to review the variety of criticisms that Parsons's work has faced (for example, Lockwood, 1956; Dahrendorf, 1958; Mills, 1959; Horowitz, 1962; Gouldner, 1970). But it is significant that a number of Parsons's detractors attack features of his theory that ultimately derive from the way his epistemological solution establishes general theory in the frame of analytical realism. Bershady (1973:13) unmasks the basic problem through analogy with a human face: "The dilemma lies, I believe, in the fact that all the characteristics and functions Parsons offers us, no matter how few or many are used, or how they are combined, cannot reproduce the features of any single society." What is at stake is the loss of a certain hypothetical concreteness that ideal types maintain. Because Parsons's categories conceptually break up historically individual complexes of social action into independently variable elements, they shatter the quality of meaningful historicity embedded in social life; similarly, his AGIL scheme explores functional interrelations at the system level rather than understanding societies' patterns of concrete socially meaningful action.

Parsons not only breaks up the organic quality of meaningful action but fails to achieve the organicism he himself pursued—of the action system and social system. This is because, following Kant, he admits the possibility of multiple schemata of analytical elements, each directed to different "interpenetrating spheres" of theoretical interests—political science, economics, sociology (see Munch, 1981). To avoid relativism, Parsons (SSA:601) asserted that these alternative schemes ultimately have to be " 'translatable' into terms of each other or of a wider scheme." Burger (1976:138–139; see Oakes, 1977) has shown that here Parsons creatively misconstrued Weber, who never sought to transcend the relativity of different theoretical schemata. Be that as it may, the consequences parallel those of moving to the level of general theory in the first place. Both moves go beyond the frame of reference of meaningful action and destroy the action organicism possible in comparative case analysis. They thus fragment social theory in a way that makes it difficult to study the interrelations between different analytically discernible spheres of phenomena—the economic, the political, the social (Burger, 1977:36).

Parsons (1977a) agreed that he advocated the analytic separation of spheres that Burger described, calling it the necessary outcome of an analytic, as opposed to empiricist, approach to theory. But he also insisted that he had tried to go beyond simple definition and description of functionally differentiated subsystems to specify their "inputs" and "outputs" with one another (see, for example, Parsons and Smelser, 1956:51ff.; Parsons and Platt, 1973). Even with this solution, basic problems persist. If Parsons found the empiricist Weber's "methodological atomism" to create difficulties in reconstituting the empirical totality, such problems surely must be compounded on the theoretical level: Parsons's "theoretical atomism" generates a mosaic of subsystem theories. The solution to this difficulty within the Parsonian framework is, as Parsons suggested, to specify a more comprehensive theoretical system that establishes the linkages and interpenetrations between subsystems. But such a synthesis cannot be achieved by systems analysis at the level of general theory.

General theory, to be worthy of the name, has to stand on its own terms, as an integrated set of propositions about relations between categories. But if, as Weber asserted and Parsons agreed, the meaningful interpretability of social action is a key element in social scientific explanation, then it is not possible to establish general theory on a strictly abstracted basis while remaining true to the postulate of *Verstehen*. Parsons's general theory does have a basis in categories about meaningful action (SSA:750-751), but this does not prevent violation of the postulate of *Verstehen*, for the significance of social actions cannot always be discerned in the formal, or derivative, properties, specified through analytic categorization. This is because the connections between subsystems, for example, are not always discernible at the formal theoretical level. Except for atemporal cultural meanings, the "interpenetrations" that Munch (1982) emphasizes are not simply formal theoretical relations of inputs and outputs between analytically real systems and subsystems; instead, they often involve lifeworldly connections of meaningful actions. Even theoretically atemporal cultural meanings, as Bourdieu (1977) has convincingly shown, cannot be theorized adequately as objectivities existing independently of the temporal practice (that is, action) which sustains and modifies them and by which they come into play socially. Meaningful content of actions, and the specific linkages of content across a potentially diverse set of "interpenetrating spheres" of action, create affinities and conjunctures between complexes of action that may remain formally distinct on the level of general theory. A given action, for example, may be oriented toward both economic and religious ends. The connections between spheres are historically established and emergent, and they do not always fit easily within a model that would describe them either as "inputs" and "outputs" or as interpenetrations of analytic subsystems. In short, isolated general theory is a flawed enterprise from the start, for even when it employs intersystemic analysis of substantive phenomena, it cannot capture certain decisive, meaningful elements of the phenomena about which it purports to theorize. It is thus detached from the social action perspective that gave rise to it.

Insofar as general theory becomes isolated from the voluntary action schema, there is a further—and, no doubt, from Parsons's viewpoint in *The Structure of Social Action,* perverse and unintended—consequence. The more a general theory transcends its base in interpretive categories of social action, the more easily it becomes aligned with other theoretical positions at odds with the voluntary action schema—namely, "pure functionalism" (that is, functionalism devoid of comparative structural analysis) and sociological positivism (which posits society as a reality *sui generis* subject to laws to be discovered scientifically through progressive testing of hypotheses in relation to empirical facts).

To the degree that a general theory of social action becomes shorn of its meaningful action-type concepts, its propositions take the same forms as those of other universalistic theories, and indeed, as Parsons (SSA:727; 1954:212ff., especially p. 218) optimally seems to have intended, the whole range of variables comes to be specifiable in a set of interrelated equations (see Munch, 1982:791). It is the parallel structure of variables in general and Parsons's analytic elements derived from an action perspective that makes possible the striking synthesis initially established in *The Structure of Social Action,* whereby the whole range of the means/ends continuum, from materially causal processes to teleological ones, can be integrated into a single theoretical model. This synthesis in turn paves the way for Parsons's (for example, 1951, 1978) later work on action theory and social systems.

But the costs of the synthesis are potentially great, for the solution is an inherently problematic result of Parsons's compelling urge to rectify ostensibly incompatible approaches to social theory (see Bershady, 1973:163; Menzies, 1976:38–39). Parsons's general theory is situated in an unstable dual alignment: The axis of a social action perspective would require a limited form of general theory and a particular set of relations to empirical analysis, whereas alignment with other forms of general theory (for example, positivism, utilitarianism, pure functionalism) eclipses the ontological and epistemological assumptions that delimit the action perspective. This dual alignment of Parsons's work with mutually incompatible theoretical positions forces resolution in one direction or the other. At various points in his scholarly career, Parsons developed the possibilities in each direction, heightening the contradictions, so to speak. Typically, Parsons (for example, 1954, 1967, 1978) wrote either substantive essays employing his theoretical framework at its current stage of development, often discussing action in terms of roles, or theoretical essays on the constitution of the "action system," its components, and their relations to other systems. Intellectually he and his students seem to have been capable of transcending the tensions between disparate phases of his work. Others, less agile, tend for the sake of consistency to opt for one alignment or the other, either working within an empiricist *verstehende Soziologie* that relegates general theory to a subsidiary role or proceeding within the frame of a positivism that subsumes the whole range of general theory.[12] It is the latter approach that poses serious difficulties.

Parsons himself began his career by seeking to offer an alternative to utilitarianism and positivism, and he no doubt lamented their predominance in sociology. Nevertheless, as an unintended consequence, the character of general theory in his work parallels the form of sociological positivism in a way that has solidified its position, rather than challenging it. Parsons was perhaps the central figure in the "sea change" of European social thought in the 1930s; in the United States his translations and interpretations of the European generation of 1890 stood practically unchallenged for decades. But on the American scene, those oriented toward an empirical and positivist sociology were ill prepared to deal with the nuances of the heterogeneous sources of European social theory. Thus, the tendency has been to subsume concepts from a variety of theoretical perspectives by "operationalizing" them. Unfortunately, the procedures of operationalization have often violated the basis of concept formation in the perspectives from which the concepts were borrowed. Perhaps the most glaring examples of this tendency have been the conceptualizations of "status" and "class" as continuous, interval-level variables.

Parsons himself did not engage in such "operationalizations." But the eclipse of *Verstehen* in a system theory alters the basis of concept formation in a way that is not incompatible with such practices. Thus, both Parsons's (1954:69-88, 386-439) original and revised approaches to the theory of stratification posit shared social values that give rise to scales of social ranking, in a way that parallels the positivist approach of W. Lloyd Warner and Paul Lunt (1941), for example. Similar approaches ecilpsing *Verstehen* emerge at the teleological end of the means/end continuum, where socially meaningful actions are subsumed under categories of pattern variables and system exigencies (that is, Parsons's AGIL problems) or the like, under a pure functionalism in which consequences are studied independently of the complexes of meaningful actions that give rise to them (for example, see Kanter, 1972).

All variables, functionalist ones and the others, come to be measured quantitatively and studied by means of a set of statistical procedures basically geared to the analysis of correlations of variables across cases and sets of cases. These modes of statistical analysis typically are based on a mathematical assumption about transitivity that is not often tenable in a social action perspective.[13] As Weber (1977:20-21) argued, averages and all statistics based on averages have application only where there is a concern with differences occurring "with respect to action which remains qualitatively the same, while in the majority of cases of action important to history or sociology the motives which determine it are qualitatively heterogeneous." But this argument has fallen on deaf ears, if indeed it has ever reached the *Umwelten* of positivist sociologists.[14] The dictates of a positivist social science require that the "variables" derived from a social action perspective be subsumed within a model alien to its assumptions.

Parsons should not be held accountable for these developments. But it must be recognized that if Parsons's general theory version of the action schema becomes isolated from ideal-type analysis, it tends to become aligned with general social theory as a whole in a way that does not countervail these tendencies but, rather, parallels them, by deriving dimensions of analytical variation in violation of the action perspective's postulate of *Verstehen*.

The Path of a Comprehensive Action Schema. Despite Parsons's predilections toward formulating a general theory of action that, in isolation, transcends the perspective from which it is derived, Parsons clearly showed that he also wanted to retain the case analysis that is the fountainhead of a *verstehende Soziologie*, but within a more encompassing epistemology. This is evidenced in the way he asserted the limitations of a "pure" functionalism. In this matter, he compared Durkheim unfavorably with Weber: Whereas Durkheim "saw clearly only the functional side of institutions, their relation to the determination of individual action, Weber saw their structural aspect on a tremendous 'architectonic' panorama" (SSA:653). To focus on structures is to focus on cases, and indeed, Parsons (SSA:742–743) insisted that his analytic-factor approach depends on the comparative method in order to discern the "independent variation of the values of analytical elements."

Whatever the tendencies to isolate Parsons's analytic-factor approach and subsume it within a more general positivist theoretical system, and however much this tendency is set up by Parsons's passage beyond an interpretive approach, this was not Parsons's intention. He applied his own efforts to maintaining analytical realism in a different alignment, one that incorporates Weber's ideal-type approach in a methodology directed toward analysis of empirical social phenomena.[15] In this alignment, so long as the continuity of analysis between analytic elements and ideal types (and thus between functions of action and meanings and structures of action, and between general theory and empirical analysis) is maintained, Parsons's divergence from Weber is not so great. Weber too used concepts of an analytic sort (for example, open and closed relationships [1977:43]) to build his ideal types. Moreover, as Guenther Roth (in Schluchter, 1981:xxiii) has pointed out, Weber employed analytic factors in combination with ideal types both in his developmental history and in case analysis. Although Weber did not construct formal batteries of ideal types derived from categorical variations of analytic elements, as Parsons and others have done, Parsons (SSA:640ff.) and, in a quite different way, McIntosh (1977) have shown that many of Weber's broadest types *could* be generated by such a procedure, and Schluchter (1981) has recently used such an approach to clarify and extend Weber's secular theory of Western rationalism, notably in a way that offers some rapprochement with Parsons's social systems theory. There is no inherent reason *not* to vary analytic elements as a way of generating skeletal ideal types, so long as they can be made to parsimoniously reflect complexes of socially meaningful action.[16] But this approach places the focus back on ideal-type analysis, within the action perspective. And it suggests that Parsons's commitment to a focus on action was something else than a stepping stone to a totally self-contained general theory.

For all his claims about the potential of universal lawlike propositions, Parsons did not go far in that direction, no doubt to the dismay of those who seek to build a "science of society." Instead, he used his approach of analytical realism to establish a sort of bootleg (that is, meaning-transcendent) ideal type, "the system," as a set of theoretical abstractions that can be used to describe empirical "systems" in general, as well as subcategories of them and individual cases. Weber used ideal types in part to generalize about historical formations and their developmental tendencies; Parsons used "types" of systems to generalize about evolutionary stages of social organization. Thus, that Parsons (for example, 1954, 1977b) was able to move back and forth between his conceptual systems and cases shows that the lifeworld—the everyday world in which we all live and act—was for him, like Weber and Schutz, the ultimate referent of social theorizing.

Reprise

Talcott Parsons's solution to the intertwined problems of concept formation and analytic strategy for social science within the social action perspective is vastly more sophisticated than what is possible under a pure positivism or pure functionalism (much less idealism, one-sided materialism, or historicism). Nevertheless, the "tilt" of his solution is skewed in the wrong direction. By establishing a general theoretical system of analytic elements rather than ideal types as the preeminent pole of analysis within his voluntary action schema, Parsons violated the postulate of *Verstehen*.

The consequences were not trivial. Parsons then could theorize society as an organic whole composed of analytically distinguishable "subsystems" that interpenetrate with one another (Burger, 1977; Munch, 1981). As Burger explains, Parsons thus was able to establish sociology as a discipline focused on the normative, give a one-sided reading to Weber (Cohen, Hazelrigg, and Pope, 1975), and assert a convergence between two theorists—Durkheim and Weber—whose "divergence is still characteristic of the field" (Bendix, 1971:283; see Collins, 1968; Pope, Cohen, and Hazelrigg, 1975).[17] Although the conceptualization of a "social system" established at least the potential for analysis of relations between spheres, the system approach involved what Weber doubtless would have regarded as an unfortunate reification. Given the constitution of the "system" from analytic categories, the interpenetrating social action complexes that connect analytically distinct spheres in actual social relations tend to drop out of the analysis, and the very approach that would claim to emphasize emergent properties of totalities in effect fragments their analysis, relegating different spheres to investigation within different social sciences. The result, as widely noted, is a social theory that tends to emphasize order, consensus, equilibrium, and teleology over the relativity of means and ends of diverse differentially located social actors. Although Parsons began with the problematic that emerged out of the assertion of relativity in the German historical school, to the degree that his solution reestablishes a totality as unity (especially in his last major work—Parsons, 1978), it reasserts idealist historicism, but on a different theoretical basis.

In the final analysis, it must be asserted that, for all its merits, Parsons's epistemological solution has serious limitations. Because it was advanced as a comprehensive solution to methodological problems of the action perspective, it stands as a real obstacle to theoretical progress, and it must be modified. But Parsons was not so far wrong as to make modification laborious. He drew on all the right elements for an epistemology appropriate to the action perspective; he simply integrated them in a way that violates the social action perspective's central postulate of *Verstehen*. Once the flawed position at the heart of Parsons's epistemological difficulties is altered, many of Parsons's concepts, insights, and analyses—both methodological and theoretical—may be retained. For

Sociological Theory

example, there is no reason not to generate ideal types out of analytic elements. And, as Weber recognized, there is no reason not to consider functional consequences of social structures in preliminary and sensitizing phases of analysis. Many parts of Parsons's theoretical work—the means/ends continuum, pattern variables, and the AGIL approach to functional analysis—remain useful as tools of substantive analysis. But Parsons's substantive analyses will have to stand on their own, disjoined from the methodology that once undergirded them.[18]

And the essential flaw in Parsons's epistemology must be modified in a way that changes the basic ontology of his work. Parsons's tilt toward analytical realism undermines the whole corpus of his work in certain ways, through the reification of the "system," a presumption of equilibrium, teleological tendencies, and an immanent evolutionism. These difficulties flow from the attempt to constitute a system causality at the level of theory. Once this project is abandoned, and concomitantly the postulate of *Verstehen* is respected, sociological interpretation and explanation can proceed only on a substantive theoretical basis. There, ideal types—however derived—will have to carry the burden of analysis. Under these conditions, it is only the social actors who reify "systems" and invoke teleology; under these conditions, social evolution would have to be discerned, if at all, in the flux of social action. Thus, Parsons's theoretical assertions would become transferred to the plane of substantive analysis, where they are forced into a confrontation with the conflicting and uneven tendencies of actual social developments.

Notes

1. Parsons was at pains to emphasize, however, that Pareto was *not* an empiricist, since facts were understood to be generated out of theoretical categories.

2. See the recently published correspondence of Parsons and Schutz (Grathoff, 1978) for their methodological confrontation (and see Embree, 1980).

3. The focus on "historical individuals"—that is, cases (SSA: 594)—must be taken to encompass empiricist explanations of concrete courses of action, not just in individual cases but also in com-

parative analysis, such as Weber's studies of the world religions. This is so because the search in the latter kind of analysis is not for general laws but for the specific and distinctive features of alternative complexes that may be used to explain their unique paths of development. Parsons seems to have recognized this, for although he described Weber's "systematic typology of religion" (SSA: 563ff.), he avoided the term *law* and acknowledged the strategy as one concerned with "*differentiating* elements in social development" (SSA:567).

4. The related issue of the connection between values and problems of relativity of knowledge in *verstehende Soziologie* is best understood as tied to the problem of parsimony.

5. Parsons restricted himself to a methodological critique of historicist arguments about the uniqueness of social phenomena. But O'Neill (1961:296) has alluded to a parallel issue that Parsons did not consider—namely, the historicist phenomenology of knowledge (see Shiner, 1969; Kellner, 1975). This issue could not easily be resolved to Parsons's advantage, but it does not directly concern Parsons's approach to concept formation and thus lies beyond the scope of present consideration.

6. Parsons made a great deal of the way Weber's focus on *rational* capitalism involved an atomistic separation of the organic whole that constituted the emergence of distinctively modern capitalism. Specifically, Parsons (SSA:631) pointed to the interaction between rational and adventurer capitalism as a key factor—a point well taken but one that belies the strategic importance of Weber's methodology, for it is only by conceptually distinguishing the two forms by means of ideal types that their interrelations can be analyzed. Weber (1977:20) was quite clear on the point that most phenomena involve complexities beyond the range of any single ideal type, but he argued that, analytically, the best way to unpack such complexities is through use of sociologically coherent and internally consistent models, which may serve as benchmarks of interpretation. It is somewhat of a testament to the power of this argument that Parsons engaged in ideal-type analysis—distinguishing rational and adventurer capitalism—while purporting to show its difficulties!

7. Haas (1982) has recently argued that most supposedly scientific sociology really does not operate in a way that can test

general hypotheses; although it shrouds its activities in a cloak of legitimacy marked by the claimed search for scientific laws, it really samples in a way that establishes historically conditioned complexes of relationships. It thus amounts to quantitative empiricism—an approach that, with proper concept formation, would come closer to Weber's type/case dynamic analysis (and to Parsons's analogue, the social system) than to Parsons's general analytic theory.

8. This tendency is exemplified by Parsons's selective translation of Part I of *Wirtschaft und Gesellschaft* (Weber, 1947). In choosing to translate Part I, Parsons provided the English-speaking audience with the key to Weber's work: Weber's last major effort to pull his wide-ranging discourse together with an integrating set of definitions and distinctions. Parsons's selection shows he attributed greatest significance to *Economy and Society* for its formal systematization. Part II, written by Weber *before* Part I, provides historical generalizations about major types of social groups, their relations to one another and to the economy, and the developmental tendencies of those structures (see Roth, in Weber, 1977:lxii ff.; Roth, in Schluchter, 1981:xxv–xxvi). The patchwork structure of *Economy and Society* evidences an enduring problem: Weber did not make his work particularly accessible to posterity. He scattered elements of his developmental theories in diverse books and articles that were major studies in their own right, and he often built on and encapsulated earlier ideas in later formulations, sometimes buried in obscure paragraphs of *Economy and Society*. For one effort to contend with Weber's theoretical development, see Collins's (1980) account of Weber's "last" theory of capitalism.

9. Indeed, it is the use of ideal types keyed to the postulate of *Verstehen* that allows Weber, in a different solution from Parsons's, to transcend the dichotomies between action and structure and between micro- and macrosociology. Thus, Weber was able to conceptualize individual action, "average" courses of action, complexes of interrelated action (for example, modern bureaucracy), institutionalized complexes of interrelated action (for example, feudalism), and institutionalized cultural "recipes" of action (for example, the Protestant Ethic), all by using ideal types that cut across so-called levels of analysis by retaining the significance of action at all points (see Hall, 1981:134–135). The oft-heard ar-

gument that because Weber was concerned with subjective action, his sociology was necessarily "individualistic" is quite an empty claim.

10. Zaret (1980) has shown that both Parsons and Schutz tended to eclipse history in their quests for generalizations. An important difference between the two should be noted here. As I have argued elsewhere (Hall, 1977, 1980, 1981), Schutz's phenomenology advances Weber's concern with *Verstehen* and retains a methodology of ideal-type analysis, in part by underscoring the alternative temporal structures of action. This emphasis on subjective temporality permits Schutz (1967) to theorize historicity. Thus, although Schutz himself did not engage in substantive historical analysis, it does not seem impossible to use his categories to do so.

11. Burger (1976:172–173) sustains this thesis in a parallel argument about the nontranslatability of ideal-typical generalizations into nomic universal statements within a voluntaristic theory of action. Interestingly, Parsons (1951:152ff.) and Parsons and Shils (1951:93) later began to recognize that not all logical combinations (in the case they were considering, of pattern variables) are likely to be equally significant empirically. Indeed, some combinations might be found impossible within given systems of action. One possible reason might be the meaningful incompatibility of certain combinations. This would vindicate an ideal-type approach based on *Verstehen,* but it is a possibility that Parsons and Shils did not pursue.

12. Parsons's students mostly have used elements of Parsons's approach either in their own, relatively independent theoretical work (for example, Smelser, 1963) or in empirical analyses (for example, Bellah, 1957; Smelser, 1959). There have been relatively few efforts by others to extend and refine Parsons's analytical system. Notable exceptions are the *Festschrift* by Parsons's former students (Loubser and others, 1976) and Warner's (1978) proposal to incorporate more fully into the action schema the key element of cognition. The most systematic effort to maintain the dual alignment of action and system in the tradition of Parsons is Niklas Luhmann's (1982) recent study of general theory and modern society. A somewhat different approach is that of Schluchter (1981), who maintains the Weberian emphasis on ideal-type analy-

sis of action, organization, and their dynamics but attempts to clarify and extend Weber's theory of rationalization, in part through a functional schema (1981:34) resembling that of Parsons.

13. The transitivity assumption is that if X is greater than Y, and Y is greater than Z, then X is greater than Z. In the case, for example, of status, defined in Weber's terms, such an assertion makes little sense. Given that status is ascribed by social others in groups that may overlap to various degrees, if X has greater status than Y, and Y has greater status than Z, Z may still have greater status than X in a different social context. Since there is no "objective" status, but only meaningful status, the assumption of transitivity cannot be made. More generally speaking, in terms of a quantitative measurement model, in the social sciences there are real problems in assuming that cases with the same score gain it for the same reasons (Stephanson, 1953:48).

14. To be sure, not all quantitative social science seeks to test a general set of interrelated lawlike propositions. To the degree that it follows a series of numbers generated by qualitatively similar actions, as historians in the *Annales* school have often done, it meets Weber's criterion. Moreover, certain external causal processes that condition social action can be modeled quantitatively (Weber, 1977:12-13). For a brief discussion of quantification within ideal types, see Rex (1974:62-65).

15. Munch (1982, for example, p. 787), more than some commentators, recognizes the important continuities between theoretical system and empirical case analysis in Parsons's work. But Munch's tilt toward the pole of general theory and his emphasis on formal interpenetration of theorized "systems," rather than action interpenetration of spheres, embody the same difficulties as Parsons's, described throughout this chapter.

16. Parsons's occasional bows in the direction of a phenomenology of essences (for example, SSA:750) suggest a fruitful avenue for the generation of ideal types. For an explicit effort in this direction, see my phenomenologically generated and structurally elaborated typology of utopian communal groups (Hall, 1978).

17. There is little doubt that Durkheim and Weber were substantially at odds in their substantive foci and emphases. But Parsons (1975) and Warner (1978) both suggest that critics fail to see convergence because they search for isomorphism.

18. It may be argued that many of Parsons's substantive analyses are contingent on his methodological approach. In some cases, the analyses may be conditioned by the functionalist and analytic realist ways in which they are developed as topics. This possibility is worthy of study in its own right. For one such effort on "the family" as a social institution, see Lasch (1977). An alternative dialectical approach to families in capitalist societies (Zaretsky, 1976) implicitly demonstrates the theoretical atomism of Parsons's approach applied to phenomena that cross-cut his analytic spheres.

References

ALEXANDER, JEFFREY C.
   1978   "Formal and Substantive Voluntarism in the Work of Talcott Parsons." *American Sociological Review* 43: 177–198.

BELLAH, ROBERT N.
   1957   *Tokugawa Religion: The Values of Pre-Industrial Japan.* Boston: Beacon Press.

BENDIX, REINHARD
   1971   "Two Sociological Traditions." In Reinhard Bendix and Guenther Roth (Eds.), *Scholarship and Partisanship*. Berkeley: University of California Press.

BERSHADY, HAROLD L.
   1973   *Ideology and Social Knowledge.* New York: Wiley.

BOURDIEU, PIERRE
   1977   *Outline of a Theory of Practice.* (Translated by Richard Nice.) Cambridge: Cambridge University Press.

BURGER, THOMAS
   1976   *Max Weber's Theory of Concept Formation.* Durham, N.C.: Duke University Press.
   1977   "Talcott Parsons, the Problem of Order in Society, and the Program of an Analytic Sociology." *American Journal of Sociology* 83:320–334.

COHEN, JERE, HAZELRIGG, LAWRENCE E., AND POPE, WHITNEY
   1975   "De-Parsonizing Weber: A Critique of Parsons' Interpretation of Weber's Sociology." *American Sociological Review* 40:229–241.

COLLINS, RANDALL
  1968   "A Comparative Approach to Political Sociology." In
         Reinhard Bendix and others (Eds.), *State and Society.*
         Berkeley: University of California Press.
  1980   "Weber's Last Theory of Capitalism: A Systematiza-
         tion." *American Sociological Review* 45:925-942.
DAHRENDORF, RALF
  1958   "Out of Utopia: Toward a Reorientation of Sociologi-
         cal Analysis." *American Journal of Sociology* 74:115-
         127.
EMBREE, LESTER
  1980   "Methodology Is Where Scientists and Philosophers
         Can Meet: Reflections on the Schutz-Parsons Ex-
         change." *Human Studies* 3:367-373.
GEHLAN, ARNOLD
  1963   *Studien zur Anthropologie und Soziologie.* Berlin:
         Luchterhand.
GERSTEIN, DEAN R.
  1975   "A Note on the Continuity of Parsonian Action The-
         ory." *Sociological Inquiry* 45(4):11-15.
GIDDENS, ANTHONY
  1979   *Central Problems in Social Theory.* Berkeley: Univer-
         sity of California Press.
GOULDNER, ALVIN
  1970   *The Coming Crisis of Western Sociology.* New York:
         Basic Books.
GRATHOFF, RICHARD (ED.)
  1978   *The Theory of Social Action: The Correspondence of
         Alfred Schutz and Talcott Parsons.* Bloomington: In-
         diana University Press.
HAAS, DAVID
  1982   "Survey Sampling and the Logic of Inference in Sociol-
         ogy." *American Sociologist* 17:103-111.
HALL, JOHN R.
  1977   "Alfred Schutz, His Critics, and Applied Phenomenol-
         ogy." *Cultural Hermeneutics* 4:265-279.
  1978   *The Ways Out.* London: Routledge & Kegan Paul.
  1980   "The Time of History and the History of Times." *His-
         tory and Theory* 19:113-131.

1981 "Max Weber's Methodological Strategy and Comparative Lifeworld Phenomenology." *Human Studies* 4: 131-143.

HOROWITZ, IRVING LOUIS
1962 "Consensus, Conflict, and Cooperation: A Sociological Inventory." *Social Forces* 41:177-188.

HUSSERL, EDMUND
1962 *Ideas.* New York: Collier. (Originally published 1913.)

1964 *The Phenomenology of Internal Time Consciousness.* Bloomington: Indiana University Press. (Originally published 1905.)

1970a *The Crisis of European Sciences and Transcendental Phenomenology.* Evanston, Ill.: Northwestern University Press. (Originally published 1936/1954.)

1970b *Logical Investigations.* (Translated by J. N. Findlay.) New York: Humanities Press. (Originally published 1901.)

KANTER, ROSABETH MOSS
1972 *Commitment and Community: Communes and Utopias in Sociological Perspective.* Cambridge, Mass.: Harvard University Press.

KELLNER, HANS D.
1975 "Time Out: The Discontinuity of Historical Consciousness." *History and Theory* 14:275-296.

LASCH, CHRISTOPHER
1977 *Haven in a Heartless World.* New York: Basic Books.

LOCKWOOD, DAVID
1956 "Some Remarks on 'The Social System.'" *British Journal of Sociology* 7:134-146.

LOUBSER, JAN J., AND OTHERS (EDS.)
1976 *Explorations in General Theory in Social Science: Essays in Honor of Talcott Parsons.* New York: Free Press.

LUHMANN, NIKLAS
1982 *The Differentiation of Society.* New York: Columbia University Press.

MCINTOSH, DONALD
1977 "The Objective Bases of Max Weber's Ideal Types." *History and Theory* 16:265-279.

MARTINDALE, DON
  1959   "Talcott Parsons's Metamorphosis from Social Behaviorism to Macrofunctionalism." *Alpha Kappa Deltan* 29:38-46.
MENZIES, KEN
  1976   *Talcott Parsons and the Social Image of Man.* London: Routledge & Kegan Paul.
MERTON, ROBERT K.
  1980   "Remembering the Young Talcott Parsons." *American Sociologist* 15:68-71.
MILLS, C. WRIGHT
  1959   *The Sociological Imagination.* New York: Oxford University Press.
MUNCH, RICHARD
  1981   "Talcott Parsons and the Theory of Action: I. The Structure of the Kantian Core." *American Journal of Sociology* 86:709-739.
  1982   "Talcott Parsons and the Theory of Action: II. The Continuity of the Development." *American Journal of Sociology* 87:771-826.
OAKES, GUY
  1977   "The *Verstehen* Thesis and the Foundations of Max Weber's Methodology." *History and Theory* 16:11-29.
O'NEILL, JOHN
  1961   "The Hobbesian Problem in Marx and Parsons." In Max Blach (Ed.), *The Social Theories of Talcott Parsons.* Englewood Cliffs, N.J.: Prentice-Hall.
PARSONS, TALCOTT
  1937   *The Structure of Social Action.* New York: Free Press.
  1951   *The Social System.* New York: Free Press.
  1954   *Essays in Sociological Theory.* New York: Free Press.
  1965   "Unity and Diversity in the Modern Intellectual Disciplines." *Daedalus* 94(1):39-65.
  1967   *Sociological Theory and Modern Society.* New York: Free Press.
  1975   "Comment on 'Parsons' Interpretation of Durkheim' and on 'Moral Freedom Through Understanding in Durkheim.'" *American Sociological Review* 40:106-111.

1977a "Comment on Burger's Critique." *American Journal of Sociology* 83:335–339.

1977b *The Evolution of Societies.* Englewood Cliffs, N.J.: Prentice-Hall.

1978 *Action Theory and the Human Condition.* New York: Free Press.

PARSONS, TALCOTT, BALES, ROBERT F., AND SHILS, EDWARD A.

1953 *Working Papers in the Theory of Action.* New York: Free Press.

PARSONS, TALCOTT, AND PLATT, GERALD M.

1973 *The American University.* Cambridge, Mass.: Harvard University Press.

PARSONS, TALCOTT, AND SHILS, EDWARD A. (EDS.)

1951 *Toward a General Theory of Action.* Cambridge, Mass.: Harvard University Press.

PARSONS, TALCOTT, AND SMELSER, NEIL J.

1956 *Economy and Society: A Study in the Integration of Economic and Social Theory.* New York: Free Press.

POPE, WHITNEY, COHEN, JERE, AND HAZELRIGG, LAWRENCE E.

1975 "On the Divergence of Weber and Durkheim: A Critique of Parsons' Convergence Thesis." *American Sociological Review* 40:417–427.

REX, JOHN

1974 *Sociology and the Demystification of the Modern World.* London: Routledge & Kegan Paul.

ROTH, GUENTHER

1971 "Sociological Typology and Historical Explanation." In Reinhard Bendix and Guenther Roth (Eds.), *Scholarship and Partisanship.* Berkeley: University of California Press.

1976 "History and Sociology in the Work of Max Weber." *British Journal of Sociology* 27:306–318.

1979 "Charisma and the Counterculture." In Wolfgang Schluchter and Guenther Roth, *Max Weber's Vision of History.* Berkeley: University of California Press.

SAVAGE, STEPHEN P.

1981 *The Theories of Talcott Parsons.* New York: St. Martin's Press.

SCHLUCHTER, WOLFGANG

1981 *The Rise of Western Rationalism: Max Weber's Devel-*

opmental History. (Translated by Guenther Roth.) Berkeley: University of California Press.

SCHUTZ, ALFRED
1967   *The Phenomenology of the Social World.* Evanston, Ill.: Northwestern University Press. (Originally published 1932.)
1973   *Collected Papers I.* The Hague: Martinus Nijhoff.

SCOTT, JOHN F.
1963   "The Changing Foundations of the Parsonian Action School." *American Sociological Review* 28:716-735.

SHINER, LAWRENCE
1969   "A Phenomenological Approach to Historical Knowledge." *History and Theory* 8:260-274.

SMELSER, NEIL J.
1959   *Social Change in the Industrial Revolution: An Application of Theory to the British Cotton Industry.* Chicago: University of Chicago Press.
1963   *Theory of Collective Behavior.* New York: Free Press.

STEPHANSON, WILLIAM
1953   *The Study of Behavior.* Chicago: University of Chicago Press.

TURNER, JONATHAN H., AND BEEGHLEY, LEONARD
1974   "Current Folklore in the Criticisms of Parsonian Action Theory." *Sociological Inquiry* 44(1):47-63.

WARNER, STEPHAN R.
1978   "Toward a Redefinition of Action Theory: Paying the Cognitive Element Its Due." *American Journal of Sociology* 83:1317-1349.

WARNER, W. LLOYD, AND LUNT, PAUL S.
1941   *The Social Life of a Modern Community.* New Haven, Conn.: Yale University Press.

WEBER, MAX
1947   *The Theory of Social and Economic Organization.* (Edited by Talcott Parsons.) New York: Oxford University Press.
1975   *Roscher and Knies.* New York: Free Press.
1977   *Economy and Society.* (Edited by Guenther Roth and Claus Wittich.) Berkeley: University of California Press.

ZARET, DAVID
1980 "From Weber to Parsons and Schutz." *American Journal of Sociology* 85:1180–1201.
ZARETSKY, ELI
1976 *Capitalism, the Family, and Personal Life.* New York: Harper & Row.

One of the most important contributions of the Parsonian tradition has been its conceptualization of the relative autonomy and mutual interpenetration of culture and social systems. The first part of this chapter defines three ideal types of empirical relationships between culture and society: specification, refraction, and columnization. Each is related to different configurations of social structure and culture and, in turn, to different degrees of social conflict. The second part of the chapter uses this typology to illuminate critical aspects of the relationship between conflict and integration in the Watergate crisis in the U.S.

☙ 10 ❧

THREE MODELS OF CULTURE AND SOCIETY RELATIONS: TOWARD AN ANALYSIS OF WATERGATE

Jeffrey C. Alexander

UNIVERSITY OF CALIFORNIA, LOS ANGELES

The problem of the relation between systems theory and social conflict remains unresolved. Within conflict theory, the problem has unfortunately been linked to the emphasis of systems theory on the relative autonomy of ideas—that is, to its emphasis on the value segment in social systems. In part, systems theorists themselves are to blame for this false link between an emphasis on equilibrium and social values, since Parsons in particular—as well as theorists like Shils—tended to illustrate "analytically differentiated" social systems by referring to such societies as the United

I would like to thank Jeffrey Broadbent, Randall Collins, and an anonymous reader for their instructive readings of earlier drafts of this chapter.

States, in which there is an unusual amount of consensus within the differentiated value segment (Parsons, 1971). Parsons, moreover, often explicitly conflated (see note 1) the *analytical* problem of the relation between social system level and cultural system level with the *empirical* problem of consensus and the concrete structure of value systems (Parsons, 1971).

On the one hand, Parsons used the term *specification* in a very clear analytical way to argue that any social system configuration involved the application or utilization of cultural patterns that were necessarily more general than any particular institutional form of concrete behavior. The way concrete behavior utilized general forms inevitably involved a process of "specification." Social system behavior, in other words, always involved some cultural reference. Yet Parsons also applied the notion of specification to the actual empirical instance of a historical nation. He often portrayed the values of the political and social actors in the system as specifications of a common value system. Although this may indeed have been the historical fact, the use of the same term, *specification,* to cover both analytical and empirical instances is an illegitimate conflation of a particular historical situation with a general analytical point.[1] For even if a society contained competing general value systems and no common value system with which these were integrated, it would nonetheless be analytically correct to say that each of the political or social subgroups in conflict with one another derived its own specific form of values by a process of specification from the more general values of a cultural system. These more general values would, nonetheless, be antagonistic to other systems of values on the cultural level. Thus, in this kind of empirical case, analytical specification and empirical polarization and conflict are perfectly reconcilable. Conflict theory is wrong: Systems theory can both allow the autonomy of values and illuminate the instability of social systems.

Once we have understood the fundamental dangers and fallacies of this conflationary strand in Parsonian work we can develop a more satisfactory approach to the analysis of values in empirical social systems. I will try to demonstrate in this chapter that the seminal theoretical advances of functionalist theory in analyzing the relation between cultural and social systems can, in fact, help us to develop a theory of conflict in empirical historical systems.

Three Models of Culture/Society Interrelation

First, I will introduce an ideal-typical schema for analyzing the relation between values and social structure. Three models can describe the relation between conflict and consensus in advanced societies—models that refer to different relations between the social and the cultural system. The first model assumes harmony and consistency on both the cultural and the social levels. Particular functions and groups in the social system do "specify" cultural patterns in concretely different ways, but these diverse value groupings are not in conflict with one another in any sense beyond the immediate one of a division of labor. This model I will call "cultural specification."

The second model assumes that there are more fundamental conflicts on the social system level but sees the cultural system as still fairly integrated. In this model conflicting social groupings and functions can and do develop antagonistic subcultures, not just complementary cultural "specifications," but because these subcultures still draw on an integrated value system at the cultural level, there remains between these subcultures substantial if unacknowledged commonality. We might call this the model of "cultural refraction," following Evans-Pritchard's (1953) analyses of harmony and conflict among the Nuer. Why refraction? Because we can say that different interests have been refracted through the same cultural lens.

Finally, the third model I introduce describes fundamental antagonism in both social and cultural systems. Thus, rather than simply subcultural conflicts, genuinely antagonistic cultures emerge in a society, interest groupings that have no significant common beliefs. One might call this "cultural columnization" because interest groupings occur in hermetically sealed cultural columns, vertical spaces between which there is no horizontal integration.[2]

Examples of Specification, Columnization, and Refraction

In the recent literature in sociology, the prototypical account of cultural specification is Parsons and Platt's (1973) analysis of the relation of the cultural value of rationality to social systems. Parsons and Platt argue that there is a dominant cultural theme of rationality in American society and that this theme operates at a very general, cultural level. They suggest, further, that there are more specific, institutionalized versions of rational orientations in each of the four subsystems of society: economic rationality in the adaptive sector, political rationality in the polity, citizenship or solidary rationality in the integrative system, and value rationality in the pattern maintenance system.

Pluralist theorists, or theorists who emphasize the disintegrative aspects of modern life, such as those in the Frankfurt school, would portray these concrete institutionalizations of rationality as in fundamental conflict with one another, arguing, for example, that the economic rationality that emphasizes efficiency in the business world is totally antithetical to the cognitive rationality that inspires scientific truth in the world of the university. Parsons and Platt, by contrast, argue that although the systemic exigencies of such concrete institutions are certainly different, the cultural rationality that guides them is derived from a common "rationality" theme in the culture at large. They assume, moreover, that these social-system-level functions are not particularly antithetical—indeed, that they usually support one another through a process of complementary exchange. With neither functional nor cultural antipathies, then, the patterns of behavior motivated by economic rationality and political rationality are basically cooperative: There is no long-term basis for division or conflict. Such a model need not examine the detailed structure of subcultural traditions, for each more detailed tradition is principally derived from the roots and structures of a single more generalized cultural theme. Not surprisingly, therefore, for Parsons and Platt it is rationality itself that is the object of analysis. When problems of disequilibrium are analyzed, as they are in some detail, the issue of intersystemic conflicts is given rather short shrift, for such an analysis would lead to an emphasis on cultural refraction. Disequilibrium is analyzed, rather, in terms of the inadequacies in the generalized value pattern itself, in this case the overly instrumental aspects of contemporary Western rationality.

This analysis of *The American University* in terms of the specification model should not be taken as purely pejorative. To the contrary, it seems to me that in American culture instrumental

rationality is, in fact, a widely shared value, one that different institutions often merely specify in different ways without substantially challenging or refracting. In part this occurs because American society is, compared with others, functionally well integrated.
This specification pattern also occurs because this particular value,
rationality, is widely shared in American life. Despite this empirical
applicability, however, one wonders whether Parsons and Platt
may not have underemphasized the possibility that economic and
political rationality form competing subcultures, or similarly,
underplayed the conflict between ethical or value rationality and
instrumental political expediency that Weber so profoundly articulated as the tension between the politics of responsibility and the
politics of expediency and faith.[3]

The difficulties of such a pure specification perspective are
most apparent when it is more directly applied to political mobilization and group conflict. The functionalist tradition has emphasized the significance of the cultural generalization that occurs
during periods of intense political and social conflicts, when the
anxiety produced by disequilibrium pushes significant elements of
the population to focus on the most fundamental and simplified
value concerns—that is, on the general cultural themes from which
the society's specific institutionalized patterns have been derived.
This analytical theory of generalization is a fundamentally important contribution, but insofar as it has been applied empirically
only in the context of an insistence on cultural specification, it has
been treated in a flawed and partial way. The flaw is apparent in
the ease with which such generalization is assumed to proceed and,
hence, the ease with which particular social crises are seen to be resolved. In Parsons and Smelser's (1956) account of the Progressive
period in the United States at the end of the nineteenth century,
for example, movements to reform the business structure are presented without sufficient attention to the fundamental social and
cultural polarizations of the day. In Smelser's own first book
(1959), the problem is much the same. The issue is not whether,
as Smelser rightly insists, an activist Protestant culture is widely
shared, but whether the competing economic groups during the
early industrial period developed sharply divergent subcultures to
express this common value. If such subcultural development took
place, and I believe it did, then the process of cultural generaliza-

tion that Smelser describes could have occurred only under conditions that would have allowed the end of such subcultural conflict: either some kind of genuine reintegration—produced, for example, by the decline of group conflict or by ritual renewal—or the dominance of one subcultural position over another. In the particular English case, I suspect, there were elements of both.

At the opposite end of the continuum from such cultural specification is what I have called cultural columnization. The situation portrayed here could not be more different, for not only is a much more fundamental conflict on the social system level portrayed, but this conflict is seen as building on fundamentally divergent themes in the general national culture. Such columnization brings to mind, of course, societies subject to revolutionary upheaval from either the left or the right; indeed, my theory of columnization is, in part, an attempt to help illuminate such processes. In his *Ancien Régime* Tocqueville portrayed France as radically divided on the cultural level between a new tradition of critical rationality, carried by the bourgeoisie and intellectuals, and a culture of tradition, deference, and hierarchy, carried by the church and the aristocracy. These cultural groupings were presented as radically heterodox, as emerging from antagonistic cultural developments such as feudalism and the Enlightenment. They were, moreover, viewed as cultures that were specified by fundamentally conflicting institutional interests—estates whose economic and political positions were in fundamental functional antagonism. In this situation of columnization, it is clear, no common ground could be found. Raymond Aron's (1960) theory of modern functional elites as completely segmental and fragmenting can be seen as the contemporary French analogue to such earlier columnization theories. That Aron completely ignores the cultures of his elites demonstrates merely that they are, indeed, so columnized that they offer no integrative support.[4]

The extreme polarization of columnization most likely occurs in societies where traditional and modernizing cultures are carried by vigorous and contentious social groups. In Italy, for example, Robert Bellah (1980) has described "five civil religions," suggesting that the Italian cultural system contains sharply divergent traditions that extend all the way from a form of primitive naturalism to an ultrarationalistic Marxism. The case of pre–World War II

Germany has been more extensively documented. Guenther Roth (1963) has written about the "negative integration" of the German working class. It seems indisputable that in Germany the sharply antagonistic class groupings became organized around traditions that were felt to be radically antagonistic: The small radical intelligentsia and the large socialist working class followed a self-consciously rationalistic and modernizing Marxism, while the middle classes, state-supported intellectuals, and aristocracy followed a strong antimodern traditionalism fundamentally influenced by Lutheranism. Ernst Nolte (1966) has described the conservative side of this polarization as culturally "antitranscendent," a description that effectively portrays its radical antipathy to the Enlightenment tradition. It is no wonder that in such columnized situations the unified "generalization" so necessary for cultural and social reintegration in crisis situations can hardly ever occur. It is not simply that functional interests diverge, but that the anxiety that leads to value ritualization and to the urge for renewal occurs within the "column" of divergent cultural groupings rather than within some more general and widely shared cultural belief. Cultural celebrations in 1848 revolutionary France did occur, but they engaged a cultural heritage fundamentally at odds with the commitments of a significant, if not at that time dominant, segment of the French nation. Four years later, the ascension of Louis Bonaparte allowed generalization to occur in another cultural "column," that of tradition or at least the column of modernity very traditionally defined. The "two cultures" in a columnized society, then, provide ritual experiences that serve merely to reinforce the different faiths and interests of already polarized groups.[5]

For the middle case of cultural refraction, divergent social tasks and interests are portrayed as drawing on fundamentally similar cultural themes. It should not be surprising that the United States has been considered a prime example within which such refraction occurs. The famous dichotomy in American culture between "equality of opportunity," a theme that emphasizes equality in an individualistic way, and "equality of results," a theme that combines equality with more collectivist concerns, is a good example of such refraction. In this case the common cultural commitment to equality is accepted, while conservative and liberal groupings are described—for example, in the work of Lipset (1965)

—as refracting this commitment through the more individualistic or collectivist interests of different economic and political groups. The implication is that sharp conflicts do in fact occur in American society but that even such polarized groupings as conservative businesspersons and liberal trade unionists share a commitment to the value of equality, a shared commitment that allows for some ultimate consensus and cooperation. Louis Hartz (1955) has applied the same kind of refraction analysis to the value of individualism rather than equality. Arguing that the bedrock of all American ideology is the commitment to a Lockean emphasis on individual liberty and rights, he suggests that trade unionists and business-persons, for example, merely offer interest-bound refractions of individualism in their purportedly radically different ideologies.[6] Similar arguments have, of course, been made for the conflict groupings of countries other than the United States. Jesse Pitts (1964), for example, has suggested that the sharply divergent themes of French society can be traced back to internally contradictory themes within Catholicism.

It should be clear that when cultural refraction is the model used for an empirical case, the opportunity for reintegration of cultural and social conflicts is presented in a more complex and open-ended way than for the two other ideal types. Because sharp subcultural conflicts exist, generalization to a shared common culture is by no means automatic, for powerful general themes do underlie the subcultures themselves, and these subcultural themes may become the object of polarizing ritual and generalization. Reintegration certainly is a possibility, however, for with refraction, in contrast to columnization, strong common themes do exist. Whether generalization will actually lead to convergence on these shared general cultural themes is a matter for particular analysis of specific empirical circumstances. Although close attention must be paid to divergent interests and to subcultural values, common commitments cannot be ignored. I will present some aspects of such an analysis in the discussion of the American Watergate crisis that follows.

Watergate: A Case Study in Refraction and Reintegration

Although every advanced industrial society experiences elements of specification, refraction, and columnization, the structural and cultural characteristics of each national society incline it in one direction or another. For the United States, with the possible exception of racial conflicts today and the definite exception of sectional conflict before 1865, the refraction model seems most appropriate. American conflicts have been serious, but they have rarely produced ideologies that have seriously violated the consensual framework composed by America's principal cultural themes.

The Watergate crisis[7] must be placed into the context of social conflict in America in the 1960s. If we want to understand the situation in America in that time, we must recognize both the intensity of social system conflict and the areas of common perception. That is, what we have to recognize is the fundamental fact of refraction in American society in the sixties.

In its broad outlines, the decade of the sixties was a period of intense, modernizing social change. It was a period of rationalization and differentiation in every institutional sphere, in politics and education, family, law, religion, civic solidarity, and economic life. The reforms introduced in these spheres revolved around issues that might be called late modernization. They demanded and involved more equality, more participation, the expansion of the notion of the individual, and the rationalization and secularization of values. In sum, they revolved around a radical kind of universalism that created and unleashed pervasive criticism of all traditions and authority and that demanded continual change of self and institutions.

The groups that initiated these changes might be called vanguard modernists—middle-class, highly educated reformers, both whites and racial minorities, government planners, intellectuals and students, liberal church men and women, and selected professionals, for example, activist lawyers and teachers. These groups sometimes draped themselves in antimodernist garb, harking back to the *Gemeinschaft* and community, to the need for affectivity. Although these traditionalistic strands are not irrelevant, I think that, considered as a whole, the subcultural orientation of these groups presented a radicalized left-wing version of the mainstream of American political culture—namely, critical universalism tied in with activism.

Against this culture of critical rationality there emerged a backlash that was more of a departure from the dominant American civic tradition, although in no sense was it a complete repudiation. This backlash promoted the drastic reduction of universalism and transformative values. It promoted particularistic values such as loyalty to family, to race, to ethnicity, to the nation—in the form of excessive patriotism—and loyalty to the authorities that represented and ruled each of these diffuse collectivities. It was anti-intellectual and often explicitly and fundamentally, or rather fundamentalistically, religious. The backlash tended toward deference and obedience. Hence, it was termed the "silent majority," as opposed to the group that emphasized critique and dissent. It emphasized stability and order, not change.

Yet this broad outline of social division conceals common cross-cutting ties that remained salient sociologically even if they were not experientially salient to citizens of the day. The social changes so spectacular in the 1960s actually can be traced back to changes initiated in the late 1950s, the later years of the Eisenhower administration. The establishment of the U.S. Civil Rights Commission, vigorous educational expansion and upgrading, religious ecumenicism, economic expansion and rationalization—all these initiatives commanded an extremely wide consensus. This social cohesion continued in the early 1960s, during which time the radical left and right continued to be marginal groups. This consensus broke down only gradually and in complicated ways.

The intensification of change in the 1960s created increasing polarization into right and left. The first phases of this division proceeded in a fairly straightforward, Hegelian way, with reformers grouped together under critical universalism and reactors grouped under more conservative, backlash particularism. Liberals moved leftward, renewing their emphasis on equality and remaining united in their support of political, integrative, educational, and religious change. Conservatives united around the backlash libertarianism of the Goldwater campaign. Modernizing groups championed equality and tied their critical position to universalism; conservative groups championed liberty and tied their defensive position to particularism. Both groups, all the same, embraced at a more general level certain common notions. Opinion polls of the 1960s show that support for inclusion and economic democracy expanded in every segment of the society. For the emerging left, indeed, equality did not seem to deny liberty; in fact, the left often championed equality in the name of greater individual freedom. For the right, liberty was often seen merely as emphasizing a particular kind of equality, the equal rights of individuals to buy and sell and to be protected from government intrusion. The tension these commitments produced within both backlash and frontlash moralities are clear in retrospect, but they had not yet surfaced at the time.

This invisible, generalized common ground became concretely explicit in the later phases of 1960s polarization. During the period from 1966 to 1969 various forms of critical particularisms emerged within the modernizing movement, producing uncomfortable combinations of modernity and primordialism within the left itself. Racial separatism and color consciousness opposed norms of universal inclusion; the revolutionary culture of violence and confrontation produced significant strands of internal authoritarianism opposed to critical rationality; the diffuse affectivity of the counterculture counteracted the impersonal standards on which other strands of the modernizing movement were based. None of these developments, however, completely undermined the critical activism, inclusiveness, and universalism on which so much of the earlier liberal-left movement had depended. The black power movement still demanded equal rights; the militant student left mobilized its movements in the cause of critique; the hippies envisioned universal brotherhood and championed the autonomy of the individual at all costs.

Nonetheless, the lines of polarization had become significantly blurred. It was in the same period of 1966–1969, partly in response to this further leftward movement in the party of reform and partly in response to the changes that actually initiated it, that a distinctly more moderate segment of the liberal movement emerged. This more conservative group of *Commentary* liberals and politicians such as Moynihan vacillated between upholding the liberalism of the earlier phase and moving toward some accommodation with backlash values.

This splitting of the left was mirrored—indeed, directly related to—equally significant changes in the right. In the wake of Goldwater's defeat and increased leftist activism, the conservative movement became fissured into more and less radical forms of backlash antimodernism. In the later 1960s, an explicitly reactionary strand emerged under the banner of nationalism and anticivility, calling for social order at all costs and the abandonment of constitutional protections for dissent. Other rightists stressed not simply antimodernist anxiety but the loss of liberty as well. This latter group sought to maintain its connection to the "center," forcing its backlash views into the mainstream. Its moderation allowed it to make growing alliances with the rightward-moving segment of liberal reformers, and the neoconservative movement was born.

This refracted character of the 1960s polarization is crucial for understanding the orientations out of which Watergate arose and the resources that allowed it eventually to be resolved. On the one hand, there was the fact of intensely polarized social groupings, the antagonism between particularistic backlash and vanguard modernist frontlash. Little conscious sense of commonality existed in the America of that day, and this climate of confrontation produced exclusionary and conspiratorial politics. Demands for total political control were encouraged, each side making efforts to silence the opposition. Sectarian politics became the order of the day, and this sectarian politics threatened the common normative of rules of the game, which often seemed threatened and about to give way. On the other hand, behind this polarization, I maintain, there was a less conscious backdrop of common culture, "modernist" commitments to forms of universalistic activism that were accepted without regard to the particular stands of any conflict group.

To see the relation between this political-cultural refraction and Watergate, we have to turn to Richard Nixon and the presidency. Nixon brought both strands of the backlash movement to power. He had always conceived of himself as a victim of social change and a champion of grass-roots movements against it. At the same time, he conceived of himself as a cosmopolitan, educated, enlightened figure, a modernist whose duty it was to control the lunatic fringe of the right wing as well as the left—so his slogan to build a "new American majority" was not a lie. His administration coopted and sponsored certain issues of the left, particularly environmentalism and to a lesser degree economic equality (welfare reform) and women's rights; it brought American troops home; it called for quiet in the streets and a renewed dedication to "tradi-

tional" forms of American activism, such as reform. This was the
Nixon who gained support from the growing neoconservative
movement and who put Moynihan in his cabinet.

It is true, nonetheless, that Nixon was also elected in 1968
as the factional leader of the backlash culture. He appealed to
patriotism over dissent, tradition over modernity; he invoked
paternalistic authority and attempted to wield it against the forces
of change in the name of the nation, in the name of the family,
and in the name of "the people." Drawing on the authoritarian resources of the American presidency, Nixon sought to push his
"new American majority" in a backlash direction. He emphasized
the pomp and circumstance of the office. He remained remote, in-
accessible, and mysterious. He utilized the extraordinary instrumental power of secrecy and the powers of coercive control that
were at his command. He tried to set in motion a movement of
counterchange against the agencies, leaders, and ideas of vanguard
liberalism. Spiro Agnew took the role of spear carrier in this, rally-
ing "the folks" against "the cosmopolitans," initiating a sectarian
politics that was unprecedented for the presidential center and
connecting the powerful and factious behavior of the backlash
movement to the personalistic, quasi-patrimonial form of presidential authority. The result was a presidency that often showed
little regard for the abstract and generalized rules of the game that,
according to a consensual model, govern conflict in the political
system. It is not surprising that this combination of power and will
led to a series of illegal and dangerous abuses of power.

The moderate and extreme dimensions of the Nixon presidency were by no means sharply demarcated. This was precisely
its great danger. While more right-wing, anticivil elements could be
pushed toward cooperation and reform, the support of more traditional movements often legitimated the administration's most anticivil trends.

Nixon and his staff began immediately in 1969 to try to
control cosmopolitan and dissident enemies. They justified their
actions—some of which were visible, others private and concealed
—on the grounds that they were dealing with enemies outside the
boundaries of civil society. These actions ranged from illegal arrests and extensive bugging of subversives to spying and provoca-
tion and to the infiltration even of their own eastern-educated

staffs, and, finally, to extensive institutional maneuvers to restrain liberal institutions and their elites—for example, the news media. It is important to understand that such illegal tactics received at least passive consent from the silent majority that they helped to shape. There was a more general moral code to justify these actions: The president's illegal, conspiratorial tactics were justified in terms of the conservative subculture. The "refraction" made liberals and radicals into an "other" with whom, Nixon's supporters believed, they had little in common.

The break into the Democratic headquarters in the Watergate Hotel in the summer of 1972 was simply one part of this overall activity. McGovern was the symbol of aggressive modernization and radical change, not only for Nixon but for the silent majority itself, and it was McGovern and his potential supporters who were the objects of the Watergate break-in. It was for this very reason—the refracted atmosphere of the time and the legitimation it gave to activities like the break-in—that Watergate received scant attention and generated little outrage at the time. There were no cries of outraged justice. There was the acceptance of Nixon's rationales, respect for his authority, belief that his version of the facts was correct despite strong evidence to the contrary. With important exceptions, the media did not even pick up the story, not because they were coerced not to do so, but because they subjectively felt it to be an unimportant story. Even after a long, hot election, 80 percent of the American people found Watergate hard to believe; 75 percent felt it was just plain politics; 84 percent said that what they had heard had not influenced them.

Two years later, it was generally agreed, this same incident, still called "Watergate," had initiated the most serious institutional crisis in American history. It had become a riveting moral symbol that was responsible for the first resignation by a president.

How and why did this perception of Watergate change? To understand this, we must first see what this extraordinary contrast in these two public perceptions indicates—namely, that "Watergate" in itself was nothing. It was a mere fact, and contrary to the positivist persuasion, facts do not speak. Watergate could not, as the French might say, tell itself. It had to be told by society; it was, to use Durkheim's famous phrase, a social fact.

To understand how this telling of a crucial social fact changed, I must introduce a notion that was implicit in my earlier discussion of generalization—namely, that there are different levels at which every social fact can be told. These levels are linked to different kinds of social resources, and the focus on one level or another can tell us much about whether a system is in crisis, is in a period of great conflict, or is operating routinely and in equilibrium. Here I draw on Parsons.

First and most specific is the level of goals. Political life occurs most of the time on this relatively mundane level of goals, power, and interest. Above this, as it were, at a higher level of generality, are norms—the conventions, customs, and morals that regulate this political process and struggle. At a still higher point there are values: those aspects of the culture that inform the codes which regulate political authority and the norms within which specific interests are resolved. When politics operates routinely, the conscious attention of political participants is on goals and interests; that is, it is relatively specific attention. Routine politics means, in fact, that these interests do not seem to violate more general values and norms. Nonroutine politics occurs when tension between these levels is felt—either because of the shift in the nature of political activity or because of a shift in the general commitments that are held to regulate it. In this situation, a tension between goals and higher levels develops. Public attention shifts from political goals to more general concerns, to the norms and values that are now perceived as in danger. In this instance we can say there has been the generalization of public consciousness I referred to earlier in this chapter.

It is in light of this analysis that we can understand the shift in the telling of Watergate. It was first viewed merely as something on the level of goals, "just politics," by 75 percent. Why? Because it was legitimated by the general values of each political subculture. The silent majority felt that such behavior was justified by the times. The left thought it merely confirmed their own views on the politics of the right. For both groups, therefore, the event remained simply political because it was compared only to the refracted subcultural expectations, not to the broader universalism and constitutionalism that, unacknowledged, remained hidden beneath these polarized beliefs and that would have viewed Watergate in a more critical way.

Two years after the break-in, in summer 1974, public opinion had changed sharply. From purely political goals Watergate was now regarded as an issue that violated fundamental customs and morals, and eventually—by 50 percent of the voters—as a challenge to fundamental values, the fundamental values that sustained political order itself. By the end, almost half of those who had voted for Nixon had changed their minds. Two thirds of all voters thought the issue had now gone far beyond politics. What had happened was a radical "generalization" of opinion. The known facts were not very different, but the social context in which they were seen had been transformed.

In the two-year transformation of the context of Watergate, we see the creation and resolution of a fundamental social crisis, an extraordinary generalization of opinion vis-à-vis a political threat that was initiated by the very center of established power, and the successful struggle not just against that social power but against the powerful cultural rationales it mobilized. We see, in other words, a movement beyond cultural refraction to genuine reintegration and renewal. On what does such a successful process of crisis creation and resolution depend? Let me lay these factors out generally, and then I will discuss briefly how each became involved in the instance of Watergate.

First, sufficient consensus must exist so that the label of deviant can be applied to the disequilibrating event. If this occurs, the event will disturb more than a mere fragment of the population; to this extent, "society" itself is aroused and indignant.

Second, significant groups in this emerging consensus must perceive that the event threatens the "center" of society.

Third, institutional social controls must be invoked or operationalized. These further legitimate attacks on the source of this disequilibrium—which is presented throughout as somewhat frightening and powerful—and these controls also begin to mobilize force and the threat of force to bring it to heal.

Fourth, elites and publics that are differentiated and relatively autonomous from the structural center of society must be drawn into the struggle. "Countercenters" must be formed.

Finally, there must be effective processes of symbolic interpretation—that is, ritual and pollution processes that continue the labeling process and enforce the strength of the symbolic center of society at the expense of the now deviant structural center. In so doing, such processes not only demonstrate conclusively the deviant qualities that are the sources of this threat, but they constitute social control processes that help to correct them.

In briefly elaborating how each of these five factors came into play in the course of Watergate, I will be illuminating how cultural refraction provides the possibility of reintegration, a reintegration that, far from being automatic, relies on the contingent outcomes of particular historical circumstances.

First, the factor of consensus. Between the Watergate break-in and the election, the necessary consensus did not occur. This continued to be a time of intense polarization politically, although the social conflicts of the sixties had begun to cool. McGovern was the very symbol of vanguard modernism on which Nixon built the backlash elements of his presidency. McGovern's continued presence allowed Nixon to continue to promote these politics and to continue to keep his moderate/conservative coalition together. It was because of this continued dissensus—the continued refraction—that the process of generalization could not take place. There could be no movement upward toward shared general values; because there was no generalization, there could be no societal sense of crisis; because there was no sense of crisis, it became impossible for the other forces I have mentioned to come into play. There was no perception of the threat to the center. There was no mobilization of social control, for those who exercised social control were afraid to act. There was no struggle by differentiated elites against the threat to and by the center—they were divided, afraid, and immobilized. Certainly, there were no deep symbolic processes emerging, for these would respond only to tensions generated by the first four factors.

Yet during the six months following the election, the situation began to be reversed. First, consensus did begin to emerge. The end of an intensely divided election period allowed the realignment that had been building since the late sixties to continue; once McGovern was eliminated, the more centrist elements of Nixon's presidency were not nearly so eager to align themselves with the extreme right. Yet this movement was itself part of a larger development that had been building since at least two years before Watergate. The social struggles of the sixties had long been over. Left groups had largely disappeared from public view. Social change had decelerated, and reactive movements had less of an immediate base. Critical universalism could now be readopted by centrist forces without its being linked to the specific ideological themes or goals of the left. With this emerging consensus the refraction of common politics into abrasive, distinctive subcultures began to dissipate. The possibility for a common feeling of normative violation emerged, and with it began the movement toward generalization vis-à-vis the Watergate events. Once this first resource of crisis creation and renewal had become available, the other developments could be activated.

What of the second factor, perception of threat to the center? With the new public redefinition and generalization processes beginning, anxiety about the threat that Watergate posed to the center began to frighten significant publics and elites. The question about proximity to the center preoccupied every major group during this early postelection Watergate period. "How much did the president know, and when did he know it?" became the telling phrase of the day. This anxiety about the threat to the center, in turn, only intensified the ongoing sense of normative violation; it increased consensus and contributed to generalization.

The third factor concerns the bringing into play of institutional social control. The developments during the early postelection months provided a much more congenial, legitimate atmosphere for the operation of social controls. I am thinking here of the activity of the courts, the justice department, various bureaucratic agencies, and special congressional committees. These social control institutions, in turn, legitimated the growing public feeling that Watergate was in fact a serious crime. They also forced more facts to surface. Of course, the ultimate level of generality and Watergate's final relationship to the center still remained undetermined.

The fourth factor is elite conflict. The generalization process I described, pushed by consensus, by fear of the center, and by the activity of new institutions of social control, was during the postelection period fueled by desire for revenge against Nixon by alienated institutional elites. Most functional elites were on the side of reform, and insofar as Nixon had supported the particularism of the radical right, he had done battle against them. During the postelection period, these elites constituted themselves as countercenters—professional associations such as the American Bar Association, newspaper reporters, intellectuals, universities, liberal religionists, many corporate figures, and last but not least, authorities in various public agencies who represented the modernists whom Nixon had earlier moved against.

By May of 1973, then, all these forces for crisis creation and resolution were in motion. Significant changes in public opinion had been mobilized, and powerful structural resources were being brought into play. It is only at this point that the fifth crisis factor emerged—namely, the deep processes of symbolic patterning, particularly ritual and pollution/cleansing processes, although there had certainly been important symbolic developments all along.

The first fundamental ritual event of the Watergate crisis occurred in May of 1973, the Senate Select Committee's televised hearings. This event had tremendous repercussions on the symbolic patterning of the entire affair. The decision to hold and to televise the Senate Select Committee hearings responded to the tremendous anxiety that had built up within important segments of the population. The symbolic process that ensued functioned to channel this anxiety in certain distinctive and more consensual symbolic directions. The hearings constituted a kind of civic ritual that revived very general yet crucial currents of critical universalism in the American political culture. Through television, tens of millions participated symbolically and emotionally in the deliberations. Viewing became obligatory for many. Old routines were broken, new ones formed. What these viewers saw was a highly simplified drama—heroes and villains formed in due course. But this drama created a deeply serious symbolic occasion. It re-created a generalized morality by evoking the mythic level of national understanding in a way that few other televised events have.

The senators who were the "stars" of the Watergate hearings managed to isolate and condemn the backlash values that had motivated and legitimated Watergate. They coupled a strategy of "bracketing" the 1960s with a ringing and unabashed affirmation of the universalistic myth that is the backbone of the American civic religion. Through their questions, statements, references, gestures, and metaphors, the senators maintained that every American, high or low, rich or poor, acts virtuously in terms of the pure universalism of the civic republican tradition. Nobody is selfish or inhumane. No American is concerned with money or power at the expense of fair play. No team loyalty is so strong that it violates the common good or neutralizes the critical attitude toward authority that is the basis of the democratic society.

The senators' questioning of administration witnesses focused on three main themes, each fundamental to the moral anchoring of a civic democratic society. First, they emphasized the absolute priority of office obligations over personal ones: "This is a nation of laws, not of men." Second, they emphasized the embeddedness of such office obligations in a higher transcendent authority: "The laws of men" must give way to the "laws of God." Or as Sam Ervin put it to Maurice Stans, "Which is more important, not violating laws or not violating ethics?" Finally, the senators insisted that this transcendental anchoring of interest conflict allowed America to be a true *Gemeinschaft,* in Hegel's term, a true "concrete universal." As Lowell Weicker said in a famous statement: "Republicans don't bug, Republicans don't cheat. They regard their fellow Americans as people to be loved and not as enemies."

The hearings ended without laws or specific judgments of evidence, but they nevertheless had profound effects. They established the framework that would henceforth give Watergate its meaning. They accomplished this by organizing the actual political events of the Watergate episode in terms of the higher antitheses between the sacred and profane elements of American civic religion. The hearings resacralized the Constitution, laws of fairness, and solidarity. They profaned sectarianism, self-interest, and particularism, and with these profaned elements they aligned Richard Nixon, his staff, and backlash values in general. The presidential party and the elements of civic sacredness had now become antithetical to each other, so antithetical that the American public now found them more and more difficult to bring together. It was this symbolic patterning, along with the other pressures I have described, that eventually drove Nixon from office one year later.

That Watergate did not prevent conservatism, after four short years of respite, from continuing its relentless assault on liberal reform misses the meaning of that fateful crisis entirely. Even the best of societies will move back and forth between left and right, change and reaction. The decisive question is not whether but how. Will the polarization produced by social change be so severely divisive that conflict is transformed into antidemocratic civil war? This has, indeed, been the fate of most modern and modernizing nations. Why it has not been so for the United States —as yet—is a cause for study. The place to begin such a study, I have suggested, is Watergate. That Reaganism sometimes feels drawn to anticivil extremism is clear from the morning newspaper. That, for now, fairly strict limits are set against this inclination is also manifest. These limits reside not only in "structure" but in the minds of men and women; they represent values that in crises are reproduced, extended, and internalized in turn. That Reaganism is democratic conservatism is thanks to Watergate.

Conclusion

This chapter began with a rather esoteric theoretical problem and concluded with a detailed case study of a gaudy and famous political scandal. My point has been, first, that social system conflict cannot be analyzed without reference to deeply felt social values, and, second, that the relation between such values and social integration can by no means be easily understood. I have offered three ideal-typical models of this relation, each of which presents different possibilities for reintegration in social crisis. I have tried to indicate, with this concluding analysis of Watergate, not only some of the empirical details that such models imply but, further, the more specific social processes on which the institutionalization of specification, refraction, and columnization depend.

Perhaps I may conclude on a more general note. The last two decades have witnessed a massive assault on functionalist theory. Much of this criticism was richly deserved; much of it also was misguided. Those who would wish to reclaim the most important contributions of that functionalist tradition are faced with a choice. They can focus on the undeserved and misguided elements of the critique, drawing further into themselves and developing a rigid orthodoxy, or they can learn from the accurate criticisms, developing a more flexible and sensitive variation of functionalist analysis. The latter path leads toward a neofunctionalism, and it is based on a combination of critique and inclusion. Conflict theory, neo-Marxism, interactionism, phenomenology—all make significant contributions. Yet functionalism, broadly defined as continuous with the traditions of Durkheim and Weber, still remains the most viable general sociological theory. It is the only theory that, at its best, can be fully multidimensional, combining individual voluntarism with structural determinism. It is the only theory that promises to successfully interweave value and force. Neofunctionalism must demonstrate that this general framework places no a priori limitations on the actual structure of any society. Conflict must be analyzed as successfully as change. The question, once again, is not whether but how.

Notes

1. "Conflation" is a concept I developed (Alexander, 1982) to explain the very common tendency to eliminate the relative autonomy of different levels of theoretical commitment. The discussion here takes off from a general criticism I made of Parsons (Alexander, 1983, particularly chaps. 6–7), that Parsons often cross-cut his differentiated understanding of order with a more "reduced" and conflated one, in which three relatively autonomous aspects of order are viewed as synonymous: presuppositional order in the sense of nonrandomness, model order in the sense of systematicity, and empirical order in the sense of cooperation and harmony.

2. It can be argued, if only on logical grounds, that there is a fourth ideal type, one in which social system integration is maintained despite cultural conflict. This combination is often implicit in the sociological literature on modern societies, for though formally acknowledging the cultural level, it makes this level actually impotent: Social life can proceed its merry way no matter what the condition of "culture." Among the classical theorists, Simmel's theorizing about conflict and the network of plural associations would seem to support this view, yet even Simmel makes residual reference to culturally integrative "forms" and "concepts" —for example, the "rules of the game" whose presence distinguishes competition from more brutal conflict. In contemporary discussions, the "politics of accommodation" evinced by Dutch society (Lijphart, 1974) would seem to be another such case. I be-

lieve, however, that this fourth possibility is a logical illusion, sociologically unfounded. If social system processes bring people together in cooperative ways, they either draw on earlier cultural commonality or will soon produce some. The literature on the Dutch case, for example, contains frequent references to Dutch nationalism, to shared material values and democratic ethos (Coleman, 1978). Whether this process issues in refraction or columnization remains an empirical question. Even societies in which there is columnization, of course, can be stable given a temporary balance of forces (see, for example, Rex's, 1961, discussion of the "truce situation").

3. Schluchter (1979), for example, writes about these as the "paradoxes" of rationalization produced by differentiation rather than as specifications. His Weberianization of Parsons's theory adds another dimension to it. Still, the notion of paradox should not entirely replace specification; this would reintroduce the type of atomism of which Parsons rightly complained. "Specification" must be retained as an *analytical* concept, even while its empirical application is limited. Even value "paradoxes" are specified, in this analytical sense.

4. For a good contrast between columnization and specification theory, one might compare Aron's analysis with the cultural emphasis of Suzanne Keller's (1963) theory of functional elites, which argues that they carry out complementary functions of the same general culture.

5. By the time of his second book (1963), Smelser had already realized this important fact, for he acknowledges that a significant element of revolutionary movements is their production of widely divergent value patterns. Although Smelser ascribes this value divergence primarily to structural rigidity, it should be linked to cultural as well as structural arrangements.

6. For an extremely acute discussion of American conservative ideology as a variation on individualism, see Nakano (1981).

7. The following analysis draws from an ongoing research project I am conducting on Watergate, including examination of the complete news reports from 1972-1974, review of the televised hearings, review of the extant secondary literature, analysis of the links between 1960s movements and Watergate, study of elite relations to the presidency during the Nixon era, and quanti-

tative analysis of public opinion between 1972 and 1974. The research has been supported by the Guggenheim, Ford, Markle, and Sage foundations (and conducted, in part, at the Vanderbilt Television Archives in Nashville, Tenn.) and by grants from the UCLA faculty senate. To document the generalizations offered here would require a great deal more space than this chapter provides. For this reason, the facts must be offered in terms of their "plausibility" in light of the theoretical considerations presented.

References

ALEXANDER, JEFFREY C.

1982   *Theoretical Logic in Sociology.* Vol. 1: *Positivism, Presuppositions, and Current Controversies.* Berkeley: University of California Press.

1983   *Theoretical Logic in Sociology.* Vol. 4: *The Modern Reconstruction of Classical Thought: Talcott Parsons.* Berkeley: University of California Press.

ARON, RAYMOND

1960   "Social Class, Political Class, Ruling Class." *European Journal of Sociology* 1:260–281.

BELLAH, ROBERT N.

1980   "The Five Religions of Italy." In Robert N. Bellah and Phillip E. Hammond, *Varieties of Civil Religion.* New York: Harper & Row.

COLEMAN, JOHN A.

1978   *The Evolution of Dutch Catholicism, 1958–1974.* Berkeley: University of California Press.

EVANS-PRITCHARD, E. E.

1953   "The Nuer Concept of the Spirit in Its Relation to the Social Order." *American Anthropologist* 55:201–241.

HARTZ, LOUIS

1955   *The Liberal Tradition in America.* New York: Harcourt Brace Jovanovich.

KELLER, SUZANNE

1963   *Beyond the Ruling Class.* New York: Random House.

LIJPHART, AREND

1974   *The Politics of Accommodation.* Berkeley: University of California Press.

LIPSET, SEYMOUR MARTIN
1965 *The First New Nation.* New York: Basic Books.
NAKANO, HIDEICHIRO
1981 "Conservatism as a Political Ideology in Contemporary America." *Kwansei Gakuin University Annual Bulletin* 30:95–108.
NOLTE, ERNST
1966 *The Three Faces of Fascism.* New York: Holt, Rinehart and Winston.
PARSONS, TALCOTT
1968 "On the Concept of Value-Commitments." In Talcott Parsons, *Politics and Social Structure.* New York: Free Press.
1971 *The System of Modern Societies.* Englewood Cliffs, N.J.: Prentice-Hall.
PARSONS, TALCOTT, AND PLATT, G. M.
1973 *The American University.* Cambridge, Mass.: Harvard University Press.
PARSONS, TALCOTT, AND SMELSER, NEIL J.
1956 *Economy and Society: A Study in the Integration of Economic and Social Theory.* New York: Free Press.
PITTS, JESSE
1964 "Continuity and Change in Bourgeois France." In Stanley Hoffman (Ed.), *In Search of France.* Cambridge, Mass.: Harvard University Press.
REX, JOHN
1961 *Key Problems in Sociological Theory.* London: Routledge & Kegan Paul.
ROTH, GUENTHER
1963 *The Social Democrats in Imperial Germany.* New York: Bedminster Press.
SCHLUCHTER, WOLFGANG
1979 "The Paradoxes of Rationalization." In Wolfgang Schluchter and Guenther Roth, *Max Weber's Vision of History.* Berkeley: University of California Press.
SMELSER, NEIL J.
1959 *Social Change in the Industrial Revolution: An Application of Theory to the British Cotton Industry.* Chicago: University of Chicago Press.
1963 *Theory of Collective Behavior.* New York: Free Press.

In attempting to learn more about the relationship between social structure and behavior, this chapter identifies the transforming conditions that promote an actor's acquisition of a noninstitutionalized role. The role concept is modified to be seen not only as an aspect of social structure, but connected to the life situation of a performer, constituting a person-role formula. Being defined according to the degree of involvement an actor will have with the proffered role, a person-role formula may be based on embracement, integration, downgrading, or avoidance. Roles are transformed into one of these possible relationships through three stages (1) role discrepancy, (2) role typification, and (3) role validation.

11

TOWARD A THEORY OF ROLE ACQUISITION

Arnold Birenbaum

ST. JOHN'S UNIVERSITY, JAMAICA, NEW YORK

A role may be traditionally defined as a set of expectations about the way individuals with special social identifications will probably act in special situations in contact with others who also have a special identification. A role, then, is seen as part of a division of labor, constituting a set of projected behaviors that are external and constraining to the actors. The social-fact approach to role locates the behavior of people in such a way that their own conceptions of what they do are largely irrelevant: "It consists of ways of acting, thinking, and feeling, external to the individual, and endowed with a power of coercion, by reason of which they control him" (Durkheim [1895], 1964:3).

The social-fact approach is a powerful argument for the reality of society, but it leaves much of the interplay between person and social structure outside its scope. It is useful, therefore, to consider interpretive behavior as important in producing the stability, modification, or dissolution of organized social life. It is reasonable to suggest that in order to perpetuate everyday social life, actors must regard their performances as willful, purposive, and subject to human intervention and judgment. A behavior has to be recognized by self and other as part of a performance and therefore a social act. It is this recognition that gives social acts their factual quality. In contrast, the social-fact approach falsely separates person and social structure, reducing social interaction to an outcome of forces beyond the control of human beings.

Ralph Turner (1962:24) has argued that when human beings are engaged in almost any set of behaviors, they are regarded as conveying information about themselves that cues others that they are playing a role. What is attended to is consistency in performance rather than absolute conformity to norms or expectations. In a similar way, Goffman (1974:38) asserts that primary frames are used as models for organizing experiences, "thereby forming conjectures as to what occurred before and expectations of what is likely to happen now."

Some behaviors appear to require little attention. Some roles, by virtue of their institutionalization, can easily be anticipated; they are part of some organized social establishment. In turn, other persons connected through a social network can recognize the future sequence of activities to be engaged in by the actor and formulate their expectations accordingly. Institutionalized roles can easily be understood, and the rightness of the designation of the social identity is rarely questioned. For example, when people become sick, they are excused from work or other responsibilities, since all concerned know full well that "these things do happen." The framework of everyday life hardly encourages examination of role acquisition as much as does an unusual or unanticipated situation. Under this condition, it is possible to locate the properties found in ordinary situations more readily, particularly the mechanisms that transform roles along the path of the ordinary, with a past and a future.

Following this line of inquiry, it would appear that despite the obligatory character of role performances, which any competent member of society would recognize, there is a shared cognitive basis for interpreting behavior. Therefore, when cues are forthcoming that are not consistent with the putative role, a redefinition of the actor's role will occur.

What are the transforming conditions that promote an actor's acquisition of a role? There are many roles that people acquire which start as unexpected or fortuitous events. From the actor's point of view, becoming a lottery winner or becoming physically handicapped is an unanticipated circumstance, yet actors who experience such events are enjoined to respond to obligations that are sometimes initially perceived almost as a case of mistaken identity.

Goffman defines these common-sense concepts as *keys,* or "sets of conventions by which a given activity, one already meaningful in terms of some primary framework, is transformed into something patterned on this activity but seen by the participants to be something quite else" (1974:43–44). Keying involves regrounding events to make them fully understandable and manageable. Keying makes possible several strategies for how to perform a role, depending on the alignment between the person, the role performed, and some ongoing social organization. The key will express the importance of the events or activities in question, tying this construction to some general cultural concern. Goffman identifies the points of contact where formulas for organizing experience are required: "Whenever an individual participates in an episode of activity, a distinction will be drawn between what is called the person, individual, or player, namely, he who participates, and the particular role, capacity, or function he realizes during that participation. And a connection between these two elements will be understood. In short, there will be a *person-role formula.* The nature of a particular frame will, of course, be linked to the nature of the person-role formula it sustains. One can never expect complete freedom between individual and role and never complete constraint. But no matter where on this continuum a particular formula is located, the formula itself will express the sense in which the framed activity is geared into the continuing world" (1974:269).

Preparation for role acquisition makes the fit between persons and roles continuous and consistent. Turner suggests that an embracement of a role is most likely to occur when the actor has worked hard at getting a role proffered. In his complete and lucid summary and commentary on Ralph Turner's contribution to role theory, Jonathan Turner (1978:387) (no relation) amplifies this insight: "People must receive reinforcement, whether this be confirmation of self, bolstering of self-esteem, an equitable ratio of rights to duties, or some other consideration."

Unanticipated roles are those that actors do not find viable; yet they may be required to perform a role proffered. It is useful to consider that actors may then have to develop a person-role formula appropriate to their situation. Defined according to the degree of involvement an actor will have with the role that is proffered, a person-role formula may be based on (1) *embracing* the role as a major source of identity, (2) *integrating* it into an array of existing roles, (3) *downgrading* it to the extent of keeping others from knowing about it, and (4) *avoiding* all connection with it (see Figure 1).

Figure 1. Degree of Involvement with Newly Acquired Role.

High *Involvement*			*Low* *Involvement*
Embracement	Integration	Downgrading	Avoidance

The task now is to examine the various ways in which unanticipated roles are framed, transforming them from the extraordinary to the ordinary, but at the same time sometimes increasing the problematic character of role performances. In seeking to reduce a role's problematic character, actors invoke various conventions to eliminate awkwardness, confusion, and ambiguity. Transformation through the use of convention does not imply that a one-to-one identity exists between the primary frames and frames that resemble them, only that continued comparisons are made.

Role Discrepancy

A role discrepancy may be defined as an actor's realization that his or her concepts of what behaviors are appropriate in the role do not match what others expect. Continued application of the same frame of understanding to organize one's experience may not maintain meaning, and one cannot continue to maintain involvement in the role (Goffman, 1974:304). Discrepancies between person and role exist when original frames are applied in situations where they no longer create meaning, as for example, when a couple divorces or when a family member joins a religious sect. Consequently, past, present, and future behaviors require a new key.

There are two ways that rekeying occurs, focusing on different features of the behavior under consideration. Each feature is tied to either the person or the roles a person performs. Roles can be rendered discrepant, requiring rekeying, (1) when behavior fails to affirm the identity of the role performer—that is, when activities raise doubts about the person's right to perform an already established role—or (2) when previously irrelevant behaviors become required for continued role performance.

Organizational reassignments of personnel provide examples of the first role discrepancy, as when those who had considerable authority and responsibility consciously or unwittingly attempt to exercise it despite demotion (Goldner, 1965). The second type of role discrepancy is illustrated by roles in which certain behaviors become obligatory. Becoming disabled makes unmanageable roles previously performed, as when a person must now be "accepted" among colleagues or in places where entry was never questioned. New behaviors such as anger, rage, grief, and acceptance are now required, even encouraged, through ritual expression.

The timing of the discovery of the role discrepancy provides an important key to subsequent behavior. Events that are part of the life cycle acquire natural interpretations but are also linked to the person-role formula, which deepens emotional involvement through either embracing the role or avoiding all connection with it. To be challenged on critical occasions, rather than through graduated recognition of the discrepancy, reduces commitment decisions but increases the likelihood of viability questions—that is, Is selfhood possible with (or without) this new role?

Timing is a subject that other sociologists have discussed. Garfinkel (1956) has considered this variable under the subject of the conditions for successful degradation ceremonies. Goffman identifies this variable as affecting an actor's information state, or "the knowledge an individual has of why events have happened as they have, what the current forces are, what the properties and intents of the relevant persons are, and what the outcome is likely to be" (1974:133–134). Graduated, as opposed to critical, timing permits the actor to acquire the new role as one of many, thereby integrating it or downgrading it, without awkward and embarrassing scenes. In a formal organization, an actor may never be told that he or she has no right to be present at a meeting or conference, but the name may disappear from lists of personnel to be notified or called in during emergencies.

In sum, role discrepancies promote the dissociation of the person and the role, creating a demand for new ways of organizing behavior and ultimately being based on a new key to the frame. Actors focus on the meaning of the events that have altered their lives and, in so doing, are engaging in actions that bring their own and others' responses into line. The demonstration of concern with the meaning of the events separates the social facts of what happened from the actor's motives, intentions, and feelings. These actions help to align the actor with new roles that are to be performed, preserving the person despite the loss of a role that connects up to other roles performed. Stokes and Hewitt say that aligning actions sustain "a relationship (but not necessarily an exact correspondence) between ongoing conduct and culture in the face of recognized failure of conduct to live up to cultural definitions and requirements" (1976:844).

Role Typification

Typification is the placement of an actor into a recurrent social category, complete with an explanation of why that fit between role and person was made. Typification, though constraining the actor to accept a certain social identity—often an undesired identity—allows the actor to reduce involvement with the role. Actors can develop a model of expected responses of others to themselves and, consequently, a model of their responses to others. Alfred Schutz designated these models "course of action" types. "We impute to the more or less anonymous actors a set of supposedly invariant motives which govern their actions. This set is itself a construct of typical expectations of the Other's behavior and has been investigated frequently in terms of social role or function or institutional behavior" (1962:25).

Actors recognize that others' expectations of them result from their being placed in recurrent social categories, rather than from supposedly unique qualities they possess. Through their typifications of others, actors typify themselves as well: "In defining the role of the Other, I am assuming a role myself. In typifying the Other's behavior I am typifying my own which is interrelated with his, transforming myself into a passenger, consumer, taxpayer, reader, bystander, etc." (Schutz, 1962:19).

Once roles are typified, rules are no longer ambiguous and ircomplete. Information is available to the role performer and others; social relationships between the performers and others will be maintained, modified, or dissolved, not remain in doubt. In other words, disorder is replaced by the potential for routine performance even if the roles to be performed are unpredictable according to the cultural recipes available to actors in that society. A new set of shared meanings emerges (Mead, 1959:209), based on belief in what Schutz called the "reciprocity of perspectives" (1962:29-30). Such recipes are so certain that if roles reversed themselves for the actors involved, each would be able to act out completely the newly acquired role.

The information available to performers and others locates the role in various organized settings, as well as, sometimes, in unconventional ones. Thus, the performer and others are able to assess the rewards and costs of complying with the norms of identity and norms of action arrived at through typification. At the same time, when roles become typified, they are located in one's personal history as well as in relations with others. Accordingly, a set of justifications for including or excluding certain acts and actors is also produced. These may be designated as "accounts"—statements that explain, justify, or excuse the fit between the characteristics of the performer and the role he or she is now expected to perform (Scott and Lyman, 1968:46-62).

It can be seen that embracement of a role is more likely to occur after typification because of the relief from uncertainty provided in the newly established unambiguous and complete rules. In this stage the availability of membership in preestablished collectivities or the use of social relationships for those who perform the newly typified role creates even more certainty by locating the role in an extensive social network. Insofar as such networks exist, contact with those in similar situations will occur, producing additional confirmation that routine performance of unexpected roles is possible.

The study of disability suggests similar embracements of un-desired or stigmatized roles, since these roles are associated with orderly accounts of the events that produced or were connected with the unexpected and undesired condition. Such accounts help to reduce self-blame when the discrepancy from "normal" people is recognized (Birenbaum, 1969:379). When mental retardation is diagnosed in children, "mothers are encouraged to accept both a naturalistic explanation of the child's origins and a continued af-firmation of their own normality" (Birenbaum, 1969:379). This process of typification follows a period of great uncertainty during which the lack of development in the child was interpreted as a sign of permanent disability.

As a result of participation in the organized world of retarda-tion, the birth of an abnormal child is adequately ordered into "the same symbolic universe that encompasses the reality of everyday life" (Berger and Luckmann, 1966:91). While the moth-er of a retarded child is encouraged to perform the tasks of con-ventional mothering, she is enjoined also to engage in activities re-lated specifically to the child's disability. The inability of conven-tional medical practice to be of service to the mother of a retarded child promotes her entry into the organized field of mental retar-dation. Here she finds a knowledgeable staff and other parents in the same situation. Membership in voluntary associations devoted to aiding the mentally retarded provides mothers with a further and extended opportunity to interact with others in the same sit-uation. First encounters with such organizations are often retro-spectively described by members as "turning points" in their ca-reers. At such meetings, speakers often emphasize the common but accidental quality of the birth of a retarded child. The appeal for solidarity is based on the similarity of conventional identity and the unpredictability of the event that took place. Thus, a naturalistic interpretation of the unexpected and undesired condi-tion of the child replaces any teleological explanation, such that it was God's plan to test the parents. This orderly account goes far beyond mere certainty because it is also an operating code for per-forming this role, making less problematic and more routine what was once highly problematic and uncertain.

When the issue of "turning points" is raised, the question of the permanence or transitoriness of the role being typified becomes crucial to the performer. Part of the process of typification involves developing a usable perspective on how long performance of the role will continue. Temporarily acquired roles can be supported by suspensions of the demands others place on the actor and may involve little in the way of redefinition of the social relationship. Permanently acquired roles are not supportable by others in the same way. Temporary roles can be downgraded (and sometimes avoided), and others may be kept from knowing about them. Yet following this strategy prevents others from either supporting the performance of the new role by suspending demands or engaging in a redefinition of the social relationship between the actor and others. Moreover, if efforts at dissimulation are discovered, then sources of support that are potentially realizable will evaporate or be overtly withdrawn, since such an act will be regarded as a more serious violation of trust in the relationship than a change in identity of an undesirable and/or unexpected kind would have been. The sequence of events surrounding Senator Thomas Eagleton's withdrawal from candidacy in July 1972, or Nixon's resignation in August 1974, demonstrates how important others are in the process of typification.

The likelihood that any one of the four strategies of performance of a newly acquired role will be adopted over others varies by whether the role is found out about suddenly or gradually and whether the role is perceived as temporary or permanent. Embracement is most likely to occur when the role is acquired suddenly and is regarded as permanent; measured in terms of consequences, it is the most disruptive of prior social relationships; and it encourages the greatest efforts, in the form of aligning actions, to explain, justify, or rationalize the role acquisition. This kind of role acquisition may be likened to a religious or political conversion experience. The "radicalization" of students in the 1960s took this form. Avoiding the role is most likely to occur when the role is acquired gradually and is defined as temporary because few others will know about it. Even when acquired suddenly, roles perceived as temporary are downgraded, while those acquired gradually but regarded as permanent are integrated among all other roles performed. Although embracement, integration, downgrading, and avoiding may be conceived of as points along a continuum, they may also be discrete cells in a classification of possible stages or temporal sequences, as in Figure 2.

The question still remains, What are the conditions under

Figure 2. Conditions Under Which a Role Is Acquired and Response.

	Sudden	*Gradual*
Permanent	Embracement	Integration
Temporary	Downgrading	Avoidance

which a role becomes defined as permanent or temporary? This is an important problem because short-lived roles such as a prison sentence or a visiting professorship have a residue of permanence, which can be expressed in the form of other roles—for example, "the ex-convict"—or translated into prestige—for example, having been a "scholar in residence." What is known about an actor can be stigmatizing or prestigious, depending on the reactions of others.

Role Validation

It is suggested here that the institutionalized character of a role, whether permanent or temporary, known about gradually or suddenly, is derived from intersubjective meanings shared by the actor and others. In order for an actor to maintain a typification of a role as a course of action, that typification must be validated. Validation is the confirmation by relevant others that a particular course of action is appropriate to their expectations for the actor. Thus, role validation is seen here as a continual process of establishing or altering the actor's self-typification. The way in which validation is arrived at accounts for the way in which roles become typified according to the four adaptations suggested earlier—embracement, integration, downgrading, or avoidance.

Permanent roles may be disruptive of one's membership in other collectivities, or they may be nondisruptive. The more a collectivity is organized on the basis of "organic solidarity" (Durkheim [1893], 1960), the more likely acquired roles will be either integrated or downgraded but not embraced or avoided. In contrast, in a collectivity organized on the basis of "mechanical solidarity," acquisition of a noninstitutionalized role may be disruptive.

Memberships in collectivities characterized by organic solidarity, such as families, work teams, and other adaptive organizations, are based on interdependent performances of fairly formal and specific roles such as husband, wife, foreman, assembly line worker, clerk, or manager. In contrast, friendship groups or even voluntary associations of people who are similarly situated are held together on the basis of mechanical solidarity. Role performance in these collectivities is generally complementary and expressive rather than interdependent and instrumental. Acquisition of a new role, even an institutionalized one, may destabilize relationships based on similarity of life-style or affection, as when friendships may be lost when a friend marries or divorces.

I propose that the extent to which newly acquired roles will be validated by others in any given network has little to do with the cultural value placed on the role and more to do with whether the new role can be perceived as potentially manageable along with other roles performed. Acquisition of unexpected roles affects all members of the collectivity, insofar as they share beliefs, not just those who are immediately involved. Therefore, it can be hypothesized that with unanticipated roles efforts will be made to restore belief in that culture as a source of order in the lives of all members.

A question remains: What kinds of aligning actions are possible in different kinds of collectivities? Examination of these conditions that make for uniform patterns of conduct would indicate the direction of validation of the role taken, according to one of the four suggested strategies. Some of the verbal behaviors of parents of disabled children are aligning actions that affirm their membership in various collectivities by disclaiming that they are different from other families. Persons who cannot live up to the cultural standards of the collectivity are still required to support those standards, and their participation in various collectivities remains an ongoing obligation.

In this way the social structure is able to gain support from those undergoing culturally induced psychological strain. Opportunities to engage in these aligning actions, such as *quasi theorizing* (Hewitt and Hall, 1973), permit newly acquired, though often undesired, roles to be explained within the same cultural framework that accounts for the stability of identity of those who did not acquire new roles. "Quasi theorizing constitutes an aligning action because it relates culture to observed and ongoing action by explaining discrepancies between the two. If what is observed is problematic and cannot be resolved into the nonproblematic, it can at least be made sensible in cultural terms that all recognize" (Stokes and Hewitt, 1976:846).

Role validation will occur when interpretive efforts are recognized by significant others as taking place. In these instances it would be expected that integration or downgrading will follow. Responses from others that raise doubt about whether others have recognized or have believed these efforts may lead to embracement or avoiding the role. Responses from others that raise doubts about the actor's right to continue previously performed roles produce embracement of the new role. The developmental patterns of religious and political movements demonstrate that efforts at sanction and control of innovation merely reinforce the beliefs that were put forth tentatively about the nature of the "established" religious and political authorities, providing occasions for revealing to future followers just how repressive these collectivities really are. Similarly, in the early history of psychoanalysis, practitioners were often accused by other physicians of being "obsessed with sex." The efforts and language of critics of psychoanalysis provided a way of substantiating the utility of Freudian concepts.

Avoiding a role is likely to occur when performers of newly acquired roles anticipate awkward situations rather than actually have doubts raised about their capacities to perform. The strategy of avoiding seeks to prevent others from finding out about the newly acquired role. Here it can be predicted that disclaimers will be proffered to prevent positive role validation. Dissimulation covers up avoiding and involves managing information about one's self as well as the potential discovery of the effort to avoid performance. Sociologically, this kind of validation results in an inverted performance. The carrier of a secret tries to act as if he or she carried no secret.

Conclusion

Problematic roles provide the sociologist with a strategic research site not available in more conventional settings. I have suggested that much can be learned about the relation between social structure and behavior through examining how noninstitutionalized roles are managed. Similarly, the origins of norms, both of action and of identity, can be studied through the ways in which unusual and unconventional identities and actions are responded to in face-to-face interaction.

The concepts and hypotheses developed here are applicable to many ranges of behavior. In illustrations selected from several substantive fields, the certainty and security of everyday life were created by the emergence of shared meanings when the operations described in the discussion of role acquisition (discrepancy, typification, and validation) were performed.

Indeed, it can be inferred that continuous revalidation of typifications through aligning actions occurs all the time as a way of preventing discrepancies from reemerging. Shared meanings about the rules for conduct or identity are never constant if they are to remain unambiguous and incomplete. Social competency, then, may be based on an implicit recognition of the fragility and danger of organized social life, a kind of knowing when and where one can be taken to be competent.

References

BERGER, PETER L., AND LUCKMANN, THOMAS
  1966   *The Social Construction of Reality: A Treatise in the Sociology of Knowledge*. New York: Doubleday.
BIRENBAUM, ARNOLD
  1969   "How Mothers of Mentally Retarded Children Use Specialized Facilities." *Family Coordinator* 18:379–385.
DURKHEIM, ÉMILE
  1960   *The Division of Labor in Society*. (Translated by George Simpson.) New York: Free Press. (Originally published 1893.)
  1964   *The Rules of the Sociological Method*. New York: Free Press. (Originally published 1895.)
GARFINKEL, HAROLD
  1956   "Conditions of Successful Degradation Ceremonies." *American Journal of Sociology* 61:420–424.
GOFFMAN, ERVING
  1974   *Frame Analysis: An Essay on the Organization of Experience*. New York: Harper & Row.

GOLDNER, FRED
    1965   "Demotion in Industrial Management." In Gerald D.
            Bell (Ed.), *Organizations and Human Behavior*. Engle-
            wood Cliffs, N.J.: Prentice-Hall.
HEWITT, JOHN P., AND HALL, PETER M.
    1973   "Social Problems, Problematic Situations, and Quasi-
            Theories." *American Sociological Review* 38:367–374.
MEAD, GEORGE H.
    1959   *The Social Psychology of George Herbert Mead*. (Edited
            by Anselm Strauss.) Chicago: University of Chicago
            Press.
SCHUTZ, ALFRED
    1962   *Collected Papers*. Vol. 1: *The Problem of Social Real-
            ity*. (Edited by Maurice Natanson.) The Hague: Marti-
            nus Nijhoff.
SCOTT, MARVIN, AND LYMAN, SANFORD
    1968   "Accounts." *American Sociological Review* 33:46–62.
STOKES, RANDALL, AND HEWITT, JOHN P.
    1976   "Aligning Actions." *American Sociological Review* 41:
            838–849.
TURNER, JONATHAN
    1978   *The Structure of Sociological Theory*. (Rev. ed.)
            Homewood, Ill.: Dorsey Press.
TURNER, RALPH
    1962   "Role Taking: Process vs. Conformity." In Arnold M.
            Rose (Ed.), *Human Behavior and Social Processes: An
            Interactionist Approach*. Boston: Houghton Mifflin.

*Sociology is split into two antagonistic or mutually oblivious
wings: quantitative and nonquantitative. Statistics does not
occupy a privileged methodological position vis-à-vis qualitative,
verbal sociology. Probability is a theory like any other, and each
statistical method contains its particular theoretical bias. Such
biases should be brought into the open and tested. Statistics
may continue to be useful, though, as a substantive theory of
change processes in the social world. A reorientation in our views
of statistics may bring mathematical and antimathematical
branches of sociology back into a common enterprise.*

☙ 12 ☙

STATISTICS VERSUS WORDS

Randall Collins

SAN DIEGO, CALIFORNIA

A struggle continues within sociology, as well as elsewhere
in the intellectual world, between the proponents and opponents
of mathematics. Proponents have often defined themselves, in
keeping with positivist philosophy, as the sole practitioners of the
scientific method. All other efforts at sociology are dismissed as
"nonempirical" or "nonscientific." Antimathematical critics, from
C. Wright Mills (1959) to Lewis Coser (1975), have charged their
opponents with concentrating on irrelevant formalisms and dis-
tracting attention from the real theoretical questions of the discipline.

In recent years, the antipositivist side has become much
more prominent within sociology, as well as more militant. There
has been the revival of Marxism, which typically condemns posi-

I am indebted for comments on an earlier draft to Albert James Bergesen, Rod Harrison, Barbara Laslett, Sal Restivo, Arthur L. Stinchcombe, and
Robert Philip Weber.

329

tivism as a symptom of our alienated capitalist society. Many of the more intellectual sociologists have been attracted to French structuralism, social phenomenology, ethnomethodology, and other sophisticated positions that are openly scornful of traditional science. Historical sociology, which is largely nonquantitative, is in a golden age, and interpretive approaches abound. However, positivist sociology has certainly not retreated. Increasingly technical approaches have been elaborated, usually of a statistical nature, ranging from the once-faddish path analysis to log-linear models and recent hits like LISREL.

In short, sociology seems to be splitting, more than ever before, into separate cocoons that scarcely occupy the same intellectual universe. Recent statistical sociology makes no concessions of intelligibility toward outsiders and shows almost no interest in linking up with larger theoretical concerns. On the other side, antipositivists, once a somewhat embarrassed minority, militantly advocate their own programs of interpretive, historical, Marxist, structuralist, or ethnomethodological sociology and condemn their positivist opponents *in absentia*. Which side one sees as the true sociology depends almost entirely on what social circle one happens to frequent.

In what follows, I examine a particular form of mathematical sociology, the use of statistics. In general, statisticians are the worst offenders in imposing a narrowly positivist orthodoxy on the field. Other forms of quantitative sociology, such as purely descriptive presentation of numerical data, on the one hand, or creation of mathematical models, on the other, are actually not so hard to harmonize with the theoretical and empirical interests touted by antipositivists. Militant Marxists are happy to bolster their historical arguments with figures on the profits of imperialism; their antipositivism does not arise at the level of sheer counting. Similarly, mathematical theories of social processes, such as network analysis, do not carry the antitheoretical tone found in so much statistical sociology. On a deeper level the ideas within some mathematical models are not dissimilar to the deep structure of arguments in the structuralist and phenomenological realms.

The problem arises primarily because of the vogue of statistical methods, with its accompanying canons of how research is to be carried out and theories to be tested. In anticipation of my argument, I will say that there is a good deal of validity in the complaints of the antipositivist side. Historical sociology and numerous other fields are not flawed because of intrinsic limitations on their use of statistics. On the contrary, they can proceed best without inroads from the statistical side. This point can be established, moreover, by going into the foundations of statistical theory itself—an area in which most statistical practitioners turn out to be surprisingly naive. I will attempt to show that the place of statistics in sociological methodology has been grossly inflated.

At the same time, though, I will say something in defense of statistics—not of statistics as methodology but of statistics as a *substantive theory* of how chance processes operate in the social world. The great mistake is to regard statistics simply as a neutral method. As such, it is always permeated by hidden theoretical assumptions. Statistics is not method but theory. It is best to get the theory out in the open and let it stand on the same ground with other substantive theories of how society operates. Instead of an intellectual straitjacket, let it operate as a boost to our theoretical imagination.

What Is Statistics: Method or Theory?

Statistics is widely regarded as a method, a way of describing relationships and testing theories, not of formulating them. A statistical test compares some given distribution, which one would like to interpret as resulting from some particular cause, against the range of distributions that could be regarded as produced by chance. Only if the null hypothesis is rejected (that the observed distribution is the result of chance) is the substantive theory accepted. It is also held that for such a test to be valid, the sample must be drawn in such a way as to avoid contamination by some systematic bias in drawing data, by preknowledge on the part of the theorist, and so on. In short, statisticians aim at a kind of untouched-by-human-hands mechanism by which theories can be "neutrally" tested against an objective world.

Such a procedure focuses attention on *our* theory, the one that is being tested, and makes it seem as if it were the only theory under consideration. But another theory is also implicitly present —the theory that, in fact, certain distributions are produced by chance.

What, then, is "chance"? Generally we regard "chance" as

merely a negative category, the absence of any determination. Commonly, when we cannot assign a reason that something happened, we describe it as happening by sheer accident, or "chance." This is more or less the same thing as "plain dumb luck," which (unless you are a gambler or other superstitious person) we resist any efforts to personify or otherwise reduce to anything beyond a blind nullity.

But a moment's reflection suggests that "chance" is not indeterminate at all. It would be sheer "accident," we would say, if a rock fell off a roof and hit you on the head. It could have fallen at any time, it could have hit a thousand other spots on the ground around you, and so forth. Hence we tend to say (somewhat vaguely and picturesquely), "The chances against that happening are about a million to one." But in fact the fall of the rock can be analyzed very easily into causal connections. The path that it described through the air follows quite precisely the law of the acceleration of gravity; where it hit was due to the direction and velocity with which it left the roof, which way the wind was blowing, and so forth. The fall of the rock onto your head was thus not at all uncaused. It was an accident only in that we did not know the initial conditions under which it fell.

Exactly the same thing can be said about social processes that appear to us as random matters of "chance." Social mobility studies that concentrate on the series of variables leading up through completion of formal education can explain only about 40 percent of the variance in occupational attainment. Does that mean the other 60 percent (as Jencks and others, 1972, have suggested) is purely a matter of chance? Only if we mean by this that, knowing as much as a conventional survey tells us about what has happened up through school graduation, we can predict occupational outcomes several decades later no more closely than within a certain range. But the other variation is not necessarily mysterious; it is likely determined by other facts (personal friendship networks, on one level; structural changes in the economy, at a larger level; see Collins, 1975:430-436, 445-456) that are simply not entered into the individual-level theory.

"Chance," then, does not mean the absence of causality. It means the absence of causality that we know about, from the point of view of what we are looking at. More generally, it also

means that the different orders of causality are essentially unconnected. The fact that you were walking by the building when the
rock fell off the roof is also the product of a series of causes: your
intention to go to a certain place, to see a certain person, say,
which can be further analyzed into such factors as your social class
culture, which made this person attractive to you as a friend (see
Collins, 1981c). There need be nothing uncaused about any aspect
of the situation, either in the social motivation that made you
walk by or in the physics that carried the rock down onto your
head. But the two causal orders are unconnected. There is no relation (or, if any, the most trivially remote one) between your walking there at that time and the rock falling when it did. *It is this un-
connectedness of different causal orders in the universe that gives
rise to the phenomenon of chance.*[1]

Chance, in an important sense, is not just a matter of "luck."
Chance has its own laws, which are precisely what the discipline of
statistics is founded on. These are the laws of *how various distributions arise from the combination of events that are causally independent.* It is not surprising that the mathematical theory of statistics should have arisen from the investigations of Pascal, Bernoulli,
and others into the principles of games of chance, for gambling
games are physical situations that have been deliberately devised
so that outcomes are independent of each other. A series of rolls
of the dice are independent physical acts; further, each die is constructed so that each side reacts the same way to shaking in a hand
or cup. The mechanical flipping of a coin, the pulling of black or
white balls from an urn, the mixing of numbers in a bingo machine: all of these are mechanical situations in which independent
elements are produced in a long series. Counting the distribution
of outcomes under these circumstances gave rise to empirical generalizations, to which various mathematical models were then
fitted. Later the model was extended to other physical situations
(to heated particles, by Poisson; to observational errors of astrono-
mers and to human demographic patterns, by Quetelet; to the
characteristics of biological populations, by Fisher and Pearson;
and so on). These applications gave the distributions against which
observed hypotheses are tested in order to reject the null hypothesis of causation as "merely" the result of chance.

The interpretation of statistical distributions has been a

matter of shifting debate over the years. The traditional "frequency theory of probability" (formulated by Bernoulli, among others) regarded distributions as empirical facts. However, since distributions can be mathematically derived merely by making the assumption that there are certain independent elements, that their combination obeys the additive property, and a few other axioms, there has been a tendency to regard statistics as simply the working out of a logical rather than an empirical system. Recently, even the assumption of independent *elements* has been dropped, and statistical distributions can be shown to be generated merely by having independent *observations*. One tendency has been in the direction of defining statistics subjectively rather than objectively. John Maynard Keynes's *Treatise on Probability* (1921) began this trend, taking a more extreme position than most subsequent statisticians about the theoretical, nonquantifiable subjective elements involved in any judgment of probability. De Finetti and Savage produced the modern subjective approach to statistics. Kolmogorov and Chaitin have carried along a subjective (but quantitative) approach by defining randomness in terms of the number of bits of information that a computer would need in order to reproduce a given number (see Hacking, 1975; Fine, 1973; Gillies, 1973; Savage, 1954; MacKenzie, 1981).

Nevertheless, I would argue that even though our *use* of statistics can be regarded as a subjective phenomenon, it implies a theoretical model of the external world. That model is what Keynes characterized as the "atomic character of natural law": "The system of the material universe must consist . . . of bodies which we may term (without any implication as to their size being conveyed thereby) *legal atoms,* such that each of them exercises its own separate, independent, and invariable effect, a change of the total state being compounded of a number of separate changes each of which is solely due to the separate portion of the preceding state" (1921:249). Hence (describing Cournot's theory of statistics): "No one . . . seriously believes that in striking the ground with his foot he puts out the navigator in the Antipodes, or disturbs the system of Jupiter's satellites. . . . Every event is causally connected with previous events belonging to its own series, but it cannot be modified by contact with events belonging to another series. A 'chance' event is a complex due to the concurrence in

time or place of events belonging to causally independent series"
(1921:283).

Keynes points out that this model is assumed rather than
proved, because it is not clear how we can know that the events
are not completely unconnected: "Just as it is likely that we are
all cousins if we go back far enough, so there may be, after all, remote relationships between ourselves and Jupiter" (1921:283).

Nevertheless, as Keynes remarks, it may be necessary to accept the "atomic" model for practical purposes. Notice that this
does not endorse the position that the universe consists entirely
of atoms or that there are no "field" or "contextual" effects in
subatomic particles, electricity, biological organisms, or human societies. But these are all orders of causality. Each of them implies
a certain set of interrelations, which we can formulate in a theory.
The theory can then be tested statistically against an underlying
model of independent "atoms" of causality, *at whatever level.*
Statistical test theory always implies that there are at least two
different causal mechanisms: One of them is the mechanism that
produces "random" distributions, wherever certain aspects of the
world consist of independent orders of causality; the other is
whatever laws we think we discern in the world (that is, our explicit theory).

I would draw two conclusions from the fact that statistics
implies a substantive theory of the world. (1) *Statistical testing is
much less important as a methodological criterion of theoretical
validity than we have supposed.* Statistical testing is more a matter
of faith than an ultimate criterion of truth; there are more important ways to validate a theory than exclusive reliance on statistical
tests against an empty null hypothesis. The fact that we do rely so
much on statistics is more an indication of the social relationships
that exist in the community of researchers than a sign of scientific
progress. (2) *The greatest value of statistics is as a theory rather
than as a method.* Statistics should not be thrown out entirely, although it does need to be put in its place. That place is in understanding the statistical "bingo machine" processes of causality that
often operate in the social world, especially at the macrostructural
level.

Statistics as Intellectual Distrust. Whenever one carries out a
statistical test of the "significance" of a given pattern of relations

found in the world, one is actually comparing one theory with another: the theory one has in mind versus the theory that some sort of "bingo game" structure to the universe produced the observed results. If in fact one does not reject the null hypothesis, does that mean the phenomenon is unexplained? On the contrary, it usually implies that one has extended the range of application of a statistical model of the universe. A major portion of our understanding of the world, then, is assumed on logical grounds, rather than proved by statistical test. There is no way to test a statistical model statistically; one simply demonstrates that the pattern of data is consonant with it. One cannot test the validity of a theory of statistical distributions by comparing it against another statistical distribution; this procedure leads only to a logical regress. As Keynes (1921) pointed out, the theory of probability itself is not based on probability. As long as we assume the theory of probability—and we do this whenever we use it for methodological purposes—we accept it as a structural given, not as something to be tested in itself.

For this reason, statistical tests are not nearly so important for the advancement of scientific truths as we have taken them to be. A considerable number of assumptions are required before we can decide that statistical tests fit the matter at hand. As Keynes (1921:21-30) pointed out, the application of a statistical test requires judgments of relevance to the matter at hand. To calculate a probability distribution requires a set of exclusive and exhaustive alternatives of equal probability. But many (or most) instances of scientific evidence for any larger problem cannot be judged strictly against this background. Suppose one has three researches on the same problem. The first contains the most experiments; the second has varied the control conditions most thoroughly and widely; the third produces the widest generalization. Which of the three generalizations is most probable? The answer cannot be stated quantitatively, because there are no grounds for comparison.

How, then, is scientific evidence actually weighted in developing a theory? In the physical sciences, the three sets of experiments just described might be evaluated and integrated according to how well their various principles fit together logically; special weight would be given to how closely these implications tie in with other principles that have been widely established as basic components of other theories. (It is here, rather than in statistical tests, that mathematics plays its principal role in scientific theories.) It is these judgments of relevance that count most, not some meeting of, or failure to meet, an arbitrary level of statistical "significance."

How much evidence it takes to prove or disprove a theory, then, varies with the logical relations of that theory to our other knowledge (Keynes, 1921:225). Some principles are much better founded than others and need much less evidence for us to accept them. Keynes (1921:383) illustrates this by commenting that if we take just human experience as a criterion, the probability of the sun's rising tomorrow is something like 1,826,214 to 1, which seems like a very high probability. But the same reasoning concludes that the probability of the sun's rising every day for the next 4,000 years is only 2/3, which is a good deal less than we would accept. We *know* the sun is going to rise every morning for the next 5 billion years or so, barring certain astronomical events which are possible but whose probability distribution is nevertheless nowhere in the range of 1/3. In short, the principles of astronomy are so well founded, and mesh together from so many angles of observation and logic, that we do not have to rely on any simple calculation of probabilities based on counting past occurrences.

The conundrum has been raised in the social sciences that if we use the .05 level of probability as our criterion of significance, then one out of twenty findings is actually invalid, having arisen solely by chance. But in fact this is a good deal less worrisome if one does not hold such a superstitious veneration for the "level of significance." Findings that fit logically into the larger pattern of scientific explanation are well established thereby—indeed, much more so than a purely isolated finding that may present itself under the guise of some very high level of significance.

Choosing .05 or .001, or any other level, is arbitrary. The habit of reporting results as "significant" or not, without giving the actual probability level, simply reduces the range of information by which, together with all our other theoretical and empirical information, one might decide on the usefulness of this particular finding. Nor is level of significance the only unfounded dogma in the use of statistics. Much information is also lost if one takes too seriously the prevailing beliefs about the order in which hypotheses are to be tested. It is often taken as a canon of scientific validity that a hypothesis must be proposed before the evidence is examined. If the explanatory principle is inducted from the evidence, then it cannot be tested on that evidence. (This is often asserted in critiques of historical generalizations in sociology, which necessarily depend on a very small number of apparently unique cases.)

Keynes (1921:304-306) gives the following example. If one happens to open a biographical dictionary of poets and finds that the first five persons listed alphabetically died at ages 48, 76, 84, 48, and 45, then one could formulate a mathematical principle that related the digits of this sequence. But that formula would not be valid for the next poets listed in the dictionary, since it was inducted only from the first five.

But, Keynes goes on to argue, if one formulates a principle based on the atomic weights of, say, the first dozen chemical elements, that principle turns out to be valid for succeeding elements in the periodic table. According to the conventional methodological criterion, neither the ages of the poets nor the characteristics of the chemical elements can be established by induction from the first part of the sequence. But in fact the principle so inducted does turn out to be true for the chemicals, though not for the poets; *and we could have known this in advance.* For if we view the circumstances surrounding the induction, we see that the poets' list is ordered simply by the alphabet (and we see this right away, without having to sample the whole dictionary), and hence we know that the relations among their ages are going to be arbitrary. However, if we know enough about the chemical structure of a dozen elements, we have a full-fledged theory about how their structural properties relate to one another; hence we have more grounds than a purely statistical probability for expecting that these properties will continue through the remainder of the sequence. Investigation of the later part of the sequence is less a test that proves the theory than a confirmation and extension of a theory in which we can already rest sufficient confidence that it is true.[2] As Keynes puts it:

> The peculiar virtue of prediction or predesignation is altogether imaginary. The number of instances examined and the analogy between them are the es-

sential points, and the question as to whether a particular hypothesis happens to be propounded before or after their examination is quite irrelevant. . . . If a theory is first proposed and is then confirmed by the examination of statistics, we are inclined to attach more weight to it than to a theory which is constructed in order to suit the statistics. But the fact that the theory which precedes the statistics is more likely than the other to be supported by general considerations—for it has not, presumably, been adopted for no reason at all—constitutes the only valid ground for this preference. If it does *not* receive more support than the other from general considerations, then the circumstances of its origin are no argument in its favor. The opposite view, which the unreliability of some statisticians has brought into existence—that it is a positive advantage to approach statistical evidence *without* preconceptions based on general grounds, because the temptation to "cook" the evidence will prove otherwise to be irresistible—has no *logical* basis and need only be considered when the impartiality of an investigator is in doubt   [1921:305-306; see also Gillies, 1973:65-66].

The point is an essential one. We set stringent statistical criteria not because logically they are crucial for establishing the truth of a theory but *because our intellectual community is socially distrustful of the honesty of investigators.* Galileo's investigations of the law of the acceleration of falling bodies consisted in experiments rolling balls down inclined planes. From this he induced a valid scientific law, which he did not attempt to test statistically. It would have made no difference had he been able, or required, to do so. The fact that we emphasize such tests in sociology, almost to the exclusion of all else, indicates the degree of competitiveness and institutionalized distrust in our intellectual community, rather than our scientific standing. The burden of the proof is placed by our social customs on the investigator to show that he or she is not cheating or deluding himself or herself. The community of researchers is less concerned with whether a given finding is true than with whether it can pass the hurdle of a very high level of ritual distrust imposed on it.[3]

There are, moreover, some important areas in sociological research where such methods are almost never applied. Not surprisingly—from my point of view—these are areas in which a great deal of substantive progress has been made. Prime among them is the field of historical sociology. It deserves special consideration because it illustrates how valid theoretical principles can be established without statistics.

Much of the best work in sociology has been carried out using qualitative methods and without statistical tests. This has been true of research areas ranging from organizational and community studies to microstudies of face-to-face interaction and macrostudies of the world system. Nor should such work be regarded as weak and initial "exploratory" approaches to these topics. The work of Erving Goffman, for example, or (on an entirely different scale) Immanuel Wallerstein would not have been improved by carrying it out under a rigid program of statistical measurement and hypothesis testing. Indeed, it is clear that someone following such methods would not have been able to do it at all.

Historical sociology occupies an especially important place here because of its strategic role in building genuine sociological theory. There are several reasons it has this significance.

1. Often only historical evidence can provide the comparisons necessary for the development of explanatory theory. To explain something, we need to know the conditions under which it occurs in one form and those under which it occurs in another—in short, its variations. For macrostructures such as the state, these variations can be seen with a sufficient and full range only if they are treated historically.

2. The same may also be true of smaller-scale social structures. There are certainly numerous empirical cases of the family in a contemporary society, for example; but without historical comparisons we fall all too easily into simplified assumptions about the range of family forms and hence about the conditions that produce them. The belief that the nuclear family is to be explained by its functional relationship to modern industrial society was based on a limited historical view that examined only modern societies and took everything else as a residual category. Broader historical evidence (see, for example, Macfarlane, 1978) has shown us that the nuclear family has existed more widely, spurring the search for more adequate theoretical explanation.

3. A different line of argument is that local phenomena within particular societies are not explicable by themselves, because they are part of a larger world system. Such arguments have been applied with much plausibility to economic "development" (Frank, 1967; Wallerstein, 1974), political change (Bendix, 1978), revolution (Skocpol, 1979), and state power as related to external geopolitics (Collins, 1981a). Such conceptions, however, raise a methodological problem: If there is only one world system, how can one test a theory? The number of historical instances reduces to one case, because everything is connected together. Taken to its extreme, this position amounts to the philosophy of historicism, in which history is seen as a constantly changing flow of particulars. In this view, no generalizations are possible, but only interpretations of particular parts of this endless flux.

The problem reduces to this: The essence of the scientific method for producing generalizations is comparison. But how does one compare without an adequate number of cases? If one takes the world-system view or the historicist one, there is only one case we can deal with. Even if we take a more limited view (1 or 2 above), usually we find that the number of cases we can examine is far smaller than the number conventionally used to establish statistical significance. And this limitation may be inalterable. History presents us with only a certain number of instances of revolution, let us say, and there is nothing one can do about it. That is all the data there are.

If these arguments are simultaneously true, sociology as a science is doomed. It cannot be a real explanatory science without history, but history appears not to allow sufficient comparisons.

Nevertheless, I am suspicious of this conclusion. For one thing, there are analogous problems in the natural sciences. The physical world is also a seamless web, yet we have been successful in piecing out various parts of it in abstraction from the others. This is true even in areas such as biology, geology, and astronomy, where the problems of historicism and the small number of instances of large-scale phenomena (such as geological epochs, evolutionary phyla, or cosmological universes) are similar to those in macrosociology.

The part of the conundrum that most easily comes undone is the assumption that generalizations cannot be made without a large random sample of cases. We are often told that historical analysis is invalid science because the number of variables exceeds the number of cases; or that once you have induced a pattern from a given number of cases, the theory cannot be accepted as true if you do not have another (unexamined) set of cases left over on which to test it. But these methodological doctrines are artificial and unnecessary.

Consider the latter principle. It states quite literally that the more you know about history, the less you know of it scientifically. Presumably you would be better off knowing less, so that you would have materials on which you could test and thereby establish your theories.

Suppose that you had 100 historical cases. If you examined all of them and drew a generalization from them, it would allegedly be worthless because you would have produced only a tautological explanation, really a description masquerading as an explanation. But if you made the same generalization based on examining 50 cases, while carefully averting your eyes from the other 50, and then found that it fit the other 50 as well, the generalization would be true. Notice: It is the same generalization, and the same total amount of evidence; only in one case, according to the conventional method, the generalization would be rejected, in the other case accepted.

Extrapolated, this means that the more you know of history, the more ignorant you are of how to explain it. Someone who knew virtually all of world history (say, Max Weber or William McNeill) would know much less than someone (say, a highly specialized statistician) who knew virtually none of it.

As we have seen, the methodological theory in question is invalid. The statistical formalities proposed do not operate to increase our objective knowledge of the world but only to express our suspicions against theorists who might cheat or who cannot examine their own presuppositions. This is a social criterion, not a logical one.

Fortunately, we do have resources on the logical and the social levels for increasing confidence that the theory we have induced from a small number of instances, or have exhausted the universe of cases in formulating, is in fact a valid picture of the underlying causal processes that govern our world. On the social level, we can reduce biases by making sure there is mutual criticism among rival theories. On the logical level, the most important techniques involve increasing our precision and our theoretical consistency.

A theory based on a small number of historical instances (or even one) can be accepted with confidence to the extent that we can accumulate more detailed evidence in keeping with our model. Here, mathematics can make its reappearance, but in a nonstatistical guise. It increases our confidence to be able to say that 75 percent of the peasants were becoming impoverished in an area of increasing peripheralization, compared with 42 percent in a nonperipheral area, instead of merely asserting that the one group is more impoverished than the other. This shows that the researcher has looked more carefully, and it also provides a basis on which mathematical relations could be built. Thus a theory based on a small number of macroinstances would be further validated if it proved fruitful for subsequent elaborations with unforeseen degrees of precision.[4]

The most important way in which the validity of a theory can be established, however, is by showing the coherence of its explanatory principles with other well-grounded theory. This involves raising the explanatory structure of any particular historical theory to a more abstract level and then showing that the principles invoked are consistent with principles and evidence found elsewhere. A theory about the French Revolution (Moore, 1966) can be validated to the extent that it is shown to be formally related to theories and evidence about peasant revolts (Paige, 1975) or about other revolutions (Skocpol, 1979) and these theories are consistent with principles induced from the study of geopolitics (Collins, 1981a, 1981b). The process of making theories coherent with one another simultaneously strengthens all of them. Ultimately, theories on highly macro levels can be further strengthened if they can be tied to theories on smaller (for example, organizational or even more micro interactional) levels of analysis (as proposed in Collins, 1975; see also Stinchcombe, 1978).

Here, too, mathematical formulation has a potential place—not that mathematical theory is essential at any particular stage of this process of demonstrating theoretical coherence; but clearly theories that can be formulated in axiomatic and deductive form, that can be shown to produce results consistent with a wide range of empirical applications, will have an especially strong claim to have been shown to be true. Again, the future of mathematics in sociology should be much more significant on the theoretical side than in the merely methodological form of statistical tests.[5]

What I have said about historical sociology, moreover, is fully applicable to every area of sociological research. Qualitative microsociology, for example, or participant-observation organizational studies do not depend on statistics. Their validity and their considerable contributions to our knowledge come from their degree of coherence with all our accumulated theoretical principles. The same is even true of quantitative research itself. The validity of statistical analyses of social mobility data, for example, does not come from whether the data have met some particular significance test; it comes from whether a coherent model has been established that is consistent among various researches and ramifies into other areas of sociology. Social mobility research, in fact, is rather weak on this side, precisely because its practitioners (especially within the so-called status attainment tradition) have placed so much reliance on statistical technique in place of understanding its own theoretical implications.[6]

In fact, as I have argued, statistics *is* a theory. It needs to be treated as such if it is truly to make a significant contribution to sociology.

Statistics as Hidden Theoretical Constraint. The use of statistics in sociology has gone through a number of phases, which bear many of the characteristics of fads. During the 1940s and 1950s, it was popular to construct scales, such as questionnaire measures of attitudes or of socioeconomic status. A related phenomenon was that instead of searching for unidimensional structures, batteries of such items were subjected to factor analysis, which produced multidimensional structures. Around the late 1950s, such techniques were gradually displaced by multivariate analysis. Whereas scales and factor analyses tended to produce descriptive results, multivariate analysis placed the emphasis on establishing causal conditions and testing them for independence of each other. Here we had the construction of various measures of association and significance (for interval, ordinal, and nominal variables and the like). This, in turn, gave way in the late 1960s to a wave of popularity of path diagrams, measuring the contributions to some outcome (most typically occupational status) of a series of causes occurring in time. More recently there has been the fashion of log-linear analysis, which returns to parceling out particular influences within the context of numerous others.

The replacement of one technique by the next has usually been touted as a methodological advance. Each solves some problem previous methods had been unable to handle. But this "advance" is by no means absolute, for theoretical biases are associated with each technique. *The abandonment of some techniques in favor of others can thus constitute a theoretical loss.*

A good illustration of the theoretical biases underlying particular techniques is provided by the kind of scale that once was popular in the study of stratification. An SES scale typically combined respondents' education, occupation, income, ethnicity, and other features into a single score, which purportedly represented their relative standing in that society. Aside from methodological issues (how much difference in ethnicity, for example, was worth how much difference in income?), such scales constrained one theoretically by the assumption that stratification is in fact unidimensional, that there is a single hierarchy in any society. Once such a decision is made methodologically, there is no way that the evidence can disprove it. An even greater obstacle in the way of advancing a theory of stratification was the fact that such scales were used mainly for description rather than for explanation. If in fact a major part of a theory of stratification consists in showing how various conditions of inequality produce differences in individuals' behavior and attitudes (that is, how social classes differ), then an SES scale makes it impossible for us to see just what are the operative variables—for all variables are lumped together. Hence, the shift to multivariate analysis, as practiced, for example, by Lipset and Bendix (1959), was not merely a methodological shift but a change to another theoretical scheme, one in which more significant theoretical questions could be asked and answered.

Multivariate analysis was most appropriate for developing a theory of such things as the determinants of individual attitudes and behaviors, such as a theory of class cultures. A good deal of evidence of this sort has in fact been amassed, and I would claim that a theory of class cultures is on reasonably firm grounds (see Collins, 1975:61–89). This kind of static cross-sectional analysis, however, was not good for analyzing relations in time, and it was to elucidate this problem that path models were devised. These have been successful in their special area of application: understanding how such factors as parental income, peer-group aspirations, or high school graduation affect later portions of an individual's career. But along with these gains, there have been theoretical losses.

Path diagrams, for example, rule out studies of the macrodimension, for one motive in developing the path model of status attainment was to overcome difficulties in the earlier type of mobility table, related to the parceling out of "structural" effects (such as so-called forced mobility) from "circulation mobility." Duncan (1966) argued that such tables confounded population change with mobility as such. His solution was to eliminate the concern for structural conditions entirely and concentrate instead on the chain of causes leading up to individual occupational attainment. But although this method has yielded some good results, it has ignored, rather than solved, questions of the larger, structural level. It assumes away by statistical manipulation the possibility that the opportunity structure of the society as a whole may affect the amounts and directions of mobility found within the system. Left to the path model, it becomes impossible to ask whether a society with a large elite will have more upward mobility than one with a small elite, or whether demographic conditions have significant effects on mobility, or whether capitalist as compared with socialist economic structures have any mobility effects. The entire macrohistorical dimension is simply ruled out of consideration by this method. (See Horan, 1978.) More generally, methods that aggregate characteristics across individuals destroy all structural information about social networks, like running them through a centrifuge (Wellman, 1983:165–166, 169).

The popularity of particular methods may have much to do with their ideological resonances. Macrolevel analyses of mobility explicitly pointed to the historical dimension: They were connected with the questions whether some societies are "fairer" than others, whether there has been a historical trend toward greater or lesser "openness," and so forth. This may be the source of the concern to find that somewhat mythical "circulation mobility," that part of the mobility table that is not caused by anything structural but reflects the meritocratic grade-point average of the society in question. Duncan appears to have reacted against this with an almost zealotic insistence that the topic to be studied is not "mobility" but "status attainment." The very term, as well as its substance, carries the implication that the picture to be kept before our eyes is to be nothing but a never-ending success story (though, of course, with varying degrees of success for its participants).

Every method has its strengths and weaknesses, its theoretical resonances and ideological biases. Our stance should not be to elevate one particular method (that is, the latest to come down the pike) to the status of a scientific cult; instead, we should regard the various methods as a tool box, to be used when appropriate for different problems. In particular, we should keep in mind that a scientific theory of any complex phenomenon (above all, something like social stratification) must cover a number of dimensions and levels of analysis. We cannot simply follow the faddish tendency to regard old methods as outdated because interest has focused on something else for the present. The underlying theoretical perspectives themselves must be juxtaposed and, where necessary, made into complementary views on a larger reality. The purpose of scientific research is, above all, to formulate theoretical principles of proven generality and power. Statistical sociology has been used, on the contrary, for the most part within the context of parochial social problems issues (for example, did American blacks make more progress in the 1960s than in the 1950s?). Because of this narrow focus, plus the self-blinding effect of absorption in purely methodological issues, most statistical sociology seems oblivious to the theoretical assumptions involved in choosing a statistical method.[7]

Statistics as Substance

Precisely the kinds of issues that have been treated by statistics are the areas of sociology that seem most in need of theoretical clarification. And in fact statistical models can play a theoretical role here, provided they are seen as a substantive theory instead of being relegated to the methods textbook and to the routinization that prevails in so much quantitative research.

In the physical sciences, a statistical model is not simply a basis against which to test some other theory; it provides the model of the phenomenon itself. Poisson provided a model for the propagation of heat as a process involving the independent interaction of numerous small particles; it is only methodological statisticians with other interests who have transformed this from a substantive model into a purely procedural one. But such substantive statistical models can have wide application in sociology.

One clear example is in the field of social mobility, when viewed on the structural level. It is well known that the total amount of mobility in any mobility table is partly determined by changes in the occupational distribution. At one time this was called "forced" mobility, although it would be more accurate to say this is mobility that is *the same thing as* the historical processes that make up occupational change. (That is to say, the changes in the marginal distributions did not cause the mobility observed, because those marginal distributions are not prior to the mobility: They are simply another way of describing it.) Concern with "forced" mobility (I would prefer to say "historical-change mobility") has been primarily methodological. Such mobility was treated primarily as an artifact that we had to remove with a suitable measure of the "true" amount of mobility. But the search for "pure" mobility has been largely a search for an ideological category, not something that exists to any great degree in the world. As Lipset and Bendix (1959) pointed out, much more mobility is "forced" (that is, is historical change) than is "pure." Hence, a theory explaining the causes and consequences of mobility should make an especially prominent place for the historical process of occupational change rather than try to put this aside as a methodological problem. Duncan's (1966) criticism of measures of "forced" mobility ceases to carry weight once we take away the implication that the change in the marginals "forced" the mobility and instead consider this as mobility produced by the larger processes of historical change that bring about occupational transformations.[8] As long as change in the marginals was considered mere interference in the research, it was controlled by mathematical manipulation and put aside. It constituted a background against which a "pure" mobility effect was to be measured. Notice that, in doing so, sociologists assumed the unconditional validity of the underlying substantive theory. They did not test to see whether historical changes in the occupational distribution were associated with mobility; this was simply assumed.

Here we have an instance in which an important substantive phenomenon was ignored by being made into something merely "methodological." A second instance can be found when we consider the effects on mobility, not of changes in the marginal distributions but of the initial sizes of the various occupational categories relative to one another. It is easy to show (Marsh, 1963; Connor, 1979:106-176) that countries with a relatively large upper class are going to have more upward mobility into the elite, and less downward mobility out of it, than countries with a small upper class. Similarly, mobility across the white-collar/blue-collar line is affected by the sheer size of those categories when the process we are measuring begins (see Collins, 1975:447).

This is a rather pure instance of a "bingo game" effect on social mobility. It is analogous to taking a small jar of white balls and a large jar of black balls, mixing them together, and then filling the two jars again. A greater proportion of white balls are going to end up in the black jar than vice versa, simply because of the size of the jars.[9] A good deal of structural mobility is thus accounted for by the static, relative sizes of different occupational strata. Indeed, there is a good deal more of this sort of mobility than there is of the long-sought "pure" or "circulation" mobility.

What I would emphasize is that this "bingo game" mobility is not a statistical artifact. It is not merely something to be controlled away so that "real" mobility can be measured. It is time we stopped worrying about "real" mobility, for all forms of it are equally real. Persons living through an occupational career have no sense of whether the mobility they experience is simply a change in the occupational distribution, a "bingo game" resulting from living in a country with a large or small white-collar sector, or some sort of "pure" meritocratic movement. On the individual level, the question does not make sense; the individual knows only whether he or she has moved up or down or stayed the same, and individuals are just as happy to be carried upward by a historical process of expanding upper occupational brackets as they would be by making it on the superior "openness to merit" of their society. This "openness," in fact, may be only a sociologist's myth; it is a residual category of unexplained mobility for which we have an ideological fondness but which recedes steadily with each advance of explanatory theory.[10]

The propensity to turn substantive causes into methodological artifacts to be held constant mathematically is one of the major obstacles to theoretical advance in such areas as social mobility. A great deal of mobility can be explained on the structural level—indeed, much more, I would say, than can be explained by the level of individual careers, the focus of path analysis. But this means turning statistics into substance, not reducing it to methodology. The general probabilistic perspective has potentially many applications. In numerous aspects of social life there are large numbers of smaller events or units, each of which has its own causal structure toward the microlevel but which are independent of one another. The macro-outcomes of such an aggregation can be predicted by an appropriate statistical model. This distribution is produced by chance, if you like; but here "chance" is not just a matter of chance. To speak plainly, chance or random distributions are not uncaused; they are caused by well-known mechanisms. And these mechanisms ought to be given a significant place in sociological theory.[11]

Mathematics Is Embedded in Words

I have argued that sociologists have badly misconceived the place of mathematics in their field. Its primary application has been taken to be statistical method. In this sphere, I would say, its claims are almost entirely unfounded. The greatest progress in sociological explanation has occurred in precisely those areas that have not become hung up on the rituals of statistical validation. However, I have pointed out two areas in which mathematics can be quite useful for the advancement of sociology. The statistical theory itself can be used as a substantive model for certain macrolevel processes in society, involving the movement of large numbers of independent individuals. And mathematical formalization may be useful as a means of showing the coherence of theoretical principles involved in particular areas of research, thus serving to validate studies that draw on a very small number of unique instances, as so often happens in historical sociology. Mathematics, including statistics, is valuable in sociology primarily as theory, not as research method.

The stress I have given to coherence among theoretical principles, however, raises the question whether there are limits to how much coherence can be introduced, especially in mathematical form. The answer, it appears, is that there are certain very fundamental limits.

The ideal of producing a completely self-consistent theory by means of mathematical formalization has been attempted in other fields. Leibniz's plan to eliminate all inconsistencies by replacing words with unambiguously defined symbols was actually carried out by Whitehead and Russell in *Principia Mathematica* (1910) for elementary mathematics and was sketched out as a program for all of physical science by Russell in his *Principles of Mathematics* (1904). The trial, however, proved the impracticability of the enterprise. Not only did Russell turn up a logical paradox at the root of his system, which led to Godel's proof of the impossibility of a closed and consistent system of the sort Russell envisioned; but even the effort to displace words by mathematics was a failure. For the *Principia Mathematica* itself, despite its avowed intent to replace words with formal symbolism, begins with some twenty pages made up almost entirely of words. And even after this, the bulk of the argument is no more than 50 percent mathematical symbols. Russell's more wide-ranging *Principles of Mathematics* is almost entirely verbal, containing virtually no symbolism at all.

One finds the same thing if one turns to mathematical journals. Mathematical problems are still introduced in words; discussions are almost always concluded by words; mathematical articles always have verbal titles rather than simply announcing some formula as their heading. Mathematicians, in fact, frequently use verbal expressions within their technical arguments to summarize some complex formal results known to mathematical readers (for example, Banach spaces or Lebesgue integrals).[12] One arrives at the paradoxical conclusion that although mathematics has often advanced by creating new formalisms that clarified the ambiguities of ordinary language and allowed the mechanical performance of otherwise impossible complex calculations, nevertheless mathematics keeps resurfacing into the world of words from which it starts its plunges. Words seem to be a necessary and inescapable frame within which mathematics is embedded.[13]

Godel's proof can be interpreted as showing why mathematical symbols depend on a surrounding structure of less precise but more evocative words. Godel demonstrated that any formal system is formally incomplete and that efforts to correct it and to prove its consistency entail adding yet another frame of reference, which itself is outside the system (Kramer, 1970:447-454). This indeterminacy or incompleteness of the "outermost" frame, in fact, is exactly what we find in mathematical articles: The mathematical formalisms have to be introduced by words (as when Whitehead and Russell spend twenty pages explaining how and why their symbolism will work). The intent of mathematical activities is framed in words; it is announced in a verbal title that draws attention to what is being done; and successful mathematical calculations come out the other end as verbal catchwords (Banach spaces and so on) that can now enter into other mathematicians' mental universes. For this reason, historians of mathematics write, for the most part, not in formalisms but in words, and not merely for purposes of simplification. The most fundamental developments of mathematical ideas cannot be grasped if one is too closely enmeshed in the formal calculations themselves; words are necessary to establish their significance in relation to other mathematical ideas.

One of the main characteristics of verbal language, of course, is its multidimensionality and open-endedness. It is precisely these qualities that motivated mathematicians and philosophers like Leibniz and Russell to seek for a perfect symbolic system that would not have these "liabilities." Wittgenstein, whose early work was an attempt to carry the Russellian program into the realm of language itself, later reversed himself and devoted his mature years to analyzing language as a system that is necessarily multileveled. To borrow Austin's term, language consists of various kinds of *speech acts* rather than merely of signs with a referential content, and different kinds of speech acts can be embedded within one another (see Goffman, 1974, 1981). Language thus has precisely the qualities of potentially endlessly expandable frames-around-frames, which Godel finds at the root of any system of logic.[14]

My conclusion, then, is that words will always be with us. If mathematics itself cannot arrive at total formalization (or total formal consistency and coherence), how much the less will sociology attain it? Such formalization as may take place in sociological theory will always be dependent on a larger frame of words that surrounds it and makes sense of it. Formalization is always subservient to the larger purposes of the argument. Words are not only more fundamental *intellectually*; one may also say that they are necessarily superior to mathematics in the *social* structure of the intellectual discipline. For words are a mode of expression with greater open-endedness, more capacity for connecting various realms of argument and experience, and more capacity for reaching intellectual audiences. Even mathematicians must lapse into words to show what are the most important things they are talking about. One might even describe mathematics as a particular form of words, operating within a context specially prepared for it by the use of some other language-game. And the open-endedness of words may also reflect the empirical open-endedness of the process of theorizing, which may approach some ideal degree of coherence without ever reaching it absolutely. Finally, this open-endedness of words is in keeping with the open-endedness of the historical world, continuously unfolding into the future.

Verbal, qualitative theory, then, will always be more fundamental in sociology than mathematics is—even if we make progress toward the proper uses of mathematics and statistics that I have outlined. In fact, in order to produce genuinely valuable mathematical theory, one probably needs to be equally adept at using words (as Russell was, and as a very few of the most mathematically sophisticated sociologists are today). At the same time, theorists and researchers whose work is purely or predominantly verbal are likely to lead our field for a long time to come. As Keynes (1921: 19) put it:

> This question . . . is in my opinion much more a question of style . . . than is generally supposed. There are occasions for very exact methods of statement, such as are employed in Mr. Bertrand Russell's *Principia Mathematica*. But there are advantages also in writing the English of Hume. . . . But those writers,

who strain after exaggerated precision without going the whole hog with Mr. Russell, are sometimes merely pedantic. They lose the reader's attention, and the repetitious complication of their phrases eludes his comprehension, without their really attaining, to compensate, a complete precision. Confusion of thought is not always best avoided by technical and unaccustomed expressions, to which the mind has no immediate reaction of understanding; it is possible, under cover of a careful formalism, to make statements, which, if expressed in plain language, the mind would immediately repudiate. There is much to be said, therefore, in favor of understanding the substance of what you are saying *all the time,* and of never reducing the substantives of your argument to the mental status of an x or a y.

Notes

1. The type of theory of probability that I am describing falls within the general category of objective theories of probability. Even within this approach, *complete* causal determinism at all levels may be nonexistent. (This is consistent with the discussion of Godel's theorem later in the chapter.) There may be *absolute* microrandomness at the subatomic level, and some theorists argue that macrorandomness is an amplification of this (Gillies, 1973: 133-137). But this residue of randomness does not affect the practical conclusions I am drawing about sociological theories. And even subatomic microrandomness may be merely another instance of the independence of causal orders—in this case, among subatomic particles or fields. See also Bohm (1971).

2. This runs contrary to our commonly accepted beliefs. After all, we were all told in our graduate methods course that the pattern one finds the first time one looks at the data may be there just by accident; one needs another sample to rule out this possibility. But in fact the second sample (or any number of subsequent samples) hardly overcomes the initial problem. As David Hume pointed out centuries ago, our knowledge of the past is never a strictly logical basis for inferences about the future. The entire universe up till now may be simply one gigantic accidental

sample; if we think otherwise, it is because we *impose* a pattern of causality on it. Statistics does not avoid this; it simply imposes a model of chance distributions, which themselves were induced from past experience. If we feel sufficiently confident to accept *any* theory (including the theory of probability), it is because our theories rest not on a method of blind prediction but on what Keynes calls "general considerations"—that is, on the pattern of theoretical coherence. The reason that, in the graduate school example, it would not be wise to accept a theory that was immediately induced from one sample is that the pattern was induced in the rawest way, without any general theoretical considerations or efforts at larger theoretical coherence.

3. The dogmatism of most sociological practitioners about statistical tests contrasts sharply with the attitude of professional statisticians regarding their own foundations. A recent overview of the field, for example, concludes:

> Reflection upon the many difficulties that beset current theories of probability leads us to wonder whether we can dispense with probability and use alternative methodologies to carry out our tasks. In support of such a position is the observation that probability by itself has not been sufficient for most applications. In practice we most often make inferences, reach conclusions (estimates), or select decision rules only after adjoining an *ad hoc* statistical methodology . . . to a theory of probability. Why not ignore the complicated and hard to justify probability-statistics structure and proceed "directly" to those, perhaps qualitative, assumptions that characterize our source of random phenomena, the means at our disposal, and the task? This suggestion, which has a radical element, has a long tradition to support it and examples of nonprobabilistic approaches are easily found in recent work. . . .
>
> Judging from the present confused status of probability theory, the time is at hand for those concerned about the characterization of chance and uncertainty and the design of inference and decision-making systems to reconsider their long-standing dependence on the traditional statistical and proba-

bilistic methodology. Hitherto, most of the efforts at reevaluation have focused on the development of statistics without due regard for the inadequacies of the conception of probability that underlies statistics. . . . Clearly much remains to be understood about random phenomena before technology and science can be soundly and rapidly advanced. It is not only the "laws" of today that may be in error but also our whole conception of the formation and meaning of laws [Fine, 1973:249-250].

4. See Hamblin, Jacobsen, and Miller (1973) for instances of such principles based on historical time sequences. Barbara Laslett (personal communication) points out that confidence can also be improved by using several operationalizations of the same historical concept.

5. The problem of how an established physical science deals with theorizing about a single case is illustrated by theories of the origins and overall structure of the universe. An astrophysicist outlines his strategy of test: "We need to do more detailed quantum mechanical calculations of how bubbles behave in de Sitter space. If it became a nice, self-consistent theoretical framework, that would stand it in good stead.

"The most important observational test is the large-scale structure of the universe," he adds. "This theory might allow us to calculate the initial spectrum of random fluctuations, and see if those fluctuations could grow up into the large-scale structure we see today" (J. Richard Gott, quoted in *Science* 215 (26 February 1982), p. 1083).

6. Featherman (1981) has argued that the status attainment tradition has made the most cumulative scientific progress of any subfield of sociology. This may be true in the sense that there has been a string of researches cumulating on the technical issues raised by earlier studies using path analysis. But one can hardly say that the result is anything approaching a general theory of the causes (let alone the effects) of mobility, even confined to the level of individual career determinants and leaving aside the structural level of analysis. Instead, such research seems to be digging deeper and deeper into a rut, producing no surprises and little theoretical insight. It is not a question of a research field having to

link up with classical theories. It is quite possible for a research area to develop its own theories without outside help; this happened, for instance, in organizational research between 1930 and 1970 (see Collins, 1975:286–347). But I would say the reason organizational research was able to make a genuine theoretical advance was that much of the research was carried out without any particular methodological dogma, especially a statistical one. Thus, it was able to use a variety of methods, adapting them to the materials of most interest for the theoretical questions to be investigated. The success story of organizational theory against the mediocrity of status attainment research points a significant methodological moral.

7. Other methodological losses can be illustrated by the use of log-linear analysis. Here the mode of presentation gives us an array of numerical coefficients that mean nothing except from the point of view of the statistical analysis proposed. One finds whether certain hypotheses are significant according to a certain criterion; the table tells us nothing else. Thus, the utility of a piece of research is limited to those particular questions that the investigator has asked of the data. Reading a log-linear analysis of female mobility, for example, gives us no clue to what percentages of women have moved from certain occupational backgrounds into certain other positions. Such a table no longer has any descriptive significance (unlike earlier mobility tables or multivariate tables); similarly, it cannot be used by another investigator as raw data from which some other analysis might be computed. Here the methodological fad gives us less information, overall, than some of the methods it displaced.

8. Duncan's problem of demographic changes confounding mobility can also be dealt with on the structural level, rather than by abandoning that level of analysis entirely.

9. One could make this model more complex and more realistic by having both jars change absolute size over time; this would model population growth. One could also add the historical-change dimension by changing the *relative* sizes of the two jars before and after mixing. This merely makes the model into a multivariate one and does not change the basic logic of the argument.

10. In short, the major causes of mobility appear to be, in

descending order of importance: (1) historical changes that produce new occupational positions or eliminate old ones; this implies an entire theory of social change; (2) the "bingo game" structure of absolute-size relations among occupational categories; this is another result of past history; (3) networks, as well as cultural and emotional capital operating at the level of individual careers (see Collins, 1981c). The residual of "meritocracy" beyond these orders of determination is vanishingly small.

11. Mayhew and Schollaert (1980) provide a good example of a substantive theory, in this case a theory of the distribution of wealth, which shows how chance processes operating under certain simple constraints produce various patterns of inequality. See also Mayhew and Levinger (1976). Other such applications are likely to be especially valuable in dealing with the micro/macro problem, since this involves the aggregation of many microevents in time and space. (See Collins, 1981c.)

12. For example, the 1976–1977 volumes of two physics journals, *Journal of Low Temperature Physics* and *International Journal of Heat and Mass Transfer,* devote an average of 40–50 percent of their total printed space to abstract symbols, the rest consisting of words. The proportion of symbols is not strikingly higher in pure mathematics. The 1976–1977 volumes of two mathematics journals (*Journal of Differential Geometry* and *Duke Mathematical Journal*) contain an average of 50–55 percent symbols in each article. The way technical calculations are embedded in verbal discourse can be seen from the following comparisons. In the physics journals, symbols (including numbers) range from 0 to 3 percent of the total length of titles, 3 to 8 percent of article abstracts, and 1 to 10 percent of introductory paragraphs. Concluding paragraphs emerge from the technical symbolism of the midsections of these papers back into words, but not to the same degree as their beginnings: Concluding paragraphs average 1–27 percent symbols in these physics journals. Mathematics journals show a similar pattern but with proportionately more symbols: 13–23 percent in first paragraphs, 40–45 percent in concluding paragraphs. (These journals include no abstracts.) But mathematics titles contain even fewer symbols than physics titles: Only 13 percent of the titles contain any symbols at all, and these are all of the simplest (for example, "2-dimensional" or "n-dimensional");

and less than 1 percent of total title space consists of symbols. Mathematicians, in fact, are strikingly fond of verbal designations for the results of technical analyses in their literature.

13. In the history of mathematics, the relative place of words and symbols has fluctuated several times. Ancient and early modern mathematics was argued out almost entirely in words; this was a major limitation on its capacity for abstraction and for making complex calculations. In the 1600s and again in the 1800s, there were movements, especially in England, toward a total notational system. In the 1700s there was a reaction back toward the tendency to argue entirely in words, like the ancient Greeks. Russell represents another wave of total formalization, which has subsequently receded. Most major mathematicians have avoided these extremes; Descartes, Euler, and others have argued in a mixture of words and symbols (Cajori [1928], 1974).

14. Ethnomethodologists' "indexicality" (Garfinkel, 1967), as well as their critiques of the limitations of mathematics in sociology (Cicourel, 1964), can be seen as hinging on just this issue.

References

BENDIX, REINHARD
  1978 *Kings or People: Power and the Mandate to Rule.* Berkeley: University of California Press.
BOHM, DAVID L.
  1971 *Causality and Chance in Modern Physics.* Philadelphia: University of Pennsylvania Press.
CAJORI, FLORIAN
  1974 *A History of Mathematical Notations.* La Salle, Ill.: Open Court Publishing Co. (Originally published 1928.)
CICOUREL, AARON V.
  1964 *Method and Measurement in Sociology.* New York: Free Press.
COLLINS, RANDALL
  1975 *Conflict Sociology.* New York: Academic Press.
  1981a "Long-Term Social Change and the Territorial Power of States." In *Sociology Since Midcentury: Essays in Theory Cumulation.* New York: Academic Press.

1981b "Geopolitics and Revolution." In *Sociology Since Mid-century: Essays in Theory Cumulation*. New York: Academic Press.

1981c "The Microfoundations of Macrosociology." In *Sociology Since Midcentury: Essays in Theory Cumulation*. New York: Academic Press.

CONNOR, WALTER D.

1979 *Socialism, Politics, and Equality*. New York: Columbia University Press.

COSER, LEWIS

1975 "Two Methods in Search of a Substance." *American Sociological Review* 40:691–700.

DUNCAN, OTIS DUDLEY

1966 "Methodological Issues in the Analysis of Social Mobility." In Neil Smelser and Seymour Martin Lipset (Eds.), *Social Structure and Mobility in Economic Development*. Chicago: Aldine.

FEATHERMAN, DAVID L.

1981 "Stratification and Social Mobility: Two Decades of Cumulative Social Science," in James F. Short, Jr. (Ed.), *The State of Sociology*. Beverly Hills, Calif.: Sage.

FINE, TERRENCE L.

1973 *Theories of Probability: An Examination of Foundations*. New York: Academic Press.

FRANK, ANDRÉ GUNDER

1967 *Capitalism and Underdevelopment in Latin America*. New York: Monthly Review Press.

GARFINKEL, HAROLD

1967 *Studies in Ethnomethodology*. Englewood Cliffs, N.J.: Prentice-Hall.

GILLIES, D. A.

1973 *An Objective Theory of Probability*. London: Methuen.

GOFFMAN, ERVING

1974 *Frame Analysis*. New York: Harper & Row.

1981 *Forms of Talk*. Philadelphia: University of Pennsylvania Press.

HACKING, IAN

1975 *The Emergence of Probability*. Cambridge: Cambridge University Press.

HAMBLIN, ROBERT L., JACOBSEN, R. BROOKE, AND MILLER, JERRY L. L.
1973   A Mathematical Theory of Social Change. New York: Wiley.

HORAN, PATRICK
1978   "Is Status Attainment Research Atheoretical?" American Sociological Review 43:334-341.

JENCKS, CHRISTOPHER, AND OTHERS
1972   Inequality: A Reassessment of the Effect of Family and Schooling in America. New York: Basic Books.

KEYNES, JOHN MAYNARD
1921   A Treatise on Probability. London: Macmillan.

KRAMER, EDNA E.
1970   The Nature and Growth of Modern Mathematics. Vol. 2. New York: Hawthorn Books.

LIPSET, SEYMOUR MARTIN, AND BENDIX, REINHARD
1959   Social Mobility in Industrial Society. Berkeley: University of California Press.

MACFARLANE, ALAN
1978   The Origins of English Individualism. Oxford: Basil Blackwell.

MACKENZIE, DONALD A.
1981   Statistics in Britain, 1865-1930: The Social Construction of Scientific Knowledge. Edinburgh: Edinburgh University Press.

MARSH, ROBERT M.
1963   "Values, Demand, and Social Mobility." American Sociological Review 28:567-575.

MAYHEW, BRUCE H., AND LEVINGER, ROGER
1976   "On the Emergence of Oligarchy in Human Interaction." American Journal of Sociology 81:1017-1049.

MAYHEW, BRUCE H., AND SCHOLLAERT, PAUL T.
1980   "The Concentration of Wealth: A Sociological Model." Sociological Focus 13:1-35.

MILLS, C. WRIGHT
1959   The Sociological Imagination. New York: Oxford University Press.

MOORE, BARRINGTON, JR.
1966   Social Origins of Dictatorship and Democracy. Boston: Beacon Press.

PAIGE, JEFFERY

    1975   *Agrarian Revolution.* New York: Free Press.

RUSSELL, BERTRAND

    1904   *The Principles of Mathematics.* Cambridge: Cambridge University Press.

SAVAGE, LEONARD J.

    1954   *The Foundations of Statistics.* New York: Wiley.

SKOCPOL, THEDA

    1979   *States and Social Revolutions.* New York: Cambridge University Press.

STINCHCOMBE, ARTHUR L.

    1978   *Theoretical Methods in Social History.* New York: Academic Press.

WALLERSTEIN, IMMANUEL

    1974   *The Modern World System: Capitalist Agriculture, and the Origins of the European World-Economy in the Sixteenth Century.* New York: Academic Press.

WELLMAN, BARRY

    1983   "Network Analysis: Some Basic Principles." In Randall Collins (Ed.), *Sociological Theory 1983.* San Francisco: Jossey-Bass.

WHITEHEAD, ALFRED NORTH, AND RUSSELL, BERTRAND

    1910   *Principia Mathematica.* Cambridge: Cambridge University Press.

THEORY NEWS:
REPORTS ON RECENT
INTELLECTUAL EVENTS

THE CRITIQUE
OF WORLD-SYSTEM THEORY:
CLASS RELATIONS
OR DIVISION OF LABOR?

Albert Bergesen

UNIVERSITY OF ARIZONA

World-system theory, as represented by I. Wallerstein, A. G. Frank, and S. Amin, has come under attack from a number of Marxists who claim that the conceptualization of the capitalist world economy as a core/periphery division of labor does not adequately deal with social relations of production (class relations), which they claim are the defining feature of capitalism as a mode of production.

What exactly is the argument all about? It begins with Wallerstein's conception of the capitalist world economy as a world division of labor: "As a formal structure, a world economy is defined as a single division of labor" where "production is for exchange; that is, it is determined by its profitability on a market" such that "production proceeds as long as it seems more profitable to produce than not produce" (Wallerstein, 1979:159, 275). The key problem here centers on the definition of capitalism. Brenner (1977) and other traditional Marxists define capitalism in terms of its social relations of production, whereas Wallerstein's capitalism is defined by its division of labor. Brenner asks: Where are the class relations in this formulation? Finding none, he depicts this core/periphery scheme as a kind of "neo-Smithian Marxism," after Adam Smith, who placed the idea of the division of labor at the center of his theory of capitalist development.

Brenner argues that it was the transformation of class relations in Europe that brought about the transition from feudalism to capitalism, not changes in exchange relations, such as the emergence of a world division of labor, à la Wallerstein. He argues that trade had expanded before, but that did not bring about capitalism. What was different with capitalism was a change in the relations of production, the concentration of ownership of the means of production in the hands of a few and the proletarianization of the many through the development of wage labor. "Such flowerings of commercial relations cum divisions of labor have been a more or less regular feature of human history for thousands of years. Because the occurrence of such 'commercial revolutions' has been relatively so common, the key question which must be answered by Sweezy and Wallerstein is why the rise of trade/division of labor should have set off the transition to capitalism in the case of feudal Europe" (Brenner, 1977:40).

Changes in exchange relations, such as the emergence of a world system, do not fundamentally affect the production process in a way that would produce capitalism. Changes in class relations, though, can produce a new mode of production, and that is why one must focus on them and their transformation if one claims to explain the rise of, and inner logic of, capitalism as a historical system. "Thus, a historical transformation of class structures, which the market itself cannot induce, is at the center of the feudalism-capitalism transition" (Brenner, 1977:55). From this point of view both development and underdevelopment are products of the outcome of class struggles in their respective areas and, most important, are not causally linked. "Capitalist economic development [is] a function of the tendency toward capital accumulation via innovation, built into a historically developed structure of class relations of free wage labor. . . . From this vantage point, neither economic development nor underdevelopment are *directly* dependent upon, caused by, one another. Each is the product of a specific evolution of class relations. . . . At every point, therefore, Frank—and his co-thinkers such as Wallerstein . . . failed to focus centrally on the productivity of labor as the essence and key to economic development. They did not state the degree to which the latter was, in turn, centrally bound up with historically specific class structures of production and surplus extraction. . . . Hence, they did not see the degree to which patterns of development or underdevelopment for an entire epoch might hinge upon the outcome of specific processes of class formation, of class struggle" (Brenner, 1977:61, 91).

For Brenner, the development of the core and underdevelopment of the periphery are not a product of their mutual interaction in a core/periphery division of labor. Each is uniquely determined by the historical evolution of its own class relations. To understand seventeenth-century Spain, you have to examine *its* class relations. To understand seventeenth-century colonial Mexico, you have to understand *its* class relations. But how can the autonomous evolution of Aztec and Inca class relations have created Spanish Latin America? Aztec and Inca class struggle did not create plantations, haciendas, mines, large-scale ranches, and all the other infrastructure of underdevelopment. The problem with Brenner's argument is that indigenous class struggle in Latin America could not have produced the class relations of an underdeveloped colonial society. Without understanding relations with Spain or, for the colonial underdeveloped world in general, relations with the European core, one cannot understand the class structure of underdevelopment. Therefore, any theoretical understanding of underdevelopment must take relations with the core into consideration. Brenner is on firmer ground when speaking of the historical transition from feudalism to capitalism in Europe. Here the argument about class relations makes more sense, although, of course, it is still debatable. But it makes no sense at all when applied to the underdeveloped periphery.

Contact with the core is vital. But does this mean we must adopt the theoretical scheme of the world-system theorists? Must core/periphery relations be in the form of an unequal exchange of commodities constituting a world division of labor? The answer, I think, is no. Core/periphery relations need not be seen as only unequal exchange relations, for they are also *class* relations. Yes, class: *global class relations*. What transformed the social relations of colonial societies was conquest and domination, not the unequal exchange of commodities. It was not unequal exchange between Europe and Aztec and Inca social formations that resulted in underdevelopment but forceful conquest and the continued ownership and control of these areas, their people, and their labor power by the core.

From this point of view the traditional Marxists and the world-system theorists are both right and wrong. The Marxists rightly point to the importance of class relations but wrongly to class relations only *within* regions or societies. The world-system theorists rightly emphasize the global core/periphery relation but wrongly conceive of that relation as one of exchange and not power dependence—that is, class.

There have been two general replies to the charge that class analysis does not receive sufficient attention in world-system theory. The first is that relations of production (class) and exchange (sometimes called circulation) are part and parcel of the same economic whole, so that it is foolish to give one primacy over the other. This position is adopted by Wallerstein, who argues that it makes no sense "to assume that one can analyze spheres of production and circulation as anything more than 'different moments' of one 'organic whole'" (1977:104). Wallerstein also suggests that focusing on world trade is central to understanding capitalism, a point, he emphasizes, made by Marx himself. "I am no more a 'circulationist' than Marx was when he argued that 'competition on the world market [is] the vital element of capitalist production.' Marx repeats this point specifically in the context of sixteenth-century Europe: 'And when in the sixteenth and partially still in the seventeenth century the sudden expansion of commerce and emergence of a new world market *overwhelmingly* contributed to the fall of the old mode of production and the rise of capitalist production, this was accomplished conversely on the basis of *already existing* capitalist mode of production. The world market itself forms the basis for this mode of production.' I dislike appeals to authority. I am not right because Marx also said it. But it is surely not the case that Marx can be persuasively cited against me on this point (which is after all fundamental to my argument) —some Marxists, yes; but Marx himself, no" (Wallerstein, 1977: 104).

André Gunder Frank understood the problem as follows: "How then can we analyze the 'internal' mode of production and accumulation or nonaccumulation in the colonies and still take due account of colonial dependence on the 'external' relations of exchange and capital flows between the colony and its metropolis?" (1979:2-3). For Frank the solution was to focus on both sets of relations—a sort of halfway position: some exchange and some class. His analysis focuses on " 'exchange' relations between the metropolis and the periphery, and then goes on to analyze the associated transformation of the dependent 'internal' relations of production and the development of underdevelopment in each of the principal regions of Asia, Africa, and the Americas" (Frank, 1979:xi).

Neither Wallerstein's response nor Frank's seems very satisfying. One says that because exchange and production are part of the same whole, there is no argument, and the other acknowledges the importance of internal class relations and incorporates them into the process but still clings to obvious trade that goes on between core and periphery. The reason I feel neither response is sufficient is that neither Wallerstein nor Frank (nor, for that matter, Brenner) really understood what each other had uncovered. The debate between the so-called internal and external has stagnated: The Marxists repeat their charge that class is ignored, and the world-system theorists repeat their claim that the unequal exchange of the core/periphery division of labor is the central fact of the world economy. To get beyond this argument, we have to probe deeper, to the latent theoretical assumptions that underlie both positions. To move beyond this moribund debate, we must rethink the whole idea of class and realize that the question of ownership and control of the means of production is not just a societal question. There is also the question of who owns/controls the world's means of production.

What is at stake here is the development of a truly globological theory, one based on those structures that are global, not social, and assuming that global dynamics determine intrasocietal dynamics, including intrasocietal class dynamics. From this point of view both the traditional Marxists and world-system theorists are trapped in the theoretical structures of the nineteenth century. The emphasis on class is correct, but traditional class relations (between bourgeoisie and wage labor) were central to the transformation of Europe, not the transformation of the periphery by the core. The "rise of wage labor out of indigenous class struggles" among precapitalist modes of production in pre-Columbian America or Africa or Asia was not the source of tea and rubber plantations, gold and silver mines, haciendas, cotton or sugar plantations, let alone the enslavement of Africans for coerced labor in the Americas or the almost complete destruction of the indigenous Indian populations in Mexico and Peru.

All of that came about through struggle, but not the localized class struggles Brenner refers to; rather, through the struggle between core and periphery, between those who conquered and colonized and those who lost control not only of their political destiny but of their very means of production. The question of who owns the means of production is still central. But who is the who? Since 80 percent of the world's people were or had been under colonial control by 1914 (Fieldhouse, 1973), colonialism represented *the* defining socioproductive relation for the world economy as a singular global mode of production. When you own a region—for example, a colony—you own its means of production, making colonial relations a kind of world class relation. Since the sixteenth century, the social relation that has affected the greatest number of the world's people and labor power, and transformed their local modes of production, has been the colonial relation, the power-dependence relation linking core and periphery.

There is, then, no "internal" and "external." There is only *one* world economy, *one* social formation, and, most important, *one* world or global mode of production. Contrary to Wallerstein, it is not defined by the unequal exchange of a core/periphery division of labor; nor, contrary to Brenner, do its class relations exist only within states. The global mode of production is defined by the global class relation of core ownership and control over peripheral production, which occurred in the past through formal colonial rule and persists today through a variety of less formal mechanisms (foreign investment, penetration by multinationals, arms dependence, periodic military interventions, and so on). The core/periphery relation is a power-dependence relation and only secondarily an exchange relation. To see the flow of commodities and miss the power-dependence relation that has made, and continues to make, these flows possible is to mystify the inner workings of the world economy, making it a Robinson Crusoe–like fiction of autonomous islanders unequally exchanging commodities. There is unequal exchange, yes, but it exists only because of a priori global power-dependence relations (global class relations) that frame these exchanges.

Similarly, those who cling to the wage relation remain locked at the intrasocietal level of analysis and are unable to grasp the workings of the world economy as a singular whole. To continue to see the hands that harvested cotton in the antebellum American South as part of one mode of production (slavery) and the hands that wove it into cloth as part of yet another (wage-labor capitalism) is to mystify the singularity of the world economy under the guise of remaining faithful to a nineteenth-century theoretical structure designed to separate Greco-Roman antiquity (slavery) from the Middle Ages (feudalism) and nineteenth-century industrial Europe (capitalism). The separation of modes of production into these categories reflects the Eurocentric bias of the nineteenth-century theorists (including Marx) who established the theoretical parameters through which we presently view the world. But separating slavery from wage labor makes sense only when one is differentiating the flow of European history or else is concerned only with the organizational features of particular regions, such as the American South or industrial Britain. That the hands that pick and the hands that spin are part of a singular economic process, formation, and mode of production would be obvious to all if we were not so preoccupied with retaining the category schemes of the past and afraid to see the world as it is.

References

BRENNER, ROBERT
1977   "The Origins of Capitalist Development: A Critique of Neo-Smithian Marxism." *New Left Review* 104 (July/Aug.):25–92.

FIELDHOUSE, DAVID
    1973   *Economics and Empire, 1830-1914*. Ithaca, N.Y.: Cornell University Press.
FRANK, ANDRÉ GUNDER
    1979   *Dependent Accumulation*. New York: Monthly Review Press.
WALLERSTEIN, IMMANUEL
    1977   "How Do We Know Class Struggle When We See It? Reply to Ira Gerstein." *Insurgent Sociologist* 7(Spring): 104-106.
    1979   *The Capitalist World Economy*. New York: Cambridge University Press.

❧ B ❧

FEMINIST SOCIAL THEORIZING AND MORAL REASONING: ON DIFFERENCE AND DIALECTIC

Roslyn Wallach Bologh

ST. JOHN'S UNIVERSITY, JAMAICA, NEW YORK

The question of difference raises uncomfortable issues for feminism. Difference is that which distinguishes us and hence separates us from others, while similarity identifies us with others and hence unites us. Much feminist theorizing has attempted to discredit attributions of difference that circumscribe female identity. Objects of feminist critique have included theories and practices that disregard, degrade, or demean women as well as those that set women apart as deserving of special regard, protection, and deference because of their alleged natural differences.

Feminist theorizing has also considered socialization practices that contribute to the development of a "feminine" mode of interaction described as expressive and compassionate, placating and deferential, subservient and subordinate.[1] The differences that

373

feminists have been likely to acknowledge, therefore, have been linked with female powerlessness and dependence, differences that needed to be remedied or overcome. Even when women's strengths and men's weaknesses were acknowledged, it was generally felt that to affirm those differences was to engage in the same kind of gender-based character assassination and attribution of difference that feminists were committed to fighting.

This view was premised on the assumption that all gender differences, those that favor women and those that do not, are due not to biology but to social arrangements, which ultimately derive from women's subordination to men.[2] The title of Elizabeth Janeway's (1981) book, *Powers of the Weak,* suggests this association of women's strengths with women's oppression. The view that differences are due ultimately to a relationship of domination leads logically to the view that if domination is eliminated, then gender difference will be eliminated along with it. Hence, there is no point in stressing female strengths and superior qualities.

According to this reasoning, although it might feel liberating to experience and express pride in being womanly, just as men have traditionally experienced and expressed pride in being manly, such pride must ultimately either recommend separatism, which is unrealistic if not undesirable, or fall back on the traditional notion of separate spheres, division of labor, and complementarity. If difference is rooted in social life, not nature, and assuming that men cannot be persuaded or forced to alter their world to reward womanliness over manliness, then women must remain in the female world in order to retain their womanly qualities. A rejection of that reactionary position seems to require a corresponding rejection of all stress on female strengths and superiorities. Feminist theorizing ought logically, then, to continue to uncover the variety of ways in which differences and inequality are perpetuated and to struggle against those. Because gender differences all ultimately derive from a situation of subordination and domination, they are therefore to be overcome, neither sentimentalized nor celebrated. This perspective becomes an assimilationist approach to gender difference.

Nevertheless, feminist theorizing in all the disciplines is more and more reconceptualizing gender differences with an emphasis on women's unique strengths. Part of this movement focuses on women's experiences in the female world (for example,

Bernard, 1981), where submissiveness and inferiority are not cultivated but various strengths and capabilities specific to women are. Such work is generally uncontroversial, for it highlights the strengths of women while filling the gap in public knowledge of the female world, a gap that has been tantamount to the obliteration of women and their experience from public consciousness. However, it does not question or challenge the given social arrangements that require separate worlds.

Keohane, Rosaldo, and Gelpi (1982) consider the focus on women's strengths and women's experiences in the female world to fall within the category of female consciousness, which they distinguish from feminine consciousness. (Feminine consciousness encompasses the experience of being an object to another and the self-definition that is based on the male gaze, male desire, and male construction.) Recent work that calls attention to female consciousness includes Sara Ruddick's "Maternal Thinking" (1982) and Jean Bethke Elshtain's *Public Man, Private Woman* (1982b). Elshtain affirms women's experience in giving and preserving life, nurturing and sustaining, the experiences and ways of relating that have traditionally characterized women's lives in the private domestic world. She argues that the introduction into the public political sphere of female consciousness and ways of life is the only viable and radical strategy for feminism to take.

Although Elshtain connects female consciousness to feminist theory and practice, Keohane, Rosaldo, and Gelpi distinguish female consciousness, which takes the form of acknowledging the strengths of women's experience, from feminist consciousness, which they identify with reflection on the asymmetries in power, opportunity, and situation, drawing attention to "the pervasive patterns of subordination, limitation, and confinement that have hampered and crippled the development of the female half of humankind" (p. x). Thus, for their version of feminist consciousness, difference is that which handicaps women. The stress on women's strengths would not express a feminist consciousness. Included in their category of feminist consciousness is the exploration of how sexuality is constructed, deconstructed, and reconstructed, particularly in terms of powerlessness vis-à-vis men (MacKinnon, 1982). This aspect of feminist theorizing brings in the political significance of lesbianism and the controversy over separatism.

The controversial element in feminist theorizing about difference has always been the radical feminist critique of the male world, male ways, and the male ethos as well as its affirmation of the female world, female ways, and the female ethos. Accused of advocating separatism and lesbianism, the radical feminist perspective (for example, Daly, 1978) has produced some of the most interesting and trenchant analyses of gender differences and relationships. This perspective has also been effective in getting lesbianism accepted not just as a tolerable variant in sexual preference but as a politically desirable one. Separatism represents the alternative position to assimilation with respect to gender difference.

The radical feminist approach to gender difference has challenged the earlier feminist orientation toward overcoming difference. Within every discipline there has been a movement from a feminist concern with correcting male bias to a recognition of the irremediable nature of that bias—a recognition that to see and speak as a man differs from seeing and speaking as a woman. Dorothy E. Smith (1979) argues that one necessarily speaks from a position in the world, that it is not possible to be a body that does not take up space or endure over time. Hence, to claim objectivity, to claim to speak from no particular position, is to claim to be no body. Feminists have challenged that claim and have shown how male objectivity expresses a male perspective, suggesting that any claim to pure objectivity is questionable (MacKinnon, 1982). Within sociology there has been a call to bring in women's voice and to create a sociology for women (Smith, 1979). Within literary criticism (for example, Abel, 1982; Pearson and Pope, 1981), historiography, philosophy (Gould, 1975; Osborne, 1979), the arts (Kimball, 1981), science (Keller, 1982), and political discourse (Elshtain, 1982a) as well as the other social sciences (Spender, 1981), feminists are challenging the dominant perspective in their disciplines and struggling to identify a perspective that affirms the female voice.

Thus, the approach to gender has taken two forms within feminism: that gender difference is something to be overcome because it ultimately implies women's subordination or that gender difference is something to be identified and affirmed because it reveals women's strengths and virtues. Into the controversy over gender difference has entered the work of a theorist whose explicit, or manifest, analysis resembles that of the least controversial and least divisive kind of theorizing: correcting the absence or mistreatment of women within some established theory or body of literature. However, the absence that this theorist documents points beyond a mere correction of male bias or misperception. It leads us straight to a reconsideration of the issue of difference.

The work to which I make reference is Carol Gilligan's (1982) *In a Different Voice*. The difference that Gilligan describes is of critical significance; it is a difference that makes a difference. Unlike other work that documents difference without claiming either superiority or inferiority, this work cannot be treated as merely adding to our knowledge, filling a gap, or correcting misperceptions. Although it does all that, it also makes us face the question of difference and reconsider the two alternative feminist strategies of either overcoming and denying difference by means of assimilation and conquest or preserving and asserting difference by means of segregated spheres or separatism.

The difference that Gilligan describes is a difference in moral reasoning. Whether the difference actually or statistically does distinguish women from men[3] is less significant than the very fact of the difference. Furthermore, this difference has traditionally been associated with gender. The difference corresponds to feminist psychoanalytic descriptions of gender difference as well as to stereotypical conceptions. Therefore, there is good reason to conceive of the two kinds of moral reasoning as masculine and feminine, regardless of whether a statistical correlation with sex could be established.

Nancy Chodorow's (1978) theory of gender difference provides a psychoanalytic context for understanding the difference that Gilligan analyzes. Chodorow claims that feminine personality comes to define itself in terms of attachment and interdependence more than does the masculine personality, which comes to define itself in terms of separation and autonomy. Chodorow attributes this difference to the fact that women, universally, are largely responsible for early childcare, a situation that Isaac Balbus (1983) calls mother-monopolized childrearing. Chodorow stresses the negative effects of this process on the female sex, although she does show its harmful effects on male development as well. Isaac Balbus stresses the negative effects on the male sex and on the masculine world of public, political, and economic life. Both see the solution to lie with the politics of childrearing.

According to Balbus, if fathers shared equally in the rearing of children, boys would not become contemptuous of women and women's ways and would not be possessed of an objectifying consciousness that treats all that is other (including nature as well as women) as an object to be used and exploited rather than as another subjectivity to be respected and treated with care. Here we see a reversal of the usual sociological perspective. The psychodynamics of microinterpersonal relationships are to blame for the ills of the macro–political economy. However, this analysis begs the question of how it comes to be that women "monopolize" childraising while men monopolize political economy.

According to Chodorow, if fathers shared equally in the raising of children, girls and women would be able to develop an individuated and autonomous sense of self (p. 212). Furthermore, she contends that the sexual division of labor and women's responsibility for childcare are linked to and "generate" male dominance, which includes a psychological need on the part of men to be superior to women (p. 214). Again we have the political issue of male dominance attributed to the domestic situation of female mothering. According to James A. Doyle (1983:81), such psychological explanations for male dominance blame women, in the final analysis, for their own domination. "If women were not so creative, fear-provoking, dreadful, or easy to identify with, men would not have a psychological need to dominate them."

Furthermore, the analysis begs the question of how it comes to be that mothers and daughters, as well as fathers and sons, come to identify with each other as sharing a specific gender identity. Does sexual (biological) difference produce gender? Chodorow does not answer the question of how gender itself is created. Yet we have research that indicates that the seeing and constructing of gender is an ongoing social accomplishment (Kessler and McKenna, 1978). Feminist psychoanalyst Juliet Mitchell (Mitchell and Rose, 1982) interprets Lacan's work as providing a compelling critique and alternative to theory that attributes gender difference to either biology or socialization as generally understood. Lacan's psychoanalytic theory suggests instead that the origins of both language and gender can be traced to the incest taboo (Mitchell and Rose, 1982) and that gender is therefore coeval with language and culture. Nevertheless, Balbus and Chodorow seem to assume that gender difference is a problem that can and ought to be overcome or at least ameliorated by changing parenting patterns.

Gilligan begins from a different concern. She wants to show the problem that arises with the suppression of gender difference. Chodorow's work seems to imply a static character to the gender difference. Women have one problem with which they struggle all their lives, men another. Masculinity is defined through separation and individuation from the mother, femininity through attachment to and identification with the mother. "Male gender identity is threatened by intimacy while female gender identity is threatened by separation. Thus males tend to have difficulty with relationships, while females tend to have problems with individuation" (p. 8). Chodorow implies that each gender has its own unique identity that continues through the life cycle; change requires an external agent, such as psychoanalysis on the individual level or shared parenting on the societal level. Shared parenting, according to her theory, should produce offspring without such marked gender differences.

Gilligan implies that although each gender has its own particular mode of moral reasoning, each undergoes change and transformation over time. Gilligan's analysis is more in keeping with a dialectical view of gender, not only in its recognition of self-change but in its identification of the source of such change. An examination of Gilligan's material reveals that movement from one stage of moral development to the next, which she and Kohlberg (1981) document, derives from crises and contradictions that lead to reflection and the creation of a higher synthesis that resolves the contradiction and overcomes an inner conflict. Finally, Gilligan's work implies a dialectical relation between the genders, as each begins by denying or repressing the moral concerns of the other and yet each ultimately requires and depends on the other for its own realization. Each then comes to acknowledge and develop the moral strengths of the other.

Gilligan also dissolves the neat boundaries used by Keohane, Rosaldo, and Gelpi for creating the categories of feminist, female, and feminine consciousness. Gilligan shows how they are dialectically related: "Sensitivity to the needs of others and the assumption of responsibility for taking care lead women to attend to voices other than their own and to include in their judgment other points of view. Women's moral weakness, manifest in an apparent diffusion and [difficulty in making a definitive] judgment, is thus inseparable from women's moral strength, an overriding concern with relationships and responsibilities" (pp. 16–17).

A similar claim could be made that men's moral strength is likewise inseparable from their moral weakness. Nevertheless, male writers have tended to see only the weakness of the female's moral reasoning in relation to that of the male.

Freud's criticism of women's sense of justice, seeing it compromised in its refusal of blind impartiality, is echoed implicitly in the work of Kohlberg. As in Piaget's work (1965), which omits "boys" altogether because "the child" is assumed to be male, in Kohlberg's research, from which he derives his theory of human moral development, females simply do not exist (Gilligan, p. 18). However, studies by others, using Kohlberg's six-stage model, have found that women appear to be deficient in moral development when measured by Kohlberg's scale. Women's judgments seem to exemplify the third stage of his six-stage sequence. Kohlberg and Kramer (1969) imply that only if women enter the traditional arena of male activity will they recognize the inadequacy of this moral perspective and progress, like men, toward higher stages where relationships are subordinated to rules (stage 4) and rules to universal principles of justice (stages 5 and 6).

This conclusion corresponds to earlier feminist work that sees women's difference as a form of inferiority due to their subordination to or exclusion from the male world. Gilligan challenges the feminist position that regards female gender identity as inferior. She argues that feminine moral reasoning differs qualitatively from the masculine model. Feminine morality assumes a world in which people are attached to and dependent on one another, hence vulnerable to one another. Because of mutual vulnerability, there must be mutual caring and responsiveness. There must be mutual listening in order to understand one another's needs and feelings, spoken and unspoken. The female approach requires dialogue.

Kohlberg's version of moral development reflects the importance of individuation in men's lives. For men the moral problem arises from competing rights of separate individuals and is resolved by a mode of thinking that is formal and abstract. Gilligan's research on moral development reveals the importance of attachment in women's lives. For women the moral problem arises from conflicting responsibilities due to attachment to others. The moral problem is resolved by a mode of thinking that is contextual and narrative.

Because females consider it a moral responsibility to be responsive to the needs of others, Kohlberg sees women as remaining at the stage he has labeled interpersonal, as opposed to societal. Gilligan's research reveals that females *are* concerned about the interpersonal, but the reason for that concern changes from concern for approval (which is what Kohlberg originally intended by *interpersonal*) to a concern with group life (which corresponds to Kohlberg's law-and-order stage) and ultimately to a universal concern for human justice that transcends the societal level—the same sequence of development that males undergo, but with a different content. Gilligan shows the limits of the masculine ethic of rights and noninterference as well as of the feminine ethic of responsibility and caring.

The masculine morality of noninterference, premised on a notion of individual autonomy, untempered by a positive commitment to caring and responsibility for others, presupposes and (re)produces indifference to inequalities of power and situation. The morality of responsibility for others, premised on a notion of mutual caring, untempered by a commitment to human autonomy, leads to exploitation and oppression in the form of self-sacrifice[4] and to human manipulation and interference as ways of vicariously living through the other.

Male moral development involves learning the limits of a morality of rights and noninterference; female moral development involves learning the limits of a morality of responsibilities and caring.

In addition to highlighting the difference and the strength of feminine moral reasoning, and enabling us to better appreciate women's difficulties in adjusting to the public, male world, Gilligan's work shows the significance of the new feminist concern with discovering women's voice and affirming women's difference.

Such a concern must include as well a critique of the male perspective that sets itself up as the voice of authority and objectivity. Gilligan's critique of Kohlberg's work implies a similar critique that is occurring in all the disciplines: "As long as the categories by which development is assessed are derived within a male perspective from male research data, divergence from the masculine standard can be seen only as a failure of development. As a result, the thinking of women is often classified with that of children" (Gilligan, 1977:490).

Feminist theorizing in the various academic disciplines began as an attempt to correct male bias, to refute male attempts at "defining" the female, and to make the problems, presence, and absence of women more salient. However, this attempt seems to be giving way to a view of the irremediable nature of male bias, a view that subjectivity cannot be avoided, that one always views and speaks (that is, interprets the world) from some perspective, and that the male perspective may differ from the female—that what is salient to the female and the way in which it is salient may differ for the male. Furthermore, for the female to be forced to perceive the world and to speak from within a male frame of reference may do violence to her own sense of self. To adopt a male language is to effectively silence the female voice. Thus, feminists have come to understand the social construction of knowledge and its implications in terms of power relations. As Spender (1981:2) summarizes: "Because it has been primarily men who have determined the parameters, who have decided what would be problematic, significant, logical, and reasonable, not only have women been excluded from the process *but the process itself can reinforce the 'authority' of men and the 'deficiency' of women.*"

Feminist theorizing promises not only to fill the gaps in knowledge about women but to provide an alternative perception of the world, a perception that men, because of their (dominant) position, could not possess. How alternative perceptions of the world are to be accommodated becomes the critical issue for theorizing, an issue that raises the question of power and paradigms. As Annette Kolodny (1981) in her discussion of literary criticism reminds us: "Graduate schools, at their best, are training grounds for competing interpretive paradigms or reading techniques" (p. 33). The problem becomes one of the power to establish one paradigm, or set of concerns and mode of perception, to the exclusion or denigration of another.

Kolodny suggests that, instead of a choice between accepting or rejecting particular esthetic values, interpretations, and judgments, the choice is between having some awareness of the bases of those values and going without such awareness. Only by questioning our perceptions and interpretations can we begin to develop awareness of the foundations of those perceptions and thus to develop self-consciousness. A concern with the foundations of human knowledge and perceptions, with developing self-consciousness, and with overcoming the polarized dichotomy between objectivity and subjectivity also characterizes phenomenological theorizing.

The question of gender difference involves not only a question of suppression or affirmation of difference, denial or assertion of difference, but one of what difference difference itself makes. Does difference mean conflict and violence, with each trying to conquer the other and assimilate the other to itself? Does difference mean separation, with each asserting its own superiority within its own spheres and in its own terms? Or does difference mean an opportunity for self-knowledge through confronting another who calls one's own truth into question, whose difference helps us to appreciate the limits of our own perceptions, knowledge, and actions? The last seems to be the most reasonable and most appealing choice, the one most in keeping with a phenomenological commitment to self-consciousness. However, this third choice is not as unproblematic as it may appear.

Can women enter the public realm as women, assert a female perspective in the context of male-defined activity, and engage in dialogue such that each perspective calls the other into question, forcing each to confront its own limits and hence to grow and change? The male world of political economy as it is presently constituted presupposes and (re)produces competitive, independent, and separate actors. Such actors must be indifferent to the sufferings that their actions might occasion for others. They must stifle or repress compassion in order to act in a way that will promote their survival and success within that world. Therefore, the world of political economy, in addition to providing actors with the political and economic resources necessary for a sense of independence and autonomy, also intensifies any feelings of indifference to others that such independence and autonomy might engender. Thus, the public world of political economy that women seek to enter is predicated on stifling the female voice. Claudine Hermann (1981:89) reflects, "It means nothing to allow women to participate in society if it robs them of everything that makes them different."

A public world in which it is necessary to repress the female voice in order to survive, a public world that requires the repression of compassion, will not be changed by having men share equally in childraising, for the public world is not merely a world in which men act according to their own personal masculine inclinations, as if such inclinations were independent of the need to enter and be successful in that public world. Introducing actors with feminine predispositions, whether these be men or women, will not of its own change that world. The world is more than the actors who make it up; it is a form of life structured by the rules for reproducing that world. Changing the world means changing the rules of the game. Altering the childraising experience or the personal predispositions of men would not, therefore, by itself be sufficient.

Today's public world precludes dialogue between masculine and feminine perspectives and hence precludes dialectical change. Dialectical change would not be change from femininity to masculinity or from masculinity to femininity but an ongoing change in the nature of each, something like a feminizing of masculinity and a masculinizing of femininity.

The existence of public and private worlds as presently constituted contributes to stereotypical masculine and feminine personalities and to the stunting of human moral development. The domination of formal, instrumental rationality that characterizes the modern public world has been a theme of critical sociological theory. Modern critical theory, as well as classical social theory, is characterized by the concern that "the ever-expanding patterns of instrumental rationality will 'erode' their expressive, communal opposites" (Glennon, 1979:197). Most Marxist theorizing sees feminism as peripheral or at best supplementary to this crisis and to the struggle for radical social change. Linda Glennon provides a needed corrective to such theorizing. She locates feminism at the center of this crisis because feminists typically find themselves caught between the "public and private duality engendered by the modern social structure, and between the expressive and instrumental orientations dualistically allocated to these spheres" (p. 172).

Glennon discovers within feminist discourse four possible solutions to the crisis of modernism and dualism: instrumentalism, expressivism, synthesism, and polarism. Instrumentalism and expressivism reflect the assimilationist solution, with either the male model dominating and obliterating the female or the female obliterating the male. Polarism reflects the solution of separatism: the creation by and for women of a separate, independent world to be run by women. The synthesis solution is the one closest to the dialectical alternative that we have been seeking. However, it is the least well formulated by Glennon, and one that she herself finds problematic.

A more adequate conceptualization of the problem and its possible dialectical resolution is provided by Kathy Ferguson (1980), who draws on the work of George Herbert Mead to develop a dialectical model of social life. Social life in this model resembles dialogue; it requires and presupposes the ability both to take the role of the other and to define one's situation for oneself. The ability to apprehend and appreciate the perspective of the other constitutes the possibility of compassion. The ability to define one's own situation constitutes the possibility of freedom. Traditionally, women have been denied the opportunity to define for themselves their own situation; they have been denied the resources necessary for so doing; their voice has been silenced as they have been excluded from political and economic power. Thus they have been denied their capacity for freedom. However, they have developed the capacity for taking the perspective of the other, so much so that compassion is the hallmark of femininity. Men, in contrast, have developed their capacity to define the situation to the extent of assuming their own definition to be the only one; they traditionally and typically are egoistic. Their capacity to take the role of the other tends to be as atrophied as women's capacity to speak in their own voice and articulate their own vision.

Ferguson identifies domination with being in a situation that has been defined by another and forced to operate within that situation without being able to effect one's own definition of it. Liberation, therefore, requires as a first condition the ability to define one's own situation and to control the necessary resources for so doing. The second condition for liberation, according to Ferguson, is the ability to take the role of the other (pp. 105-106): "The ability to relativize one's perspective, to take the world of the other and appreciate the other as a unique durational being, is crucial to liberation because it opens us to the possibilities that others offer" (p. 109).

Her work suggests also that we come to know ourselves in relation to another. Hence, to cut ourselves off from another is to cut ourselves off from learning about and appreciating the self that we could be in relation to the other. These two aspects of social life, of dialogue, and of the human self constitute a dialectical unity in which neither aspect suppresses the other or assimilates the other to itself. However, there may be a conflict between these two conditions for liberation. "Since we depend on the other as the very source of our self-identity, when the relation with the other is also the source of our domination then we are put in an intolerable bind" (p. 123).

To pursue compassion within such a context would mean "to embrace the present spatiality of social relations, the 'being' that exists with others, and to sacrifice ['becoming,'] the pursuit of one's own autonomous definition of the situation" (p. 124). It is necessary to recognize the tension and tragedy inherent in the dilemma of oppression in order to avoid destructive oversimplification in recommendations for liberation. Ideally, a liberated life would involve a dialectical unity of the two: "in which one is able to affirm oneself and the other simultaneously, to work out an authentic self-identity in the context of one's social relations. We ultimately seek the process through which being and becoming might dialectically coincide—when that which we are, in our relations with others, supports and affirms us in our attempts to move toward that which we wish to become" (p. 125).

Unfortunately this dialectical unity is denied us when we face an intransigent other, one who refuses to hear and insists on imposing his definition of the situation on us. In such a situation we are faced with the choice of either assimilation, which does violence to our being, or separatism, which does violence to our becoming. Assimilation means living within the other's definition of the situation, the other's frame of reference. It requires seeing the world through the other's eyes while denying one's own vision. Separatism provides the opportunity for women to listen to one another, to articulate their own vision, to develop their own voices, to define their own situation.

However, defining our situation is ultimately as one-sided, restrictive, and confining as assimilation. As Ferguson and Gilligan show, it is one moment in a larger dialectic in which it is necessary to learn from difference. We can learn our strengths, our limits, and our possibilities only in relation to that which is other. Without experiencing resistance in the form of difference, we become excessive. Only by having our ways called into question can we become conscious of our strengths as we reflect on, articulate, and persuade others of the reasonableness and desirability of those ways; and conscious as well of our limits as we learn the possibility and reasonableness of other ways.

Separatism, as a struggle to empower the powerless, an occasion for articulating and displaying the rightness of one's values, must lead to dialogue and the possibility of dialectical transcendence. Such possibility requires transforming a world that precludes dialogue, a world that requires assimilation as a condition for speaking. The struggle for women's voice to be heard is a struggle for a world in which men and women can assert their truths, respect their differences, and learn from each other. This means women must become powerful enough to speak and be heeded, powerful enough to overcome the power and privilege that make possible indifference, derision, and silencing of the female voice. Feminists must challenge and struggle to transform a repressive social world that requires silencing the female voice, and must challenge and struggle to transform social theories that overlook a female perspective.

The work of feminists like Gilligan and Ferguson suggests that the choice of either assimilation or separatism—and a dualistic world that requires and presupposes such a choice—is ultimately self-defeating. They show how that kind of world is stifling of human development. Their work recommends dialogue, as opposed to either separatism or assimilation. Jane Gallop (1982), a feminist psychoanalyst who attempts to construct a dialogue between Lacanian psychoanalysis and feminism, compares that dialogue, and by implication all dialogue, to marriage: "The radical potential in their marriage is not a mystical fusion obliterating all difference and conflict, but a provocative contact which opens each to what is not encompassed by the limits of its identity" (p. xxi).

The question of difference is one with the question of identity. It is becoming the critical question for feminist theorizing in all the disciplines including social science research methods (Roberts, 1981; Hunt, forthcoming) as feminists begin to question and challenge the implicit male perspective of the dominant paradigms, methodological strictures, and theoretical assumptions of the various disciplines (Rosaldo, 1983). As feminists struggle to come to terms with gender identity, they attempt to articulate a theoretical perspective that is liberating to women. Some deny gender difference; some affirm it. Others adopt a dialectical position best expressed by Jane Gallop (1982:xii): "I hold the Lacanian view that any identity will necessarily be alien and constraining. I do not believe in some 'new identity' which would be adequate and authentic. But I do not seek some sort of liberation from identity. That would lead only to another form of paralysis—the oceanic passivity of undifferentiation. Identity must be continually assumed and immediately called into question."

Similarly, we may conclude that difference, like identity, must be continually affirmed (for example, articulating a feminine or masculine perspective) and immediately called into question (for example, engaging in dialogue with its opposite). Such must constitute a feminist, dialectical, phenomenological mode of theorizing[5] that respects difference and aims at self-consciousness and self-change—in short, human growth. In order to achieve a world in which dialogue and dialectical self-change are possible and their importance recognized, the current repressive world must be challenged and transformed. Thus the issue of gender difference, the question of assimilation, separatism, or dialectical human growth, implies differences in feminist politics.

Notes

1. The earlier work on gender differences in communication includes Eakins and Eakins (1978), Henley (1977), and Lakoff

(1975). For a review of the more recent work on language and gender see West (1983).

2. Anthropologist Peggy Sanday (1981) finds that male subordination of women and the emphasis on gender difference varies with societal conditions of stress and survival in conjunction with myths of origin that attribute creative power to one or the other sex.

3. We must avoid reifying the conceptions of female and male identity. Women have masculine concerns and capacities, just as men have feminine ones. However, according to most conceptions of gender, women tend to stress the feminine and suppress (and even repress) the masculine, just as men tend to do the opposite.

4. The importance of the feminine ideal of selflessness and its consequences for women has led to rigorous philosophical analysis and critique of this ideal by feminist philosophers (Blum and others, 1975; Tormey, 1975).

5. An analysis of dialectical phenomenology as a method of theorizing can be found in Bologh (1979). A more recent discussion can be found in Bologh and Marsh (1983).

References

ABEL, ELIZABETH (ED.)
   1982   *Writing and Sexual Difference.* Chicago: University of Chicago Press.

BALBUS, ISAAC
   1983   *Marxism and Domination: A Neo-Hegelian, Feminist, Psychoanalytic Theory of Sexual, Political, and Technological Liberation.* Princeton, N.J.: Princeton University Press.

BERNARD, JESSIE
   1981   *The Female World.* New York: Free Press.

BLUM, LARRY, AND OTHERS
   1975   "Altruism and Women's Oppression." *Philosophical Forum* 5(1-2):222-247.

BOLOGH, ROSLYN WALLACH
   1979   *Dialectical Phenomenology: Marx's Method.* London: Routledge & Kegan Paul.

BOLOGH, ROSLYN WALLACH, AND MARSH, JAMES L.
    1983   "Phenomenology, Marxism, and Feminism." *Journal of Social Philosophy* 14(4).

CHODOROW, NANCY
    1978   *The Reproduction of Mothering: Psychoanalysis and the Sociology of Gender.* Berkeley: University of California Press.

DALY, MARY
    1978   *Gyn/Ecology: The Metaethics of Radical Feminism.* Boston: Beacon Press.

DOYLE, JAMES A.
    1983   *The Male Experience.* Dubuque, Iowa: William C. Brown.

EAKINS, BARBARA, AND EAKINS, R. GENE
    1978   *Sex Differences in Human Communications.* Boston: Houghton Mifflin.

ELSHTAIN, JEAN BETHKE
    1982a   "Feminist Discourse and Its Discontents: Language, Power, and Meaning." *Signs* 7(3):603-621.
    1982b   *Public Man, Private Woman.* Princeton, N.J.: Princeton University Press.

FERGUSON, KATHY
    1980   *Self, Society, and Womankind: The Dialectic of Liberation.* Westport, Conn.: Greenwood Press.

GALLOP, JANE
    1982   *The Daughter's Seduction: Feminism and Psychoanalysis.* Ithaca, N.Y.: Cornell University Press.

GILLIGAN, CAROL
    1977   "In a Different Voice: Women's Conceptions of Self and of Morality." *Harvard Educational Review* 47(4): 481-517.
    1982   *In a Different Voice.* Cambridge, Mass.: Harvard University Press.

GLENNON, LINDA
    1979   *Women and Dualism: A Sociology of Knowledge Analysis.* New York: Longmans.

GOULD, CAROL
    1975   "The Woman Question: Philosophy of Liberation and the Liberation of Philosophy." *Philosophical Forum* 5(1-2):5-44.

HENLEY, NANCY
1977 *Body Politics: Power, Sex, and Nonverbal Communication.* Englewood Cliffs, N.J.: Prentice-Hall.

HERMANN, CLAUDINE
1981 "The Virile System." In E. Marks and I. de Courtivron (Eds.), *New French Feminisms.*

HUNT, JENNIFER
Forth- "The Development of Rapport Through the Negotia-
coming tion of Gender in Field Work Among Police." *Human Organization.*

JANEWAY, ELIZABETH
1981 *Powers of the Weak.* New York: Morrow/Quill.

KELLER, EVELYN FOX
1982 "Feminism and Science." *Signs* 7(3):589-602.

KEOHANE, NANNERL O., ROSALDO, MICHELLE Z., AND GELPI, BARBARA C. (EDS.)
1982 *Feminist Theory: A Critique of Ideology.* Chicago: University of Chicago Press.

KESSLER, SUZANNE J., AND MCKENNA, WENDY
1978 *Gender: An Ethnomethodological Approach.* New York: Wiley.

KIMBALL, GAYLE (ED.)
1981 *Women's Culture: The Women's Renaissance of the Seventies.* Metuchen, N.J.: Scarecrow Press.

KOHLBERG, LAWRENCE
1981 *The Philosophy of Moral Development.* San Francisco: Harper & Row.

KOHLBERG, LAWRENCE, AND KRAMER, R.
1969 "Continuities and Discontinuities in Child and Adult Moral Development." *Human Development* 12:93-120.

KOLODNY, ANNETTE
1981 "Dancing Through the Minefield: Some Observations on the Theory, Practice, and Politics of a Feminist Literary Criticism." In Dale Spender (Ed.), *Men's Studies Modified: The Impact of Feminism on the Academic Disciplines.* Elmsford, N.Y.: Pergamon Press.

LAKOFF, ROBIN
1975 *Language and Woman's Place.* New York: Harper & Row.

MACKINNON, CATHARINE A.
1982 "Feminism, Marxism, Method, and the State: An Agenda for Theory." *Signs* 7(3):515–544.

MARKS, ELAINE, AND DE COURTIVRON, ISABELLE (EDS.)
1981 *New French Feminisms.* New York: Schocken Books.

MITCHELL, JULIET, AND ROSE, JACQUELINE (EDS.)
1982 *Feminine Sexuality: Jacques Lacan and the École Freudienne.* New York: Norton.

OSBORNE, MARTHA LEE (ED.)
1979 *Woman in Western Thought.* New York: Random House.

PEARSON, CAROL, AND POPE, KATHERINE
1981 *The Female Hero in American and British Literature.* New York: Bowker.

PIAGET, JEAN
1965 *The Moral Judgment of the Child.* New York: Free Press.

ROBERTS, HELEN (ED.)
1981 *Doing Feminist Research.* London: Routledge & Kegan Paul.

ROSALDO, MICHELLE Z.
1983 "Moral/Analytic Dilemmas Posed by the Intersection of Feminism and Social Science." In Haan and others (Eds.), *Science as Moral Inquiry.* New York: Columbia University Press.

RUDDICK, SARA
1982 "Maternal Thinking." In B. Thorne (Ed.), *Rethinking the Family.* New York: Longmans.

SANDAY, PEGGY REEVES
1981 *Female Power and Male Dominance: On the Origins of Sexual Inequality.* Cambridge: Cambridge University Press.

SHERMAN, JULIA A., AND BECK, EVELYN TORTON (EDS.)
1979 *The Prism of Sex: Essays in the Sociology of Knowledge.* Madison: University of Wisconsin Press.

SMITH, DOROTHY E.
1979 "A Sociology for Women." In J. A. Sherman and E. T. Beck, (Eds.), *The Prism of Sex: Essays in the Sociology of Knowledge.* Madison: University of Wisconsin Press.

SPENDER, DALE (ED.)
    1981   *Men's Studies Modified: The Impact of Feminism on the Academic Disciplines.* Elmsford, N.Y.: Pergamon Press.

TORMEY, JUDITH
    1975   "Exploitation, Oppression, and Self-Sacrifice." *Philosophical Forum* 5(1–2):206–221.

WEST, CANDACE
    1983   "Language and Gender." *Contemporary Sociology* 12 (Jan.):30–35.

℀ C ℀

THE PARSONS REVIVAL
IN GERMAN SOCIOLOGY

Jeffrey C. Alexander

UNIVERSITY OF CALIFORNIA, LOS ANGELES

The following observation appeared in a recently published work of German social theory:

> Max Weber, George Herbert Mead, and Emile Durkheim are indisputably accepted as classical figures in the history of sociological theory—thanks, not least of all, to the work of Talcott Parsons. That one still occupies oneself with these authors today as if they were one's contemporaries needs no explicit justification. Yet however highly one may rate the work of Talcott Parsons, his status as a classical thinker is not so uncontroversial that one may choose his work

I would like to thank Richard Münch for his generous contributions of information and insight about this topic of mutual interest. He cannot be held accountable, however, for the opinions I have expressed.

as the starting point of systematic sociological explanation without justifying this choice.

To begin with the obvious: there is no one among his contemporaries who developed a social theory of comparable complexity. The autobiographical intellectual history that Parsons published in 1974 gives an initial insight into the consistency and the cumulative success of the effort which this scholar of more than fifty years has put into the construction of a single theory. As it stands today, the work is unparalleled in regard to its level of abstraction, internal differentiation, theoretical breadth and systematicity —all of which is, simultaneously, connected to the literature of each particular empirical field. Although the interest in this theory has slackened since the mid 1960s, and though Parsons's later work has at times been pushed into the background by hermeneutically and critically oriented investigations, no social theory can be taken seriously today which does not—at the very least—clarify its relationship to Parsons's. Whoever deludes himself about this fact allows himself to be captured by contemporary issues rather than rationally confronting them. That goes also for a neo-Marxism which wishes simply to bypass Parsons—in the history of social science, errors of this type are normally quickly corrected.

This spirited justification of Parsons's continuing importance—indeed, his classical stature—may seem too wearily familiar. Slightly defensive and a little too strident, it is written, one might suppose, by one of the aggrieved orthodoxy, another former student of Parsons flaying hopelessly against the tide of intellectual history.

But such a supposition would be wrong. This passage was written by Jürgen Habermas, Germany's leading social theorist and, many would argue, the leading critical social theorist in the world today. With this ringing justification Habermas introduced his analysis of Parsons in the second volume of his *Theories des Kommunicativen Handelns* (1981b:297), a discussion of some 200 pages that holds center stage in the work. When this work—*Theories of Communicative Action*—appeared in December 1981, it sold out its first edition of 10,000 copies within the month. Has Parsons become bedtime reading for German social theorists?

When Talcott Parsons traveled to Heidelberg in 1926, he was making a pilgrimage to the home of sociological theory, for Germany had the greatest theoretical tradition in sociology by far. This tradition had effectively ended by the time of Parsons's arrival: The social and cultural basis for significant theory was destroyed by the deluge of 1915–1945. After the Second World War, sociology was reintroduced to Germany by scholars like König and Schelsky who had substantive rather than theoretical interests. Some older critical theorists like Adorno and Horkheimer returned, but the only distinctively sociological theorist of this early period whose work became influential was Ralf Dahrendorf, who had received his training outside Germany, at the London School of Economics. Dahrendorf, of course, helped create conflict theory, and his presence, added to the influence of the older critical theorists, gave to what there was of German sociological theory a distinctly antifunctionalist bent. Yet perhaps the most distinctive quality of this theory was the very fact of its paucity—this in the land that had given sociological theory its birth. Dahrendorf did not found a school or train significant theorists, and the politics of the early postwar period was not fruitful for the growth of critical sociological theory.

With the rebirth of political activity in the 1960s, and the growing distance that separated German intellectual life from the ravages of the inter-war period, German sociological theory revived. At first this revival was almost entirely within the framework of critical theory. The best-known German theoretical discussions undoubtedly were the celebrated arguments over positivism, in which critical theorists like Adorno and Horkheimer debated critical rationalists like Popper and Albert. The student movement of the late 1960s gave added force to this theoretical-cum-political revival, pushing it, in the process, toward a more orthodox and deterministic brand of Marxism, a framework within which the bulk of substantive German sociology remains.

Yet German theoretical development continued to grow and change. The most distinguished younger member of the Frankfurt school, Habermas also took part in the early positivism dispute, which helped revitalize the younger generation of German theorists.

Habermas, however, was a sharp critic of the student movement and was opposed to Marxist orthodoxy. For reasons I will elaborate below, during the late 1960s and the 1970s his theory became more expansive and complex. Habermas was quickly drawn into a dialogue with leading nonMarxist theories, particularly those of Weber and Parsons. This initial dialogue was decisive; not only did it give vital impetus to the further growth of German sociological theory, but it significantly affected its form.

In 1980 the University of Heidelberg gave Parsons an honorary doctorate of philosophy. The speeches honoring him, serious and appreciative in tone, were delivered by some of the leading lights in German sociological theory—by Habermas, Niklas Luhmann, and Wolfgang Schluchter, among others. (They are collected in Schluchter, 1980.) Once a pilgrim to the theoretical mecca, Parsons was now the object of a theoretical homage himself. In some manner he had managed to give back to German theory as much as he had earlier received. Although sociological theory in Germany is unlikely ever to regain its earlier domination over the field, it certainly is now a major force to be reckoned with in sociology. As it is increasingly translated and read, theorists in the English-speaking world are learning that critical theory is far from its only achievement. In fact, with the exception of the continuing strand of Marxist orthodoxy, German sociological theory has become dramatically "Parsonized." Every major branch —critical theory, systems theory, action theory, phenomenology, Weberian theory—has absorbed some of Parsons's most important lessons; each has, indeed, often assumed a distinctively Parsonian form. How has this come about, and what does it mean?

As compared with the situation in the United States—Mertonian injunctions notwithstanding—the cultural studies tradition in Europe has been much more sharply differentiated into separate theoretical and practical strands. Sociological theory in Europe has tended toward the philosophical and speculative rather than the explanatory. This has been nowhere more true than in Germany, the country Marx scorned as a nation of philosophers. Marx's criticism, of course, was motivated not only by his country's philosophical penchant, for the German inclination for social philosophy is usually combined with an inclination toward idealism. German theorists want their philosophy to be explicitly normative; it should make the world more meaningful, providing answers to the basic problems of existence. Traditionally, German theory has accomplished this task in one of two ways: (1) it has argued that the world is not a fragmented and individualized world of material constraints but a unified, organic community of spiritual ties; (2) it has argued that although the world is in fact materialistic and fragmented, it need not be, and that a more spiritualized existence is possible.

This penchant for philosophy and ambivalent idealism is German theory's strength and its weakness. It provides the German tradition with a richness and depth that often make the Anglo-American tradition seem shallow by comparison. At the same time, it makes German theory often frustratingly far removed from mundane explanatory concerns, and it also leads, in many cases, to an either/or approach to epistemological and ideological dilemmas. Theory should focus *either* on norms *or* on interest; modern societies should be *either* utilitarian and modern *or* romantic, in either the conservative or the radical sense. Rather than an agnostic position that, rather sloppily, says "a little of each," German social theory often insists that a choice be made.

Although German social theory today continues to reflect the strengths and weaknesses of this double heritage, it has moved closer to sociological theory in the American and English sense. Marxism, of course, has been one important bridging mechanism, for it can encourage explanatory empirical efforts while providing both metaphysical anchoring and the indictment of a normless and despiritualized world. A second, and recently a more important, bridge has been provided by Parsonianism. American and English readers may find this ironic, for Parsons is often viewed in the Anglo-American world as espousing mere speculative philosophy and idealistic ideology. This very philosophical and normative bent makes him attractive to German theory. Yet for all his similarities, Parsons remains part of a very different intellectual tradition. His is an explanatory theory, albeit at a high level of generality, and although he emphasized the normative aspects of society, he often demonstrated their interpenetration with the material world. What Parsons sought, in fact, was to overcome the either/or choices posed by the German tradition: He tried to transform the polar choices of modernism and romanticism, norms and interests, into interpenetrating positions on a single continuum.

This is where Habermas's interest in Parsons began. Habermas was always uncomfortable with the dichotomizing aspects of the Marxist tradition, and long before he had overtly taken his "Parsonian turn" he sought to incorporate aspects of Parsons's conceptual synthesis. In his famous essay "Science and Technology as Ideology" (1970), for example, he brought the pattern variables into the center of "critical theory." The pattern variables had been developed by Parsons to break down the dichotomy that Tönnies had established between *Gemeinschaft* and *Gesellschaft*. Against Tönnies, Parsons argued that modern society included both community and society—indeed, that different combinations of rationality and affectivity existed in different institutional spheres. Yet, although Habermas was attracted to the pattern-variable schema, he revised it in a revealing way. On the one hand, he used the schema to complicate and differentiate the conceptual apparatus he had inherited from critical theory; on the other, he used the pattern variables to reinstate the very dichotomy that Parsons had sought to avoid. Habermas claimed that affective neutrality, universalism, and specificity were the principal norms of instrumental capitalist society; only in some postinstrumental society would the alternative pattern-variable choices come into being.

This double-sided attitude toward Parsons's theory set the framework for much of the rest of Habermas's development. Absorbing more and more of Parsons's vocabulary, he steadily gains more insight into the complex structuring of the modern world; at the same time, his insistence on the merely instrumental character of this world leads him to turn Parsons's synthetic theory inside out. In his masterly *Legitimation Crisis* (1975), for example, Habermas implicitly appropriates Parsons's AGIL model, which views society as composed of the interacting subsystems of polity/law/economy/values, and he relates this differentiation, as Parsons did, to the three-system model of personality, culture, and society. Because of the complexity with which Habermas traces the interworking of the subsystems of capitalism, this work is a landmark of neoMarxist theory. Yet Habermas maintains, all the same, that capitalism cannot really establish reciprocal interactions between cultural patterns, social system demands, and psychological needs, and the familiar polarity of instrumental rationality versus human value is reestablished. In his latest work, *Theories of Communica-*

tive Action, Habermas examines Parsons in systematic detail for the first time, for only in this most recent phase has he consciously set out to develop a new, post-Marxist theory. Yet his conclusions here are much the same. Parsons, he acknowledges, poses the crucial question of the relation between lifeworlds—worlds of experience and symbolic discourse—and system or structure. But he insists that Parsons, particularly in his later work, reduces symbolic experience to an instrumental reflection of impersonal "systems" life (for at least a partial summary of his views in English, see Habermas, 1981a). Habermas once again revises Parsons so the theory reflects the problems he himself sees in "modernity."

Habermas's "critical Parsonianism" seems to me one-sided and wrong. He has drastically depersonalized the social system and overly moralized the lifeworlds of culture and experience. His theory finds answers to the problems of existence, and it does so in a philosophically brilliant and satisfying way. Yet in doing so, Habermas has reintroduced the epistemological and ideological dichotomies of idealism. But it is really not enough to locate Habermas by placing him within this broad tradition. To understand the evolution of his relation to Parsons, we must appreciate the specific dialogue through which his later attitude toward Parsonian theory developed. We must turn, for this, to Niklas Luhmann.

In the early 1970s, Habermas and Luhmann engaged in a major debate over the relative advantages of "critical" versus "systems" theory. Is the essence of modernity the freedom and order allowed by the differentiation of systems or the gap between a universalized culture and a rationalized society? Whereas Habermas argued that systems theory technologized society and actually eliminated choice, Luhmann argued that all societies are in fact subject to certain "technical" constraints and that by conceptualizing these demands, systems theory can transcend ideology and provide an objective framework for social analysis. (For a collection of his essays spanning the period 1964–1976, see Luhmann, 1982. For two longer analyses, see Luhmann, 1979. Columbia University Press is publishing a translation of the Habermas–Luhmann debate.) Many observers agreed that Luhmann had the better of this debate and that Habermas's historicism seemed to place him on weaker ground. It is certainly true that after this exchange Habermas took up the systemic aspects of Parsonian theory in a much more assiduous and explicit way. In some sense this was an enormous victory for Parsonianism, for this debate paved the way for the tremendously expanded interest in Parsons's work among younger German theorists. At the same time, however, Habermas's "conversion" may actually have been a defeat. The problem lay with Luhmann's presentation of the essence of Parsons's work.

Luhmann is an enormously accomplished social theorist whose work ranges as easily across disciplines as it does across historical time. Trained in jurisprudence and administration, he came only later in life to academia, and a crucial element in this transition was a year spent in the early 1960s with Parsons at Harvard.

Where Parsons starts with the voluntary character of choice and derives norms from the necessity for such choice to be carried out according to general standards of evaluation, Luhmann starts from the phenomenological insistence on the lack of real choice in human affairs, on the "natural familiarity" that brackets the range of any individual's experience. By adding Heidegger to Husserl, however, Luhmann begins to establish the necessity for artificial, more social mechanisms of control, because the temporal contingency of experience creates anxieties about encounters with new individuals, new experiences, and future events. The growing complexity of modern society adds further to this necessity for the control or systematization of experience, for increasing complexity threatens to eliminate the interpersonal basis of trust that phenomenology assumes. For all these reasons, modern society places a new premium on abstract and general mechanisms of control. The most general such mechanism is the existence of a "system" as such. The depersonalized world of modernity demands system organization, and actors must trust in the system itself. Systems reduce the untenable complexity of the modern world. They simplify reality, first, by becoming internally differentiated; increasing the range of institutions and processes opens up options for society while reducing options and anxieties for particular actors. Systems also create trust by establishing "media of communication." Money, power, love, and truth are mechanisms that concentrate and simplify information about society and social interaction; by providing standards that are accepted on faith, they allow interaction to proceed in what would otherwise be a chaotic and fundamentally incomprehensible world.

Some of the recent introductions to Luhmann's work suggest that he has "radicalized" Parsons, and Luhmann himself stresses the distance from Parsons and the advances he has made. Certainly Luhmann has "advanced" in certain significant ways. His writing is pithy, and he moves from common experience to esoteric argument with astonishing ease. For these reasons he is able to demonstrate some of the essential structures of Parsonian thinking with a clarity and richness Parsons never approached. The phenomenological and Heideggerian dimensions of Luhmann's work expand Parsons in important ways—they converge here with the early Garfinkel—and his close attention to empirical and historical literature is salutary. Yet to speak of "advance" as such, let alone of "radicalization," seems wholly premature.

Luhmann has changed Parsons, but not always for the better. His phenomenological focus has costs as well as benefits, and his explicit and omnipresent focus on "systems" can be dangerous as well. These analytical difficulties are exacerbated by distinctive ideological differences, for Luhmann, unlike Parsons, has definite conservative leanings. Where Parsons supported the New Deal, Luhmann works for the Christian Democrats.

Systems in Luhmann's work have a mechanistic and naturalistic cast. Parsons avoided this danger because he insisted that social systems were always interpenetrated by meaning and culture. Luhmann does not; he rarely talks about meaning as such, preferring to discuss culture as an epiphenomenon of the need to reduce system complexity through trust. Luhmann poses the dichotomy of theories of meaningful action *versus* systems analysis; Parsons's theory starts with meaningful action and derives the concepts of culture and social system from the need to coordinate it. For Luhmann, systems are reified, they have purposes. When Parsons's systems are reified, he misspeaks himself; he is usually conscious that "system" is an intellectual abstraction. In Luhmann's work there can be no question of ethics or morality being opposed to system demands, since there is no internalized source of moral conflict outside of system demands. For Parsons, by contrast, culture is always a system analytically separated from society, and as differentiation and complexity increase, this distinction is accentuated. For Luhmann, *dis*trust is a residual category; for Parsons, it is not only an ever-present possibility but something that modern society systematically encourages even while it seeks its control. For Luhmann, people are primordially experiential; Parsons's people certainly are affectual as well, but they are also thinking, moral beings who have the potential for rationality and complex judgments. Here is the difference, perhaps, between Husserlian psychology and neo-Kantian liberalism.

Luhmann too, therefore, has used Parsonianism to reintroduce the dichotomies that Parsons sought to avoid. His dichotomies seem at first to be directly opposite from those Habermas posits, yet in actuality they complement them. Luhmann tells us that truth, love, and trust are part of everyday bourgeois life, and in this he could not be more different from Habermas's critical Parsonianism. Still, he locates the "base" of this society in intrinsically nonmeaningful system demands. The structures of society and the processes that change them exist "behind the backs" of actors, independent of their will. And society can become only more differentiated and atomized, so despite the presence of media, meaningful integration and community are increasingly difficult. There is in Luhmann's theory a strain of *Realpolitik,* a strain reinforced by his relative conservatism about activism and change. He has escaped from idealism, but *Realpolitik,* with its weary and often cynical acceptance of workaday demands, has always been the other side of idealism in the German tradition.

We have now found one of the hidden reasons for Habermas's idiosyncratic use and misuse of Parsons's work. If Luhmann is, after all, "the German Parsons," then systems theory may indeed be viewed as embodying a form of instrumental rationality, and the lifeworld and symbolic discourse may appear as legitimate counterweights. True, such a reading would not be entirely fair to Luhmann, but his work certainly can more easily be misread this way than Parsons's own. Both Habermas and Luhmann, then, re-dichotomize Parsons's thought, creating forms of Parsonianism that represent different strands of their national traditions. Each version, it is now clear, is symbiotically related to the other. Each needs the other, moreover, for its own justification.

Luhmann's and Habermas's creative misreadings of Parsons, and of each other's work, form the background for the variations on Parsonianism created by the two other major participants in the new German revival, Richard Münch and Wolfgang Schluchter.

Both theorists are aware of the dichotomizing results of this Habermas–Luhmann debate, yet in remedying them each moves in significantly different ways.

Although Münch himself once theorized from within Luhmann's systems framework, he is now very critical of Luhmann's work. Against Luhmann he stresses the Kantian elements in Parsons's theory (see Münch, 1981b, 1982), its openness to human intervention, and its commitment to universalism and rationality. For him, Parsons's theory has a "Kantian core," not the kind of systems infrastructure that Luhmann implies. And, in truth, Münch gets much closer to "the real Parsons" than Luhmann or Habermas. His essays are enormously rich and limpid expositions of Parsons's thought, and he has a feel for its empirical relevance that allows him to embrace Parsons's formalism without in any way being formalistic. For the most part, Münch follows up on the theoretical directions Parsons laid out. He amplifies Parsons's continuous but still creative relationship to different strands of the classical tradition (see, for example, Münch, 1980, 1981a). He writes powerfully and persuasively, and his ongoing research program into the comparative structures of modern society is promising indeed.

Yet Münch, too, has revised Parsons while purportedly only explicating and following him, and despite his truer reading, he has followed Luhmann and Habermas in producing a Parsonianism more in line with the traditions of German thought than Parsons's own. In his reaction against the atomizing and mechanistic aspects of Luhmann's theory, Münch suggests an explicit normative emphasis in Parsons's vision of society that was not really there. Münch presents Parsons as overwhelmingly concerned with maintaining the "whole" through the interpenetration of society's parts. This is undoubtedly a theme, and an important one, in Parsons's writing. Yet it does not represent his only normative commitment, nor does it do justice to what at least was Parsons's overweening conscious concern: the mundane ambition to explain historical and empirical variation as such.

For Parsons, subsystem differentiation is the most outstanding historical fact. It is an empirical separation that corresponds to generalized analytical divisions, and the interchange relations that connect different subsystems have the same "everyday" character.

If exchange is not broadly reciprocal, equilibrium cannot be maintained; if disequilibrium occurs, conflict ensues, and change processes develop; eventually more differentiation occurs, and exchange reciprocity is temporarily restored. Münch's emphasis is quite different. Rather than the fact of differentiation, it is the subsystem interrelationships that focus his attention, and he calls these relationships of "interpenetration" rather than exchange. Although he recognizes the explanatory possibility of Parsons's AGIL model for illuminating empirical equilibrium and change, it is the moral implications of the model that he finds powerfully attractive. He moralizes Parsons's analytical scheme, discussing system exchanges as positive, "dynamizing" processes; the boundary relation of economic and cultural life, for example, allows, in Münch's view, for the energizing expansion of both moral and economic possibilities. Reciprocal exchange is not simply equilibrating, it is also healthy, representing the balance and interpenetration of a good society. Unequal exchange is not, for it represents the possibilities for hyperspecialization, domination, or isolation that eventually undermine social well-being.

We hear in the back of Münch's Parsonianism the echoes of recent German experience. If the subsystems of "latency" (L) and "integration" (I) are functionally interpenetrated, Münch writes, then the intellectual culture of the latency dimensions will provide rationality and direction to social integration and group life, while the integrative pressures of group life will, in turn, ensure that social responsibility controls the intellect. If, however, the "L" subsystem dominates this exchange with "I," then intellectuals have become isolated from society and form a self-interested elite. If, by contrast, "I" dominates the exchange with "L," then powerful social groups are given free rein to manipulate ideas for their own purposes. Münch cites China and other historical cases by way of illustration, but Germany's Mandarin intellectuals and its dominating Prussian aristocracy seem not far behind. Yet although such examples of the consequences of uneven interchange are opportune, they do not in themselves provide the basis for conflating moral judgments with Parsons's analytical schema. Parsons was well aware that differentiation would lead to tension, uneven development, and an endemic lack of equal return. This unevenness, however, could itself be viewed as a sign of dynamism and health;

it could lead to social reform, not reaction, and to self-respect rather than deference. Reciprocity is a norm for explaining variance, not necessarily a norm for characterizing and evaluating it. Thus, although this kind of direct moral relevance is what makes Münch's work so appealing—in contrast to the dreary scientism of so many orthodox followers—it also compresses dimensions that Parsons would have left intact.

But there is also a problem in Münch's characterization of Parsons's morality as such. More than Münch seems to allow, individuation and differentiation were for Parsons very positive goods. If he had written a philosophy of history, and at times it lies barely concealed in his evolutionary work, he would have insisted at least as much on separation and autonomy as on wholeness and interpenetration. Münch has overemphasized the organicist metaphysics in Parsons's work. By underplaying the critical importance of utilitarianism and liberalism, he has developed what is still a distinctively German Parsons, although it is a far more accurate and more richly illuminating Parsons than his colleagues have yet to find.

It would not be fair if I failed to indicate that behind this German revival of Parsons there stands an earlier figure who also sought to undermine the traditional dichotomies of German thought: Max Weber. In their movement beyond purely critical theory and orthodox Marxism, German theorists have become increasingly interested in Weber's work, even as they have been increasingly attracted to Parsons's. Wolfgang Schluchter has been central to the Weber revival and has emerged as one of the premier Weberian scholars and theorists on the contemporary scene.

In the spring of 1981, Schluchter gave a talk at UCLA entitled "Current Trends in German Sociological Theory." These trends, he suggested, were the critical communications theory of Habermas, the systems theory of Luhmann, the action theory of Münch, and the Weberian theory of developmental history. This last theoretical strand is his own, and Schluchter has skillfully dedicated himself to demonstrating its superiority over the other three. Schluchter argues that these three movements are independent and antagonistic to one another; I have argued here to the contrary, that they can also be seen as three variations on Parsonian thought. So, I would also argue, can a major thrust of Schluchter's own work. Just as neoMarxism is becoming Parsonized in contemporary German theory, so is its Weberianism. If Habermas can be seen as fighting against Luhmann from a Parsonized systems theory of his own, so Schluchter must be seen as battling his three opponents at least in part on the Parsonized ground they all share.

Münch has opposed Habermas's instrumentalist, "decision-ist" theory of capitalism by criticizing the way in which his view of Parsons and modern systems theory has been overly affected by Luhmann. Habermas is much more Schluchter's target than he is the target of Münch, and Schluchter adopts a somewhat similar strategy of critique, though from an explicitly "Weberian" point of view (see, Roth and Schluchter, particularly Schluchter's "Value-Neutrality and the Ethic of Responsibility," 1979). His criticism is two-fold: he argues first against Habermas's insistence that modern society is merely instrumentally rational and "deci-sionist," and second, against Habermas's suggestion that Max Weber's historical sociology explains and legitimates this. While Münch finds the symbolic and normative resources to oppose Habermas in Parsons's work, Schluchter ostensibly finds them in Weber's. He insists that Weber is neither instrumental nor deci-sionist, and he elaborates a "Weberian" historical theory that dem-onstrates that modernity is neither as well.

The problem with Schluchter's argument is that Weber's theory, taken by itself, cannot carry this heavy burden; without Parsons, Schluchter would not find the symbolic and normative re-sources he needs. He realizes that the hinge of his argument against Habermas is Weber's rationalization thesis, the key to a normative and multidimensional understanding of which rests, in turn, on Weber's sociology of religion (see especially Schluchter's "The Paradox of Rationalization" in his 1979 volume with Roth). The interpretation of Weber's sociology of religion, therefore, becomes crucial to Schluchter's argument. He suggests that Weber's reli-gious sociology traces cultural differentiation rather than rationali-zation as such, the growing independence of meaning, cognition, and affect rather than the elimination of meaning and affect by cognition. Weber writes of the systematization and abstraction of religious symbolism, Schluchter argues, not its reduction and in-strumentalization. Finally, Weber's practical and postreligious understanding of modernity must be seen as an "anthropocentric dualism" that maintains the tension between the "is" and the "ought," not a theory of *Realpolitik* that eliminates it.

Every point in this crucial interpretation of Weber's religious sociology, it is clear, has been filtered through the evolutionary cultural theories of Parsons and Bellah. Yet, while Schluchter amply footnotes the Parsonian corpus, he presents his multidimensional version of the rationalization thesis as if it were Weber's own. Much the same can be said for his brilliant later analysis of legal and political rationalization (see Schluchter, 1981, especially chaps. 3-4). Here Schluchter "elaborates" Weber's theory of rational-legal society by connecting Weber's concept of "the ethic of responsibility"—the political embodiment of anthropocentric dualism—to his notion of rational, enacted law. Schluchter makes this connection by describing political ethics and law as complementary dimensions whose relationship was established through the functional differentiation of a broader political morality.

Schluchter has made good use of Parsons's synthetic achievement to overcome the dichotomies of Habermas's (and Weber's!) thought. The politics of the German theoretical debate, however, have caused him partly to conceal this good use. Similar "political" considerations lead him to speak very openly about Parsons when criticisms are due. For Schluchter is not simply Habermas's antagonist; he aligns himself with Habermas against the "wholism" of Parsonians like Luhmann and Münch. Indeed, one of the most telling polemics of his rationalization discussion is Schluchter's argument against the Parsonian idea that differentiation leads to complementary political and cultural strands. He suggests that Parsons underemphasizes the "paradoxes of rationalization," the real tensions generated by the conflicts between science and morality, between the politics of responsibility and the politics of conviction. This underemphasis, Schluchter believes, is linked in turn to Parsons's idealism, to his neglect of the pressure from "real interests."

In this open criticism, however, Schluchter is both right and wrong. In terms of epistemology, there certainly are strands in Parsonianism that are antirealistic, strands that mar large parts of the corpus of work. Yet to lump Parsons together with Friedrich Tenbruk—the German Weberian who produced an elegant but overtly emanationist reading of Weber's religious sociology—goes much too far. Tenbruk, for example, while drawing on Bellah's evolutionary theory, completely neglected its very real emphasis on politics and class. And Parsons's brilliant introductory essay to Weber's *Sociology of Religion* (1964)—on which Schluchter himself relies—systematically incorporates Weber's discussion of the impact of material experience on religious orientation.

In terms of his more empirical point, Schluchter's criticism is also valid in significant ways. Weber had a much surer sense of the tragic difficulties of modern life. Parsons—and, as we have seen, certain strands of German Parsonianism as well—was much too inclined to equate the fact that values are differentiated from a common value system with their complementarity in either a cultural or a social sense (on this point, see my own critique of Parsons's theory earlier in this volume). Yet Schluchter oversteps himself here as well. The very notion that modernity is characterized by substantive moral and political paradoxes is available to Schluchter only because he used Parsons's differentiation theory to enrich Weber's own approach to modern life. Parsons's more integrated theory allows Schluchter to overcome Weber's dichotomies. Only once these analytical dichotomies are overcome can Schluchter successfully speak of modernity's ideological and empirical "paradoxes"! If I have suggested that Schluchter, more than any of the other theorists, steps outside the German tradition, it is because he has one foot on Weber's shoulders but one on Parsons's as well.

If German sociological theory is blossoming today, it is at least in part because of its vivid encounter with Talcott Parsons. Parsons is read and studied in Germany today not because of his "Germanness"—the abstraction and generality that so bothers Americans—but because he has succeeded in bringing to German theory synthetic and explanatory perspectives that its native traditions often lack. It is this specifically theoretical dimension of Parsons that the Germans seek out. They regard Americans' political readings and denunciations of Parsons as naive and intellectually immature. They are right. The younger German scholars interested in Parsons today are leftists and liberals.

In America, of course, the relationship of sociological theory to Parsons has been burdened with much more historical and psychological freight. It was here that Parsons once exercised his much-disputed domination. If sociology were to be free to develop, this domination had to be overthrown. The attacks on Parsons, which spanned the three postwar decades of his life, were often significant. Anti-Parsonian attacks spawned every major movement of theoretical reform, each of which initially presented itself vis-à-vis some particular dimension of Parsons's work.

Now that Parsons is gone, however, and the status of his corpus in American theory severely diminished, these new theories stand as radically incomplete. Each concentrates on one strand of Parsons's original work, and when considered together they revive all the significant dichotomies that Parsons's framework was designed to resolve. If these theoretical pieces are ever going to be put back together again, it will take more than the king's men. Only another equally synthetic theory could do the job. This theory, I believe, would have to be a neofunctionalism modeled generally after Parsons's own: It would have to refer to system while recognizing will; it would have to maintain components of norms and of interests; it would have to explain conflict and cooperation. To simply bypass Parsons, as Habermas has reminded us in the passage that begins this essay, would be a serious intellectual mistake. Trying to discuss the relation between action and structure or between micro- and macrosociology without reference to Parsons is like trying to reinvent the wheel. If Parsons is to be transcended, it can be only by a true *Aufheben,* through what Hegel called a concrete rather than abstract negation.

It is tempting to say that the current American "stupidity" about Parsons's work will be overcome by the continuing translation of these new German texts and that this will be one result of the new Europeanization of American social theory, along with the ideologicalization of our debates and our introduction to *tout Paris.* Certainly this is partly true. Durkheim came back to France via American sociology and English anthropology. Weber was brought back to Germany through Parsons and Bendix. Yet it is also clear, I think, that the renewal of serious interest in Parsons has already begun here at home. There is some talk and some handwringing about an incipient "Parsons revival." One reason is the growing interest in theory itself. The bloom is off the rose of quantitative sociology, and more historical and comparative work is back in fashion. Another reason is decreasing excitement over

Marxist and critical work, for even while the competent practice of Marxist sociology has spread enormously, the social and cultural reasons for its ideological renewal have begun—in every western nation—to wither on the vine. And finally, if there is the beginning of a Parsons revival here at home, it is due in no small part to the intrinsic quality of Parsons's intellectual work, a quality that German sociological theory has recently come to appreciate.

References

HABERMAS, JÜRGEN
    1970   "Science and Technology as Ideology." In J. Habermas, *Towards a Rational Society*. Boston: Beacon Press.
    1975   *Legitimation Crisis*. Boston: Beacon Press.
    1981a "Talcott Parsons: Problems of Theory Construction." *Sociological Inquiry* 51:173-196.
    1981b *Theories des Kommunicativen Handelns*. Frankfurt: Suhrkamp.

LUHMANN, NIKLAS
    1979   *Trust and Power*. New York: Wiley.
    1982   *The Differentiation of Society*. New York: Columbia University Press.

MÜNCH, RICHARD
    1980   "Uber Parsons zu Weber." *Zeitschrift für Soziologie* 9: 18-53.
    1981a "Socialization and Personality Development from the Point of View of Action Theory: The Legacy of Durkheim." *Sociological Inquiry* 51:311-354.
    1981b "Talcott Parsons and the Theory of Action, I: The Kantian Core." *American Journal of Sociology* 86: 709-739.
    1982   "Talcott Parsons and the Theory of Action, II: The Continuity of the Development." *American Journal of Sociology* 87:771-826.

ROTH, GUENTHER, AND SCHLUCHTER, WOLFGANG
    1979   *Max Weber's Vision of History*. Berkeley: University of California Press.

SCHLUCHTER, WOLFGANG
    1979   *Verhalten, Handeln, und System*. Frankfurt: Suhrkamp.

1981 *The Rise of Western Rationalism.* Berkeley: University of California Press.

WEBER, MAX

1964 *Sociology of Religion.* Boston: Beacon Press.

NAME INDEX

SUBJECT INDEX